CRITICAL SURVEY

OF

LONG FICTION

Novelists
with
Feminist Themes

Editor

Carl Rollyson

Baruch College, City University of New York

D1715586

SALEM PRESS

Ipswich, Massachusetts • Hackensack, New Jersey

CONTENTS

CONTRIBUTORS

M. D. Allen
University of Wisconsin-Fox Valley

Mary A. Blackmon
Hardin-Simmons University

Virginia Brackett
Triton Community College

Karen Carmean
Original Contributor

Thomas Cassidy
South Carolina State University

C. L. Chua
California State University, Fresno

Wilton Eckley
Original Contributor

Miriam Fuchs
University of Hawaii at Manoa

Kristine Ottesen Garrigan
Original Contributor

Elsie Galbreath Haley
Metropolitan State College of Denver

Renata Harden
Fort Valley State University

Melanie Hawthorne
Original Contributor

Earl G. Ingersoll
SUNY-College at Brockport

Archibald E. Irwin
Original Contributor

Rebecca Kuzins
Pasadena, California

Brooks Landon
University of Iowa

Ralph L. Langenheim, Jr.
University of Illinois at Urbana-Champaign

Robert Emmet Long
Original Contributor

Joanne McCarthy
Tacoma, Washington

Mary E. Mahony
Wayne County Community College

Lois A. Marchino
University of Texas at El Paso

Charles E. May
California State University, Long Beach

Laurence W. Mazzeno
Alvernia College

Sally Mitchell
Original Contributor

Sherry Morton-Mollo
California State University, Fullerton

George O'Brien
Original Contributor

Rosemary M. Canfield Reisman
Charleston Southern University

Mark Rich
Cashton, Wisconsin

Dorothy Dodge Robbins
Louisiana Tech University

DaRelle M. Rollins
Hampton University

R. Baird Shuman
University of Illinois at Urbana-Champaign

Sharon Spencer
Original Contributor

Brian Stableford
Reading, England

Karen F. Stein
University of Rhode Island

Shawncey Webb
Taylor University

Judith Weise
Original Contributor

Donna Glee Williams
North Carolina Center for the Advancement of Teaching

FEMINIST LONG FICTION

Feminist long fiction features female characters whose quest for self-agency leads to conflict with a traditionally masculinist and patriarchal society. These novels have been harshly criticized and dismissed—and even ridiculed—for their nontraditional female characters.

Feminist ideology in the Western world traces its roots to the late eighteenth century. One particular work considered foundational to feminism is *A Vindication of the Rights of Woman, with Strictures on Political and Moral Subjects* (1792), by English writer Mary Wollstonecraft (1759-1797). Not until the twentieth century, more than one hundred years later, would women begin to reap some of the benefits of a long campaign for basic human rights. Feminism led to radical changes for women in politics, the public sphere, the workplace, the home, and the cultural realm, including the arts and literature. Popular literature, especially, began to reflect women's previously silenced voices.

As early as the end of the seventeenth century, however, women were publishing works of literature. Aphra Behn (1640-1689), likely the first Englishwoman to support herself through writing, published the highly popular *Oroonoko: Or, The History of the Royal Slave* (1688), a prose romance. This novel was the first in English to express sympathy for the plight of slaves.

THE EIGHTEENTH CENTURY

Fiction, a genre that did not fully develop until the eighteenth century, provided a perfect vehicle for women who sought a voice through writing. The first long fiction in England consisted of what may generally be termed "romances." Men traditionally received credit for developing long fiction and, eventually, the novel form. Touted examples include Samuel Richardson's epistolary novel, *Pamela: Or, Virtue Rewarded* (1740-1741), and Henry Fielding's *The History of Tom Jones, a Foundling* (1749). However, earlier novels were written by women, a fact not widely acknowledged until the twentieth century. Mary de la Rivière Manley (c. 1670-1724) published *The Secret History of Queen Zarah and the Zarazians* in the early eighteenth century (1705). The novel is a version of the roman à clef. This type of fiction featured real-life personalities thinly disguised as its characters. Eliza Haywood (c. 1693-1756), a highly political figure, also wrote romances, including *The History of Jemmy and Jenny Jessamy* (1753). She is now frequently mentioned as an important figure in the development of the novel.

THE NINETEENTH CENTURY

The nineteenth century became a golden age of writing for women. Jane Austen (1775-1817) wrote seven novels, often called novels of manners, that parody the ludicrous activities of genteel society and criticize inequitable social rules. *Sense and Sensibility* (1811), *Pride and Prejudice* (1813), *Mansfield Park* (1814), *Emma* (1816), *Persuasion*

(1818), and *Sanditon* (1925) uncover the oppressive lives of women, including confining environments, a shameful lack of education, and pitiful dependence upon male relatives for survival. Austen's *Northanger Abby* (1818) satirizes as sentimental its heroine's love for the gothic genre, fiction that offers readers mysterious castles or mansions with secret passages, dark shadowy beings, a damsel threatened by death, a hero with an obscure past, and visions and ghosts.

Mary Wollstonecraft Shelley (1797-1851) would rejuvenate the public's appreciation for the gothic in her 1818 novel *Frankenstein*. Rather than emphasize the traditional elements of the gothic, Shelley produced a complex psychological study of her characters, imbuing her horror and science-fiction story with disturbing imagery of aborted creations and multiple deaths. Feminist critics link these elements to Shelley's real-life experiences.

By midcentury, Charlotte Brontë (1816-1855) and Emily Brontë (1818-1848) were producing novels featuring a new hero based on the Romantic ideals of the English poet Lord Byron (1788-1824). Named for the poet and the heroes of his poetry, the Byronic hero most generally had a brooding, dark, independent, and sometimes abusive personality. Charlotte Brontë's *Jane Eyre* (1847) includes a Byronic hero in the form of Edward Rochester. More important, however, the novel introduces a never-before-seen heroine in the shape of a plain, small governess, whose values for truth and justice lead to her rejection of the romantic attentions of Rochester, her master. The character of Jane undercuts the popular female stereotypes of fiction: the angel of the house, the "invalid," or the whore.

Although Charlotte Brontë's novel was well received by her contemporaries, Emily Brontë's masterpiece, *Wuthering Heights*, also published in 1847, was not. With its metaphysical suggestions that bordered on the gruesome and with an abusive, vengeful Byronic hero, its messages proved too strong for its time (especially so because they came from a woman). By the next century, however, this novel took its rightful place in the canon not only of feminist long fiction but also long fiction in general.

THE TWENTIETH CENTURY

Feminist fiction writer Kate Chopin (1851-1904) published *The Awakening* in 1899, a novel that many libraries refused to shelve, despite Chopin's earlier popularity as a writer of "traditional" fiction. Her book shocked readers with its heroine who took pleasure in sexual relations and its suggestion of the connections between the imagination, the artist, and sex. The hostile criticism it received centered on its heroine's rejection of the traditional oppressive role of wife and mother, causing even Chopin's hometown library in St. Louis, Missouri, to ban the book.

In 1920, the year women won the vote in the United States, Edith Wharton (1862-1937) published *The Age of Innocence*. She became the first woman to win a Pulitzer Prize in fiction for the novel in 1921, even though the work focuses on society's inequitable treatment of women.

As Wharton's career flourished in the United States, the English feminist Virginia Woolf (1882-1941), who was also an essayist and editor, also enjoyed popularity. She began her publishing career in 1915 with the novel *The Voyage Out*, which required seven years of work. In early adulthood, Woolf studied Greek, an unusual subject for a young woman of her time; taught at a college for working women; performed menial chores for the suffrage movement; and wrote for the *Times Literary Supplement*, a prestigious publication. All these experiences influenced her feminism.

In *Night and Day* (1919), Woolf shaped a heroine not unlike herself, who had experienced the trials of a young female writer. After *Jacob's Room* (1922), Woolf produced a highly influential novel, *Mrs. Dalloway* (1925). Departing from traditional novel structure, Woolf designed an analysis of post-World War I London society by moving, over a twenty-four-hour period, from her heroine's point of view to that of Septimus Warren Smith, a kind of insane alter ego for Mrs. Dalloway. Woolf's *To the Lighthouse* (1927), often studied by feminist critics, critiques the Victorian social mores that create an environment at once suffocating and stimulating for young women.

Woolf's intimate relationship with writer Vita Sackville-West likely inspired her 1928 novel *Orlando: A Biography*. *Orlando* is written as a biography of a character who lives more than four hundred years, during which time her gender evolves from that of a man to that of a woman. The novel represents the history of the aristocratic Sackville-West family and also the development of English literature. In 1929, Woolf produced a long essay published as *A Room of One's Own*, which focuses on the writing life of women; historians agree it represents the first major work of feminist criticism in English. Her most experimental novel, *The Waves* (1931), was labeled by Woolf herself a "poem-play." Made up of a number of monologues, the novel presents six characters, all lamenting the death of a young man named Percival, supposedly fashioned on Woolf's own brother, Thoby, who died many years before.

Additional works by Woolf include the nonfiction *Three Guineas* (1938), considered the most radical of her feminist writings in its examination of social oppression. Her final novel, *Between the Acts*, appeared in 1941, following Woolf's suicide in the same year.

Woolf's contemporary, English writer Rebecca West (1892-1983), was an actor, journalist, and suffragist. Born Cicily Isabel Fairfield, West adopted as her name that of a radical feminist character from Henrik Ibsen's play *Rosmersholm* (pb. 1886; English translation, 1889). Although much of West's work is in journalism and nonfiction, she published several important fictional works, despite some negative reactions to her writings and to her as an individual. Accounting for a portion of the hostility was her love affair with English novelist H. G. Wells, an affair that led to an illegitimate son. The two writers' relationship challenged the conservative values of their society. After West gave birth to her son in 1914, she took a great interest in the situation of unwed mothers, leading her to write *The Judge* (1922). This novel featured the suffragist struggle with additional consideration of issues such as rape, illegitimacy, and motherhood.

In 1930, West produced more novels, expressing an enthusiasm for writings by Woolf. West's *The Harsh Voice* (1935), a collection of novellas, concerned economic and financial matters and focused on the 1929 global economic crisis. Many reviewers of the book declared its subject too harsh and its tone too pessimistic for a female writer. Others, however, noted with interest that West shaped female characters who differed from those in her earlier works. These heroines were strong, taking an active part in the determination of their own fate, something women were not encouraged to do in real life. This same strength of character informed West's most popular novel, *The Thinking Reed* (1936). Although some found the novel's heroine, Isabelle, ruthless, the book garnered much critical acclaim. In the novel, West criticized French, English, and American societies in a manner that some found offensive but most declared accurate.

By the 1950's, West departed from her feminist-socialist view to take up a conservative anticommunist stance. Her political reversal earned her the title of Dame Commander of the British Empire, a somewhat ironic circumstance for a writer who earlier had deeply criticized imperialism in print.

A FEMALE AESTHETIC

With the exodus of men fighting the two world wars in the first half of the twentieth century, American and English women entered the workforce in record numbers to occupy positions other than that of the traditional nurse, teacher, or secretary. As women's roles in the world changed, so did the characterizations of women in novels. Female writers began to connect their work and their lives. They discovered a number of disparities between their own ambitions, ingenuity, and creativity on one hand and the limited, often secondary, roles assumed by the majority of traditional female fictional characters on the other hand. This reality was easily explained, as the majority of novelists were white men. By the mid-twentieth century, a plethora of long fiction by women began to appear, with realistic female characters. Women's fiction transformed from products of imitation of a male aesthetic to protests against that aesthetic, eventually becoming self-defining works of literature.

The success of these new novelists was propelled by the work of feminist literary critics, especially scholars in academia. In the 1960's, critics began questioning the characterizations of women as either angels or monsters. They also questioned the representation of women in popular literature written by men and, most important, refused to accept the exclusion of women from literary history. Their diligence in rediscovering female novelists from previous centuries and decades helped propel authors such as Woolf, George Sand (1804-1876), George Eliot (1819-1880), and West to their rightful place in the literary canon.

Feminist critics also traced the historical connections of recurring images, themes, and plots in women's writing that reflected their social and psychological experience in a culture dominated by men. One recurring image, for example, is that of the caged bird, which represents the suppression of female creativity or the physical and emotional imprisonment of women in general. Slowly, writings by women began to be accepted not only in the classroom but also the marketplace. Virago Press, which publishes the writings of women, reprinted, for instance, West's novels in affordable editions. While her work in its own day was deemed "too intellectual," feminist critics helped define a new study and a new appreciation of these works. In addition, the critical analyses of the aesthetic values that appeared in many of the novels that had long been considered classics led to a newly defined feminist novel.

Closely related to the formation of a feminist aesthetic was the development of a black women's aesthetic. Novels by African American women from the first half of the twentieth century, such as *Their Eyes Were Watching God* (1937) by anthropologist and writer Zora Neale Hurston (1891-1960), were reissued after decades of neglect. Hurston's novel—which tells the story of a young black woman involved in three abusive marriages who eventually finds redemption through her own strength and beliefs and through the support of her female friend—gained an important place in the feminist canon. Hurston's work prefigured that of Toni Morrison (born 1931), the first black woman to receive the Nobel Prize in Literature (1993). One of America's foremost novelists, Morrison is celebrated for her acute analyses of the dynamics of race and gender. Often framing her fiction in the fantastic and the mystical, Morrison is known for *The Bluest Eye* (1970), *Sula* (1973), *Song of Solomon* (1977), *Tar Baby* (1981), the Pulitzer Prize-winning *Beloved* (1987), *Jazz* (1992), *Paradise* (1998), *Love* (2003), and *A Mercy* (2008).

Like Morrison, Alice Walker (born 1944) explores the cultural inheritance of African Americans by examining universal moral issues and by celebrating supportive communities of women. In her critically acclaimed Pulitzer Prize-winning novel *The Color Purple* (1982), Walker presents her story in epistolary form, emphasizing her characters' struggles with articulating their feelings of identity from the perspective of African American experience. In her 1983 work of nonfiction, *In Search of Our Mothers' Gardens: Womanist Prose*, Walker coined the term "womanist" to describe the particular perspectives of feminist women of color.

By the 1950's, writers such as Iranian-born Doris Lessing (born 1919) were publishing works that feminists claimed as supportive of their cause. In Lessing's *The Golden Notebook* (1962), heroine Anna Wulf struggles with being a creative woman who fights solitude, has self-destructive impulses, and who practices self-censorship to conform to society. These are themes repeated in many of Lessing's novels. Lessing also is known for her vision of the writer as a morally responsible person, who criticizes capitalist inequities through a socialist philosophy.

Lessing was awarded the Nobel Prize in Literature in 2007. The Nobel Academy described her as "that epicist [writer of epics] of the female experience, who with scepticism, fire and visionary power has subjected a divided civilization to scrutiny."

Erica Jong (born 1942) wrote the widely popular *Fear of Flying* (1973). Even with its frank treatment of female sexuality, the novel sold more than five million copies by 1977 and prompted an avalanche of letters to Jong from women responding to the work as a revelation of emotions they had never encountered in fiction. The book caused a flurry of mixed critical response as well, partly in reaction to its provocative cover images and to its content, which some labeled pornographic. Expressing in no uncertain terms the anger and energy of the women's rights movement, the novel also garnered praise for its frankness but also received criticism for what some called a banal tone and weak writing style.

The second half of the twentieth century saw feminist novels addressing race and ethnicity. This focus developed out of the work of feminists of color, who argued that race, gender, and class were inextricably linked. Maxine Hong Kingston (born 1940), born to Chinese immigrants, published *The Woman Warrior: Memoirs of a Girlhood Among Ghosts* (1976), which combines autobiography and fiction in a tale of "a girl-hood among ghosts." These ghosts emerge from Chinese myth to show how the definition of "feminine" is shaped in that culture. Frankly oppressive for women, ancient Chinese culture allows Kingston to investigate challenges to female physical and emotional survival. Louise Erdrich (born 1954), who is part American Indian, interrogates the social, economic, and emotional pressures suffered by dislocated women in her novel *Love Medicine* (1984). The book won the National Book Critics Circle Award. Novelist Julia Alvarez (born 1950), in her novel *In the Time of the Butterflies* (1994), tells the story of the historic Mirabal sisters and their resistance to Dominican dictator Rafael Trujillo.

Other feminist novelists who write from a multiethnic and multicultural perspective include Yvonne Vera (1964-2005). Her novel *Butterfly Burning* (2000) examines gender inequality in Zimbabwe. Monica Ali (born 1967), a British writer of Bangladeshi descent, tells the story of a woman in an arranged married in *Brick Lane* (2003). Chinese novelist Wang Anyi (born 1954) has had several of her short novels translated into English, including those examining women's lives in contemporary China (*Xiao cheng zhi lian*, 1988; *Love in a Small Town*, 1988). Lebanese novelist Hanan al-Shaykh (born 1945) is the author of *Misk al-ghazal* (1988; *Women of Sand and Myrrh*, 1989), a novel that was banned in several countries in the Middle East for its harsh criticism of patriarchy; it was well-received in English translation.

By the beginning of the twenty-first century, it was no longer remarkable that stories about women's lives were indeed serious literature. However, much of the "seriousness" also has translated into increased sales and profits for publishers, especially because women surpassed men in terms of buying and reading novels. Books by women about women still are considered attractive primarily for female readers, whereas books by men about men are considered to have universal appeal.

Virginia Brackett

BIBLIOGRAPHY

Acampora, Christa Davis, and Angela L. Cotten, eds. *Unmaking Race, Remaking Soul: Transformative Aesthetics and the Practice of Freedom.* Albany: State University of New York Press, 2007. Collection of essays on the power of creativity—including writing—to transform the lives of women of color. Argues for the importance of "aesthetic agency" to literature and other forms of creative experience.

Gilbert, Sandra M., and Susan Gubar. *The Madwoman in the Attic: The Woman Writer and the Nineteenth-Century Literary Imagination.* New Haven, Conn.: Yale University Press, 1979. Classic text that considers nineteenth century stereotypes of female fictional characters and of the writers who created them, framing its discussion with ideas governing restrictive social mores. Essential reading for understanding feminist literature and writers.

_____, eds. *The Norton Anthology of Literature by Women: The Traditions in English.* 3d ed. New York: W. W. Norton, 2007. Comprehensive anthology of women's writing, featuring works from medieval times through the early twenty-first century. Biographies, works, and excerpts are presented chronologically, with each era preceded by introductions that examine the culture in which each woman wrote.

Lauret, Maria. *Liberating Literature: Feminist Fiction in America.* New York: Routledge, 1994. Lauret explores the writing of American feminist writers of long fiction, including Marge Piercy, Marilyn French, Tillie Olsen, Alice Walker, Kate Millett, Agnes Smedley, Zora Neale Hurston, Toni Morrison, and Maya Angelou.

Makinen, Merja. *Feminist Popular Fiction.* New York: Palgrave, 2001. Analysis of the move into popular fiction—detective fiction, science fiction, romances, and fairy tales—by feminist writers beginning in the 1980's. Includes a history of each genre and women's contributions to their formation. Also includes an introductory chapter, "Feminism and Genre Fiction: The Preliminaries."

Moers, Ellen. *Literary Women: The Great Writers.* 1976. Reprint. London: Women's Press, 1986. Moers, in part, makes visible a "subtext" in the writings of women. Argues that some works contain messages unrecognized in their own time because of assumptions and presumptions about gender. Includes a new introduction.

Robbins, Ruth. *Literary Feminisms.* New York: Palgrave, 2003. An introduction to feminist literary and critical theories in the United States and Great Britain. Examines the "pluralist" composition of feminist literary theory, which uses Marxist, postmodern, and other theories but remains centered on women. Includes readings of commonly taught feminist texts.

Whelehan, Imelda. *The Feminist Bestseller: From "Sex and the Single Girl" to "Sex and the City."* New York: Palgrave Macmillan, 2005. Overview of popular feminist fiction from the late 1960's to the end of the 1990's, examining the influence of Erica Jong, Marilyn French, and others on late twentieth century writers. Explains how these works are in dialogue with contemporary feminism.

JULIA ALVAREZ

Born: New York, New York; March 27, 1950
Also known as: Julia Altagracia Maria Teresa Alvarez

PRINCIPAL LONG FICTION

How the García Girls Lost Their Accents, 1991
In the Time of the Butterflies, 1994
¡Yo!, 1997
In the Name of Salomé, 2000
The Cafecito Story, 2001
Saving the World, 2006

OTHER LITERARY FORMS

Julia Alvarez has written in several genres, something for which, she says, "I blame my life." Her publications include the nonfiction *Once upon a Quinceañera: Coming of Age in the USA* (2007), which she was invited to write. She also has written numerous essays, including the autobiographical *Something to Declare* (1998). Her favorite genre is poetry, and she has published many poems in literary journals, plus several books of poems, including *The Other Side/El otro lado* (1995) and *Seven Trees* (1998), which features prints by her daughter-in-law, artist Sara Eichner. She also has drawn on her Latino heritage for a substantial number of books for children and young adults, notably *Before We Were Free* (2002) and *How Tía Lola Came to Stay* (2001).

ACHIEVEMENTS

Julia Alvarez's books have been published in at least eleven languages and are widely available around the world. Some are bilingual (English and Spanish) editions. She has won a number of prizes for her poetry, including from the Academy of American Poetry in 1974, and was awarded a Robert Frost Fellowship in Poetry in 1986. Three of her works, *How the García Girls Lost Their Accents*, *In the Time of the Butterflies*, and *Before We Were Free*, were chosen as Notable Books by the American Library Association (ALA); the latter also received the ALA's Pura Belpré Award, presented for an outstanding literary work for youth and children that "best portrays, affirms, and celebrates the Latino cultural experience." Alvarez has received honorary degrees from John Jay College of the City University of New York and from Union College of Schenectady, New York. Her works have contributed substantially to the Latina voice in contemporary American literature.

BIOGRAPHY

Julia Alvarez was born Julia Altagracia Maria Teresa Alvarez in New York City in 1950, the second of four daughters, but her family returned to the Dominican Republic when she was still an infant. Her mother and her father, a doctor, both came from large, affluent Dominican families that had respect for and connections to the United States. Alvarez and her sisters grew up in a large and traditional extended family; she remembers the men going to work and the children being raised with their cousins by a large group of aunts and maids. She came to recognize the restrictions these women faced: One aunt was trained as a physician but did not practice; another aunt, known as the one who read books, was unconventional and unmarried. This "reading aunt" gave Alvarez a copy of the classic collection of folktales *One Thousand and One Nights*, introducing her to her "first muse," Scheherazade, a princess who was dark-skinned and resourceful. Alvarez, fascinated by the possibilities of storytelling, would draw on her experiences with her aunts, maids, cousins, and siblings for several of her novels, notably *How the García Girls Lost Their Accents*.

Alvarez was ten years old when her father's involvement in a plot to overthrow Dominican dictator Rafael Trujillo was discovered. With the help of a U.S. agent, the family escaped and returned to New York City. Although Alvarez yearned for this "homecoming," the adjustment was difficult for all. Her father had to retrain as a physician. The family lived in a small apartment in Queens, isolated from other Dominicans and without the support of their extended family. Alvarez herself was homesick and faced the prejudice of her classmates. This experience as an immigrant would be a major focus of her writing.

Alvarez went to college in the late 1960's and early 1970's, struggling to reconcile her traditional Dominican background with her new and chaotic culture. She earned her bachelor's degree at Middlebury College in Vermont in 1971 and her master's degree in creative writing from Syracuse University in 1975. She married and divorced twice before she was thirty years old, unable to combine marriage with the life of writing that had become her passion. For a number of years, she worked at part-time and temporary academic jobs to support herself. Both Alvarez's professional and personal lives stabilized at the end of the 1980's. In 1988, she began a long-term association as a professor at Middlebury; in 1998, she entered a new arrangement with the college, becoming a writer-in-residence so that she would have more time for writing.

In 1989, Alvarez was married a third time, this time to Bill Eichner, a doctor and son of a Nebraska farm couple. This relationship gave Alvarez a new culture to negotiate, a new appreciation for farming and gardening, and a new project. She and Eichner started a sustainable organic-coffee farm and a school to teach reading and writing to illiterate coffee farmers and their families in the Dominican Republic. This project is the subject of the novel *The Cafecito Story*, which Alvarez calls an "eco-parable" and a love story, written primarily for young readers.

ANALYSIS

If Julia Alvarez's life were a novel, postmodern, postcolonial, and feminist critics, especially, would be interested in analyzing it. She has referred to herself as a "Dominican hyphen American," adding, "As a fiction writer, I find that the most exciting things happen in the realm of that hyphen—the place where two worlds collide or blend together." This is the place postcolonial writers call the liminal space, the "place between." It is the place where Alvarez has lived her life, and it is the setting of her fiction.

Alvarez considers herself an American, but her writing is concerned with both Dominican and American culture and with the dilemma of immigrants trying to bridge the gaps. Because she is aware that most of her American readers, like her young American classmates from the past, will not be familiar with anything Dominican, she also patiently works to bridge this gap as well. It is understandable, given this focus, that some scholars consider her a Caribbean writer, connecting her to Edwidge Danticat and Jamaica Kincaid, among others.

Alvarez's sense of living in liminal space and having to deal with the collision of cultures is mirrored in the fragmented form of her novels, which some scholars consider short stories; in her fluid use of time; and in her use of multiple points of view. This style results in a confusion between reality and fiction. While Alvarez addresses general concerns of the postcolonial and postmodern, her novels focus primarily on how these issues affect women. Through her numerous female characters, she examines sexism in Latino culture, pressures faced by women living in dictatorships, and misogyny in both external and internalized forms. It is not coincidental that her most intriguing characters are women who rebel against the existence of repressive boundaries (for example, Yo in *How the García Girls Lost Their Accents* and Miranda in *The Time of the Butterflies*).

Alvarez is not only interested in examining cultural, ethnic, and gender boundaries; another main concern in her work is language—its use to define and limit, especially immigrants and the lower classes, and its possibilities for a writer, especially a bilingual one. Her childhood experience in an oral culture, her own love of poetry, and her struggles to learn English and to maintain her fluency in Spanish all contribute to her thoughtful use of language in her writings.

How the García Girls Lost Their Accents

Alvarez's first novel is based on the experiences of her own family. The book is divided into three sections by time, which moves backward in this account. Each section is subdivided into five vignettes, stories focused on a single character or group of characters. To aid her readers, Alvarez provides a genealogical chart at the beginning of the book, tracing both the de la Torreses (Mami's family) and the Garcías to the conquistadores. Readers also become aware of where the four García girls—Carla, Sandra (Sandi), Yolanda (Yo), and Sofia (Fifi)—fit in these two large and important families. Alvarez has noted that Yo's name is a play on the Spanish word for self or "I"; indeed, Yo is the storyteller in this work.

The first section (1989-1972) details Yo's return to the Dominican Republic after a five-year absence, looking for a home but not finding it. This section presents the aging of the parents and the marriages and struggles, including Sandi's breakdown, of the adult "girls." The second section (1970-1960, the ten years after the family's exile) focuses on the parents' struggle to adjust to American life, the father's acceptance that conditions in his homeland mean staying in the United States, and the tensions between the parents and their daughters, who are having their own problems in the United States in the 1960's. During this period, the parents decide that summers with the family on the island will help solve the problems, but the sisters have to "rescue" Fifi from the prospect of a traditional island marriage with her sexist cousin, Manuel. The final section, 1960-1956, depicts life on the island before the family's exile, when America was represented by toys from FAO Schwarz. Because of the reverse chronology, readers get a clear picture of what the García family gained—and lost—when they were exiled.

IN THE TIME OF THE BUTTERFLIES

Alvarez's second novel is a fictionalized account of the story of the three Mirabel sisters, Patria, Minerva, and Maria Teresa (Maté), who were brutally murdered by Trujillo in November, 1960, shortly after the Alvarez family fled to the United States. *Las Mariposas* (the butterflies, which was the code name of the sisters) were among the founders of the underground resistance to which Alvarez's father belonged. Alvarez refers to this book as one she felt compelled to write.

In this account, Alvarez focuses on the characters, beginning with the surviving sister, Dede, in 1994, as she is waiting to talk to a "gringo writer," clearly Alvarez, coming to interview her about her sisters. Dede, now in her sixties, still maintains a museum in honor of *Las Mariposas*; she has become their storyteller. Although the rest of the book is written in the first person, from the rotating viewpoints of the three butterflies, Dede's sections are third-person, limited point of view, which emphasizes her distance from the others and their story.

In the Time of the Butterflies is divided into three parts, starting in the late 1930's and moving to November 25, 1960, the day the sisters were murdered. Each sister has one chapter in each of the sections; Dede speaks the epilogue, using first person for the first time. Each sister is presented clearly. Patria, the oldest, is the most traditional. A devout Catholic, she marries young and focuses on her husband, his family farm, and her children. She is brought to the revolution through the church: along with her priest and others, she is radicalized during a retreat in the mountains after they witness a government massacre of peasants, one of whom looks like Patria's young son.

Minerva is always rebellious, understanding even as a youth the nature of Trujillo and his dictatorship. She is attracted to a mournful classmate, whose sorrow she finds has been caused by Trujillo's murder of all male members of her family, including a young brother. Minerva witnesses Trujillo's seduction of the most beautiful and accomplished young woman in her school, whose life is destroyed by this attention. Minerva's own beauty attracts Trujillo's notice, and she puts herself and her family in jeopardy when she publicly slaps him. She becomes a revolutionary early, is attracted to two young radicals, and marries one of them.

Alvarez presents Maté, the youngest sister, through the pages of Maté's diary. At first, the entries seem typical of any young girl and are even a bit silly. As the story progresses, Maté matures, and the diary and its ominously torn-out pages symbolize how even innocent thoughts can be dangerous in a dictatorship.

Dede stays outside the intrigue because of the attitude of her husband, but ironically, she divorces him after the death of her sisters. Dede, though devastated by her loss, rallies to take care of her extended family, including her sisters' children. Hers is a feminist voice, criticizing the sisters' husbands, who are eventually released from prison and go on with their lives and to new families. The epilogue suggests, however, that she is finally ready to embrace her own life, including herself, "the one who survived," as part of the story.

In a postscript, Alvarez discusses her connection to the history of the Mirabel sisters and her approach to telling their story. She has also included an essay titled "Chasing the Butterflies" in *Something to Declare*, which discusses her 1986 trip to the Dominican Republic and her first interviews with people who knew the Mirabel sisters or had witnessed parts of their last day. *In the Time of the Butterflies* was made into a feature film (2001) starring Salma Hayek.

¡Yo!

Alvarez has said that *¡Yo!* is not a sequel to her successful first novel, but there is a clear connection. Yo, the writer of her own successful novel, has angered her family and friends for turning them into "fictional fodder." This novel is their answer; in fifteen separate pieces, the novel presents varied perspectives on Yo, including an ironic one from her mother, a poignant one from a landlady, a frightening one from a stalker, and a tender one from her father. Alvarez creates believable characters with distinctive voices; at the same time, she presents a complex portrait of Yo.

Elsie Galbreath Haley

OTHER MAJOR WORKS

POETRY: *Homecoming: Poems*, 1984 (revised and expanded 1996 as *Homecoming: New and Collected Poems*, 1996); *The Other Side/El otro lado*, 1995; *Seven Trees*, 1998; *Cry Out: Poets Protest the War*, 2003 (multiple authors); *The Woman I Kept to Myself*, 2004.

NONFICTION: *Something to Declare*, 1998; *Once upon a Quinceañera: Coming of Age in the USA*, 2007.

CHILDREN'S/YOUNG ADULT LITERATURE: *The Secret Footprints*, 2000; *How Tía Lola Came to Stay*, 2001; *Before We Were Free*, 2002; *Finding Miracles*, 2004; *A Gift of Gracias*, 2005.

EDITED TEXT: *Old Age Ain't for Sissies*, 1979.

BIBLIOGRAPHY

Johnson, Kelly Lyon. *Julia Alvarez: Writing a New Place on the Map.* Albuquerque: University of New Mexico Press, 2005. The first book-length examination of Alvarez's writings. Johnson explores shared themes, ideals, and issues of understanding cultural identity in a global society. Notes that Alvarez embraces the notion of *mestizaje,* the mixing of races.

Luis, William. "A Search for Identity in Julia Alvarez's *How the García Girls Lost Their Accents.*" *Callaloo* 23, no. 3 (Summer, 2000): 839-849. A study of Alvarez's tale of the search for identity in the "space" between two homelands.

Oliver, Kelly. "Everyday Revolutions, Shifting Power, and Feminine Genius in Julia Alvarez's Fiction." In *Unmaking Race, Remaking Soul: Transformative Aesthetics and the Practice of Freedom,* edited by Christa Davis Acampora and Angela L. Cotten. Albany: State University of New York Press, 2007. In this collection of essays on the power of creativity to transform the lives of women of color, Oliver explores how Alvarez's female characters use their everyday genius to counter, for example, sexism and misogyny. Oliver places this "feminine genius" on similar footing with the genius of larger-scale revolutionary acts.

Sirias, Silvis. *Julia Alvarez: A Critical Companion.* Westport, Conn.: Greenwood Press, 2001. A basic guide to Alvarez's works, with chapters on four of her novels. Includes chapters examining Alvarez's life as well as the Latino/Latina novel.

Socolovsky, Maya. "Patriotism, Nationalism, and the Fiction of History in Julia Alvarez's *In the Time of the Butterflies* and *In the Name of Salomé.*" *Latin American Literary Review* 34, no. 68 (July-December, 2006): 5-24. Socolovsky is concerned with Alvarez's ability in these novels to walk the line between remembering historical events and the risk of hagiography, or forgetting the events by overmemorializing them.

MARGARET ATWOOD

Born: Ottawa, Ontario, Canada; November 18, 1939
Also known as: Margaret Eleanor Atwood

PRINCIPAL LONG FICTION

The Edible Woman, 1969
Surfacing, 1972
Lady Oracle, 1976
Life Before Man, 1979
Bodily Harm, 1981
The Handmaid's Tale, 1985
Cat's Eye, 1988
The Robber Bride, 1993
Alias Grace, 1996
The Blind Assassin, 2000
Oryx and Crake, 2003
The Penelopiad: The Myth of Penelope and Odysseus, 2005

OTHER LITERARY FORMS

A skillful and prolific writer, Margaret Atwood has published many volumes of poetry. Collections such as *Double Persephone* (1961), *The Animals in That Country* (1968), *The Journals of Susanna Moodie* (1970), *Procedures for Underground* (1970), *Power Politics* (1971), *You Are Happy* (1974), *Two-Headed Poems* (1978), *True Stories* (1981), *Interlunar* (1984), and *Morning in the Burned House* (1995) have enjoyed a wide and enthusiastic readership, especially in Canada. During the 1960's, Atwood published in limited editions poems and broadsides illustrated by Charles Pachter: *The Circle Game* (1964), *Kaleidoscopes Baroque: A Poem* (1965), *Speeches for Dr. Frankenstein* (1966), *Expeditions* (1966), and *What Was in the Garden* (1969).

Atwood has also written books for children, including *Up in the Tree* (1978), which she also illustrated, and *Rude Ramsay and the Roaring Radishes* (2004). Her volumes of short stories, a collection of short fiction and prose poems (*Murder in the Dark*, 1983), a volume of criticism (*Survival: A Thematic Guide to Canadian Literature*, 1972), and a collection of literary essays (*Second Words*, 1982) further demonstrate Atwood's wide-ranging talent. In 1982, Atwood coedited *The New Oxford Book of Canadian Verse in English*. She has also written articles and critical reviews too numerous to list. She has contributed prose and poetry to literary journals such as *Acta Victoriana* and *Canadian Forum*, and her teleplays have been aired by the Canadian Broadcasting Corporation.

ACHIEVEMENTS

Early in her career, Margaret Atwood received critical recognition for her work. This is particularly true of her poetry, which has earned her numerous awards, including the E. J. Pratt Medal in 1961, the President's Medal from the University of Western Ontario in 1965, and the Governor-General's Award, Canada's highest literary honor, for *The Circle Game* in 1966. Twenty years later, Atwood again won this prize for *The Handmaid's Tale*. Atwood won first prize in the Canadian Centennial Commission Poetry Competition in 1967 and won a prize for poetry from the Union League Civic and Arts Foundation in 1969. She has received honorary doctorates from Trent University and Queen's University. Additional honors and awards she has received include the Bess Hoskins Prize for poetry (1974), the City of Toronto Award (1977), the Canadian Booksellers Association Award (1977), the St. Lawrence Award for Fiction (1978), the Canada Council Molson Prize (1980), and the Radcliffe Medal (1980). *The Blind Assassin* won the 2000 Booker Prize, and Atwood received Spain's Prince of Asturias literary prize for 2008.

BIOGRAPHY

Margaret Eleanor Atwood was born in Ottawa, Ontario, Canada, on November 18, 1939, the second of Carl Edmund Atwood and Margaret Killam Atwood's three children. At the age of six months, she was backpacked into the Quebec wilderness, where her father, an entomologist, pursued his special interests in bees, spruce budworms, and forest tent caterpillars. Throughout her childhood, Atwood's family spent several months of the year in the bush of Quebec and northern Ontario. She did not attend school full time until she was twelve.

Though often interrupted, Atwood's education seems to have been more than adequate. She was encouraged by her parents to read and write at an early age, and her creative efforts started at five, when she wrote stories, poems, and plays. Her serious composition, however, did not begin until she was sixteen.

In 1961, Atwood earned her B.A. in the English honors program from the University of Toronto, where she studied with poets Jay Macpherson and Margaret Avison. Her M.A. from Radcliffe followed in 1962. Continuing graduate work at Harvard in 1963, Atwood interrupted her studies before reentering the program for two more years in 1965. While she found graduate studies interesting, Atwood directed her energies largely toward her creative efforts. For her, the Ph.D. program was chiefly a means of support while she wrote. Atwood left Harvard without writing her doctoral thesis.

Returning to Canada in 1967, Atwood accepted a position at Sir George Williams University in Montreal. By this time, her poetry was gaining recognition. With the publication of *The Edible Woman* and the sale of its film rights, Atwood was able to concentrate more fully on writing, though she taught at York University and was writer-in-residence at the University of Toronto. In 1973, Atwood divorced her American husband of five years, James Polk. After the publication of *Surfacing*, she was able to support herself through her creative efforts. She moved to a farm near Alliston, Ontario, with Canadian novelist Graeme Gibson; the couple's daughter, Eleanor Jess Atwood Gibson, was born in 1979. In 1980, Atwood and her family returned to Toronto, where Atwood and Gibson became active in the Writers' Union of Canada, Amnesty International, and the International Association of Poets, Playwrights, Editors, Essayists, and Novelists (PEN).

ANALYSIS

For Margaret Atwood, an unabashed Canadian, literature became a means to cultural and personal self-awareness. "To know ourselves," she writes in *Survival*, "we must know our own literature; to know ourselves accurately, we need to know it as part of literature as a whole." Thus, when she defines Canadian literary concerns she relates her own as well, for Atwood's fiction grows out of this tradition. In her opinion, Canada's central reality is the act of survival: Canadian life and culture are decisively shaped by the demands of a harsh environment. Closely related to this defining act of survival, in Atwood's view, is the Canadian search for territorial identity—or, as literary theorist Northrop Frye put it, "Where is here?"

Atwood's heroines invariably discover themselves to be emotional refugees, strangers in a territory they can accurately label but one in which they are unable to feel at home. They are alienated not only from their environment but also from language itself; for them, communication becomes a decoding process. To a great degree, their feelings of estrangement extend from a culture that, having reduced everything to products, threatens to consume them. Women are particularly singled out as products, items to be decorated and sold as commodities, though men are threatened as well. Indeed, Canadian identity as a whole is in danger of being engulfed by an acquisitive American culture, though Atwood's "Americans" symbolize exploitation and often turn out to be Canadian nationals.

Reflective of their time and place, Atwood's characters are appropriately ambivalent. Dead or dying traditions prevent their return to the past, a past most have rejected. Their present is ephemeral at best, and their future inconceivable. Emotionally maimed, her heroines plumb their conscious and unconscious impressions, searching for a return to feeling, a means of identification with the present.

Atwood often couches their struggle in terms of a journey, which serves as a controlling metaphor for inner explorations: The unnamed heroine of *Surfacing* returns to the wilderness of Quebec, Lesje Green of *Life Before Man* wanders through imagined Mesozoic jungles, Rennie Wilford of *Bodily Harm* flies to the insurgent islands of Ste. Agathe and St. Antoine. By setting contemporary culture in relief, these primitive sites define the difference between nature and culture and allow Atwood's heroines to gain new perspectives on their own realities. They can see people and places in relation to each other, not as isolated entities. Ultimately, however, this resolves little, for Atwood's novels end on a tenuous note. Although her heroines come to terms with themselves, they remain estranged.

Supporting her characters' ambivalence is Atwood's versatile narrative technique. Her astringent prose reflects their emotional numbness; its ironic restraint reveals their wariness. Frequent contradictions suggest not only the complexity of her characters but also the antagonistic times they must survive. By skillful juxtaposition of past and present through the use of flashbacks, Atwood evokes compelling fictional landscapes that ironically comment on the untenable state of modern men and women. Still, there remains some hope, for her characters survive with increased understanding of their world. Despite everything, life does go on.

SURFACING

The first of Atwood's novels to arouse critical praise and commentary, *Surfacing* explores new facets of the bildungsroman. What might have been a conventional novel of self-discovery develops into a resonant search for self-recovery imbued with mythic overtones and made accessible through Atwood's skillful use of symbol and ritual. At the same time, Atwood undercuts the romantic literary conventions of ultimate self-realization as a plausible conclusion. To accept the heroine's final emergence as an end in itself is to misread this suggestively ironic novel.

The unnamed heroine of *Surfacing*, accompanied by her lover, Joe, and a married couple named David and Anna, returns to the Canadian wilderness where she was reared in hopes of locating her missing father. His sudden disappearance has recalled her from a city life marked by personal and professional failures that have left her emotionally anesthetized. While her external search goes forward, the heroine conducts a more important internal investigation to locate missing "gifts" from both parents. Through these, she hopes to rediscover her lost ability to feel. In order to succeed, however, she will need to expose the fiction of her life.

At the outset of her narrative, the heroine warns her readers that she has led a double life when she recalls Anna's question, "Do you have a twin?" She denies having one, for she apparently believes the elaborate fiction she has created, a story involving a spurious marriage, divorce, and abandonment of her child. As additional protection, the heroine has distanced herself from everyone. She refers to her family as "they," "as if they were somebody else's family." Her relationship with Joe is notable for its coolness, and she has known Anna, described as her best friend, for only two months.

By surrounding herself with friends whose occupation of making a film significantly titled *Random Samples* reveals their rootlessness, the heroine seeks to escape the consequences of her actions. Indeed, she describes herself both as a commercial artist, indicating her sense of having sold out, and as an escape artist. Reluctantly approaching the past she sought to escape, the heroine feels as if she is in foreign territory.

That she feels alienated by the location of her past is not surprising, for she is an outsider in a number of telling ways: of English descent in French territory; a non-Catholic, indeed nonreligious, person among the devout; a woman in a man's world. Her French is so halting that she could be mistaken for an American, representing yet another form of alienation, displacement by foreigners. Most of all, she is a stranger to herself. Rather than focusing on her self-alienation, she is consumed by the American usurpation of Canada, its wanton rape of virgin wilderness; this allows her to avoid a more personal loss of innocence.

Canada's victimization by Americans reflects the heroine's victimization by men. Having been subjected to the concept that "with a paper bag over their head they're all the same," the protagonist is perceived as either contemptible or threatening. Her artistic skills are denigrated by a culture in which no "important" artists have been women. Even her modest commercial success is treated as a personal assault by Joe, who has an "unvoiced claim to superior artistic skills." By telling herself that the wilderness can never recover from abuse, the protagonist denies her own recovery. Although she feels helpless at the beginning of the novel, she soon rediscovers her own capabilities, and as these are increasingly tested, she proves to be a powerful survivor. Thus, the wilderness, a self-reflection, provides the key to self-discovery.

Perhaps the most important lesson the heroine learns is that the wilderness is not innocent. Her encounter with and response to a senselessly slaughtered heron evoke a sense of complicity, leading her to reflect on similar collusion in her brother's animal experiments when they were children. Finding her refuge in childhood innocence blocked, the heroine goes forward with her search. Once again, nature provides information, for in discovering her father's body trapped under water, she finally recognizes her aborted child, her complicity in its death by yielding to her lover's demands. On a broader scale, she acknowledges death as a part of life and reclaims her participation in the life process by conceiving a child by Joe.

In a ceremony evocative of primitive fertility rites, she seduces her lover. Then, assured of her pregnancy, she undergoes a systematic purgation in order to penetrate to the very core of reality. During this process, the protagonist discovers her parents' gifts—her father's sense of sight and her mother's gift of life. With body and mind reunited, she takes an oath in which she refuses to be a victim. Whole, she feels free to reenter her own time, no longer either victim or stranger.

Atwood's procedure for bringing her heroine to this state of consciousness is remarkable for its intricacy. Though she distrusts language, the protagonist proceeds to tell her story by describing what she sees. Since she has lost her ability to feel, much of this description seems to be objective—until the reader realizes just how unreliable her impressions can be. Contradictions abound, creating enormous uncertainty as intentional and unintentional irony collide, lies converge, and opinion stated as fact proves to be false. Given this burden of complexity, any simple conclusion to *Surfacing* is out of the question. Clearly, Atwood hints at a temporary union with Joe, but this is far from resolving the heroine's dilemma. Outer reality, after all, has not altered. Atwood's open-ended conclusion is thus both appropriate and plausible, for to resolve all difficulties would be to give in to the very romantic conventions that her fiction subverts.

Life Before Man

Coming after the gothic comedy of *Lady Oracle*, *Life Before Man* seems especially stark. Nevertheless, its similarity with all of Atwood's novels is apparent. A penetrating examination of contemporary relationships, it peels away protective layers of deceptions, stripping the main characters until their fallible selves are presented with relentless accuracy. Lesje Green and Elizabeth and Nate Schoenhof are adrift in a collapsing culture in which they struggle to survive. As she focuses on each character, Atwood reveals unrecognized facets of the others.

In this novel, wilderness and culture converge in the Royal Ontario Museum, where Lesje works as a paleontologist and Elizabeth works in public relations. There is little need for the bush country of Quebec, since culture is something of a jungle itself. Unlike the Mesozoic, however, the present anticipates its own extinction because of abundant evidence: pollution, separatist movements, political upheaval, lost traditions, disintegrating families. Humanity is in danger of drowning in its own waste. Whatever predictability life held in the past seems completely absent; even holidays are meaningless. Still, the novel is fascinated with the past, with the behavior of animals, both human and prehistoric, and with the perpetuation of memory, particularly as it records the history of families.

As in *Surfacing*, a violent death precipitates emotional withdrawal. Most affected is Elizabeth Schoenhof, whose lover Chris has blown off his head as a final gesture of defiance, the ultimate form of escape. His act destroys Elizabeth's sense of security, which resides both in her home and in her ability to manipulate or predict the actions of others. A supreme manipulator, Elizabeth attempts to make everyone act as reasonably as she. Not surprisingly, Elizabeth has at least two selves speaking different languages, genteel chic and street argot, and what passes for "civilized" behavior is merely an escape from honest confrontation with such basic human emotions as love, grief, rejection, and anger. In fact, all of the novel's characters prefer escape to self-realization, and while they pay lip service to social decorum, they quietly rebel.

Their rebellious emotions are reflected in the larger world, a political world aflame with separatist zeal. René Lévesque, with whom Nate identifies, is gaining momentum for the separation of Quebec and the reestablishment of French as the major language, threatening to displace the English. Indeed, the world seems to be coming apart as international, national, and personal moves toward separation define this novel's movement. As a solution, however, separation fails to satisfy the characters' need to escape, for no matter how far they run, all carry the baggage of their past.

Elizabeth in particular has survived a loveless past, including abandonment by both parents, the painful death of her alcoholic mother, her sister's mental breakdown and drowning, and her Auntie Muriel's puritanical upbringing. All of this has turned Elizabeth into a determined survivor. Beneath her polished exterior is a street fighter from the slums, a primitive. Indeed, Elizabeth recognizes an important part of herself in Chris. Nate and Lesje share a different kind of past, where love created as much tension as affection.

Lesje's Jewish and Ukrainian grandmothers treated her as disputed territory, speaking to her in languages she could not understand and driving her to seek refuge in her fantasy world of Lesjeland.

Feeling like a refugee in treacherous territory, each character attempts to build a new, stable world, notwithstanding the continual impingement of the old, messy one. Nate, having forsaken his mother's futile idealistic causes to save the world, falls in love with Lesje, whom he envisions as an exotic subtropical island free from rules. For a time, Elizabeth inhabits a clean expanse of space somewhere between her bed and the ceiling, and Lesje explores prehistoric terrain, wishing for a return to innocence. When these fantasies diminish in power, the characters find substitutes, challenging the reader to reexamine the novel's possibilities.

Despite its bleak tone, its grimy picture of a deteriorating culture, its feeling of estrangement and futility, and its rejection of simplistic resolutions, *Life Before Man* is not without hope. Each character emerges at the end of this novel with something he or she has desired. Nate has Lesje, now pregnant with his child—a child who, in turn, confirms Lesje's commitment to life by displacing her preoccupation with death. Having exorcised the evil spirits of her past, Elizabeth experiences a return of direct emotion.

There is, however, a distinct possibility that the apparent resolution is as ambivalent as that of *Surfacing*. What appears to be a completely objective third-person point of view, presiding over chapters neatly cataloged by name and date, sometimes shifts to the first person, an unreliable first person at that. Through her revolving characters, their identification with one another, and their multiple role reversals, Atwood creates contradictory, problematic, and deceptive human characters who defy neat categorization. Taken separately, Nate, Elizabeth, and Lesje can easily be misinterpreted; taken as a whole, they assume an even more complex meaning, reflecting not only their own biased viewpoints but also the reader's. Atwood's ability to capture such shifting realities of character and place is one of her chief artistic distinctions.

BODILY HARM

Rather like the narrator of *Surfacing*, Rennie Wilford in *Bodily Harm* has abandoned her past, the stifling world of Griswold, Ontario, to achieve modest success as a freelance journalist. To Rennie, Griswold represents values of duty, self-sacrifice, and decency found comic by modern-day standards. It is a place where women are narrowly confined to assigned roles that make them little better than servants. Rennie much prefers city life, with its emphasis on mobility and trends such as slave-girl bracelets and pornographic art. In fact, Rennie has become an expert on just such trends, so adept that she can either describe or fabricate one with equal facility. Having learned to look only at surfaces, Rennie has difficulty accepting the reality of her cancerous breast, which *looks* so healthy.

Her cancer serves as the controlling metaphor in the novel, spreading from diseased personal relationships to a political eruption on St. Antoine. Indeed, the world seems shot through with moral cancer. The symptoms are manifest: Honesty is a liability, friends are "contacts," lovers are rapists, pharmacists are drug pushers, and no one wants to hear about issues. What should be healthy forms of human commerce have gone out of control, mirroring the rioting cells in Rennie's breast. When confronted by yet another manifestation of this malaise, a would-be murderer who leaves a coil of rope on her bed, Rennie finds a fast escape route by landing a magazine assignment on St. Antoine.

Her hopes of being a tourist, exempt from participation and responsibility, are short-lived as she is drawn into a political intrigue more life-threatening than her cancer. Before reaching St. Antoine, she learns of its coming election, ignoring Dr. Minnow's allusions to political corruption and makeshift operations. What puzzles her most about their conversation is his reference to the "sweet Canadians." Is he being ironic or not, she wonders. Her superficial observations of island life reveal little, though plenty of evidence points to a violent eruption. Rennie seems more concerned about avoiding sunburn and arrest for drug possession than she is about the abundant poverty and casual violence. Her blindness allows her to become a gunrunner, duped by Lora Lucas, a resilient survivor of many injurious experiences, and Paul, the local connection for drugs and guns, who initiates Rennie into genuine, albeit unwilling, massive involvement.

As a physical link to life, Paul's sexual attention is important to Rennie, who appreciates the value of his touch. His hands call forth the "missing" hands of her grandmother, her doctor's hands, and Lora's bitten hands, hands that deny or offer help. Paul's "aid" to the warring political factions, like Canada's donation of canned hams and Rennie's assistance, is highly questionable, and the results are the reverse of what was planned. Trying to escape from his botched plan, Rennie is brought to confront her own guilt.

Again, Atwood uses flight as a route to self-discovery and deprivation as a source of spiritual nourishment. In Rennie's case, however, these are externally imposed. In her underground cell, with only Lora as company, Rennie ultimately sees and understands the violent disease consuming the world, a disease growing out of a human need to express superiority in a variety of ways and at great spiritual expense. Rennie becomes "afraid of men because men are frightening." Equally important, she understands that there is no difference between *here* and *there*. Finally, she knows that she is not exempt: "Nobody is exempt from anything."

If she survives this ordeal, Rennie plans to change her life, becoming a reporter who will tell what truly happened. Once again, however, Atwood leaves this resolution open to questions. Rennie is often mistaken about what she sees and frequently misinterprets events. Her entire story may well be a prison journal, an account of how she arrived there. When projecting her emergence from prison, she uses the future tense. For Atwood's purposes, this is of relative unimportance, since Rennie has been restored in a way she never anticipated. In the end, stroking Lora's battered hand, Rennie finally embodies the best of Griswold with a clear vision of what lies beneath the surface of human reality.

THE HANDMAID'S TALE

In *The Handmaid's Tale*, Atwood's fiction turns from the realistic to the speculative, though she merely takes the political bent of the 1980's to its logical—and chilling—conclusion. Awash in a swill of pollution, promiscuity, pornography, and venereal disease, late twentieth century America erupts into political and religious battles. Rising from the ashes is the Republic of Gilead, a theocracy so conservative in its reactionary bent that women are channeled into roles as Daughters, Wives, Marthas (maids), Econowives, or Handmaids (mistresses).

The narrator, Offred (referring to her status as a possession *of* her master), is among the first group of Handmaids, fertile women assigned to high-ranking government officials. Weaving between her past and present in flat, almost emotionless prose, Offred draws a terrifying picture of a culture retreating to religious fundamentalist values in the name of stability. At first her prose seems to be accurate, a report from an observer. Deeper in the story, readers come to understand that Offred is numb from all that has changed in her life. Besides, she does not trust anyone, least of all herself. Still, as a survivor, she determines to stay alive, even if that means taking risks.

Her loss of freedom and identity create new hungers in Offred: curiosity about the world, a subversive desire for power, a longing for feeling, a need to take risks. In many ways, *The Handmaid's Tale* is a novel about what loss creates. Gilead, in fact, is created partially in response to men's loss of feeling, according to Fred, Offred's Commander. Offred, however, takes little comfort in his assurance that feeling has returned.

As she knows, feeling is ephemeral, often unstable, impossible to gauge. Perhaps this is why her characterization of others in the novel seems remote. While Offred observes gestures, facial movements, and voice tone, she can only guess at intent. Implicit in the simplest statement may be an important message. Offred thus decodes all kinds of communication, beginning with the Latin inscription she finds scratched in her wardrobe: "Nolite te bastardes carborundorum." Even this injunction, however, which becomes her motto, is a corruption. Though desperate for communication, Offred cautiously obscures her own message. Her struggle to understand reflects Atwood's familiar theme of the inability for an individual truly to understand another person, another situation.

By having Offred acknowledge the impossibility of accurately decoding messages, Atwood calls attention to the narrative itself. Another fictional element is the narrative's remove in time. Offred tells her story in the present, except when she refers to her life before becoming a Handmaid. Ironically, readers learn that not only is she telling her story after events, but her narrative has been reconstructed and presented to an audience at a still greater temporal remove. All of this increases the equivocal quality of the novel and its ambiguity.

While Atwood demands attention, she provides direction in prefatory quotations. Most revealing is her quotation from Jonathan Swift's "A Modest Proposal." Like Swift's satire, Atwood's skates on the surface of reality, often snagging on familiar actions and only slightly exaggerating some attitudes, especially those commonly held about women.

Perennial issues of a woman's place, the value of her work, and her true role in society are at the center of this novel.

CAT'S EYE

These concerns appear again in *Cat's Eye*, but in a more subdued form. In subject and theme, *Cat's Eye* is an artistic retrospective. Elaine Risley, a middle-aged painter, is called to Toronto to prepare for her first artistic retrospective. Risley takes the occasion to come to terms with the dimensions of self in time, which she perceives as a "series of transparencies, one laid on top of another." Her return to Toronto, where she grew up, gives her an opportunity to look through the layers of people and events from her present position on the curve of time. This perspective, often ironic and tenuous, allows Risley to accept herself, including her foibles.

Cat's Eye takes full advantage of Atwood's visual style as it reiterates the importance of perspective in relation to change. The novel's art theme emphasizes interpretation while simultaneously satirizing the kind of inflated yet highly subjective criticism published for public consumption. Atwood's most personal novel to date, *Cat's Eye* tackles the physics of life and art and arrives at Atwood's least ambiguous conclusion. Returning to her family in Vancouver, Risley notes that the starlight she sees is only a reflection. Still, she concludes, "it's enough to see by."

THE ROBBER BRIDE

In *The Robber Bride* communication as a decoding process occurs both figuratively and literally, as one of the four protagonists, the historian Antonia "Tony" Fremont, seeks to discover the underlying meaning of the past. In her own storytelling she sometimes uses a reverse code, transforming herself into her imagined heroine Ynot Tnomerf. In fact, each of the women in the novel has renamed herself to gain distance from past traumas: Karen becomes Charis to cast out the memory of sexual abuse; Tony hopes to escape the "raw sexes war" that characterized her family; Roz Grunwald becomes Rosalind Greenwood as her family climbs the social ladder.

Although cast in comic form, the novel explores issues of identity, reality versus fiction, and women's friendship. The three friends meet for lunch and reminisce about their betrayal at the hands of Zenia, a mysterious femme fatale who seduced Tony's and Roz's husbands and Charis's lover. Zenia has multiple stories about her origins, all dramatic but plausible. She ensnares her victims by preying on their fears and hopes. Speaking about the novel, Atwood has remarked that Zenia is the equivalent of the fiction writer, a liar, a trickster who creates stories to captivate her audience.

ALIAS GRACE

Alias Grace is a historical novel based on the real case of Grace Marks, a nineteenth century Irish immigrant to Canada who was accused of being an accomplice in the murder of her employer and his housekeeper-mistress. The novel combines gothic elements, social commentary, and conventions of nineteenth century fiction to tell its story. Spinning out several parallel courtship plots, the novel elucidates the implications of class and gender: Servant women were often the victims of wealthy employers or their employers' bachelor sons. Grace's friend Mary Whitney dies of a botched abortion when she becomes pregnant.

The story is told through letters and narration by Grace and Dr. Simon Jordan, a young physician who has been employed by Grace's supporters to discover the truth of the murder. Dr. Jordan is a foil to Grace: As her fortunes rise, his fall. Hoping to win a pardon from her prison sentence, the shrewd Grace narrates her life story in great detail but claims she cannot clearly remember the events surrounding the murder. Dr. Jordan hopes to restore her faulty memory and to learn the facts of the case. However, in an ironic twist of plot, he becomes embroiled in a shabby romantic liaison and, to avoid the consequences, flees Canada in haste. He is injured while serving as a physician in the American Civil War and loses his recent memory. Grace is released from prison, given a job as a housekeeper, and marries her employer. Dr. Jordan remains in the care of his mother and the woman she has chosen to be her son's wife. At the end of the novel all the plot threads are conveniently tied together as in the conventional nineteenth century novel, but at the heart of the story Grace herself remains a mystery.

THE BLIND ASSASSIN

Some of Atwood's loyal readers may have looked to *The Blind Assassin* as an opportunity for the Nobel Committee to grace the author with its literature prize. It is a "big novel," not merely because it runs well over five hundred pages but also because it offers a large slice of Canadian history in the twentieth century—or, perhaps more accurately, modern history, in its sweep through the two world wars and the Great Depression. It is a family chronicle of at least three generations of the Chase family, a wealthy, socially prominent family whose progenitor enriched his heirs from the manufacture of buttons and underwear. Stylistically, *The Blind Assassin* is an especially complex text, a series of nested narratives, for the most part under the control of the novel's octogenarian narrator, Iris Chase Griffen, telling the story as a memoir of essentially how she has survived the rest of her family. Because she has a heart condition, Iris is racing against time to finish her story, the most important prospective reader of which is her lost granddaughter Sabrina.

Iris begins with the blunt statement, "Ten days after the war [World War II] ended, my sister Laura drove a car off a bridge," which this memoir promises to explain. Many readers of *Alias Grace* were disappointed because they expected to know eventually whether or not Grace was guilty of murder, but the opening pages of *The Blind Assassin* give a strong sense that Iris not only knows "whodunit" but will eventually divulge that information.

Before Iris can do so, she must explain everything that led up to that fatal day in 1945.

She tells how her father survived World War I—unlike his brothers—and struggled with his business through the Depression to save his workers' jobs, only to accept a merger that cost them those jobs and doomed Iris to a loveless marriage with his business rival, who delighted in leaving bruises on her body where only he could enjoy them as the stigmata of his domination. In rapid fashion Iris loses the only man she ever loved, then her sister and her husband to suicide, and finally her daughter is taken from her as well—a tragic sequence of events reminiscent of Greek tragedy.

ORYX AND CRAKE

Atwood has encouraged readers to approach *Oryx and Crake* as a "bookend" to *The Handmaid's Tale*. *Oryx and Crake* is also set in a future United States. It involves speculation concerning humankind's uses of science, but Atwood rejects the term "science fiction" for this novel as well as for *The Handmaid's Tale*, preferring instead to call them "speculative fiction." She has been adamant in arguing that all the scientific elements she needed for *Oryx and Crake*'s future world, in which global warming and genetic engineering are the dominant forces, are either already in play or merely extensions of the present.

Oryx and Crake represents a new departure for the author as her first novel with a male viewpoint character. Snowman, short for "The Abominable Snowman," struggles to survive in a postapocalyptic world. Snowman was once "Jimmy," the childhood chum of Crake, a boy wonder of bioengineering. In its earlier stages, bioengineering was a boy's game of dreaming up hybrids such as the "rakunk," a mixture of raccoon and skunk. Now the field has developed into procedures such as NooSkins, which gradually replace human skin for a youthful appearance.

As a young man, Crake moves into a powerful position in which he seduces Oryx, whom Jimmy and Crake "met" as boys surfing child pornography online, as well as Jimmy, as his instruments in a master plan to eradicate humanity and replace it with the Children of Crake, creatures he has genetically engineered to survive, as *Homo sapiens* no longer can, in the global swamp generated by contamination of the atmosphere and the melting of the polar icecaps. These Frankenstein's "monsters" will inherit a brave new world from which Snowman and a few remaining humans will soon depart.

THE PENELOPIAD

Commissioned by Canongate Books for its series The Myths, *The Penelopiad* offers the long-suffering wife of Odysseus an opportunity to tell her side of the story from the Underworld more than three millennia after her death. Half of the novel is her memoir, a genre to which Atwood has become attracted in her later years.

Penelope begins with her unhappy childhood as the daughter of an indifferent water spirit and a royal father who foolishly sought immortality by attempting to drown her when the Oracle prophesied that Penelope would weave his shroud—actually it was her father-in-law whose shroud she would famously weave—but she was saved by a flotilla of ducks, thus earning the nickname "Duckie." From childhood she was tormented with the name by her beautiful cousin Helen, whose abduction by or elopement with Prince Paris would start the Trojan War.

Accordingly, if Penelope would cast herself as a figure in Greek tragedy—Atwood's theater adaptation has been successfully staged—Helen is the nemesis who brought about a fall from the good fortune of her early married life with Odysseus, whom she grew to love, even if she could never trust him because he was a "storyteller" and because he had his eye on Helen. Like Iris with her writer-lover, Penelope learned to tell stories after making love. Almost obsessed with her cousin as rival for Odysseus's love, Penelope devotes her energies to managing Ithaca so well that Odysseus upon his return will tell his wife she is worth a thousand Helens.

Atwood has stated that she took the Canongate assignment because she had been haunted as an early teenager by the summary execution of Penelope's twelve maids by Odysseus and Telemachus. The maids function as a Greek chorus of cynical commentary on the royals. They are Penelope's confidants, spies, and helpers with the unweaving of the shroud their mistress must finish before choosing a new husband. At least one disclosed the shroud ruse, and Penelope may have feared they would accuse her of adultery. The big question is whether Penelope colluded in their murder. Like Grace, Penelope never reveals any guilt.

Atwood's vision is as informed and humane as that of any contemporary novelist. Challenging her readers to form their own judgments, she combines the complexity of the best modern fiction with the moral rigor found in the works of the great nineteenth century novelists. Atwood's resonant symbols, her ironic reversals, and her example challenge readers and writers alike to confront the most difficult and important issues of today's world.

Karen Carmean; Karen F. Stein
Updated by Earl G. Ingersoll

OTHER MAJOR WORKS

SHORT FICTION: *Dancing Girls, and Other Stories*, 1977; *Bluebeard's Egg*, 1983; *Murder in the Dark: Short Fictions and Prose Poems*, 1983; *Wilderness Tips*, 1991; *Good Bones*, 1992 (also known as *Good Bones and Simple Murders*, 1994); *Moral Disorder*, 2006.

POETRY: *Double Persephone*, 1961; *The Circle Game*, 1964 (single poem), 1966 (collection); *Kaleidoscopes Baroque: A Poem*, 1965; *Talismans for Children*, 1965; *Expeditions*, 1966; *Speeches for Dr. Frankenstein*, 1966; *The Animals in That Country*, 1968; *What Was in the Garden*, 1969; *The Journals of Susanna Moodie*, 1970; *Procedures for Underground*, 1970; *Power Politics*, 1971; *You Are Happy*, 1974; *Selected Poems*, 1976; *Two-Headed Poems*, 1978; *True Stories*, 1981; *Snake Poems*, 1983; *Interlunar*,

1984; *Selected Poems II: Poems Selected and New, 1976-1986*, 1987; *Selected Poems, 1966-1984*, 1990; *Poems, 1965-1975*, 1991; *Poems, 1976-1989*, 1992; *Morning in the Burned House*, 1995; *Eating Fire: Selected Poems, 1965-1995*, 1998; *The Door*, 2007.

NONFICTION: *Survival: A Thematic Guide to Canadian Literature*, 1972; *Days of the Rebels, 1815-1840*, 1977; *Second Words: Selected Critical Prose*, 1982; *Margaret Atwood: Conversations*, 1990; *Deux sollicitudes: Entretiens*, 1996 (with Victor-Lévy Beaulieu; *Two Solicitudes: Conversations*, 1998); *Negotiating with the Dead: A Writer on Writing*, 2002; *Moving Targets: Writing with Intent, 1982-2004*, 2004 (also known as *Writing with Intent: Essays, Reviews, Personal Prose, 1983-2005*, 2005); *Waltzing Again: New and Selected Conversations with Margaret Atwood*, 2006 (with others; Earl G. Ingersoll, editor); *Payback: Debt and the Shadow Side of Wealth*, 2008.

CHILDREN'S LITERATURE: *Up in the Tree*, 1978; *Anna's Pet*, 1980 (with Joyce Barkhouse); *For the Birds*, 1990; *Princess Prunella and the Purple Peanut*, 1995 (illustrated by Maryann Kowalski); *Bashful Bob and Doleful Dorinda*, 2004 (illustrated by Dusan Petricic); *Rude Ramsay and the Roaring Radishes*, 2004 (illustrated by Dusan Petricic).

EDITED TEXTS: *The New Oxford Book of Canadian Verse in English*, 1982; *The Oxford Book of Canadian Short Stories in English*, 1986 (with Robert Weaver); *The CanLit Foodbook: From Pen to Palate, a Collection of Tasty Literary Fare*, 1987; *The Best American Short Stories 1989*, 1989 (with Shannon Ravenel); *The New Oxford Book of Canadian Short Stories in English*, 1995 (with Robert Weaver).

MISCELLANEOUS: *The Tent*, 2006.

BIBLIOGRAPHY

Bloom, Harold, ed. *Margaret Atwood*. Philadelphia: Chelsea House, 2000. Collection of essays by literary critics provides analyses of Atwood's major novels. Includes brief biography, chronology of Atwood's life, and an informative editor's introduction.

Brown, Jane W. "Constructing the Narrative of Women's Friendship: Margaret Atwood's Reflexive Fiction." *Literature, Interpretation, Theory* 6 (1995): 197-212. Argues that Atwood's narrative reflects the struggle of women to attain friendship and asserts that Atwood achieves this with such reflexive devices as embedded discourse, narrative fragmentation, and doubling.

Cooke, Nathalie. *Margaret Atwood: A Biography*. Toronto, Ont.: ECW Press, 1998. Although this is not an authorized biography, Atwood answered Cooke's questions and allowed her access, albeit limited, to materials for her research. A more substantive work than Sullivan's biography *The Red Shoes* (cited below).

Howells, Coral Ann. *Margaret Atwood*. New York: St. Martin's Press, 1996. Lively critical and biographical study elucidates issues that have energized all of Atwood's fiction: feminist issues, literary genres, and her own identity as a Canadian, a woman, and a writer.

_____, ed. *The Cambridge Companion to Margaret Atwood.* New York: Cambridge University Press, 2006. Collection of twelve excellent essays provides critical examination of Atwood's novels as well as a concise biography of the author.

McCombs, Judith, ed. *Critical Essays on Margaret Atwood.* Boston: G. K. Hall, 1988. Indispensable volume comprises thirty-two essays, including assessments of patterns and themes in Atwood's poetry and prose. Discusses her primary works in chronological order, beginning with *The Circle Game* and ending with *The Handmaid's Tale.* An editor's introduction provides an illuminating overview of Atwood's writing career. Includes a primary bibliography to 1986 and a thorough index.

Stein, Karen F. *Margaret Atwood Revisited.* New York: Twayne, 1999. Presents a thorough overview of Atwood's writings in all genres. Includes references and a selected bibliography.

Sullivan, Rosemary. *The Red Shoes: Margaret Atwood, Starting Out.* Toronto, Ont.: HarperFlamingo Canada, 1998. Biography focuses on Atwood's early life, until the end of the 1970's. Attempts to answer the question of how Atwood became a writer and to describe the unfolding of her career.

Wilson, Sharon Rose. *Margaret Atwood's Fairy-Tale Sexual Politics.* Jackson: University Press of Mississippi, 1993. One of the most extensive and thorough investigations available of Atwood's use of fairy-tale elements in her graphic art as well as her writing. Covers her novels up to *Cat's Eye.*

_____, ed. *Margaret Atwood's Textual Assassinations: Recent Poetry and Fiction.* Columbus: Ohio State University Press, 2003. Collection of scholarly essays examines Atwood's work, with a focus on her writings published since the late 1980's. Includes discussion of the novels *Cat's Eye, The Robber Bride, Alias Grace,* and *The Blind Assassin.*

DJUNA BARNES

Born: Cornwall-on-Hudson, New York; June 12, 1892
Died: New York, New York; June 18, 1982
Also known as: Djuna Chappell Barnes

PRINCIPAL LONG FICTION
Ryder, 1928
Nightwood, 1936

OTHER LITERARY FORMS

Although primarily known for her singular novel *Nightwood,* Djuna Barnes wrote in many genres throughout her long life. She initially earned her living in New York City as a freelance reporter and theater critic, publishing articles in the *Brooklyn Daily Eagle, New York Morning Telegraph, Vanity Fair, The New Yorker, New York Press, The Dial,* and other periodicals. Her artistic skills showed in her drawings, some of which appeared as early as 1915 in *The Book of Repulsive Women,* her first published chapbook. Her artwork also appeared as illustrations for *Ladies Almanack,* a roman à clef about lesbian circles in Paris, a book she cleverly structured in the format of an almanac. Another collection of her drawings was published in 1995 as *Poe's Mother: Selected Drawings of Djuna Barnes.* Her first collection of short stories, *A Book* (1923), was reissued as *A Night Among the Horses* in 1928 with a number of additional stories.

Barnes also was a dramatist. Her one-act plays were performed at the Provincetown Playhouse in Greenwich Village, New York City. She wrote and rewrote the full-length verse drama, *The Antiphon,* over a twenty-year period before poet T. S. Eliot, in his position as a literary editor with publisher Faber and Faber, approved the manuscript for publication. The action of the play occurs in a fictional township in England during World War II, as family members from America reunite; family drama ensues. Their memories of love and aggression probably reflect Barnes's own upbringing and family dynamics.

Barnes's last book before she died was *Creatures in an Alphabet* (1982), a collection of short rhyming poems. Since her death in 1982, collections of her journalism, short fiction, poetry, short plays, previously published work, and manuscript selections have appeared, confirming her versatile talents in many literary and artistic forms.

ACHIEVEMENTS

Djuna Barnes was initially known as a literary modernist, someone who wrote formally and linguistically complex and allusive works. In the 1970's, critics began to examine her work in the context of feminist studies and feminist literary theory. They also began researching Barnes, long known for her role in the American expatriate literary scene in Paris in the 1920's. Like Gertrude Stein, Barnes is now appreciated as a formative figure in studies of modernism and of lesbian and gay cultural history. The concessions she made to adhere to U.S. censorship regulations are less widely known, but the published typescript of *Nightwood* shows what Eliot deleted while editing. *Ryder*, in this regard, also was problematic, and Barnes used asterisks in the text to indicate the changes that she was forced to make.

Because her protagonists often refer to individuals that Barnes knew from her years in Paris or from childhood, her books lend themselves to biographical, psychobiographical, and life-writing approaches. Barnes was knowledgeable about women's rights, and her fiction investigates the nature of sexuality, gender, sexual expression, equality, and choice. Barnes received recognition for her role in American literature when she was elected in 1961 to the National Institute of Arts and Letters.

BIOGRAPHY

As a child, Djuna Chappell Barnes received no formal education, but she was educated at home in Cornwall-on-Hudson. She was one of five children in a difficult and polygamist family structure. She left for New York City after a brief and inappropriate marriage and then studied art at the Pratt Institute (1912-1913) and the Art Students League (1915-1916). While living in Greenwich Village, she became a reporter and covered political issues such as women's suffrage (her grandmother had been a suffragist), and wrote popular feature stories and conducted interviews.

Barnes moved to Paris and by the early 1920's was well established in expatriate circles on the Left Bank. She came to know James Joyce, Stein, Eliot, and many others. Memoirs from this period describe her as a dramatic, striking woman with an acerbic wit and strong will. Her *Ladies Almanack* both celebrates and satirizes the women she knew in Natalie Clifford Barney's lesbian salon on the rue Jacob, which met regularly to read writings by women. Barnes lived in Paris for about twenty years, primarily with her lover Thelma Wood. Other individuals close to her were Peggy Guggenheim, who helped support her; Emily Holmes Coleman, a writer and exhaustive diarist; and Robert McAlmon, who was responsible for privately printed *Ladies Almanack*.

Barnes also spent time in the early 1930's at the Guggenheim manor house, Hayford Hall, in the English countryside, with Guggenheim, Coleman, writer Antonia White, and an array of male and female visitors. Hayford Hall was a supportive and lively community, and the living arrangements gave Coleman the opportunity to read and critique the manuscript of *Nightwood*. Coleman's diaries reveal something most readers of Barnes do not know: Coleman's resourceful determination and urging letters were instrumental in convincing Eliot to accept the manuscript for publication by Faber and Faber and to write his somewhat ambiguous introduction.

With the onset of World War II, Barnes returned to New York and moved to a small apartment on the historic Patchin Place in Greenwich Village. She lived there for decades, eventually in failing health and famously unreceptive to visitors, including scholars. She sold her correspondence and manuscripts to the McKeldin Library at the University of Maryland in College Park in 1972 but destroyed parts of her personal archive. According to various accounts, Barnes's neighbors at Patchin Place could smell smoke coming from her apartment, and they knew that she was methodically burning information she did not want to become part of her history and legacy.

ANALYSIS

The difficulties of negotiating identity in a culture whose moral values and cultural expectations are powerful and repressive run throughout Djuna Barnes's canon, from her satirical and witty works to the profoundly serious and dark *Nightwood*. Emotions, which run high through the generations of the families she depicts, are reflected in the struggles, violence, or loyalties of individuals. Characters across a broad Euro-American landscape try to locate and free themselves from old patterns of quest and fulfillment, seeking authentic channels of emotional and sexual intimacy. Barnes's work incorporates multiple levels of meaning and multiple layers of figurative allusiveness, which make it challenging for readers to distinguish truth from falsehood and sincerity from fabrication; the characters themselves may not articulate their positions and often may not know themselves.

From the vantage point of the early twenty-first century Barnes remains a modernist concerned with literary innovation, but she is indisputably a saboteur of traditional culture, a woman who extended her writing beyond traditional modernism and who lived according to her own standards. Like other women writers of the period, such as H. D., Jean Rhys, Anaïs Nin, and Gertrude Stein, she cared about women's freedom and was certainly a feminist. It could be said, however, that her greatest allegiance was to language, to creating it and controlling it either through elaborate expression or declared silence.

RYDER

Published in 1928 with the author's own illustrations, Barnes's first novel, *Ryder*, is an elaborately structured story about the Ryder family, extending through four generations up to the early twentieth century. There are many family members, some of whom appear briefly while others, like the patriarch and polygamist Wendell Ryder (based on Barnes's father), loom large. The book sold well for a time, but the complexities of its language (Chaucerian, Elizabethan, and Rabelaisian) and harsh portrayal of family relationships failed to sustain a readership.

Highly ambitious, *Ryder* works through literary pastiche and satire, relying also on quick changes of style, tone, and narrative points of view. On some levels it resembles a family chronicle, but it progresses episodically with part of its energy created by many embedded genres, including letters, poems, ghost stories, lullabies, parables, and epigrams. The book creates tension between patriarchy and matriarchy and gradually foregrounds women's struggles for autonomy and integrity through the mothers and daughters it portrays.

NIGHTWOOD

Nightwood is Barnes's major work of fiction and is undoubtedly the book on which her strong reputation will continue to be based. Its literary style is dazzling, and its language is highly structured. Although like other modernist masterpieces, it brilliantly undermines traditional elements of plot, character development, and linearity. The story is minimalist, taking place primarily in Europe between the two world wars and projecting a landscape of postwar disillusionment. The characters attempt to move beyond their individual despair to find new communities.

At the center is Robin Vote, whose silences make her unknowable and protean, regardless of where and with whom she goes. Felix Volkbein, a supposed Old World aristocrat, marries Robin in anticipation of producing strong progeny, but Robin leaves him and her young son and goes off with Nora Flood, the "Westerner" from the United States. Nora is devoted to Robin even after Robin abandons her. She follows Robin in her wanderings and witnesses Robin's horrific breakdown in the final chapter. Nora carries the weight of loyalty and has the equilibrium of balanced self-knowledge. In contrast, Robin is forever in flux, the "eternal momentary," and thus a source to be pursued and repeatedly lost.

The person who reigns over events is Dr. Matthew O'Connor, who functions as a modern-day Tiresias, imparting advice to the individuals who seek him out for predictions and wisdom from his private *quartier* in Paris. Matthew comes to occupy the center stage of *Nightwood* as chronology recedes and long monologues replace direct narrative action. Matthew's monologues respond to each character's questions and their own respective monologues. Increasingly, the doctor exposes his uncertain identity and own collection of self-performances.

In the chapter "Go Down, Matthew," Matthew explains the message that Robin's abandonments suggest: Life is not to be known or understood, despite the relentless attempts. Whatever one does, individually or coupled or communally, life will not reveal itself, and whatever stories the narrative seems to tell, the accounting is flawed, merely one of many possible and impossible fabrications. There are formulas for actions and prescriptions for truths, and they all fall into dissolution. These revelations have repercussion within the plot and beyond it, repercussions for *Nightwood* as a literary text: Structure rebounds on itself, and then order blurs into different orders or into disorder. In other words, *Nightwood* incorporates some of the familiar modernist conclusions, but it does so with Barnes's unique genius.

The last few pages of the novel, titled "The Possessed," depict the most pessimistic scene in the book. Robin, who has quested through marriage, childbirth, motherhood, and bisexuality, makes her way to Nora's country property in the United States. Reaching a decaying chapel on the property reminiscent of the one in Eliot's modernist poem *The Waste Land* (1922), Robin collapses and swings at Nora's dog, both of them barking before going entirely silent. The scene is open to different interpretations but is surely a reckoning of the woman, and women, whose socialized and rebellious sides fight one another in a psychic and mythic war of attrition. There are many ways to approach and understand *Nightwood*. What is unlikely to change is *Nightwood*'s central position in the evolving history of prose narrative.

Miriam Fuchs

OTHER MAJOR WORKS

SHORT FICTION: *A Night Among the Horses*, 1929; *Spillway*, 1962; *Smoke, and Other Early Stories*, 1982; *Collected Stories*, 1996.

PLAYS: *Three from the Earth*, pr., pb. 1919; *The Antiphon*, pb. 1958; *At the Roots of the Stars: The Short Plays*, 1995.

POETRY: *The Book of Repulsive Women*, 1915 (includes drawings); *Collected Poems: With Notes Toward the Memoirs*, 2005.

NONFICTION: *Interviews*, 1985 (journalism); *I Could Never Be Lonely Without a Husband*, 1987 (Alyce Barry, editor); *New York*, 1989 (journalism).

CHILDREN'S LITERATURE: *Creatures in an Alphabet*, 1982.

MISCELLANEOUS: *A Book*, 1923 (enlarged edition published as *A Night Among the Horses*, 1929; abridged as *Spillway*, 1962); *Ladies' Almanack*, 1928; *Selected Works*, 1962; *Poe's Mother: Selected Drawings of Djuna Barnes*, 1995 (Douglas Messerli, editor).

BIBLIOGRAPHY

Benstock, Shari. *Women of the Left Bank, 1900-1940*. Austin: University of Texas Press, 1986. Classic biocritical study of women artists, writers, and intellectuals. Chapter seven covers Barnes's life and writing while she lived on the Left Bank of Paris, a thriving center for American expatriates.

Broe, Mary Lynn, ed. *Silence and Power: A Reevaluation of Djuna Barnes*. Carbondale: Southern Illinois University Press, 1991. Pivotal collection of essays that emphasize the feminist and communal aspects of Barnes's life.

Chait, Sandra M., and Elizabeth M. Podnieks, eds. *Hayford Hall: Hangovers, Erotics, and Aesthetics*. Carbondale: Southern University Illinois Press, 2005. Critical essays examine the characters living and learning at Hayford Hall, the Devonshire estate in England where Barnes lived for a time.

Fuchs, Miriam. "Djuna Barnes and T. S. Eliot: Resistance and Acquiescence." *Tulsa Studies in Women's Literature* 12, no. 2 (Fall, 1993): 288-313. Uses unpublished correspondence to map the collaborative dynamics between Barnes and poet T. S. Eliot.

_____. "The Triadic Association of Emily Holmes Coleman, T. S. Eliot, and Djuna Barnes." *ANQ: A Journal of Short Articles, Notes, and Reviews* 12, no. 4 (Fall, 1999): 28-39. Examines Emily Holmes Coleman's unpublished diary entries to relate the drama behind T. S. Eliot's decision to publish Barnes's novel *Nightwood*.

Herring, Phillip F. *Djuna: The Life and Work of Djuna Barnes*. New York: Viking Press,

1995. A useful, comprehensive, and critical biography of Barnes that traces her inspirations and influences. Herring examined private papers and manuscripts and inter-
viewed family and friends for this scholarly but accessible work.

Kannenstine, Louis F. *The Art of Djuna Barnes: Duality and Damnation.* New York: New
York University Press, 1977. The first university press study of Barnes, which aligns
Barnes with James Joyce. A groundbreaking work that nevertheless has been criti-
cized by feminist and other scholars.

Review of Contemporary Fiction 13, no. 3 (Fall, 1993). Special issue on Barnes's fiction.
Features papers presented at the Djuna Barnes Centennial Conference at the University of Maryland in 1992.

Warren, Diane. *Djuna Barnes' Consuming Fictions.* Cornwall, England: Ashgate, 2008.
Study that positions itself in relation to ongoing dialogues and debates about Barnes's
work. Emphasizes her ideas of identity, language, and culture.

KATE CHOPIN

Born: St. Louis, Missouri; February 8, 1851
Died: St. Louis, Missouri; August 22, 1904
Also known as: Katherine O'Flaherty

PRINCIPAL LONG FICTION
At Fault, 1890
The Awakening, 1899

OTHER LITERARY FORMS

In addition to her novels, Kate Chopin (SHO-pan) wrote nearly fifty poems, approximately one hundred stories and vignettes, and a small amount of literary criticism. Her poems are slight, and no serious claims can be made for them. Her criticism also tends to be modest, but it is often revealing. In one piece written in 1896, for example, she discloses that she discovered Guy de Maupassant eight years earlier—that is, when she first began to write. There is every indication that Maupassant remained one of her most important models in the short-story form. In another essay, she pays tribute to Mary Wilkins Freeman, the New England local colorist whose depiction of repressed passion in women was probably an influence on Chopin's own work. Elsewhere, Chopin seems to distinguish between her own writing and that of the so-called local-color school. She is critical of Hamlin Garland for his concern with social problems, "which alone does not insure the survival of a work of art," and she finds the horizons of the Indiana local-color writers too narrow. The subject of genuine fiction is not regional quaintness, she remarks, but "human existence in its subtle, complex . . . meaning, stripped of the veil with which ethical and conventional standards have draped it." She finds no moral purpose in nature, and in her fiction she frequently implies the relativity of morals and received standards.

Chopin's most important work, apart from her novels, lies in the short story. It was for her short stories that she was chiefly known in her time. Her earliest stories are unexceptional, but within only a few years she was producing impressive work, including a fine series of stories set in Natchitoches Parish, Louisiana. Many of these mature stories are included in the two volumes published during her lifetime—*Bayou Folk* (1894) and *A Night in Acadie* (1897). All of her stories and sketches were made available with the 1969 publication of *The Complete Works of Kate Chopin*. Had she never written *The Awakening*, these stories alone, the best of which are inimitable and gemlike, would ensure Chopin a place among the notable writers of the 1890's.

ACHIEVEMENTS

Kate Chopin's reputation today rests primarily on three books: her two short-story collections, *Bayou Folk* and *A Night in Acadie*, and her mature novel, *The Awakening. Bayou*

Folk collects most of her fiction of the early 1890's set in Natchitoches (pronounced NAK-uh-tahsh) Parish. The characters it generally portrays, although belonging to different social levels, are Creole, Acadian (Cajun), or African American. In many cases they are poor. Not all of the stories in *Bayou Folk* are perfectly achieved, for when Chopin departs from realism into more fanciful writing she loses her power, but three of the stories in this volume—"Beyond the Bayou," "Désirée's Baby," and "Madame Célestin's Divorce"—are among her most famous and most frequently anthologized.

A Night in Acadie collects Chopin's stories from the middle and late 1890's. In many of the stories, the protagonists come to sudden recognitions that alter their sense of the world; Chopin's recurring theme is the awakening of a spirit that, through a certain set of circumstances, is liberated into conscious life. Passion is often the agent of liberation; whereas in the fiction of William Dean Howells, for example, characters frequently meet and fall putatively in love, in Chopin's fiction they do so from the inmost springs of their being. There is nothing putative or factitious about Chopin's characters who are brought to the point of love or desire. *A Night in Acadie* differs from *Bayou Folk* somewhat in the greater emphasis it gives to the erotic drives of its characters.

Chopin's authority in this aspect of experience, along with her concern with the interaction of the deeply inward on the outward life, sets her work apart from other local-color writing of the time. In her early novel *At Fault*, she had not as yet begun to probe deeply into the psychology of her characters. David Hosmer and Thérèse Lafirme are drawn too much at the surface level to sustain the kind of writing that Chopin does best. After she had developed her art in her stories, however, she was able to bring her psychological concerns to perfection in *The Awakening*, her greatest work. Chopin's achievement was somewhat narrowly bounded, without the scope of the fiction of manners that occupied Howells and Henry James, but in *Bayou Folk*, *A Night in Acadie*, and *The Awakening*, Chopin gave to American letters works of enduring interest—the interest not so much of local color as of a strikingly sensuous psychological realism.

BIOGRAPHY

Kate Chopin was born Katherine O'Flaherty on February 8, 1851, in St. Louis, Missouri, into a socially prominent family with roots in the French past of both St. Louis and New Orleans. Her father, Thomas O'Flaherty, an immigrant from Ireland, had lived in New York and Illinois before settling in St. Louis, where he prospered as the owner of a commission house. In 1839, he married into a well-known Creole family, members of the city's social elite, but his wife died in childbirth only a year later. In 1844, he married Eliza Faris, merely fifteen years old but, according to French custom, eligible for marriage. Faris was the daughter of a Huguenot man who had migrated from Virginia and a woman who was descended from the Charlevilles, among the earliest French settlers in America.

Kate was one of three children born to her parents and the only one to live to mature years. In 1855, tragedy struck the O'Flaherty family when her father, now a director of the

Pacific Railroad, was killed in a train wreck; thereafter, Kate lived in a house of many widows—her mother, grandmother, and great-grandmother Charleville. In 1860, she entered the St. Louis Academy of the Sacred Heart, a Catholic institution where French history, language, and culture were stressed—as they were, also, in her own household. Such an early absorption in French culture would eventually influence Chopin's own writing, an adaptation in some ways of French forms to American themes.

Chopin graduated from the Academy of the Sacred Heart in 1868, and two years later she was introduced to St. Louis society, becoming one of its ornaments, a vivacious and attractive girl known for her cleverness and talents as a storyteller. The following year, she made a trip to New Orleans, and it was there that she met Oscar Chopin, whom she married in 1871. After a three-month honeymoon in Germany, Switzerland, and France, the couple moved to New Orleans, where Chopin's husband was a cotton factor (a businessman who financed the raising of cotton and transacted its sale). Oscar Chopin prospered at first, but in 1878 and 1879, the period of the great "Yellow Jack" epidemic and of disastrously poor harvests, he suffered reverses. The Chopin family then went to live in rural Louisiana, where, at Cloutierville, Oscar Chopin managed some small plantations he owned.

By all accounts, the Chopin marriage was an unusually happy one, and in time Kate became the mother of six children. This period in her life ended, however, in 1883 with the sudden death, from swamp fever, of her husband. A widow at thirty, Chopin remained at Cloutierville for a year, overseeing her husband's property, and then moved to St. Louis, where she remained for the rest of her life. She began to write in 1888, while still rearing her children, and in the following year she made her first appearance in print. As her writing shows, her marriage to Oscar Chopin proved to be much more than an "episode" in her life, for it is from this period in New Orleans and Natchitoches Parish that she drew her best literary material and her strongest inspiration. She knew this area personally, and yet as an "outsider" she was also able to observe it with the freshness of detachment.

Considering the fact that she had only begun to have her stories published in 1889, it is remarkable that Chopin should already have written and published her first novel, *At Fault*, by 1890. The novel is apprenticeship work and was published by a St. Louis company at her own expense, but it does show a sense of form. She then wrote a second novel, "Young Dr. Gosse," which in 1891 she sent out to a number of publishers, all of whom refused it, and which she later destroyed. After finishing this second novel, she concentrated on the shorter forms of fiction, writing forty stories, sketches, and vignettes during the next three years. By 1894, her stories began to find a reception in eastern magazines, notably in *Vogue*, *The Atlantic Monthly*, and *Century*. In the same year, her first short-story collection, *Bayou Folk*, was published by Houghton Mifflin to favorable reviews. Even so, because short-story collections were not commercially profitable, she had difficulty placing her second collection, *A Night in Acadie*, which was brought out by a relatively little-known publisher in Chicago in 1897.

Although having achieved some reputation as an author of what were generally perceived to be local-color stories set in northern Louisiana, Chopin was still far from having established herself as a writer whose work was commercially profitable. Under the advice of editors that a longer work would have a broader appeal, she turned again to the novel form, publishing *The Awakening* in 1899. *The Awakening*, however, received uniformly unfavorable reviews, and in some cities it was banned from library shelves. In St. Louis, Chopin was dropped by friends and refused membership in a local fine-arts club. Chopin had never expected such a storm of condemnation and, although she withstood it calmly, she was deeply hurt by the experience. She wrote little thereafter and never published another book. In 1904, after attending the St. Louis World's Fair, she was stricken with a cerebral hemorrhage and died two days later.

With her death, Chopin's reputation went into almost total eclipse. In literary histories written early in the century, her work was mentioned only in passing, with brief mention of her local-color stories but none at all of *The Awakening*. Even in the first biography of Chopin, Daniel S. Rankin's *Kate Chopin and Her Creole Stories* (1932), *The Awakening* was passed over quickly as a "morbid" book. The modern discovery of Chopin did not begin until the early 1950's, when the French critic Cyrille Arnavon translated *The Awakening* into French and wrote an introduction to the novel in which he discussed Chopin's writing as early realism comparable in some respects to that of Frank Norris and Theodore Dreiser. In essays written in the mid-1950's, Robert Cantwell and Kenneth Eble called attention to *The Awakening* as a neglected work of classic stature.

The belated recognition of *The Awakening* gained momentum in the 1960's when Edmund Wilson included a discussion of Chopin in *Patriotic Gore: Studies in the Literature of the American Civil War* (1963), in which he described *The Awakening* as a "quite uninhibited and beautifully written [novel] which anticipates D. H. Lawrence in its treatment of infidelity." By the mid-1960's, *The Awakening* was reprinted for the first time in half a century, and critics such as Werner Berthoff, Larzer Ziff, and George Arms all praised it warmly; Ziff called the novel "the most important piece of fiction about the sexual life of a woman written to date in America." With the publication of Per Seyersted's *Kate Chopin: A Critical Biography* (1969) and his edition of her writings, *The Complete Works of Kate Chopin*, Chopin's work at long last became fully available. Chopin has been of particular interest to feminist scholars, but interest in her work has not been limited to a single group. It is now generally conceded that Chopin was one of the significant writers of the 1890's, and *The Awakening* is commonly viewed as a small masterpiece.

ANALYSIS

When Kate Chopin began to publish, local-color writing, which came into being after the Civil War and crested in the 1880's, had already been established. Bret Harte and Mark Twain had created a special ambience for their fiction in the American West, Sarah Orne Jewett and Mary Wilkins Freeman had drawn their characters in the context of a New England world in decline, and the Creole culture of New Orleans and the plantation region beyond it had been depicted by George Washington Cable, Grace King, and Ruth McEnery Stuart.

AT FAULT

A late arriver to the scene, Chopin was at first, as her stories show, uncertain even of her locale. *At Fault*, her first novel, was a breakthrough for her in the sense that she found her rural Louisiana "region." The novel is set in the present, a setting that is important to its sphere of action. Place-du-Bois, the plantation, represents conservative, traditional values that are challenged by new, emergent ones. David Hosmer, from St. Louis, obtains lumber rights on Place-du-Bois, and with him comes conflict. *At Fault* deals with divorce, but beyond that, it addresses the contradictions of nature and convention. Place-du-Bois seems at times idyllic, but it is shadowed by the cruelties of its slaveholding past, abuses created by too rigidly held assumptions. St. Louis is almost the opposite, a world as much without form as Hosmer's pretty young wife, who goes to pieces there and again at Place-du-Bois.

A problem novel, *At Fault* looks skeptically at nature but also at received convention. Intelligent and well thought out, it raises a question that will appear again in *The Awakening*: Is the individual responsible to others or to him- or herself? The characters in *At Fault* tend to be merely vehicles for ideas, but in the short stories Chopin wrote after the novel, her ability to create characters with emotional richness becomes apparent. If *At Fault* suggests the symmetrical social novels of William Dean Howells, *Bayou Folk* gives the impression of southern folk writing brought to a high degree of perfection. The dominant theme in this collection is the universality of illusion, while the stories in *A Night in Acadie* prepare for *The Awakening*, in which a married woman, her self-assertion stifled in a conventional marriage, is awakened to the sensuous and erotic life.

Comparable in kind to Gustave Flaubert's *Madame Bovary* (1857; English translation, 1886), *The Awakening* is Chopin's most elaborate orchestration of the theme of bondage and illusion. Dramatic in form, intensely focused, it makes use of imagery and symbolism to an extent never before evident in Chopin's work. The boldness of her possession of theme in *The Awakening* is wholly remarkable. Her earliest effort in the novel, *At Fault*, asks if the individual is responsible to others or to him- or herself, a question that is raised again in *The Awakening*. *At Fault*, however, deals with its characters conventionally, on the surface only, while in *The Awakening* Chopin captures the deep, inner life of Edna Pontellier and projects it powerfully onto a world of convention.

In writing *At Fault*, Chopin drew on her familiarity with two regions, St. Louis and the plantation country north of New Orleans. The hero, David Hosmer, comes to Louisiana from St. Louis, like Chopin herself, and at least one segment of the novel is set in St. Louis. The heroine, Thérèse Lafirme, proprietress of Place-du-Bois, is similar to Chopin—a widow at thirty who carries on the management of her late husband's property. Moreover, her plantation of four thousand acres is of the same size as and seems suggested by that of

Chopin's father-in-law, who had purchased it from the notorious Robert McAlpine, the model for Harriet Beecher Stowe's Simon Legree in *Uncle Tom's Cabin* (1852). In Chopin's novel, attention is called specifically to McAlpine, the former owner of the property, whose ghost is said to walk abroad at night in expiation of his cruel deeds.

Apart from its two settings, *At Fault* does not seem autobiographical. It has the form of a problem novel, reminiscent of the novels of Howells, to whom Chopin sent a copy of the work when it was published. As in certain of Howells's novels, a discussion takes place at one point that frames the conflict that the characters' lives illustrate. In this case it is the conflict between nature and convention, religious and social precept versus the data of actual experience. Thérèse Lafirme, although a warm and attractive woman, is accustomed to thinking about human affairs abstractly. When she learns that David Hosmer, who owns a sawmill on her property, is divorced from his young wife, a weak and susceptible woman who drinks, she admonishes him to return to his wife and fulfill his marriage pledge to stand by and redeem her. Hosmer admires Thérèse to such an extent that, against his own judgment, and most reluctantly, he returns to St. Louis and remarries Fanny Larimore. They then return to the plantation to live, and in due course history repeats itself. Despite Hosmer's dutiful attentions and her acceptance into the small social world of Place-du-Bois, Fanny begins to drink and to behave unreasonably. Near the end of the novel, having become jealous of Thérèse, Fanny ventures out in a storm and, despite Hosmer's attempt to rescue her, dies in a river flood.

Running parallel to this main plot is a subplot in which Hosmer's sister Melicent feels a romantic attraction to Thérèse's impetuous young nephew Grégoire but decides on the most theoretical grounds that he would not be suitable for a husband. When he becomes involved in a marginal homicide, she condemns him utterly, literally abandoning him. He then returns to Texas, where he goes from bad to worse and is eventually killed in a lawless town. At the end, a year after these events, Hosmer and Thérèse marry and find the happiness they had very nearly lost through Thérèse's preconceptions. It is clear to her that Fanny never could have been redeemed, and that her plan to "save" her had brought suffering to all parties concerned—to Hosmer, herself, and to Fanny as well. Left open, however, is the question of Melicent's responsibility to Grégoire, whom she had been too quick to "judge." *At Fault* appears to end happily, but in some ways it is pessimistic in its view of nature and convention.

At Fault shows a questioning intelligence and has an architectural competence, but it is still apprenticeship work. The St. Louis setting, especially in comparison to the southern one, is pallid, and the characters encountered there are lifeless. Fanny's associates in St. Louis include Mrs. Lorenzo (Belle) Worthington, who has dyed blond hair, and Mrs. Jack (Lou) Dawson, who has an expressionless face and "meaningless blue eyes set to a good humored readiness for laughter." These lady idlers, Belle and Lou, are stick figures. Although given stronger individuality, the more important characters also tend to be typed. Grégoire is typed by his vulnerability and impetuousness, just as Melicent is drawn to type as an immature girl who does not know her mind. The plot of *At Fault* is perhaps too symmetrical, too predictable in its outcome, with the irredeemability of Fanny Larimore a foregone conclusion. Moreover, in attempting to add emotional richness to the work, Chopin sometimes resorts to melodramatic occurrences, such as Joçint's setting fire to the mill, his death at the hands of Grégoire, the death of Joçint's father, the death of Grégoire, and the scene in which Fanny perishes in the storm. *At Fault* is essentially a realistic novel but resorts at times to romantic or melodramatic conventions. If Chopin fails to bring her novel to life, she does at times create suggestive characters such as Aunt Belindy, Thérèse's cook, who asks pointedly, "Whar you gwine live if you don' live in de worl'?" A tonal richness is also evident in the drawing of Thérèse Lafirme. Thérèse is not allowed in this work to be fully "herself," but she points the way to Chopin's later successes in fiction, the women Chopin creates from the soul.

THE AWAKENING

In *The Awakening*, Chopin achieved her largest exploration of feminine consciousness. Edna Pontellier, the heroine, is always at the center of the novel, and nothing occurs that does not in some way bear on her thoughts or developing sense of her situation. As a character who rejects her socially prescribed roles of wife and mother, Edna has a certain affinity with the "New Woman," much discussed in the 1890's, but her special modeling and the type of her experience suggest a French influence. Before beginning the novel, Chopin translated eight of Guy de Maupassant's stories. Two of these tales, "Solitude" and "Suicide," share with *The Awakening* the theme of illusion in erotic desire and the inescapability of the solitary self. Another, "Reveil," anticipates Chopin's novel in some incidents of its plot. At the same time, *The Awakening* seems to have been influenced by *Madame Bovary*. Certain parallels can be noticed in the experiences of the two heroines— their repudiation of their husbands, estrangement, and eventual suicides. More important, Flaubert's craftsmanship informs the whole manner of Chopin's novel—its directness, lucidity, and economy of means; its steady use of incident and detail as leitmotif. The novel also draws on a large fin de siècle background concerned with a hunger for the exotic and the voluptuous, a yearning for the absolute. From these diverse influences, Chopin shapes a work that is strikingly, even startlingly, her own.

The opening third section of *The Awakening*, the chapter set at Grand Isle, is particularly impressive. Here one meets Edna Pontellier, the young wife of a well-to-do Creole *negociant* and mother of two small boys. Mrs. Pontellier, an "American" woman originally from Kentucky, is still not quite accustomed to the sensuous openness of this Creole summer colony. She walks on the beach under a white parasol with handsome young Robert Lebrun, who befriends married Creole women in a way that is harmless, since his attentions are regarded as a social pleasantry, nothing more. In the background are two young lovers and, not far behind them, keeping pace, a mysterious woman dressed in black who tells her beads. Edna Pontellier and Robert Lebrun have just returned from a midday swim in the ocean, an act undertaken on impulse and perhaps not entirely prudent, in view of the extreme heat of that hour and the scorching glare of the sun. When Edna rejoins her husband, he finds her "burnt beyond recognition." Léonce Pontellier is a responsible husband who gives his wife no cause for complaint, but his mind runs frequently on business and he is dull. He is inclined to regard his wife as "property," but by this summer on Grand Isle she has begun to come to self-awareness, to recognize how she is suppressed by her role as a "mother-woman." Emboldened by her unconventional midday swim, she goes out swimming alone that night, and with reckless exhilaration longs to go "further out than any woman had ever swum before." She quickly tires, however, and is fortunate to have the strength to return to the safety of the shore. When she returns to their house, she does not go inside to join her husband but drowses alone in a porch hammock, lost in a long moonlit reverie that has the voluptuous effulgence of the sea.

As the novel proceeds, it becomes clear that Edna has begun to fall in love with Lebrun, who decides suddenly to go to Mexico, following which the Pontelliers themselves return to their well-appointed home in New Orleans. There Edna begins to behave erratically, defying her husband and leading as much as possible an independent existence. After moving to a small house nearby by herself, she has an affair with a young roué, Alcée Arobin. Lebrun returns from Mexico about the same time, and, although he is in love with Edna, he does not dare to overstep convention with a married woman and mother of two. Trapped once again within her socially prescribed role, Edna returns to the seashore and goes swimming alone, surrendering her life to the sea.

In its own time, *The Awakening* was criticized both for its subject matter and for its point of view. Reviewers repeatedly remarked that the erotic content of the novel was disturbing and distasteful, and that Chopin had not only failed to censure Edna's "morbid" awakening but also had treated it sympathetically. The reviewers failed to take into account the subtlety and ambiguity of the novel's vision, for if Chopin enters deeply into Edna's consciousness, she also stands outside it with a severe objectivity. A close examination of *The Awakening* reveals that the heroine has been involved in illusion from the beginning. Edna sometimes meditates, for example, on the self-realization that has been blunted by her roles as wife and mother, but in her rejection of her responsibilities she constantly tends toward vagueness rather than clarity.

The imagery of the sea expresses Edna's longing to reach a state in which she feels her own identity and where she feels passionately alive. The "voice" of the sea, beckoning Edna, is constantly in the background of the work. "The voice of the sea," Chopin writes, "speaks to the soul. The touch of the sea is sensuous, enfolding the body in its soft, close embrace." In this "enfolding," however, Edna discovers her own solitude and loses herself in "mazes of inward contemplation." In *Moby Dick* (1851), Herman Melville contrasts the land and the sea, the one convention bound, the other "open" and boldly, defiantly speculative, but Edna is no thinker; she is a dreamer who, in standing apart from conditioned circumstance, can only embrace the rhapsodic death lullaby of the sea. At the end of her life, she returns to her childhood, when, in protest against the aridness of her Presbyterian father's Sunday devotions, she had wandered aimlessly in a field of tall meadow grass that made her think of the sea.

Edna had married her Catholic husband despite her father's objection—or rather, one thinks, because of his objection. Later, discovering the limitations that her life with her husband imposes on her, she rebels once again, grasping at the illusion of an idealized Robert Lebrun. Edna's habit of idealization goes far back in her past. As a girl, she had fallen in love with a Confederate officer whom she had glimpsed, a noble figure belonging to a doomed cause, and also with a picture of a "tragedian." The last lines of the novel, as Edna's consciousness ends, are as follows: "The spurs of the cavalry officer clanged as he walked across the porch. There was the hum of bees, and the musky odor of pinks filled the air." Her consciousness at the end thus reverts back to its beginning, forming a circle from which she cannot escape. The final irony of *The Awakening*, however, is that even though Edna is drawn as an illusionist, her protest is not quite meaningless. Never before in a novel published in the United States was the issue of a woman's suppressed erotic nature and need for self-definition, apart from the received roles of wife and mother, raised so forcefully. *The Awakening* is a work in which the feminist protest of the present is memorably imagined.

In the mid-1950's, Van Wyck Brooks described *The Awakening* as a "small perfect book that mattered more than the whole life work of many a prolific writer." In truth, *The Awakening* is not quite "perfect." Chopin loses some of her power when she moves from Grand Isle to New Orleans. The guests at her dinner party, characters with names such as Mrs. Highcamp and Miss Mayblunt, are two-dimensional and wooden, and at times the symbolic connotations of incidents seem too unvaried. *The Awakening*, certainly, would be embarrassed by comparison with a large, panoramic novel of marital infidelity such as Leo Tolstoy's *Anna Karenina* (1875-1877; English translation, 1886). Within its limits, however, it reveals work of the finest craftsmanship, and it is a novel that continues to linger in the reader's consciousness well after it has been read.

Chopin was not prolific; all but a few of her best stories are contained in *Bayou Folk* and *A Night in Acadie*, and she produced only one mature novel, but these volumes have the mark of genuine quality. Lyric and objective at once, deeply humane and yet constantly attentive to illusion in her characters' perceptions of reality, these volumes reveal Chopin as a psychological realist of magical empathy, a writer having the greatness of delicacy.

Robert Emmet Long

OTHER MAJOR WORKS

SHORT FICTION: *Bayou Folk*, 1894; *A Night in Acadie*, 1897.

NONFICTION: *Kate Chopin's Private Papers*, 1998.

MISCELLANEOUS: *The Complete Works of Kate Chopin*, 1969 (2 volumes; Per Seyersted, editor); *Complete Novels and Stories*, 2002.

BIBLIOGRAPHY

Bonner, Thomas, Jr. *The Kate Chopin Companion*. New York: Greenwood Press, 1988. Alphabetically arranged guide provides information on the more than nine hundred characters and more than two hundred places that affect the courses of Chopin's stories. Also includes a selection of her translations of pieces by Guy de Maupassant and one by Adrien Vely. Supplemented by interesting period maps and a useful bibliographic essay.

Boren, Lynda S., and Sara de Saussure Davis, eds. *Kate Chopin Reconsidered: Beyond the Bayou*. Baton Rouge: Louisiana State University Press, 1992. Collection of essays presents extensive discussion of *The Awakening*, with several contributors also addressing such stories as "Charlie," "After the Winter," and "At Cheniere Caminada." Other topics include a comparison of Chopin with playwright Henrik Ibsen in terms of domestic confinement and discussion of Chopin's work from a Marxist point of view.

Hackett, Joyce. "The Reawakening." *Harper's Magazine* 307, no. 1841 (October, 2003). Lengthy review of the Chopin collection *Complete Novels and Stories* (2002) provides an overview of Chopin's life and career and offers analysis and commentary on *The Awakening*, which Hackett describes as "the book that both culminated Chopin's career and ended it."

Petry, Alice Hall, ed. *Critical Essays on Kate Chopin*. New York: G. K. Hall, 1996. Comprehensive collection of essays on Chopin reprints early evaluations of the author's life and works as well as more modern scholarly analyses. Begins with a substantial introduction by the editor and includes original essays by such notable scholars as Linda Wagner-Martin and Heather Kirk Thomas.

Seyersted, Per. *Kate Chopin: A Critical Biography*. 1969. Reprint. Baton Rouge: Louisiana State University Press, 1980. Provides invaluable information about the New Orleans of the 1870's while examining Chopin's life, views, and work. Devotes substantial discussion not only to *The Awakening* but also to Chopin's many short stories. Seyersted views Chopin as a transitional literary figure, a link between George Sand and Simone de Beauvoir.

Skaggs, Peggy. *Kate Chopin*. Boston: Twayne, 1985. Overview of Chopin's life and work includes a brief biographical chapter and discussion of the author's work in terms of the theme of the search for identity. Includes a chronology and a select bibliography.

Streater, Kathleen M. "Adèle Ratignolle: Kate Chopin's Feminist at Home in *The Awakening*." *Midwest Quarterly* 48, no. 3 (Spring, 2007): 406-416. Presents analysis of the character Adèle Ratignolle, arguing that she is a less radical feminist than Edna Pontellier but is admirable because of her feminine virtue and ideals of motherhood. Maintains that Ratignolle, whom Chopin portrays as a sexually confident woman as well as a mother, defied the sexist stereotypes of the period.

Taylor, Helen. *Gender, Race, and Religion in the Writings of Grace King, Ruth McEnery Stuart, and Kate Chopin*. Baton Rouge: Louisiana State University Press, 1989. Chapter on Chopin is divided between the novels and the short stories, some of which are given extensive feminist readings. Focuses on Chopin as a local colorist who uses regional and historical themes to explore gender issues. Offers invaluable discussion of Chopin's literary influences, particularly Guy de Maupassant, and the intellectual climate of the time.

Toth, Emily. *Kate Chopin*. New York: William Morrow, 1990. Definitive biography is a thoroughly documented, exhaustive work, an excellent starting point for Chopin research. Covers not only Chopin's life but also her literary works, discussing many of the short stories in considerable detail and addressing the alleged banning of *The Awakening*. Includes a bibliography of Chopin's work and a helpful chronology of her life.

————. *Unveiling Kate Chopin*. Jackson: University Press of Mississippi, 1999. Using newly discovered manuscripts, letters, and diaries of Chopin, Toth examines the source of Chopin's ambition and passion for her art, arguing that she worked much harder at her craft than previously thought.

MICHELLE CLIFF

Born: Kingston); November 2, 1946

OTHER LITERARY FORMS

In addition to being a novelist, Michelle Cliff is a poet, essayist, short-story writer, and literary critic. Her first writing was a response to an article about Jamaica that, in her opinion, contained inaccuracies. In her poems, short stories, and essays, she portrays the "real" Jamaica and what it is like to be Jamaican. A collection of her essays, *If I Could Write This in Fire*, was published in 2008. Cliff examines oppression, lost oral history, and sexual and racial prejudice, and she addresses the importance of revising official history. Her novels treat these same issues and concerns.

ACHIEVEMENTS

Michelle Cliff is recognized as one of the most significant writers of fiction exploring the complex issues of race, color, sexual orientation, and feminism as well as the postcolonial concerns of identity and heritage for people of mixed race. She has played a critical role in revealing the "other," or unofficial, history in her novels, and in a sense has been rewriting history. Cliff also is respected as a literary critic. In 1982, she received a fellowship from the National Endowment for the Arts and a fellowship for study at MacDowell College. In 1984, she won a Massachusetts Artists Foundation award and was named an Eli Kantor Fellow.

BIOGRAPHY

Michelle Cliff, the daughter of an American father and a Jamaican mother, was born on November 2, 1946, in Kingston). A light-skinned Creole, she was born into a mixed-race family that valued lightness of skin and continually insisted that she pass for white. This pressure to reject her Creole and black heritage has influenced her writing. During her childhood and adolescence, Cliff lived in Jamaica and the United States. Her family moved to the United States when she was three years old. She remained in Jamaica with other family members for some time, but she later joined the family in a Caribbean neighborhood of New York City. During the 1940's and early 1950's, Cliff often returned to Jamaica with her family for short visits; in 1956, when she was ten years old, she returned to Jamaica to attend boarding school.

After graduating from secondary school, Cliff returned to the United States and studied at Wagner College. She received a bachelor of arts degree in 1969 and then became involved in politics, including the feminist movement. She also was an active opponent of the war in Vietnam. After graduating from college, she worked in the publishing field as a reporter, researcher, and editor. She completed a master of philosophy degree in 1974 and received a doctorate from the Wartburg Institute at the University of London.

Although Cliff had been attracted to a classmate while at an all-female boarding school in Jamaica, it was during her residency in England that she realized she was lesbian. In 1976, she began a long-term relationship with American poet Adrienne Rich. That same year, Cliff began writing poetry and published her first book in that genre: *Claiming an Identity They Taught Me to Despise* (1980). From 1981 to 1983, she and Rich coedited *Sinister Wisdom*, a multicultural lesbian journal. In 1985, Cliff published another collection, *The Land of Look Behind: Prose and Poetry.*

In 1985, Cliff published her first novel, *Abeng*, which draws upon her multiracial and multicultural heritage. Her second novel, *No Telephone to Heaven*, is a sequel to *Abeng*. She began writing short stories, which were first published in *Bodies of Water* (1990). In 1993, she published her third novel, *Free Enterprise*. In 1998, she published her second collection of short stories, *The Store of a Million Items*. Cliff has had several university teaching positions as well.

ANALYSIS

Michelle Cliff writes about Jamaica and the tightly structured society of the island. She addresses problems inherent to a postcolonial culture, including prejudice, oppression, class structure, the devaluing of women, and the lost history—especially oral history—of the oppressed. Although her novels are not truly autobiographical, much of what the character Clare confronts in *Abeng* and *No Telephone to Heaven* is a reflection of her own experiences growing up in Jamaica and the United States and in living in England as a university student. Her novels display an ever-present consciousness of skin color, which is closely connected to identity, but for Cliff, the color of one's skin is both a means of identity and a means of losing identity.

Cliff's stories depict a society in which each person's place is determined by his or her skin color. This caste system is accepted simply as "the way it is." In the prejudicial thinking of her characters, skin color not only indicates certain flaws but also virtues. In *Abeng*, the character Mattie Freeman, Clare's grandmother, knows who she is. She is a Maroon, a red-skinned woman with a history that traces to Nanny, the Maroon resistor to slavery. Nanny had magical powers and spiritual insights no colonial would ever enjoy. Boy Savage, in contrast, has lost a part of his identity through his rejection of his color ancestry and his insistence on passing for white.

Language plays an important role in Cliff's novels as well. The language spoken by a character is an identifier of that character. In *Abeng*, when Clare is at her grandmother's farm with Zoe, her dark-skinned "friend," she speaks patois, which is forbidden in her middle-class existence in Kingston. For Cliff)n patois is just as viable a language as Standard English, and it is critical for readers without knowledge of patois to understand the meanings of the words. *No Telephone to Heaven* includes a glossary of patois words used in the novel.

Oral history and ethnic-specific stories, which rarely are included in the "official" accounts of the past, are integral to Cliff's novels. The novels are multilayered and create a sort of international tapestry of the history of oppressed and marginalized individuals and ethnic groups. The story of Nanny, the Maroon woman who refused to accept slavery and led her people in rebellion, is recounted or referred to in *Abeng*, *No Telephone to Heaven*, and *Free Enterprise*. In *Free Enterprise*, additional oral histories are told by minor characters.

Cliff extends this multilayering into the names she gives to her characters and to her novels. *Abeng* is an African word for conch shell. The conch shell served two purposes during the colonial period: It called slaves to the cane fields and was used by the Maroons to pass messages to one another. *Free Enterprise* refers both to the free enterprise of dealing in slaves in a capitalist market and to the enterprise of the main characters of the novel, resisters of slavery, and their freely entering into the fight.

Cliff writes her novels in a rich lyrical style reminiscent of her prose poems. Her descriptions of the Jamaican countryside are colorful and reflect the bond between the Maroons and nature. Jamaica becomes real for the reader with its mangoes, its tropical foliage, cane fields, and sun-drenched red earth.

ABENG

Abeng is the story of Clare Savage, a young girl growing up in a complex multicultural world. It is a world fraught with oppression, rejection, and denial. Her family belongs to the Jamaican middle class. Her father, James Arthur "Boy" Savage, is a light-skinned man of white-black ancestry who rejects his black heritage and insists upon passing for white. He takes pride in his white colonial ancestry, which traces back to Judge Savage, one of the most of brutal slave owners. Her mother, Kitty Savage, is a Maroon, or red-skinned, woman who is deeply attached to her color ancestry. Clare has one sister; she is younger than Clare and darker-skinned.

Boy and Kitty are an intriguing and often incomprehensible couple. They remain separate and contradictory. On Sunday mornings, the family goes to Boy's church, the John Knox Memorial Church. On Sunday evenings, they go to Kitty's church, the Tabernacle of the Almighty. They both consider Clare, the light-skinned daughter, to be Boy's child and the dark-skinned younger sister to be Kitty's child. The husband and wife have almost nothing in common and argue bitterly, which frightens Clare.

Clare spends summers in the country with Miss Mattie, her maternal grandmother. Although Miss Mattie was born after the freeing of the slaves, she had worked in the cane fields and remembers the harsh treatment by the overseers and how the cane cut her legs.

She no longer cuts cane, and is now a landowner. She is not of the same social class as the light-skinned Jamaicans; she is higher on the social scale as a landowner. Known for her kindness, she lets Miss Ruthie, a market woman, live on her land and raise produce to sell. Miss Ruthie has a daughter named Zoe, who becomes Clare's playmate. Miss Ruthie constantly warns Zoe not to get too involved with Clare because they are different and cannot really be friends. Clare is a *buckra*, a white-skinned person, who is not to be trusted.

The twelve-year-old Clare does not understand why so many things are the way they are. She enjoys the country, the lifestyle, and the connection with her mother's heritage. She has no comprehension of the necessity of not breaking the rules of her society. She resents the greater freedom afforded to the boys; she does not understand why she is admonished for considering Zoe her friend and equal. Then, one day, Clare breaks every rule that governs her life as a middle-class Jamaican female. She takes Miss Mattie's gun and sets out with Zoe to hunt Cudjoe, a legendary wild boar. Climbing to his lair proves too difficult, so they abandon the hunt and go for a swim in the river. Sunbathing nude, Clare is physically attracted to her forbidden friend. They are surprised by male cane cutters and become frightened. Clare fires the gun. The bullet ricochets and kills her grandmother's bull, Old Joe.

Clare admits to killing Miss Mattie's bull, but she is given no chance to explain how and why it happened. Her parents take her to Miss Beatrice, a widow who has buried all of her children. Kitty tells her daughter that Miss Beatrice will teach her how to be a "proper lady" so she can make something of herself. However, in the presence of Miss Beatrice, Clare also learns more about prejudice, oppression, and cruelty. She witnesses Miss Beatrice's harsh treatment of the elderly Minnie Bogle, a black woman who is hired to clean the dog feces from her yard. Miss Beatrice often strikes Minnie with her cane.

Miss Beatrice brings Clare to see her sister, who is considered mad. Clare is told not to talk to her, but the independent and rebellious Clare does. She learns what happens when she says "coons" and *buckras* mix. The sister tells Clare that as a young girl, she had a baby by a black man who worked for her family. She insists that what she did was wrong, and that her family was right in sending her to a convent. The sister has spent her life trying to expiate her sin.

The novel ends with Clare dreaming of fighting with Zoe, with blood trickling down Zoe's face and her apologizing and treating the wound. Awakening, Clare goes outside and discovers she is experiencing her first menstrual cycle. Clare is leaving the world of childhood and the magic of the Jamaican countryside and her summers with Zoe. In *No Telephone to Heaven*, she will deal with her fight to find her identity as an adult.

FREE ENTERPRISE

Free Enterprise is a novel of resistance and reclamation, the story of Annie Christmas and Mary Ellen Pleasant (M. E. P.), two women with black ancestry, who are dedicated to the abolition of slavery in the United States. Cliff draws upon the many stereotypes that envelop M. E. P. in official histories to present her in the novel as a powerful and determined individual who is feared by white society. She is very dark-skinned and uses her blackness to become a successful businesswoman in San Francisco. By being what white society expects her to be, a black madam catering to rich white men, she acquires money, which she uses to fund the abolitionist movement. Annie, in contrast to M. E. P., is light-skinned and is victimized by the white society she challenges.

Free Enterprise centers on the failure of John Brown's raid on Harper's Ferry, Virginia, in 1859. Through fortuitous circumstances, M. E. P., who was present at the raid, slips away from Harper's Ferry and returns to San Francisco. She remains active in the abolitionist movement and works for the rights of black citizens after the American Civil War. Annie is denied such good fortune. She is captured and put on a confederate chain gang. She disguises herself as a man but is soon discovered to be a woman. She becomes an amusement for her captors as a collar is placed around her neck. She is forced into sexual acts with male prisoners, while the captors watch. Annie is devastated. She had left the Caribbean to avoid being the mistress of a rich white man. She is emotionally and physically "broken," and she does not have the fortitude to continue actively in the fight. She retreats to Mississippi, where she lives a hermetical life.

Cliff also examines the lack of freedom of women regardless of their skin color. The secondary story of Alice and Clover Hooper, white abolitionists, elucidates the common bond of denial of freedom that unites all women. In their upper-class society, Alice and Clover are not free to speak their minds or pursue a career. They dream of going West and freeing themselves from male domination.

Shawncey Webb

OTHER MAJOR WORKS

SHORT FICTION: *Bodies of Water*, 1990; *The Store of a Million Items*, 1998.

NONFICTION: *If I Could Write This in Fire*, 2008 (essays).

EDITED TEXT: *The Winner Names the Age: A Collection of Writing by Lillian Smith*, 1978.

MISCELLANEOUS: *Claiming an Identity They Taught Me to Despise*, 1980 (prose and poetry); *The Land of Look Behind: Prose and Poetry*, 1985; *If I Could Write This in Fire*, 2008.

BIBLIOGRAPHY

Adisa, Opal Palmer. "Journey into Speech: Writer Between Two Worlds—An Interview with Michelle Cliff." *African American Review* 28, no. 2 (1994). In this special issue on black women's culture, essays explore Cliff's work on race and oppression in Jamaica and her ideas on resistance as a form of community and the significant role of women in the history of political resistance.

Browdy de Hernandez, Jennifer. *Women Writing Resistance: Essays on Latin America and the Caribbean.* Cambridge, Mass.: South End Press, 2003. Cliff is one of eighteen women whose work—including their writing—against all forms of oppression is examined in this book. The focus is on Latin American and Caribbean women who have used literature and other creative works to resist the political regimes of the countries in which they were born.

Edmondson, Belinda. "Race, Privilege, and the Politics of (Re)Writing History: An Analysis of the Novels of Michelle Cliff" *Callaloo* 16, no. 1 (1993): 180-191. A useful study of how Cliff seeks out obscure events of history and reworks those histories to include factors of race and oppression.

Elia, Nada. *Trances, Dances, and Vociferations: Agency and Resistance in Africana Women's Narratives.* New York: Garland, 2001. Examines Cliff's use of alternative and oral history, sexual disguise, and racial passing in her work. Chapter 3 is an analysis of the character Annie Christmas from *Free Enterprise.* Includes a bibliography.

Hudson, Lynn M. *The Making of Mammy Pleasant: A Black Entrepreneur in Nineteenth-Century San Francisco.* Urbana: University of Illinois Press, 2003. Contrasts Cliff's portrayal of M. E. P. with that character's portrayal in the novels of others.

MARYSE CONDÉ

Born: Point-à-Pitre, Guadeloupe, West Indies; February 11, 1937
Also known as: Maryse Boucolon

<small>PRINCIPAL LONG FICTION</small>

Hérémakhonon, 1976 (English translation, 1982)
Une Saison à Rihata, 1981 (*A Season in Rihata*, 1988)
Ségou: Les Murailles de terre, 1984 (*Segu*, 1987)
Moi, Tituba, sorcière noire de Salem, 1985 (*I, Tituba, Black Witch of Salem*, 1992)
Ségou II: La Terre en miettes, 1985 (*The Children of Segu*, 1989)
La Vie scélérate, 1987 (*Tree of Life*, 1992)
Traversée de la mangrove, 1989 (*Crossing the Mangrove, 1995*)
Les Derniers Rois mages, 1992 (*The Last of the African Kings*, 1997)
La Colonie du nouveau monde, 1993
La Migration des cœurs, 1995 (*Windward Heights*, 1998)
Desirada, 1997 (English translation, 2000)
Célanire cou-coupé, 2000 (*Who Slashed Celanire's Throat? A Fantastical Tale*, 2004)
La Belle Créole, 2001
Histoire de la femme cannibale, 2003 (*The Story of the Cannibal Woman*, 2007)
Victoire, les saveurs et les mots, 2006
Les Belles Ténébreuses, 2008

<small>OTHER LITERARY FORMS</small>

A prolific writer, Maryse Condé (kohn-DAY) has published extensively in many genres. She has edited collections of francophone writings from former French colonies in Africa and the Caribbean, and has written plays, one of which was produced in France in 1974 and in New York in English in 1991. She has published works of literary criticism, including a book about women novelists in the French Caribbean, as well as collections of short stories, books for children, and a childhood memoir. She also has written articles for journals and other periodicals.

<small>ACHIEVEMENTS</small>

Maryse Condé's books have been translated into six languages. She has won numerous awards, including the grand prix de la Femme and the Prix Alain Boucheron in 1986 for *I, Tituba, Black Witch of Salem*; the Anaïs Nin Prize from the French Academy for *Tree of Life* in 1988; and the Prix Carbet de la Caraibe in 1997 for *Desirada*. She was the first woman to receive the University of Oklahoma's Puterbaugh Fellowship, and in 1999 she won a Lifetime Achievement Award from New York University's Africana Studies Program and Institute of African-American Affairs. In France, she was appointed Commander of the Order of Arts and Letters (2001), Chevalier of the Legion of Honor (2003), and Commander of the National Order of Merit (2007). The two volumes of the Segu series have been best sellers, the first being a selection of the French Le Livre du Mois (book-of-the-month club). Condé has honorary degrees from Occidental College, Lehman College of the City University of New York, and the University of the West Indies at Cave Hill in Barbados.

BIOGRAPHY

The life of Maryse Condé, and the source of many of her preoccupations as a writer, is the story of relocations from an obscure French Caribbean colony to other regions of the francophone world: Paris, West Africa, back to Paris, then back to her natal island. She has earned a living by holding academic posts in Paris, West Africa, and the United States, while acquiring increasing fame as a writer.

Née Boucolon, Maryse Condé grew up in Guadeloupe, one of the two French islands in the West Indies. Her mother was the first black female instructor of her generation, and her father had been recognized by the Legion of Honor. Despite these solid achievements, the family was socially insecure, aware of being black in a racially hierarchical colony. Intelligent and critical, the young Condé was bored in Guadeloupe and found the little island suffocating. Still, she did well as a student and was sent to a high school in Paris; she was later expelled for insubordination after she reacted strongly against attitudes she regarded as racist. She moved on to the Sorbonne (the esteemed university in Paris).

Condé escaped West Indian circles, which she saw as limiting, and made friends in the African community in Paris, where she met and fell in love with Mamadou Condé, a Guinean actor. They were married in 1959 and moved to Guinea. Soon the relationship was facing difficulties, and Condé, who had defied her family by marrying Mamadou, accepted that the marriage was a failure and left her husband, supporting herself and her children by teaching in the Ivory Coast, Guinea, Ghana, and Senegal. In 1969, she met Richard Philcox, who would translate many of her novels into English. They were married in 1982. She returned to Paris in 1970 to work at the Sorbonne on a doctorate in comparative literature, which she completed in 1976. Condé stayed at the Sorbonne as a lecturer for nearly a decade, then returned to Guadeloupe.

Condé also held prestigious academic posts in the United States until her retirement in 2002. She was professor of French at the University of California (Los Angeles and Berkeley), the University of Maryland, and Columbia University, where she also was chair of the French and Francophone Institute.

ANALYSIS

Maryse Condé's works deal with themes considered central by many contemporary authors and critics. She writes in the aftermath of decolonization, in and of a realm increasingly globalized and interconnected. In the course of the eighteenth and nineteenth centuries, France had established a worldwide empire, exporting its culture and values into the Americas, Asia, the Pacific, and especially Africa, vast areas of which came under French control. French colonialism led to the building of hospitals and roads, and to the development of industry and trade. French colonialism also had a manifest "civilizing mission" (*mission civilisatrice*), not crude land-grabs but "beneficent" incursions into less developed or fortunate regions. This mission involved the export of the fruits of a high French culture; exposure to this new culture, it was believed, would benefit all, regardless of geographical or ethnic origin. France's relationship with its colonies was often strained and sometimes bloody, but the mother country, too, imbued many of its colonized subjects with an occasionally ambiguous respect for and admiration of the art, customs, and political system of the French.

This cultural and imperialist tide, having flowed, would eventually ebb. Exhausted by the bloodletting of two world wars, France had to withdraw from nearly all of its colonial possessions, sometimes, as with Indochina (in Southeast Asia) and Algeria, in circumstances that were traumatic for colonizer and colonized alike. In former colonies as well, a more or less Gallicized elite found itself in a culturally ambivalent position: not fully French, occasionally exposed to racism or other forms of discrimination, but unable, too, to embrace unselfconsciously the indigenous culture, insofar as that culture had survived. In the case of female members of that elite, perceived gender inequalities added to the sense of a false position within the former colonies. Condé's writing is a prolonged attempt to examine her position as a colonized woman of African origin situated in a world still culturally and economically dominated by Western Europe, including France, and the anglophone United States.

HÉRÉMAKHONON

Hérémakhonon, published in Paris in 1976, is Condé's first novel. The predicament of its central character is recognizably suggested by that of her creator, Condé. Veronica has spent her childhood in Guadeloupe and, after a period as a student in Paris, wants to escape that island's respectable black bourgeoisie, which she regards as secretly afraid of its own inferiority. She travels to an unnamed West African state and, while there, seeks an authentically African past with which she will be able to identify.

However, Veronica comes to see that, despite a wish she acknowledges as sentimental, this newly independent country can no more return to a precolonial past than the Sahara can return to its condition before desertification. Furthermore, the state, which encourages its people to believe in "progress," is facing political unrest: Students who demonstrate against the leader are hauled off by the army; one of Veronica's colleagues, described as a militant member of a banned party, is arrested and maltreated; and her newfound lover is a government bureaucrat who lives in the sort of luxury that is almost obscenely beyond the reach of most of his countryfolk. Indeed, Veronica is chauffeured past mud huts to and from his villa, named Hérémakhonon (Mandingo for welcome house). His own wish to preserve the past leads to his being labeled a "reactionary" and a mystifier of the people. Unable to commit to any side, Veronica returns to Paris.

An incidental paragraph reveals the inextricable confluence of cultures brought about by France's imperial ambitions: The gardener at Hérémakhonon is a member of the Fon people, from Dahomey, a former French colony. He has fought in Indochina, was a docker at Marseilles, was a truck driver in Algeria, and talks to himself in bits of French, English, and Arabic. He reads from an old copy of Victor Hugo's 1862 novel *Les Misérables*.

I, TITUBA, BLACK WITCH OF SALEM

Condé added to her fifth novel, *I, Tituba, Black Witch of Salem*, a "Historical Note," in which she explains the novel's origins. Tituba was a historical figure, a black slave from Barbados who confessed to practicing witchcraft in Salem in 1692. It is known that she survived the hysteria and was sold about one year later. However, Condé writes, because of conscious or unconscious racism, history knows little more than this.

I, Tituba, Black Witch of Salem is the fictional autobiography of a person almost erased from history because of her race and gender. Condé imagines for her a life before and after the brief period in which her existence is carefully documented only because of the malignant fear and religious bigotry of her persecutors.

Tituba is conceived in an act of real, and symbolic, violence: the rape of a black slave by a white sailor in a ship ironically named *Christ the King*. Living in Barbados, Tituba escapes slavery by running away after her mother is hanged for resisting another rape, this time at the hands of her master. For a time, Tituba leads an idyllic existence and is taught the healing power of certain plants and how to communicate with the spirits of the dead by an old woman who lives outside society, in an isolated hut. It is Tituba's desire for John Indian, another slave, that draws her back into contact with her kind, as human chattel and the wife of another.

The couple are sold to the Reverend Samuel Parris, who becomes minister in Salem village. There, despite the Puritan beliefs of the villagers, Tituba is obliged more than once to decline using her knowledge to harm others. She sees that her exotic background and abilities add "spice" to the lives of the repressed children she looks after, who listen with fascination and fear to her stories of diabolic possession. When the witchcraft hysteria strikes, Tituba is tortured and questioned. She confesses, falsely, to hurting children at the devil's behest, knowing such an admission is expected of her.

Finally released, Tituba's is sold again, this time to a Jew who becomes her lover. She returns to Barbados, becomes involved in a slave uprising, and is consequently hanged. Her spirit roams Barbados and foresees the eventual end of the suffering of enslaved Africans and their descendants.

In addition to its focus on racial, gender, and sexual oppression, *I, Tituba, Black Witch of Salem* is a postmodern novel that, in its repeated insistence on the possibility of communication between living and dead, raises doubts about the reliability of the narrator's perceptions. Furthermore, Condé playfully makes Nathaniel Hawthorne's Hester Prynne (the central character of *The Scarlet Letter*, 1850) appear as a character within her own work: Tituba is imprisoned with Hester in Massachusetts, and Hester teaches her about feminism.

THE LAST OF THE AFRICAN KINGS

Condé spoke of her admiration for Bruce Chatwin's *The Viceroy of Ouidah* (1980), a novel that, she believes, deals with themes very similar to those in her Segu series of novels. *The Last of the African Kings* tells the story of the once proud kings of Dahomey, exiled by the French from their West African fiefdom to Martinique, the second of the two French Caribbean islands. In this novel, the reader is once again confronted with the reworking of the connections among West Africa, the Caribbean, and the United States. The novel is another treatment of the confluence of cultures brought about by the African diaspora and its consequences.

In this novel, however, Condé asks whether the idea of an African origin should one day be forgotten. When should one let the past go and live in the American present? The king's illegitimate son, Djéré, is obsessed by his father's story and his own attempts to come to terms with his inadvertent abandonment in Martinique. Djéré reads as much as possible about African history, as does his son Justin. Neither Djéré nor Justin achieves anything in life, however; both spend their days drinking rum and immersed in the legends of the displaced royal family and its former glories.

The young Spero, Justin's son, begins his life just as entranced as his father and grandfather had been. However, Spero learns to live in his "American present," specifically in South Carolina, where he now lives, away from the failures and poverty of the French Caribbean. He has observed his father's wasted life. He soon marries Debbie, an African American and as much a prisoner of past events as anybody on her new husband's side of the family. Her obsessive focus is on the injustices meted out to African Americans and on post-Reconstruction American history. Political correctness is satirized as Spero rejects his wife's beliefs in a simple dualism of black "victim" and white "oppressor."

Spero chooses to name his coming child (a girl) not Jomo or Patrice or for any other heroes of African independence or African American enfranchisement, but instead for a blues singer he admires. He is banished from Debbie's bed when he has an affair with a white woman, and he loses his job at a black Catholic college because he insists on teaching about the European painters Edgar Degas and Pierre-Auguste Renoir rather than about painters of African origin.

M. D. Allen

OTHER MAJOR WORKS

SHORT FICTION: *Pays mêlé*, 1985 (*Land of Many Colors*, 1999).

PLAYS: *Dieu nous l'a donne*, pb. 1972; *Mort d'Oluwemi d'Ajumako*, pb. 1973; *Le Morne de Massabielle*, pr. 1974 (*The Morne of Massabielle*, 1991); *Pension les Alizes*, pr. 1988 (*The Tropical Breeze Hotel*, 1994); *An tan revolisyon: Elle court, elle court la liberté*, pr. 1989.

NONFICTION: *La Civilisation du bossale*, 1978; *Cahier d'un retour au pays natal: Césaire—Analyse critique*, 1978; *La Parole des femmes: Essai sur des romancières des Antilles de langue française*, 1979; *Entretiens avec Maryse Condé*, 1993 (*Conversations with Maryse Condé*, 1996); *Le Cœur à rire et à pleurer: Contes vrais de mon enfance*, 1998 (*Tales from the Heart: True Stories from My Childhood*, 2001).

TRANSLATIONS: *De Christophe Colomb à Fidel Castro: L'Histoire des Caraïbes*, 1975 (of Eric Williams's *From Columbus to Castro: The History of the Caribbean, 1492-1969*); *Tim, tim: Bois sec! Bloemlezing uit de Franstalige Caribsche Literatuur*, 1980 (of her edited texts *La Poésie antillaise* and *Le Roman antillaise*).

CHILDREN'S LITERATURE: *Haiti chérie*, 1987; *Victor et les barricades*, 1989; *Hugo le terrible*, 1991.

EDITED TEXTS: *Anthologie de la littérature d'expression française*, 1966; *La Poésie antillaise*, 1977; *Le Roman antillaise*, 1977; *L'Héritage de Caliban*, 1992; *Penser la créolité*, 1995 (with Madeleine Cottenet-Hage); *Nouvelles d'Amérique*, 1998 (with Lise Gauvin).

BIBLIOGRAPHY

Barbour, Sarah, and Gerise Herndon, eds. *Emerging Perspectives on Maryse Condé: A Writer of Her Own*. Trenton, N.J.: Africa World Press, 2006. A good resource for varied interpretations of Condé's writings. Includes several chapters that examine her novels and their recurrent themes.

Bruner, David K. "Maryse Condé: Creative Writer in a Political World." *L'Esprit créature* 17, no. 2 (Summer, 1977): 168-173. Discussion of the politics informing Condé's early work, including her first two plays and her first novel, *Hérémakhonon*.

Condé, Maryse, with VèVè A. Clark. "I Have Made Peace with My Island." *Callaloo* 12, no. 1 (Winter, 1989): 85-133. A wide-ranging interview that includes an account of Condé's life experiences and a discussion of how her political beliefs affect her writing.

Fulton, Dawn. *Signs of Dissent: Maryse Condé and Postcolonial Criticism*. Charlottesville: University of Virginia Press, 2008. In this first full-length biographical study of Condé in English, Fulton examines the "exceptional role" her writings have had "in shaping a dialogue between francophone studies and the English-dominated field of postcolonialism."

Hohl, Anne Mullen. "Maryse Condé." In *Multicultural Writers Since 1945: An A-Z Guide*, edited by Alba Amoia and and Bettina L. Knapp. Westport, Conn.: Greenwood Press, 2005. A readable account of Condé's life and works in this comprehensive, encyclopedic collection of postwar multicultural writers.

BUCHI EMECHETA

Born: Yaba, Lagos, Nigeria; July 21, 1944
Also known as: Florence Onye Buchi Emecheta

PRINCIPAL LONG FICTION
In the Ditch, 1972
Second-Class Citizen, 1974
The Bride Price, 1976
The Slave Girl, 1977
The Joys of Motherhood, 1979
Destination Biafra, 1982
Double Yoke, 1982
Adah's Story, 1983 (includes *Second-Class Citizen* and *In the Ditch*)
The Rape of Shavi, 1983
A Kind of Marriage, 1986 (adaptation of her teleplay)
Gwendolen, 1989 (also known as *The Family*, 1990)
Kehinde, 1994
The New Tribe, 2000

OTHER LITERARY FORMS

Books written by Buchi Emecheta (eh-mee-CHEH-tah) include a number of works for a juvenile audience, such as *The Moonlight Bride* (1980) and *The Wrestling Match* (1980). Two others, *Titch the Cat* (1979) and *Nowhere to Play* (1980), are based on stories by her daughters. Emecheta has also published an autobiography—*Head Above Water* (1986)—screenplays, and articles in prominent British journals and newspapers, including *New Statesman*, *The Times Literary Supplement*, and *The Guardian*.

ACHIEVEMENTS

Described by M. Keith Booker as "probably Africa's best known and most widely read woman novelist," Buchi Emecheta has gained a reputation and readership that extend far beyond her native land and her adopted country of Great Britain. Her novels have been translated into many European languages, including Danish, Finnish, Greek, Hungarian, and Swedish, and also into Korean, Tamil, and Sinhalese. She was invited by the World Population Foundation to contribute an article to its *Brief aan de 6 miljardste wereld-burger* (1999; letters to the sixth billionth world citizen). Emecheta's article, along with those of such major literary figures as Ariel Dorfman, Salman Rushdie, and Pramoedya Ananta Toer, was translated into Dutch and then published in Hebrew (*Mikhtavim le-ezrah ha-shishah-mili'ard*, 1999). She won the 1978 *New Statesman*/Jock Campbell Award for *The Slave Girl*, was named the Best Black Writer in Britain in 1980, and was named one of the best young British writers in 1983. In 2005, she was appointed an honorary officer of the Order of the British Empire.

BIOGRAPHY

Readers of Buchi Emecheta's heavily autobiographical fiction will see its inspiration in the events of her life. Florence Onye Buchi Emecheta was born July 21, 1944, in modest circumstances to Igbo parents in Yaba, near Lagos, when Nigeria was still a British colony. Her father, described in the dedication to her novel *In the Ditch* as a "Railwayman and 14th Army Soldier in Burma," died when she was nine years old. Despite economic disadvantages and racial and gender biases, Emecheta rose above her life circumstances. She won a scholarship to the Methodist Girls' High School, staying there for half a dozen years until her marriage, at the age of sixteen, to Sylvester Onwordi. Following Igbo practice, she was engaged to Onwordi at the age of eleven. In 1962, she moved to London, where Onwordi had relocated one year earlier to study accounting.

Despite an abusive marriage and the births of five children in six years, Emecheta focused on the two activities that would save her from poverty and degradation: She learned how to write, and she developed a career that would lead her to academia. From 1965, still in London, Emecheta began to work outside the home, first in the library of the British Museum and later for the Inner London Education Authority as a youth worker and sociologist. She left her husband in 1966, kept custody of her children, and entered the University of London, where she earned a bachelor's degree in sociology in 1972. She earned a doctorate from the same institution in 1991.

Emecheta's academic qualifications, coupled with increasing fame as a writer, led to several academic posts. For most of the decade after 1972, she was a visiting professor at various American universities, including Pennsylvania State; the University of California, Los Angeles; the University of Illinois at Urbana-Champaign; and Yale. She also taught at the University of Calabar in Nigeria (1980-1981) and at London University (beginning in 1982); in addition, she became a fellow at London University in 1986.

Aware from childhood that she had literary talent and ambitions, Emecheta began keeping a diary while living impoverished and being abused by her husband. She soon published short pieces about the lives of black Britons. Parts of her first novel, *In the Ditch*, an account of a single black mother living a life of precarious survival and comradeship in a squalid North London apartment, first appeared in serial form in the left-wing weekly *New Statesman*. Her work has earned her recognition as perhaps the foremost African woman writer, and one of a dozen or so of the most significant postcolonial African novelists.

In 1979, Emecheta became a member of the British Home Secretary's Advisory Council on Race. She was a member of the Arts Council of Great Britain from 1982 to 1983.

ANALYSIS

Buchi Emecheta's novels deal principally with the life experiences of Nigerian women, who are subordinated in an indigenous society deeply influenced by the Western values introduced by British colonists. Other Nigerian women, those who have relocated to England, for example, often suffer the emotional effects of being suddenly immersed into an alien country. Their lives are further complicated by the power that Nigerian men, following traditional beliefs, still have over them. Emecheta, who struggled in Nigeria to get an education and who suffered abuse in England by her Nigerian husband, reproduces these and other experiences in fictionalized form. Whether at home or in the imperial metropolis, Nigerian women in Emecheta's novels experience both sexism and racism in a world of African—and Western—traditions.

SECOND-CLASS CITIZEN

A prequel to *In the Ditch, Second-Class Citizen* explains how Adah became a single parent in a North London slum. At the age of eight she first noticed a "Presence" accompanying her, a wish to acquire education despite her inferior status as a girl. Resisting pressure to leave school at the age of eleven and eventually to marry and become a submissive wife, she wins a scholarship with full board to the Methodist Girls' School, where she does well. At the end of her stay at the school she marries Francis, but she does so simply to acquire a stable and socially acceptable home. Adah and Francis, who is studying to become an accountant, then move to London.

A defeatist Francis tells Adah that the color of her skin makes her a second-class citizen, her educational achievements notwithstanding. Adah, however, sets out to prove Francis wrong: She gets and keeps a "white man's" job in a library, where she is accepted by her white coworkers; she refuses to foster out her children, as do many African women in London, and instead finds a nursery for them; and she laments the jealousy directed at her as an ambitious Igbo by other blacks, including West Indians, considering this jealousy as harmful as white prejudice. Adah undergoes other trials. It is difficult for her family to find accommodations, as explicit racist exclusion is still legal ("Sorry, no coloreds"). Francis, unable to cope with British life, not only stops studying but is repeatedly unfaithful while demanding submission and sex from Adah. In response, Adah experiments unsuccessfully with birth control in an attempt to avoid the financial catastrophe of yet another pregnancy.

Later in the novel, Adah is introduced to black writers, including James Baldwin, by a fellow worker, and her own ambition to write begins to form. After Francis burns the manuscript of her novel, Adah takes the couple's four children and leaves him; she soon realizes that she again is pregnant.

Second-Class Citizen is unpretentiously written and compelling. It is an autobiographical story of an intelligent and resilient woman who is determined not to let sexism and racism limit her life or her talents. Although the book has been criticized for its portrayal of Nigerian society and Nigerian men, it is free of apparent bitterness and explicit special pleading. *Second-Class Citizen* captures a phase in the relationship between Britain and one of its African colonies, explaining why some Nigerians left for Britain in the late 1940's and what happened to those who failed there. The novel is also insightful in discussing the experiences of immigrants who arrived in Britain in the 1960's shortly after Nigeria's independence. Still, *Second-Class Citizen*, the work of a young writer, is lumpily episodic in structure, and its ending is disconcertingly abrupt.

THE BRIDE PRICE

The name of Aku-nna, the central character of *The Bride Price*, translates as "father's wealth." Knowing the importance her loving father places on her bride price, the sum paid to the family of a bride by the family of a suitor, Aku-nna determines to marry a rich man with a substantial bride price. However, after the death of her father, Aku-nna, her brother, and their mother move from pluralistic Lagos to traditional Ibuza, where Aku-nna's mother marries Okonkwo, her own brother-in-law, according to custom.

Okonkwo's social ambitions require money. He permits Aku-nna to continue her education because it will increase her bride price, which will now go to him, but he has no interest in her personal wishes. Meanwhile, Aku-nna and Chike, her schoolmaster, fall in love, but Chike, the descendant of slaves, is subordinated and limited by traditional views as well. When Aku-nna can no longer hide that she is menstruating, and thus marriageable, Okonkwo, in a display of male power, tells her that she must let her friendship with Chike die. Aku-nna is kidnapped for marriage by Okoboshi, a classmate, in a tradition that is tolerated by Igbo society, but she is rejected by him when she falsely claims that she is not a virgin. She is able to escape with Chike, marries him, but dies giving birth to a daughter.

Emecheta's own fears of powerlessness and loss of autonomy in a male-dominated society are here projected onto an exclusively Nigerian setting and are more extensively fictionalized than in her first two novels. There is, furthermore, the introduction of a new theme, the destructive effects of the caste system within African society: Chike, too, is marginalized. Indeed, the repressive forces that threaten Aku-nna's happiness are indigenous rather than imported.

Despised by Okoboshi and his relatives when they think she has lost her virginity, Aku-nna reflects that she will be killed by Okonkwo if she runs away from him, and that she will die of shame and rejection if she stays. The point of these psychological pressures is to bring about the very death that is traditionally predicted for those who break custom and taboo. When Aku-nna dies during labor because of her youth, physical frailty, and malnutrition, the omniscient authorial voice informs the reader that Aku-nna's story is told to every girl in Ibuza: Women who do not accept the man chosen by their people and whose bride price is not paid will die while giving birth to their first child. Ironically, even the rebel against traditional customs and constraints reinforces these traditions by the manner of her death.

THE JOYS OF MOTHERHOOD

Nnu Ego, the central character of *The Joys of Motherhood*, whose life and sufferings will dramatize the story's main points, is the illegitimate daughter, by a fiercely proud mistress, of the local chief in rural Ibuza. Nnu Ego's inability to bear children with her first husband causes her father to arrange a second marriage, to Nnaife Owulum, who works in Lagos for an English family. Nnu Ego submits to marrying a man she has never met; indeed, when she does meet him, she finds in him neither esteem nor attractiveness. When Nnaife's older brother dies, his wife, Adaku, becomes the younger brother's junior wife. Nnaife is conscripted into the British army for action in World War II, and his two wives are left to their own resources. Adaku becomes a prostitute and does well financially; Nnu Ego remains respectable and does not. When Nnaife returns, he acquires a third wife, sixteen-year-old Okpo. Nnu Ego's sons, as boys, are favored in society, and decide to continue their education in the United States and in Canada. Nnu Ego's own life continues to be subordinated to men and their privileged status. Nnaife, after serving a brief prison sentence for attacking a man of a different tribe who wanted to marry one of his daughters, returns to Ibuza, with the young Okpo. Nnu Ego, disowned, dies in Ibuza obscurely, and a shrine is built for her so any infertile granddaughters can pray to her.

A mesh of interconnected themes is developed in *The Joys of Motherhood*. At one stage, Nnu Ego thinks that if she were in Ibuza she would have her own hut and be given respect; in colonized Lagos, she has the worst of both worlds—polygamy and exploitation. She has been given to a man who is subservient before his English masters, as if he were a woman, but who still tries to exact complete obedience in the home, as if he were part of an organic social system of give and take that justified such demands. Her boys, to whom she has sacrificed everything, end up living in the New World, the epitome of modernity, and do not correspond with their mother. Nnu Ego has obeyed all the old rules but is still taken advantage of, and abandoned in old age.

M. D. Allen

OTHER MAJOR WORKS

TELEPLAYS: *A Kind of Marriage*, 1976; *Family Bargain*, 1987.
RADIO PLAY: *The Ju Ju Landlord*, 1976.
NONFICTION: *Head Above Water*, 1986 (autobiography).
CHILDREN'S LITERATURE: *Titch the Cat*, 1979; *The Moonlight Bride*, 1980; *Nowhere to Play*, 1980; *The Wrestling Match*, 1980; *Naira Power*, 1982.

BIBLIOGRAPHY

Booker, M. Keith. "Buchi Emecheta: *The Joys of Motherhood*." In *The African Novel in English: An Introduction*. Portsmouth, N.H.: Heinemann, 1998. A good account and overview of critical responses to Emecheta's novel.
Cox, C. Brian, ed. *African Writers*. 2 vols. New York: Charles Scribner's Sons, 1997. This

compilation on African writers includes a biographical and critical overview of Emecheta and her writings. Also includes a brief bibliography.

Derrickson, Teresa. "Class, Culture, and the Colonial Context: The Status of Women in Buchi Emecheta's *The Joys of Motherhood.*" *International Fiction Review* 29, nos. 1/2 (2002): 40-51. An examination of women in Igbo society and their place in colonial Nigeria. Discusses how women's status is reflected in *The Joys of Motherhood.*

Fishburn, Katherine. *Reading Buchi Emecheta: Cross-Cultural Conversations.* Westport, Conn.: Greenwood Press, 1995. A more demanding postmodernist approach. For advanced readers with some knowledge of literary and cultural theories.

Ogunyemi, Chikwenye Okonjo. "Buchi Emecheta: The Shaping of a Self." *Komparatistische Hefte* 8 (1983): 65-77. A general, and sometimes hostile, account of Emecheta's writings and themes through *The Joys of Motherhood.*

Umeh, Marie, ed. *Emerging Perspectives on Buchi Emecheta.* Trenton, N.J.: Africa World Press, 1995. A diverse collection of essays that show ever-changing interpretations of Emecheta's works.

Uwakweh, Pauline Ada. "Carving a Niche: Visions of Gendered Childhood in Buchi Emecheta's *The Bride Price* and Tsitsi Dangarembga's *Nervous Conditions.*" *African Literature Today* 21 (1998): 9-21. A comparative essay arguing, in part, that gender identity, as evidenced in Emecheta's novel *The Bride Price,* is created by socialization.

EDNA FERBER

Born: Kalamazoo, Michigan; August 15, 1885
Died: New York, New York; April 16, 1968
Also known as: Edna Jessica Ferber

OTHER LITERARY FORMS

In addition to twelve novels, Edna Ferber wrote eight plays, two novellas, eighty-three short stories, and two autobiographies. Although her novels have perhaps been the most enduring part of her work, her short stories and plays were equally or more important during her lifetime. Almost all her works, except the dramas, first appeared serially in magazines. In addition, she wrote numerous short articles and commentaries. Twenty-two Emma McChesney stories made Ferber a best-selling writer. These were first published in *The American Magazine* or *Cosmopolitan* between 1911 and 1915 and later were collected in *Roast Beef Medium* (1913), *Personality Plus* (1914), and *Emma McChesney and Co.* (1915). Emma McChesney also was the heroine of *Our Mrs. McChesney* (pr., pb. 1915), Ferber's first play, which she wrote with George V. Hobart.

The McChesney character was a significant innovation—the first successful businesswoman depicted in popular American literature. Finally, however, Ferber declined *Cosmopolitan*'s proffered contract for as many McChesney stories as she wished to write at a price she could name. Ferber saw herself, instead, as a novelist and dramatist. The plays she wrote with George S. Kaufman, especially *Dinner at Eight* (pr., pb. 1932), *The Royal Family* (pr. 1927), and *Stage Door* (pr., pb. 1936), enjoyed long Broadway runs and secured her fame as a dramatist. Her autobiographies, *A Peculiar Treasure* (1939, 1960) and *A Kind of Magic* (1963), explain her motivations and detail her writing techniques. The books also are intensely personal and revealing. The second, written after her health began to deteriorate, is rambling and repetitive but essentially completes the story of her active life.

Edna Ferber
(Library of Congress)

ACHIEVEMENTS

Edna Ferber maintained herself as a best-selling author and a popular celebrity from the appearance of the Emma McChesney stories in 1911 to the publication of *Ice Palace* in 1958. During this period, she was cited several times as America's best woman novelist, and literary notables such as William Allen Wright, Rudyard Kipling, and James M. Barrie praised her work. Her reputation, however, abruptly declined in the late 1960's. A resurgence in interest in Ferber's work began in the 1980's, fueled mostly by the publicity surrounding her participation in several social crusades. Her advocacy of social and political causes in her fiction significantly influenced public opinion and policy. Ernest Gruening, territorial senator-elect of Alaska, for example, cited Ferber's *Ice Palace* as important in winning Alaska's statehood.

Ferber's explication of regional history and culture in her novels also played a prominent part in raising pride in American culture after World War I. Her short story "April Twenty-fifth as Usual" (first published in *Ladies' Home Journal* in July, 1918) received the O. Henry Award in 1919, and in 1925, her novel *So Big* won the Pulitzer Prize for fiction. Jerome Kern and Oscar Hammerstein II's classic musical play *Show Boat* (pr. 1927), based on Ferber's novel, was the first American musical with a serious plot derived from a literary source. The story also was used in a successful radio serial program and four films; it made so much money that Ferber referred to it as her "oil well." She associated with many prominent theatrical, literary, and political figures, including members of the Algonquin Round Table, a circle of literary friends who met for lunch regularly at New York's Algonquin Hotel. At least twenty-seven films have been based on her works.

BIOGRAPHY

Edna Jessica Ferber was the second daughter of a Hungarian Jewish immigrant storekeeper, Jacob Charles Ferber, and Julia Neuman Ferber, daughter of a prosperous, cultured German Jewish family. She was named Edna because the family, hoping for a male child, had already selected the name Edward. When she was born in Kalamazoo, Michigan, her father owned and operated a general store. Soon the business faltered, and the family moved in with Julia's parents in Chicago. The family moved subsequently to Ottumwa, Iowa, then back to Chicago, then to Appleton, Wisconsin, but Jacob Ferber still failed to prosper as a storekeeper. Though intelligent, kindly, and cultured, he never acquired business skills; in addition, he soon lost his sight. Julia assumed management of the business and became the head of the family. With great personal effort and the active assistance of Edna, she stabilized the business, paid off debts, and maintained the family's independence.

Edna Ferber later described Ottumwa as narrow-minded and sordid. There she experienced anti-Semitism and witnessed a lynching. During her high school years in Appleton, in contrast, she enjoyed pleasant, tolerant, midwestern small-town life. Unable to afford college tuition in 1902, she began her professional writing career as a reporter for the *Appleton Daily Crescent*. Eighteen months later, the editor who had hired her—on the strength of her reportorial writing in her high school paper—left the newspaper, and Ferber was fired. The most credible reason given for her dismissal was her imaginative "embroidering" of news reports. She then became a reporter on the *Milwaukee Journal*. Exhausted by overwork and anemia, she returned home in 1905 and began writing fiction. High school and about five years of newspaper writing constituted Ferber's entire preparation for her literary career.

After Jacob Ferber's death in 1909, Julia sold the store and took her two daughters to Chicago. There, while her mother and sister earned their living, Edna continued writing. In 1912, after selling some of her work, she moved to New York City, but she remained closely attached to her mother. Thereafter, she and her mother resided in hotels or apartments in New York, Chicago, and elsewhere but considered themselves New Yorkers. Though they did not always actually live together, their lives were closely intertwined. In 1938, Edna, who never married, built a house for herself in suburban Connecticut, pointedly leaving her mother in a New York apartment. After Julia died, Edna sold her house and returned to New York to live, taking an apartment. During the last ten years of her life, a painful nervous disorder impaired her writing. She died of stomach cancer in New York City on April 16, 1968.

ANALYSIS

Edna Ferber was a feminist, a conservationist, a crusader for minorities and immigrants, and a staunch believer in the work ethic and American culture. Strong women characters rising above the limitations of birth and gender dominate her novels; most men in her works are weak, and many desert their women and children. Ferber's fiction describes and condemns mistreatment of African Americans, Jews, Latinos, and Native Americans. Her novels decry unrestrained capitalism and wasteful exploitation of natural resources while celebrating regional culture and history in an effective and pleasing style that clearly reflects her journalistic background. Her characterization, however, is less effective, and her plots tend toward melodrama and coincidence.

All of Ferber's novels were commercial successes, and many remained in print for decades after their first publication. Her first novels, *Dawn O'Hara* and *Fanny Herself*, are strongly autobiographical. They remain interesting because they show Ferber's literary growth. The background material in *Great Son*, a later work, is sketchy, the characters are stereotypical, and the plot is contrived. At the time of that novel's writing, during World War II, Ferber was preoccupied with writing propaganda to help in the war effort. Her final novel, *Ice Palace*, is a political tract of little literary merit; Ferber was ill at the time of its writing.

THE GIRLS

Ferber expected *The Girls* to be a best seller and considered it her best novel. The story recounts six decades of Chicago middle-class history and intergenerational conflict. Charlotte Thrift, forbidden to marry an unsuitable boy, loses him to death in the American Civil War. She never marries. Her unmarried niece, Lottie, under her mother's domination, keeps house for her mother and aunt. Lottie finally rebels, joins the Red Cross during World War I, has a brief affair, and returns with her illegitimate daughter, whom she passes off as a French orphan. Charly (Charlotte), Lottie's niece, falls in love with a poet, who is killed in World War I, and moves in with her aunt and great-aunt. All three of these women are strong personalities, whereas their men are either incompetent boors or scoundrels.

SO BIG

Ferber's first best seller, *So Big*, effectively contrasts humble life in the Halstead Street Market with that of pretentious Chicago society. A genteelly reared orphan, Selina Peake, goes to teach school in a community of Dutch market gardeners, where she must adjust to a brutal existence. Her only intellectual companion is thirteen-year-old Roelf, the artistically talented son of the family with whom she lives. After a year, she marries kindly Pervus DeJong, an unimaginative, unenterprising widower. They have a son, Dirk, nicknamed So Big. After Pervus's death, Selina makes their farm a thriving success. She sacrifices all for So Big, who, after a few years as a struggling architect, shifts to a banking career and high society. In contrast, Selina's first protégé, Roelf, becomes a famous sculptor. At the end, So Big finally realizes that his life is empty. Although the novel was critically acclaimed, the characterization barely develops beyond stereotypes, and many of the anecdotes presented in the work are clichés.

SHOW BOAT

Show Boat describes life aboard late nineteenth and early twentieth century Mississippi River showboats and addresses the cultural significance of these centers of entertainment. Magnolia Hawkes, daughter of Captain Andy and Parthenia Hawkes of the showboat *Cotton Blossom*, marries Gaylord Ravenal, a charming professional gambler. After Captain Andy's death, Magnolia, Gaylord, and their daughter, Kim, move to Chicago, where they squander Magnolia's inheritance. Magnolia, deserted by her wastrel husband, becomes a successful singer and raises Kim to become a successful serious actor. Parthenia inherits and successfully operates the showboat. Parthenia, Magnolia, and Kim are all protofeminist career women. Captain Andy, though competent and wise, defers to Parthenia in almost everything.

In *Show Boat*, Ferber depicts African Americans as patient, upright, and hardworking people. A tragic incident of miscegenation and the injustice of the laws in the American South balance the romanticized account of showboat life, which is charming.

CIMARRON

Cimarron is set in Oklahoma in the period between the 1889 land rush and the 1920's oil boom. Sabra Cravat begins life as a genteel, impoverished southern girl but ends up an assured newspaperwoman and member of the U.S. Congress. Her husband, Yancey Cravat, a flamboyant lawyer-newspaperman of dubious background, starts grandiose projects, performs heroic acts, and upholds high ideals, but he accomplishes little. Desertion of his family clears the way for Sabra's rise. These characters exemplify the tension between those who "won" Oklahoma and those who "civilized" it. In addition, in this work interaction between Native Americans and European Americans is perceptively treated.

AMERICAN BEAUTY

Ferber rhapsodically describes the Connecticut landscape in *American Beauty*, in which she also chronicles the abuse of land and resources. She presents Polish immigrant culture sympathetically, whereas she depicts the indigenous New Englanders as played-out aristocrats. Judy Oakes and her niece, Tamar Pring, are strong, stubborn women devoted to their aristocratic background and ancestral home. Their hired man, Ondy Olszak, a kindhearted, hardworking, unimaginative Polish immigrant, maintains the farm at just above subsistence level. Tamar seduces and marries Ondy, and their son Orrange combines Ondy's peasant vigor and Tamar's cultural sensibilities. Although Orrange inherits the farm, Ondy's family forces him to sell. Millionaire True Baldwin, who, as an impoverished farm lad, had aspired to marry Judy Oakes, buys it. Fortunately, Baldwin's architect daughter, Candy Baldwin, who is sexually attracted to Orrange, hires him to manage the farm.

COME AND GET IT

Ferber draws heavily on her own background in *Come and Get It*, a story of resource exploitation, unrestrained capitalism, and social contrast. After lumberjack Barney Glasgow fights his way up to a managerial position at the mill, he marries his boss's spinsterish daughter. The mill's timbering and papermaking thrive under his direction, until he is fatally attracted to Lotta Lindaback, granddaughter of his longtime lumberjack pal Swan Bostrom. Barney's daughter, frustrated by unacknowledged desire for her father, marries a dull young businessman. Bernard, Barney's son, pursues Lotta when Barney restrains his own passion for her. Barney then fights with Bernard and expels him from the house. Immediately afterward, Barney and his family are killed in an explosion. Bernard marries Lotta and builds an industrial empire in steel and paper. Lotta, meanwhile, enters international high society. The Great Depression forces Lotta's return to Wisconsin, where her twins come under the influence of Tom Melendy, an idealistic young man from a millhand family. Rejecting their parents' materialism, the twins return to the simple Bostrom ways.

SARATOGA TRUNK

In *Saratoga Trunk*, Ferber decries the evils of unrestrained capitalism and the decadent snobbery of New Orleans high society. She also promotes women's causes and the conservation of natural resources. Illegitimate Clio Dulain and Texas cowboy-gambler Clint Maroon join forces to extort money from Clio's aristocratic father. They then move to Saratoga, New York, where Clio sets out to snare a rich husband. Although she entraps railroad millionaire Van Steed, she drops him for Clint when Clint is injured fighting for Van Steed's railroad, the Saratoga Trunk. Thereafter, Clio and Clint become railroad millionaires but idealistically give their wealth to charity. Clio subtly manipulates Clint in all important matters.

GIANT

Giant, Ferber's flamboyant version of Texas history and culture, exemplifies the Texas mythology; upon publication, the novel earned violent protests from Texans. Ferber's typical strong female central character, Leslie Lynnton, daughter of a world-famous doctor living in genteel shabbiness, is swept off her feet by a visiting Texas rancher. Transported to his gigantic ranch, she finds her husband ruled by his spinster sister, Luz. Luz dies violently, and, with great skill and wisdom, Leslie guides her man through repeated crises as the great cattle and cotton "empires" are hemmed in by vulgar oil billionaires. In this novel, Ferber shows the original Texans, Mexican Americans, as deeply wronged, patient, dignified, and noble. Unfortunately, the book's ending leaves ongoing problems unsolved.

Ralph L. Langenheim, Jr.

OTHER MAJOR WORKS

SHORT FICTION: *Buttered Side Down*, 1912; *Roast Beef Medium*, 1913; *Personality Plus*, 1914; *Emma McChesney and Co.*, 1915; *Cheerful—By Request*, 1918; *Half Portions*, 1919; *Mother Knows Best*, 1927; *They Brought Their Women*, 1933; *Nobody's in Town*, 1938 (includes *Nobody's in Town* and *Trees Die at the Top*); *One Basket*, 1947.

PLAYS: *Our Mrs. McChesney*, pr., pb. 1915 (with George V. Hobart); *$1200 a Year*, pr., pb. 1920 (with Newman A. Levy); *Minick*, pr., pb. 1924 (with George S. Kaufman); *The Royal Family*, pr. 1927 (with Kaufman); *Dinner at Eight*, pr., pb. 1932 (with Kaufman); *Stage Door*, pr., pb. 1936 (with Kaufman); *The Land Is Bright*, pr., pb. 1941 (with Kaufman); *Bravo!*, pr. 1948 (with Kaufman).

NONFICTION: *A Peculiar Treasure*, 1939 (revised 1960); *A Kind of Magic*, 1963.

BIBLIOGRAPHY

Antler, Joyce. *The Journey Home: Jewish Women and the American Century*. New York: Free Press, 1997. Ferber is one of the fifty women profiled in this overview of the lives of American Jewish women in the 1890's and the twentieth century.

Batker, Carol. "Literary Reformers: Crossing Class and Ethnic Boundaries in Jewish Women's Fiction of the 1920's." *MELUS* 25, no.1 (Spring, 2000): 81-104. Analyzes the work of Ferber, Fannie Hurst, and Anzia Yezierska, focusing on how Ferber depicted African American characters and class mobility.

Bloom, Harold, ed. *Jewish Women Fiction Writers*. New York: Chelsea House, 1998. Provides biographical information, a wide selection of critical excerpts, and complete bibliographies of Ferber and nine other female Jewish American writers. Designed for high school and undergraduate students.

Botshon, Lisa, and Meredith Goldsmith, eds. *Middlebrow Moderns: Popular American Women Writers of the 1920's*. Boston: Northeastern University Press, 2003. Collection of essays examines the work of writers who were both critically acclaimed and commercially successful in the 1920's. Two chapters are devoted to Ferber: One discusses the "middlebrow regional fiction" of Ferber and Rose Wilder Lane; the other analyzes Ferber's novel *Cimarron*.

Gilbert, Julie Goldsmith. *Ferber: Edna Ferber and Her Circle—A Biography*. New York: Applause, 1999. Well-researched biography calls Ferber a romantic realist. Notes that she was not opposed to working with the system, yet she created her own unique niche within it. Includes an index.

Meade, Marion. *Bobbed Hair and Bathtub Gin: Writers Running Wild in the Twenties.* New York: Nan A. Talese/Doubleday, 2004. Offers a nonscholarly, entertaining look at Ferber, Dorothy Parker, Edna St. Vincent Millay, and Zelda Fitzgerald, chronicling the lives of these writers in the "Roaring Twenties."

Shaughnessy, Mary Rose. *Women and Success in American Society in the Works of Edna Ferber.* New York: Gordon Press, 1977. Examination of Ferber's life and work provides an assessment of the author's place in the women's movement.

Watts, Eileen. "Edna Ferber, Jewish American Writer: Who Knew?" In *Modern Jewish Women Writers in America,* edited by Evelyn Avery. New York: Palgrave Macmillan, 2007. Essay interpreting Ferber's work from the perspective of her Jewish heritage is included in a collection devoted to the discussion of American women writers whose lives and work have been influenced by Judaism.

ELLEN GLASGOW

Born: Richmond, Virginia; April 22, 1873
Died: Richmond, Virginia; November 21, 1945
Also known as: Ellen Anderson Gholson Glasgow

OTHER LITERARY FORMS

In addition to nineteen novels, Ellen Glasgow (GLAS-goh) wrote a book of short stories, *The Shadowy Third, and Other Stories* (1923); a book of poems, *The Freeman, and Other Poems* (1902); a book on her views of fiction writing (concerned primarily with her own works), *A Certain Measure: An Interpretation of Prose Fiction* (1943); and an autobiography, *The Woman Within* (1954). She also wrote a number of articles on fiction for various periodicals and magazines. Her letters were published in 1958.

ACHIEVEMENTS

Although Ellen Glasgow never felt that she had received the critical acclaim she deserved, or at least desired, she nevertheless played an important part in the development of southern letters. A significant figure in the so-called Southern Renaissance, she provided in her novels a new picture of the South, a region reluctantly ushered into the modern

Ellen Glasgow
(Library of Congress)

world. Against a sentimentalized view of the Old South, Glasgow advocated an acceptance of the inevitability of change.

Prior to 1925, Glasgow's critical reception was mixed—more positive than negative, but nothing that would mark her as a writer of the first rank. With *Barren Ground*, however, Glasgow's reputation began to grow with both critics and readers. That novel made the 1925 *Review of Reviews* list of twenty-five outstanding novels of the year. Represented also on the list for 1925 were Sinclair Lewis's *Arrowsmith*, Edith Wharton's *The Mother's Recompense*, Willa Cather's *The Professor's House*, and Sherwood Anderson's *Dark Laughter.* Glasgow's *The Sheltered Life* was a best seller and greatly enhanced her reputation. *Vein of Iron* and *In This Our Life*, which received the Pulitzer Prize in 1942, helped to ensure her position as a writer of major significance.

"The chief end of the novel, as indeed of all literature," Glasgow wrote, is "to increase our understanding of life and heighten our consciousness." To this end she directed her artistic skills, writing with care and precision, for, as she also said, "The true novel . . . is, like poetry, an act of birth, not a device or invention."

BIOGRAPHY

Born in Richmond, Virginia, in 1873, Ellen Glasgow came from a combination of stern Scotch-Irish pioneers on her father's side and Tidewater, Virginia, aristocratic stock on her mother's side. Francis Glasgow was an ironworks executive, an occupation well suited to his Puritan temperament and character. Ellen Glasgow had little positive to say about her father. Her mother was a cultivated, gracious, and humane woman. These divergent influences provided the crucible from which Glasgow's writings were to emerge.

The next to the youngest in a family of four sons and six daughters, Glasgow experienced a more or less lonely childhood, with Rebe, her younger sister, and Mammy Lizzie Jones, her black nurse, providing her only companionship. Because of fragile health and a nervous temperament that precluded adjustment to formal schooling, her isolation was increased, and most of her education came from her father's extensive library. As a child, Glasgow admired the novels of Charles Dickens, Henry Fielding, and Jane Austen. From Dickens, she gained reinforcement for her already strong aversion to cruelty, and from the latter two, she learned that only honest writing can endure. "Lesser" novelists, she felt, lacked "the creative passion and the courage to offend, which is the essential note of great fiction."

Glasgow grew up in that period following the American Civil War when, as she described it, the "prosperous and pleasure-loving" agrarians of the antebellum years were struggling for existence amid "the dark furies of Reconstruction." It was a conservative, even reactionary, time when, according to Glasgow, "being a rebel, even an intellectual one, was less exciting and more uncomfortable than it is nowadays." Rejecting the harsh Calvinism of her father and the bloodless social graces of Richmond society, she retreated even further into a life of the mind. Glasgow's growing sense of alienation and rebelliousness has been seen by critics as the wellspring of her literary vision.

By 1890, just one year after her hearing had begun to fade, Glasgow had produced some four hundred pages of a novel, *Sharp Realities* (unpublished). Putting that effort aside, she began writing *The Descendant* in 1891. Two years later, however, upon the death of her mother, with whom she had great affinity, she destroyed a good part of what she had written. Another two years passed before she returned to the novel and completed it. The following year, she made the first of numerous trips to Europe.

With the publication (anonymously) of *The Descendant* in 1897, Glasgow was launched on her prolific career, a career that saw novels appearing every two years or so. Writing became and remained her role in life, and she was ever mindful of the growth of her literary reputation, changing publishers when she felt it to her advantage and making sure that critics were fully aware of her books.

Presumably while on a trip to Europe in 1899, Glasgow fell in love with a married man, to whom she refers in her autobiography *The Woman Within* as Gerald B_____. A mystery man, Gerald B_____ was described by Glasgow as an older Wall Street man with a wife and children. There is some evidence, however, indicating that Gerald B_____ was a physician. Another serious love affair was with Henry Watkins Anderson, a Richmond lawyer. He and Glasgow met in 1915 and were engaged in 1917. In July of the next year, Glasgow attempted suicide when she learned that Anderson, who was working with the Red Cross in the Balkan States, was attracted to Queen Marie of Romania. This turbulent love affair between Glasgow and Anderson was tacitly broken about 1920. In two novels, *The Builders* and *One Man in His Time*, Glasgow incorporated aspects of her relationship with Anderson.

As Glasgow began receiving the critical recognition for which she longed, her health began to fail. A heart condition worsened, and she died on November 21, 1945, in Richmond.

ANALYSIS

Turning away from a romanticized view of her own Virginia, Ellen Glasgow became a part of the revolt against the elegiac tradition of southern letters. Although she rejected romance, she did not turn to realism; rather, she saw herself as a "verist": "The whole truth," she said, "must embrace the interior world as well as external appearances." In this sense, she strove for what she called "blood and irony"—blood because the South had grown thin and pale and was existing on borrowed ideas, copying rather than creating; and irony because it is the surest antidote to sentimental decay. Certain that life in the South was not as it had been pictured by previous writers, she produced a series of novels that recorded the social history of Virginia through three generations, picturing sympathetically the social and industrial revolutions that were transforming the romantic South.

A central theme in this record is that of change—change brought about by the conflict between the declining agrarian regime and the rising industrial system. Arguing that such change must be accepted and even welcomed, Glasgow observed

> For thirty years I have had a part in the American literary scene, either as a laborer in the vineyard or as a raven croaking on a bust of Pallas. In all these years I have found that the only permanent law in art, as in the social order, is the law of change.

In pursuing the theme of change, however, Glasgow was careful not to go to the extreme in her presentation of deterioration, feeling that "the literature that crawls too long in the mire will lose at last the power of standing erect." In this respect, her works, unlike those of William Faulkner or Erskine Caldwell, lack shocking or sensational detail and maintain an almost Victorian sense of decorum. For example, when Dorinda in *Barren Ground* goes to the city, she is first approached by a fascinating lady clad in black who wants her to enter into a disreputable house. She is then rescued by a kindly doctor who gives her money to go back to Virginia and establish a dairy farm.

This tendency toward propriety found in Glasgow's writing is explained in her plea to the novelist of the southern gothic school:

All I ask him to do is to deal as honestly with living tissues as he now deals with decay, to remind himself that the colors of putrescence have no greater validity for our age, or for any age, than . . . the cardinal virtues.

The theme of change gives a mythic quality to Glasgow's work. It is that quality that Henry Canby refers to when he says that Glasgow sees her world as always a departing and a becoming. Her instrument for this cutting away is her sense for tender and ironic tragedy, a tragedy that is, in the words of Canby, "a tragedy of frustration—the waste of life through maladjustment of man to his environment and environment to its men."

Often, too, Glasgow's works picture nobility cramped by prejudice, or beauty gone wrong through an inability to adjust to the real, or a good philosophy without premises in existing experience. A good example of the latter theme can be found in the character of John Fincastle in *Vein of Iron*. A man of deep thought, he is considered "as a dangerous skeptic, or as a man of simple faith, who believed that God is essence, not energy, and that blessedness, or the life of the spirit, is the only reality." Fincastle is a part of the constant change in the world, but he himself does not fully realize the implications of the dynamic society in which he lives. He sees nothing of any potential value in the machine age and is unable to reconcile his own philosophy to the reality of the times.

Although all of Glasgow's works contain a note of pessimism, there is also present a note of optimism. More often than not, this hope comes after a protagonist's contact with city life. Dorinda, for example, returns to Pedlar's Mill after her stay in the city, to start a successful farm and gain revenge from Jason. Then, too, there is Ada in *Vein of Iron*, who, with her cynical husband, returns to the manse that was once her home and, strengthened by the recovery of "that lost certainty of a continuing tradition," looks forward to a new beginning.

Perhaps, when compared with Faulkner or Thomas Wolfe, the theme of change, as treated by Glasgow, may seem somewhat sentimental; there is, however, a refreshing and heartening chord in her work that lends credence to the idea that the world is not destined to be one great naturalistic garbage can, but may perhaps be fertile enough for an occasional bed of flowers. At any rate, as Glasgow phrased it, "the true revolution may end in a ditch or in the shambles, but it must begin in the stars."

VIRGINIA

In *Virginia*, her first acknowledged masterpiece, Glasgow focuses on the southern woman. "As an emblem," she writes of the southern woman in *The Deliverance*, "she followed closely the mid-Victorian ideal, and though her sort was found everywhere in the Western world, it was in Virginia that she seemed to attain her finest and latest flowering." It would follow, then, that if southern women attained their "finest and latest flowering" in Virginia, that also is where they would be most affected by the winds of social change that were sweeping over the South in the late nineteenth and early twentieth centuries. Bred and reared to tradition, they faced a new order that was both challenging and perplexing. While some held firmly to the pedestal on which they had been placed, others leaped from it and immersed themselves in the new world.

Virginia Pendleton, the heroine of *Virginia*, is, like her mother, the ideal southern woman, the image of propriety and gentility. "Whenever I attempt to recall the actual writing of Virginia," Glasgow writes in *A Certain Measure*,

> and to recapture the mold in which the book was conceived, I find myself moving again in an imaginary world which was then more real to me than the world which I inhabited. I could not separate Virginia from her background, because she was an integral part of it, and it shared her validity. What she was, that background and atmosphere had helped to make her, and she, in turn, had intensified the life of the picture.

In Dinwiddie, Virginia, during the 1800's, Virginia has been reared as "the perfect flower of the Victorian ideal" and "logical result of an inordinate sense of duty, the crowning achievement of the code of beautiful behavior and the Episcopal Church." She has been taught that duty, devotion, and sacrifice are the lot of women and that husband and family must come before all else.

Virginia, educated at Miss Priscilla Battle's finishing school, the Dinwiddie Academy for Young Ladies, is indeed "finished," at least as far as any real purpose in life is concerned. The basis of her education was simply that "the less a girl knew about life, the better prepared she would be to contend with it." Thinking him an excellent choice for a husband, she marries Oliver Treadwell, son of an industrialist, and, bearing him three children, settles down to family life. Oliver, like his father, who had dominated Oliver's mother, exercises this same control over Virginia. A would-be dramatist, Oliver is unsuccessful as a serious playwright, but he does receive some financial return by writing claptrap for the New York stage. Although Virginia has become middle-aged and worn, Oliver has maintained the look of youth. Finding no understanding from Virginia, who is not equipped to give him any, he deserts her for Margaret Oldcastle, an actor. Not knowing how to fight for her husband's love, Virginia is left with her two daughters, whose independence and aggressiveness she cannot understand, and her devoted son, Harry. The purpose in life for which she and so many other southern women had been prepared is gone. "Nothing but constancy was left to her," says Glasgow, "and constancy, when it has outlived its usefulness, is as barren as fortitude."

Virginia, in her minor tragedy, represents the ideal woman as victim of change, a change for which she has not been prepared and for which there is no effective antidote. One detects at least a small tear shed by Glasgow for the Virginias of the world. Once seen as ornaments of civilization and as restraints upon the more coarse natures of men, they now must replace self-sacrifice with an assertiveness that will be more in keeping with the changing social order. In that sense, Virginia points forward to *Barren Ground*.

BARREN GROUND

Barren Ground marks Glasgow's emergence not only from a period of despondency regarding her social life but also as a novelist who has moved without question from apprentice to master. Certainly her finest work to that time, *Barren Ground* was to Glasgow the best of all her novels. One of her country novels, it deals with that class of people often referred to as "poor whites." Glasgow herself refutes this appellation, preferring instead to call them "good people," a label that distinguishes them from the aristocratic "good families." Lineal descendants of the English yeoman farmer, good people were the ones who pushed the frontier westward. In this novel, they stand as a "buffer class between the opulent gentry and the hired labourers."

Dorinda Oakley, the heroine, is the offspring of a union of opposites: her father, Joshua, a landless man whose industry and good nature do not compensate for his ineffectuality; and her mother, Eudora, the daughter of a Presbyterian minister, with a religious mania of her own. This background, says Glasgow, has kept Dorinda's heart "in arms against life." More important, however, she has also inherited a kinship with the earth. This kinship enables her to make something positive out of "barren ground."

Dorinda falls in love with Jason Greylock, a young doctor, seeing in him the promise of something more than the grinding poverty she has known. They plan to marry, but Jason cannot go against his father's wishes, and he marries Geneva Ellgood instead. Pregnant by Jason, Dorinda flees to New York, where, after being struck by a taxi, she loses the unborn baby. She works as a nurse for Dr. Faraday until she learns that her father is dying. She returns home with enough money borrowed from Faraday to start a dairy farm. Back on the land, she becomes a tough-minded spinster and makes a success of the farm. Although she marries Nathan Pedlar, a storekeeper, she remains the head of the family. After his death in a train wreck, she is again alone, but happy, rearing Nathan's child by a previous marriage and managing the farm. Jason, in the meantime, has lost his wife by suicide and is forced to sell his farm to Dorinda. Because he is ill and an alcoholic, she unwillingly provides him with food and shelter. After a few months, he dies, and once more she is alone. When a local farmer asks Dorinda to marry him, she responds, "I am thankful to have finished with all that."

A tragic figure of sorts, Dorinda sees herself trapped by fate, "a straw in the wind, a leaf on a stream." Even so, she is not content to be simply a passive victim of that fate. Unlike Jason, who through his inherited weakness, succumbs to the forces that beset him, Dorinda looks upon the land as a symbol of that fate against which she must struggle. Hardened by adversity and with a deep instinct for survival, she refuses to surrender.

Although Dorinda's life may be compared to barren ground because it has been emotionally unfulfilled, it nevertheless is a successful life in that she does master herself and in turn masters the land. Just as the broom sedge must be burned off the land, so must romantic emotions be purged from Dorinda's soul. In giving her life to the land, she, in a sense, gains it back—and is thus, ironically, both victim and victor.

THE ROMANTIC COMEDIANS

Following *Barren Ground*, Glasgow turned to the novel of manners with *The Romantic Comedians*. The first of a trilogy—the subsequent works being *They Stooped to Folly* and *The Sheltered Life*—this novel has been regarded by some critics as Glasgow's finest. After *Barren Ground*, Glasgow comments, a novel "which for three years had steeped my mind in the tragic life, the comic spirit, always restless when it is confined, began struggling against the bars of its cage." Because she never before had turned her hand to comedy of manners, *The Romantic Comedians* was written in the nature of an experiment.

The novel exhibits a high spirit of comedy with tragic overtones. "Tragedy and comedy were blood brothers" in Glasgow's image-making faculty, she writes, "but they were at war with each other, and had steadily refused to be reconciled." In *The Romantic Comedians*, says Blair Rouse, "we see people and their actions as participants in the follies of the comic genre; but we see, too, that a very slight shift of emphasis may reveal a tragic mask upon the actors."

Judge Gamaliel Bland Honeywell, the protagonist, "is a collective portrait of several Virginians of an older school," says Glasgow, "who are still unafraid to call themselves gentlemen." Living in Queenborough (Richmond), he seeks female companionship after his wife of thirty-six years dies. At age sixty-five, he is expected to marry a former sweetheart, Amanda Lightfoot. Disdaining such expected decorum, however, he falls in love with and marries Annabelle Upchurch, a young cousin of his wife. Annabelle marries him not so much for love but rather to heal the pain of being jilted by Angus Blount. As one might suspect in such a marriage, Annabelle is soon looking for greener pastures, finding them in Delaney Birdsong, with whom she goes to New York. Unable to win her back, the Judge, ill and disillusioned, believes that life holds nothing more for him. With the coming of spring, however, he looks upon his attractive young nurse and muses, "Spring is here, and I am feeling almost as young as I felt last year."

Judge Honeywell, like many of Glasgow's women, is of another tradition. More than age separates him from Annabelle. While he is the target of some satiric jibes in the book and one finds it difficult to find much sincerity in him, he is, nevertheless, a victim of the same kind of romantic claptrap that dooms other Glasgow characters.

A refreshing book when contrasted with Glasgow's previous efforts, *The Romantic Comedians* displays the author's humanity as well as her humor. While she makes the reader laugh at the actions of the judge and the other characters of the novel, she never lets them become completely ridiculous. Whatever else the judge is, for example, he is a human being—and no one recognizes that more than Glasgow.

THE SHELTERED LIFE

In *The Sheltered Life*, the last novel of her trilogy on manners, Glasgow employs two points of view—that of youth and that of age, in this case a young girl and an old man, respectively. Against the background of a "shallow and aimless society of happiness hunters," she presents more characters of Queenborough as they are revealed through the mind and emotions of Jenny Blair and her grandfather, General David Archbald.

Glasgow intended General Archbald as the central character in the novel—a character who "represents the tragedy, wherever it appears, of the civilized man in a world that is not civilized." General Archbald sees before him a changing world, a world that is passing him by. Thus, he holds to the social traditions of the nineteenth century, which have provided little shelter for him. He was never a man for his time. A sensitive person who had wanted to be a poet, he was ridiculed in his earlier years. Poetry had been his one love in life; it was lost before it could be realized. He married his wife only because of an accidental, overnight sleigh ride that, in tradition-bound Queenborough, demanded marriage to save appearances. A compassionate man, he gives up his desire to marry again after his wife dies in order not to disrupt the lives of his son's widow and her daughter, Jenny.

Jenny, too, unknowingly is caught in the patterned existence of the Archbald heritage. A willful girl, she has been sheltered from the real world by culture and tradition and can see things only in terms of her own desires. At the age of eighteen, she falls in love with an older married man, George Birdsong. George's wife, Eva, eventually finds them in each other's arms. Jenny flees the scene, only to learn later that Eva has killed George.

Eva Birdsong is another perfect image of southern womanhood, beautiful and protected all her life. A celebrated belle prior to her marriage to George, she has striven to achieve a perfect marriage. Without children, she and George are thrown upon each other. Over the years, George has been a bit of a roué, seeking pleasure where he could find it. In the end, Eva is left with the realization that what women "value most is something that doesn't exist." When Jenny realizes what she has done, she flies to the general's understanding and sheltering arms, crying, "Oh, Grandfather, I didn't mean anything. . . . I didn't mean anything in the world." Ironically enough, she is right: She did not mean anything.

The Sheltered Life is more a tragicomedy than simply a comedy of manners. It is also, perhaps, Glasgow's best work, the novel toward which its predecessors were pointed. Symbol, style, characterization, and rhythm all combine to make *The Sheltered Life* a poignant and penetrating illustration of the futility of clinging to a tradition that has lost its essential meaning.

Glasgow's goal in all of her writing is perhaps stated best in *A Certain Measure*, when she says in reference to her last novel, *In This Our Life*, that she was trying to show "the tragedy of a social system which lives, grows, and prospers by material standards alone." One can sense in such a statement a conservative regard for tradition; even though Glasgow and many of her characters struggled against a shallow romanticism, a yearning for a genuine tradition was never far from her own artistic vision. The land seems to be the single sustaining factor in all of Glasgow's novels—it was the land that gave rise to and nourished the so-called southern tradition and that provides the "living pulse of endurance" to so many of her characters.

Wilton Eckley

OTHER MAJOR WORKS

SHORT FICTION: *The Shadowy Third, and Other Stories,* 1923; *The Collected Stories of Ellen Glasgow,* 1963.

POETRY: *The Freeman, and Other Poems,* 1902.

NONFICTION: *A Certain Measure: An Interpretation of Prose Fiction,* 1943; *The Woman Within,* 1954; *Letters of Ellen Glasgow,* 1958; *Perfect Companionship: Ellen Glasgow's Selected Correspondence with Women,* 2005 (Pamela R. Matthews, editor).

BIBLIOGRAPHY

Goodman, Susan. *Ellen Glasgow.* Baltimore: Johns Hopkins University Press, 1998. A biography that demonstrates Glasgow's significance as a southern author at the end of the nineteenth century and beginning of the twentieth century. Goodman discusses the gap between Glasgow's reception by her contemporaries and her later reception.

McDowell, Frederick P. W. *Ellen Glasgow and the Ironic Art of Fiction.* Madison: University of Wisconsin Press, 1960. An interesting analysis of Glasgow's oeuvre, analyzing it primarily in terms of style, irony, and wit. Includes an extensive bibliography.

Matthews, Pamela R. *Ellen Glasgow and a Woman's Traditions.* Charlottesville: University Press of Virginia, 1994. Matthews uses feminist psychological theory to reevaluate Glasgow's work, discussing, among other topics, Glasgow's perception of herself as a female author. Includes bibliographical references and an index.

The Mississippi Quarterly 49, no 2 (Spring, 1996). A special issue on Glasgow includes essays on her novels *The Sheltered Life, The Romantic Comedians,* and *The Descendants,* as well as a discussion of her use of childbirth metaphors and the impact of her deafness upon her writing.

Nicolaisen, Peter. "Rural Poverty and the Heroics of Farming: Elizabeth Madox Roberts's *The Time of Man* and Ellen Glasgow's *Barren Ground.*" In *Reading Southern Poverty Between the Wars, 1918-1939,* edited by Richard Godden and Martin Crawford. Athens: University of Georgia Press, 2006. Argues that many of the southern writers, social scientists, activists, and others who professed to be progressive actually upheld the traditional economic and social systems that maintained poverty. The essay on Glasgow analyzes *Barren Ground.*

Patterson, Martha H. "Mary Johnston, Ellen Glasgow, and the Evolutionary Logic of Progressive Reform." In *Beyond the Gibson Girl: Reimagining the American New Woman, 1895-1915.* Urbana: University of Illinois Press, 2005. At the end of the nineteenth and beginning of the twentieth century, an image emerged of the "New Woman," who was well-educated, progressive, and white. Patterson's book describes how Glasgow and other writers challenged this image by creating women characters who were African American, southern, and in other ways different from popular notions of womanhood.

Rouse, Blair. *Ellen Glasgow.* New York: Twayne, 1962. Presents facts, analyses, and interpretations of Glasgow's life; discusses the nature and purposes of her writing; and analyzes the scope of her work and her attainment as a literary artist. Rouse, a southerner, was one of the first contemporary critics to appreciate Glasgow. Includes an annotated bibliography.

Scura, Dorothy M., ed. *Ellen Glasgow: New Perspectives*. Knoxville: University of Tennessee Press, 1995. Detailed essays on Glasgow's major novels and themes, two essays on her autobiographies, and two essays on her poetry and short stories. Includes a helpful overview in the introduction, and a bibliography.

Taylor, Welford Dunaway, and George C. Longest, eds. *Regarding Ellen Glasgow: Essays for Contemporary Readers*. Richmond: Library of Virginia, 2001. This collection includes essays about some of the novels and examinations of Glasgow's work in the context of southern history, Calvinism, depictions of southern women, and feminism. Includes a chronology, a bibliography, and an index.

Wagner, Linda W. *Ellen Glasgow: Beyond Convention*. Austin: University of Texas Press, 1982. An excellent analysis of Glasgow's work, placing it in the context of her time and place, as well as in relation to later work by other American authors.

Weaks-Baxter, Mary. "Veins of Iron: Ellen Glasgow's Virginia Farmers." In *Reclaiming the American Farmer: The Reinvention of a Regional Mythology in Twentieth-Century Southern Writing*. Baton Rouge: Louisiana State University Press, 2006. Weaks-Baxter analyzes works by Glasgow and other southern authors in the years from 1900 until 1960, focusing on how their works replaced idealized descriptions of the plantation system with a new agrarian mythology that glorified the yeoman farmer.

RADCLYFFE HALL

Born: Bournemouth, Hampshire, England; August 12, 1880
Died: London, England; October 7, 1943
Also known as: Marguerite Radclyffe Hall

PRINCIPAL LONG FICTION
The Forge, 1924
The Unlit Lamp, 1924
A Saturday Life, 1925
Adam's Breed, 1926
The Well of Loneliness, 1928
The Master of the House, 1932
The Sixth Beatitude, 1936

OTHER LITERARY FORMS

Radclyffe Hall launched her writing career in 1906 with a collection of verse, *'Twixt Earth and Stars*. This well-received collection was followed by four more volumes of Hall's poetry, which were published between 1908 and 1915. In 1907, Hall met Mabel Veronica Batten, an amateur singer and prominent socialite, who helped her set twenty-one of the eighty poems in *'Twixt Earth and Stars* to music. With encouragement from Batten, Hall published *Sheaf of Verses* in 1908. This volume included poems on lesbian sexuality, notably "Ode to Sappho" and "The Scar."

Hall published three more volumes of verse: *Poems of the Past and Present* (1910), *Songs of Three Counties, and Other Poems* (1913), and *The Forgotten Island* (1915). The narrator in *The Forgotten Island* ruminates on her past life on the island of Lesbos and bemoans her fading love for another woman.

Aside from her collections of poetry, Hall published *Miss Ogilvy Finds Herself*, a collection of short stories, in 1934. The five stories in *Miss Ogilvy Finds Herself* mirror some of the author's own inner conflicts. Its critical reception was disappointing. Her letters are collected in *Your John: The Love Letters of Radclyffe Hall* (1997), edited by Joanne Glasgow.

ACHIEVEMENTS

Although *The Well of Loneliness* is Radclyffe Hall's best-known novel, she was awarded three prestigious literary prizes for another work, *Adam's Breed*. This perceptive tale portrays Gian-Luca, a food server who becomes so disgusted with watching the gluttonous people he serves stuff themselves with rich food that he eschews food and eventually starves himself.

Adam's Breed brought Hall the Eichelbergher Humane Award in 1926 for the best novel of the year, a prize that was followed in 1927 by the Prix Femina-Vie Heureuse Prize and shortly thereafter by the much-coveted James Tait Black Memorial Prize. Only once before in the history of these awards had a novel—E. M. Forster's *A Passage to India* (1924)—received both awards in the same year.

The celebrity Hall gained through the enthusiastic critical and popular reception of *Adam's Breed* made the reading public clamor for more of her writing. She devoted October and November, 1927, to beginning her next work of long fiction with the working title "Stephen," named for the novel's protagonist. This novel, renamed *The Well of Loneliness*, appeared in 1928. In this book, Hall produced the first piece of long fiction in England to explicitly explore female homosexuality, a topic Hall touched on obliquely in her earlier work. Although most critics do not consider *The Well of Loneliness* Hall's strongest novel, the notoriety that accompanied its publication established its author in feminist and lesbian and gay circles as a social and literary pioneer.

BIOGRAPHY

Marguerite Radclyffe Hall was born on August 12, 1880, to Radclyffe Radclyffe-Hall and Mary Jane Diehl Sager Radclyffe-Hall, an American expatriate from Philadelphia. Hall's father had inherited a sizable legacy from his own father, a savvy businessman who turned his tuberculosis sanitarium into a highly profitable enterprise.

Hall's father, not needing to work, left Mary Jane shortly after his daughter's birth. Mary Jane divorced him and, in 1889, married Alberto Visetti, a voice instructor at the Royal College of Music in London. Mary Jane, hoping that her first child would be a boy, raised her daughter as a boy, often dressing her in male attire and referring to her as John, a name that Hall later adopted. As her writing progressed, Hall dropped her given name and published as Radclyffe Hall.

In her teenage years, Hall inherited a substantial fortune. She entered King's College in London but left after two terms and spent the next year in Dresden, Germany. Returning to England in 1906, she bought a house in Malvern Wells, Worcestershire. In that year she published her first book of verse and met the socially prominent Mabel Veronica Batten, known as Ladye, a woman a generation older than Hall. Batten became her mentor and, in 1908, her lover.

Batten remained a major factor in Hall's life until her death from a stroke in 1916. Hall had became infatuated with Batten's niece, Una Vincenzo Troubridge, and began a sexual relationship with her, causing Batten considerable grief. Her death left Hall and Troubridge feeling terrible guilt, which haunted them until they died.

Hall died in 1943 and was buried beside Batten in Highgate Cemetery. Hall's tombstone bears the following words from Elizabeth Barrett Browning's *Sonnets from the Portuguese* (1850): "And if God Choose I Shall But Love Thee Better After Death," a testimony to the guilt that Hall suffered because of the pain she caused Batten.

Hall's reputation as a poet and novelist increased in the two decades between the publication of her first verse collection and the publication of *Adam's Breed* in 1926. She had verged on revealing her sexuality in much of her earlier writing. In 1927, however, she wrote *The Well of Loneliness*, a lesbian-themed novel in which she argued for the right of people to be different and to marry those they love, even if the "objects" of their love are of the same gender.

Although *The Well of Loneliness* is not prurient, its morality was questioned, and it soon became the subject of much controversy. On August 19, 1927, less than one month after its publication, James Douglas, editor of the *London Sunday Express*, raised questions about the book's morality and insisted that the British home secretary ban it. Hall's publisher, Cape, withdrew the novel but arranged for its re-publication in Paris.

Charges brought under the Obscene Publications Act of 1857 were lodged against the publisher and a bookseller, Leonard Hill, who had sold copies of the novel smuggled from France. Despite court testimony from numerous literary luminaries, the book was banned in England, not to be published there for twenty-two years. A lawsuit to ban the book in the United States found in Hall's favor.

In 1934, Hall became infatuated with a Russian nurse named Evguenia Souline, who was hired to care for the ailing Troubridge. Although Hall entered into an affair with Souline that lasted until shortly before Hall's death, Troubridge, much pained by the relationship, remained loyal to Hall and was at her bedside when Hall succumbed to colon cancer in 1943. In her instructions for distributing her estate, Hall trusted Troubridge to treat Souline equitably.

ANALYSIS

Lesbian sexuality and gender expression were the dominant factors in Radclyffe Hall's life, and the topics pervaded most of her writing directly or indirectly. Hall firmly believed in freedom of choice in human relationships and was ahead of her time in being an advocate for such controversial issues as same-gender marriage.

Society's disdain for homosexuality dominated Hall's thinking, and her opinions about this disdain appear in her long fiction as well as in her early poetry. She was familiar with the studies of sexologists Richard von Krafft-Ebing and Havelock Ellis, who argued that homosexuality is congenital—or genetic—rather than a matter of choice. She felt duty-bound to promote this view in her writing.

Although *The Well of Loneliness* contains Hall's most forthright sentiments regarding female homosexuality, the theme is present in a more subdued form in her first work of long fiction, *The Unlit Lamp*, in which a close relationship, covertly homosexual, exists between Joan Ogden and her governess, Elizabeth Rodney. In Victorian England, the setting of this novel, such relationships were common, but their sexual nature was overlooked in a society that shied away from acknowledging sex, especially between women.

In her next novel, *The Forge*, Hall uses the device of writing about a heterosexual couple in coded language that reveals, to those familiar with that language, that Hilary and Susan Brent are, in actuality, lesbians. The author offers veiled hints throughout the novel of a relationship other than heterosexual.

Hall's finest work of long fiction, as many critics agree, is *Adam's Breed*, in which a fully realized protagonist, Gian-Luca, is Hall's best-realized character. Although this novel does not have the homosexual overtones of much of Hall's work, it explores other important themes, those she addresses in much of her writing: isolation, alienation from family, cruelty to animals, the effects of a troubled childhood upon one's later development, and social persecution.

THE UNLIT LAMP

The Unlit Lamp is Hall's first novel, although it was published after *The Forge*. Hall got the idea to write *The Unlit Lamp* after observing a spinster caring for her demanding mother at a seaside resort. Hall was appalled by how women, especially single women, are drawn into acting gratis as servants to demanding relatives.

As *The Unlit Lamp* begins, the adolescent Joan Ogden wants to become a physician. Her governess, Elizabeth Rodney, plans to help her achieve that end by moving to London with her so that Joan can pursue medical studies. Joan has been trapped in the small town to which her mother retreated following the deaths of Joan's overbearing military father and her younger sister.

Joan and Elizabeth make one last attempt to relocate in London, but Joan's manipulative mother again draws her daughter into her trap. Elizabeth, realizing the futility of trying to fulfill her cherished dream of taking Joan to London, runs away from the small town and is married. In *The Unlit Lamp*, Hall also deals with what one might call a retreat into heterosexuality by having Elizabeth leave Joan and marry a man. Elizabeth seeks the stability and social acceptability of heterosexual marriage over a lesbian relationship.

Joan's mother dies, leaving her without options. She becomes the spinster caregiver for an old man. The frustration, isolation, and futility that pervade this novel lead to thought-provoking questions about a woman's place in society, and they articulate strong feminist sentiments long before such sentiments were common.

ADAM'S BREED

Generally considered Hall's most successful novel, *Adam's Breed* is notable for its psychologically sound character study. The story revolves around the life of Gian-Luca, who feels abandoned and alienated in unique ways. He does not know who his father is until fairly late in his life. His mother dies in childbirth. Gian-Luca's maternal grandmother, who blames him for her daughter's death, raises him.

Isolated and lonely, Gian-Luca eventually becomes headwaiter at the Doric Restaurant and marries a simple young Italian woman. Serving in World War I as a caterer for the military, at war's end he attempts to return to his former life, but the war has changed him. He cannot adjust. Working in the restaurant, he is surrounded by greedy, gluttonous patrons whose excesses disgust him to the point that the sight of food appalls him.

In the restaurant one night, he serves an Italian poet, Ugo Doria, who turns out to be his birth father. Eventually, Gian-Luca leaves his wife and goes to the New Forest to live as a recluse. Realizing that he cannot withdraw from life, he returns to his wife, but he has become so emaciated that he dies of starvation.

In this sensitively told story, Hall pursues many of the themes that interest her most. Isolation and abandonment were major factors in her own life, and she was able in *Adam's Breed* to capture the ways these two forces impinge upon a person's life; in this case, on Gian-Luca's development.

THE WELL OF LONELINESS

Although *The Well of Loneliness* is not Hall's best work of long fiction, it is the novel that reflects her deepest emotions and most pressing concerns. The leading character in the novel is Stephen Gordon, a woman whose aristocratic parents, hoping for a son, gave her a male name and dressed her in masculine clothing. As she matures, she realizes that she is a lesbian. When she receives a marriage proposal from Martin Hallam, she rejects it and then falls in love with Angela Crossby, the wife of a businessman. As Stephen's sexual orientation becomes obvious to many, her mother forces her out of the family home. Stephen goes to London and writes a novel, and even though she spends time with other gays and lesbians, she still suffers inner conflict about her sexuality.

The time is World War I, and Stephen joins the ambulance corps, where she meets and falls in love with Mary Llewellyn, an unsophisticated young woman from Wales. At war's end, the two go to Paris together and rent a house. Mary begins to feel discomfort with Stephen's activities and the people she attracts, and they separate. Stephen generously "gives" Mary to Martin, the man whose marriage proposal Stephen rejected.

The novel ends with the proclamation "Give us also the right to our existence!," a sentiment at the heart of much of Hall's writing. *The Well of Loneliness* remains the work of long fiction for which Hall is remembered. The first novel in England to broach openly the matter of female homosexuality, the book gained sufficient notoriety to ensure its sales both upon publication and after. Two years after its release in 1928, the novel brought Hall sixty thousand dollars in royalties, a princely sum at that time. In the year of Hall's death, 1943, international sales of *The Well of Loneliness* exceeded one hundred thousand copies.

R. Baird Shuman

OTHER MAJOR WORKS

SHORT FICTION: *Miss Ogilvy Finds Herself*, 1934.

POETRY: *'Twixt Earth and Stars*, 1906; *A Sheaf of Verses*, 1908; *Poems of the Past and Present*, 1910; *Songs of Three Counties, and Other Poems*, 1913; *The Forgotten Island*, 1915.

NONFICTION: *Your John: The Love Letters of Radclyffe Hall*, 1997 (Joanne Glasgow, editor).

BIBLIOGRAPHY

Castle, Terry. *Noël Coward and Radclyffe Hall: Kindred Spirits*. New York: Columbia University Press, 1996. Castle argues that although they were seeming opposites, British playwright and composer Noël Coward and Hall were friends who contributed directly to each other's work.

Cline, Sally. *Radclyffe Hall: A Woman Called John*. New York: Overlook Press, 1998. This thorough biography of Hall discusses how she assumed essentially a masculine gender identity and chronicles as well her relationships with women, many of those relationships long term.

Dickson, Lovat. *Radclyffe Hall at the Well of Loneliness: A Sapphic Chronicle*. New York: Scribner, 1975. An incisive account of Hall's literary work on the torments of being different in a society with strict gender roles and rules about sexual expression, homosexuality in particular.

Doan, Laura, and Jay Prosser, eds. *Palatable Poison: Critical Perspectives on "The Well of Loneliness."* New York: Columbia University Press, 2001. Twenty-one essays, and a perceptive introductory essay by the editors and an afterword by literary critic Terry Castle, offer excellent analyses of the critical reception of this controversial novel.

Glasgow, Joanne, ed. *Your John: The Love Letters of Radclyffe Hall*. New York: New York University Press, 1997. This collection of 576 letters Hall wrote between 1934 and 1942 to Evguenia Souline, a Russian emigre with whom she was in love, offers keen insights into Hall's character and emotions.

Souhami, Diana. *The Trials of Radclyffe Hall*. New York: Doubleday, 1999. Of particular interest in this critical biography is Souhami's discussion of the triangulated love affair that involved both Una Troubridge, Hall's lover for twenty-eight years, and Evguenia Souline, her paramour for nearly a decade.

Troubridge, Lady Una Vincenzo. *The Life of Radclyffe Hall*. New York: Citadel Press, 1961. A reminiscence by the woman who was Hall's longtime lover. A highly subjective account that is, nonetheless, interesting and informative.

KHALED HOSSEINI

Born: Kabul, Afghanistan; March 4, 1965

PRINCIPAL LONG FICTION
The Kite Runner, 2003
A Thousand Splendid Suns, 2007

OTHER LITERARY FORMS

While Khaled Hosseini (hoh-SAY-nee) is best known for his long fiction, he has written articles for national publications including *The Wall Street Journal* and *Newsweek*. His editorial in defense of Sayed Perwiz Kambakhsh, an Afghan journalism student sentenced to death for distributing information that questions Islamic laws, is the most notable of his writings in nonfiction.

ACHIEVEMENTS

Published in more than forty languages, Khaled Hosseini's *The Kite Runner* has received widespread acclaim from critics and the general public. Awards for the book include the *San Francisco Chronicle* Best Book of the Year for 2003, the American Library Association's Notable Book Award in 2004, and the American Place Theatre's Literature to Life Award in 2005. The novel was adapted for the cinema and released in 2007. *A Thousand Splendid Suns* appeared on many best-seller lists, won a Galaxy British Book Awards—the Richard & Judy Award for Best Read of the Year—and a Book Sense Book of the Year Award in 2008 from the American Booksellers Association.

Hosseini has been honored both for his writing and humanitarian work. In 2006, the United Nations Office of the High Commissioner for Refugees named him its humanitarian of the year. In addition, *Time* magazine included Hosseini in its 2008 list of the most influential people. Former American first lady Laura Bush, an advocate for Afghan women, wrote the *Time* entry about Hosseini and his work.

BIOGRAPHY

Khaled Hosseini was born March 4, 1965, in Kabul, Afghanistan, and spent his boyhood there with his siblings and parents: his mother, a high school teacher, and his father, a diplomat. During that time, the family enjoyed prosperity in a peaceful Afghanistan. In 1976, Hosseini and his family moved to Paris, France, where his father received a new post at the Afghan embassy. The family expected to remain in Paris for only four years, the duration of his father's assignment, and then to return to Afghanistan. However, they found that returning to their country would be too dangerous after it was invaded by the Soviet Union in 1979. Thus, the family applied for and was granted political asylum by the United States. In 1980, they moved to San Jose, California.

After graduating from Santa Clara University with a degree in biology, Hosseini studied medicine at the University of California, San Diego. He graduated in 1993 with a specialization in internal medicine. He was a practicing physician until 2004, shortly after *The Kite Runner* was published.

ANALYSIS

The Kite Runner and *A Thousand Splendid Suns* explore the themes of exile, displacement, immigration, and a person's relationship to one's nation, themes commonly associated with postcolonial literature. Many nations, such as India), and Afghanistan, were once colonies of more powerful countries, including Great Britain, the Netherlands, France, and the United States, seeking to expand their wealth and territories. As the once colonized areas gained independence, they created new national identities, most visibly through art and literature. Theorists have categorized as postcolonial the literature and art that explores the relationships between colonized and colonizer.

Afghanistan has struggled for independence from various invading nations throughout its history; in the twentieth and twenty-first centuries alone, England, the former Soviet Union, and United Nations peacekeeping forces, primarily consisting of U.S. soldiers, have occupied the country. As a result, many Afghans have migrated either by force or by choice to different countries. Both *The Kite Runner* and *A Thousand Splendid Suns* describe the lives of characters who have left their homelands—either to another country or a safer part of their own country—as a result of war.

While far from a direct representation of his childhood in Kabul and young adulthood in California, to which Hosseini's family migrated, the characters in *The Kite Runner* were nevertheless inspired by Hosseini's friends and family. Hosseini acknowledges that his own father inspired the magnanimity of the character Baba, and the mother of another character, Amir, is a professor of Farsi and history, much like Hosseini's own mother, who taught the same subjects in high school. Hosseini said that one of his own family's servants in Kabul, Hossein Khan, and the relationship he had with him, inspired the characterization of Hassan and his friendship with Amir.

One of the most salient ways in which Hosseini examines the tension between selfhood and nationality is through intertextuality—drawing on other literary works to illuminate a novel or poem. In *The Kite Runner*, Amir and Hassan enjoy reading the story of Rostam and Sohrab, which comes from Persian poet Firdusi's *Shahnamah* (c. 1010), the poetic epic of Iran, Afghanistan, and other Persian-speaking countries. Much like the mythologized history of the Greco-Roman world found in classic works of poetry by Homer, the *Shahnamah* poetically narrates the creation of the Persian Empire, of which Afghanistan was once a part. Rostam, a proud and successful warrior, and Sohrab, a champion in his own right, are father and son but have never met. Fighting to protect their country from invaders, they destroy each other and save the nation. Hosseini depicts how the relationships between fathers and sons and the secrets they keep from one another have the potential to determine individual and national characters.

A Thousand Splendid Suns borrows its title from a poem by Sa'ib, a seventeenth century Persian poet. A translation of the poem's most pertinent lines reads as follows: "One could not count the moons that shimmer on her roofs/ And the thousand splendid suns that hide behind her walls."

In contrast to the main characters in *The Kite Runner*, Mariam and Laila, protagonists in *A Thousand Splendid Suns*, remain in Afghanistan throughout several invasions. Laila and her father cite the lines of this poem when thinking of the Kabul they knew before the wars. The poem conveys a strong love for the city and nation, but it also serves as a haunting lament for how Afghanistan's troubled history has impacted its peoples.

THE KITE RUNNER

In *The Kite Runner*, Hosseini employs the genre called bildungsroman, or the coming-of-age story, to follow the development of Amir, the protagonist and narrator, from his youth in Kabul through his adulthood in the area of San Francisco, California. Foils and father-son relationships unify the sprawling, yet symmetrical narrative.

As a little boy and preteen, Amir lives with his father Baba; his best friend and servant Hassan; and Hassan's father Ali, also a servant. Amir and Hassan play in Kabul's streets, watch American Westerns at the cinema, run kites together, and live, in many ways, as brothers. Similarly, Baba, a child of the upper class, grew up in the same household with Ali acting as his servant, friend, and brother figure. However, the idyllic surroundings in which Amir matures are troubled by these relationships. Amir desperately seeks Baba's attention, whereas Hassan, despite Baba not claiming him as his son, receives the praise and affection that Amir desires. At once, Amir admires Hassan's goodness, loyalty, bravery, and his relationship with Baba, but he is jealous of him. This creates tension between the two boys, as Amir often resorts to cruelty toward Hassan when he feels inadequate.

While Amir and Hassan are described throughout the novel as "milk brothers," boys who suckled from the same woman as infants, their closeness is frowned upon. Amir is a Pashtun, the majority ethnic group in Afghanistan; Hassan is a Hazara and, as a result, relegated to the servant class in Kabul. Despite their intimacy, the two boys are not supposed to be friends according to cultural beliefs. The tension in their friendship parallels national conflicts between the majority and minority ethnic groups in Afghanistan that have engendered division and war in that country.

After Amir wins a citywide kite-flying tournament, Hassan retrieves the kite for him and encounters a gang who has threatened the two boys before. The gang leader, Assef, physically and sexually assaults Hassan while Amir watches. This act of betrayal affects Amir in myriad ways: He gains Baba's affection, albeit temporarily, by having won the tournament, yet his guilt for failing to protect his best friend Hassan destroys his friendship with Hassan and plagues Amir into adulthood.

Baba and Amir are forced to leave Kabul, escaping to Pakistan and then to the United

States as a result of the Soviet invasion. Settling in Northern California, they live relatively tranquil lives in spite of diminished economic circumstances and become members of a vibrant Afghan immigrant culture. After a decade, Baba dies, and Amir, a newly published author, creates a life with his wife Soraya. When Amir receives a telephone call from Baba's best friend from Kabul, Rahim Khan, telling him that "there is a way to be good again," Amir finds that he must return to Kabul. Rahim Khan reveals to Amir that Hassan is his biological half-brother, the son of Baba and Ali's servant wife. He then asks Amir to retrieve Hassan's son Sohrab from one of the underfunded and failing orphanages in Kabul.

Amir's journey to rescue Sohrab acts as a physical and moral journey to redeem himself from guilt and from the cowardice that he and his father shared. Ultimately, he stands up to the men who have brutalized Sohrab and brings him to California. Critics have argued that the symmetrical plot and moralistic theme undercut the novel's realism. In addition, some have claimed that the narrative, if viewed as an allegory of Afghanistan's national crisis and its "redemption" by the West, reads as too simplistic and patronizing. However, it is important to remember that Amir's quest does not paint him as a savior of anyone or any nation. Any fairy-tale endings for Amir, Sohrab, or Afghanistan are quickly dismissed when one takes into account the continuing struggles of survivors and refugees.

A Thousand Splendid Suns

Hosseini's second novel has been heralded for its realistic portrayal of Afghanistan during its occupation by the Soviets, the mujahideen—Islamic guerrilla fighters—the Taliban, and U.N. peacekeeping forces. In contrast to *The Kite Runner*, *A Thousand Splendid Suns* examines relationships between women as they are influenced by customs and class.

Spanning a period of nearly thirty years, the novel describes the intertwining lives of Mariam and Laila. Mariam, the daughter of Jalil, a wealthy businessman, and his servant Nana, is raised by her mother in a hut outside Herat, one of Afghanistan's most beautiful cities. Nana, having been ousted by Jalil and disowned by her family, cultivates a pristine bitterness that she tries to pass on to Mariam. Life treated Nana cruelly, and she believes it her job to steal Mariam from the shattered hopes that she will encounter because she is a woman and a *harami*, or illegitimate child.

Despite her mother's admonishments, Mariam relishes the weekly visits Jalil makes to her home. During their time together, Jalil gives Mariam gifts, tells her she's beautiful, and listens to her in a way that Nana cannot. The intimacy between father and daughter, however, is tempered by Jalil having legitimate children and wives in Herat; thus, he cannot publicly accept Mariam as his child—the only gift that Mariam really wants from her father. When she is fifteen years old, Mariam decides to visit Jalil in the city, much to Nana's dismay, and finds that Jalil will not accept her into his home. Still angry from the shame of being forced to sleep on the street in front of her father's house, Mariam returns to her home outside Herat, only to find that Nana has committed suicide. This puts Mariam in extremely precarious circumstances: She is an illegitimate female orphan without a male protector in a culture that values the honor and chastity of women. To rectify the situation, Jalil arranges her marriage to Rasheed, a shoemaker in Kabul who is nearly twice her age.

The early days of their marriage are filled with excitement for Mariam. On the surface, it appears that her life has improved, now that she lives in a house instead of a shack and receives frequent kindnesses from her husband. Rasheed, however, forces her to wear a burka, a garment designed to cover women from head to foot. He also forbids her to leave the house without him. After Mariam miscarries several times, Rasheed begins to beat her consistently. Without a male heir to carry on the family name, he finds Mariam useless. Verses from the Qur'an taught by her friend and village mullah, or teacher of Islam, keep Mariam from sinking into despair.

Nearly two decades Mariam's junior, Laila was raised as the daughter of liberal parents in a middle-class household. Her childhood lies in stark contrast to that of Mariam, as she lived in relative freedom and luxury and aspired as a youth to attend the university. However, war infiltrates Kabul and she is left the only survivor of her family. As an act of "mercy," the now-middle-age Rasheed agrees to take adolescent Laila as his second wife. While the relationship between Laila and Mariam is strained at first, the two begin to love one another. The birth of Aziza and the mother-daughter-grandmother relationships that the women share brings purpose and meaning to their otherwise painful existence.

As conditions in Kabul worsen with the Taliban's occupation and as the family increases in size, they suffer from a privation so desperate that Rasheed forces Aziza to live in one of the city's many orphanages while his and Laila's son, Zalmai, continues to live at home. Rasheed continues to abuse Mariam; and, the Taliban, on the lookout for women unaccompanied by male protectors, beats Laila as she makes her way to the orphanage to visit her daughter. When Tariq, Laila's first love and Aziza's birth father, returns to Kabul, the women hope to escape, but it becomes clear that Rasheed will never let them do so. In an act of self-sacrifice, Mariam kills Rasheed and accepts the Taliban's sentence—death by execution—so that Laila, Tariq, Aziza, and Zalmai can live in a loving home. After peacekeeping forces control the Taliban in Kabul, Laila returns to the city and becomes a teacher in an orphanage to honor Mariam's memory and contribute to her country's recovery.

The beauty and sorrow of *A Thousand Splendid Suns* can be seen in the relationship between Mariam and Laila—two women born into vastly different circumstances who find themselves with the same abusive husband. Hosseini presents traditional customs regarding women in a relatively balanced fashion, offering in the novel that some woman accept veiling and the protection it provides. However, the contrast between Mariam's and Laila's expected fates highlights several undeniable issues, most saliently that women and children survivors are the true victims of war and that education and employment are fundamental to individual survival and national redevelopment.

DaRelle M. Rollins

BIBLIOGRAPHY

Ahmed-Gosh, Huma. "A History of Women in Afghanistan: Lessons Learnt for the Future." *Journal of International Women's Studies* 4, no. 3 (2003): 1-14. Study of the history of women in Afghanistan in the late twentieth century that also suggests ways for a freer future.

Bloom, Harold, ed. *Khalid Hosseini's "The Kite Runner."* New York: Bloom's Literary Criticism, 2009. Comprehensive study guide on *The Kite Runner* with essays written especially for students in grades 9 through 12. Part of the Bloom's Guides series of analyses of classic works of literature.

Katsoulis, Melissa. "Kites of Passage: New Fiction." *The Times* (London), August 30, 2003. Brief review of Hosseini's novel *The Kite Runner* in a renowned British periodical.

Lemar-Aftaab. June, 2004. Special issue of this Web-based magazine devoted to Khaled Hosseini and his works. Two articles explore themes in *The Kite Runner.* Also features an interview with Hosseini. Available at http://afghanmagazine.com/2004_06/.

JAMAICA KINCAID
Elaine Cynthia Potter Richardson

Born: St. John's, Antigua; May 25, 1949
Also known as: Elaine Cynthia Potter Richardson

PRINCIPAL LONG FICTION
Annie John, 1985
Lucy, 1990
The Autobiography of My Mother, 1996
Mr. Potter, 2002

OTHER LITERARY FORMS

Jamaica Kincaid first gained respect and admiration as the writer of *At the Bottom of the River* (1983), a collection of unconventional but thematically unified short stories. She has also written two important memoirs, *A Small Place* (1988), about growing up in a Caribbean vacation resort, and *My Brother* (1997), which relates the story of her brother's struggle with acquired immunodeficiency syndrome (AIDS). Additionally, as a staff writer for *The New Yorker* for twenty years, she wrote numerous "Talk of the Town" pieces and frequent articles on gardening. In 2005, she published the travel book *Among Flowers: A Walk in the Himalaya*, in which describes a trip to Nepal during which she sought out rare plants for her garden in Vermont.

ACHIEVEMENTS

Jamaica Kincaid has made writing about her life her life's work. Her finely honed style highlights personal impressions and feelings over plot development. Although she allows a political dimension to emerge from her use of Caribbean settings, her fiction does not strain to be political. Rather, she uses the political issues relating to her colonial background to intensify the most important issue of her fiction: the intense bond between mother and daughter. Her spare, personal style simultaneously invites readers to enter Kincaid's world and, by its toughness, challenges them to do so.

Although she made no specific effort to align herself with any ideology, her first book, *At the Bottom of the River* (which in 1983 won the Morton Dauwen Zabel Award from the American Academy and Institute of Arts and Letters), quickly established Kincaid as a favorite among feminist and postcolonial critics, who lauded her personal but unsentimental presentation of the world of women and of the Caribbean. Her fame continued as she received more distinguished honors, including a Guggenheim Fellowship in 1989 and honorary degrees from William College, Long Island University, and Wesleyan University. Among the awards she has received for her writing are the Lannan Literary Award for Fiction, the Anisfield-Wolf Book Award, and the Lila Wallace-Reader's Digest Award.

BIOGRAPHY

Jamaica Kincaid was born Elaine Cynthia Potter Richardson in St. John's, Antigua, the daughter of Annie Richardson and Roderick Potter, a taxi driver. Her father was not a significant presence in her life. The man she considered her father was David Drew, a cabinetmaker and carpenter whom her mother married shortly after Elaine's birth. She learned to read at the age of three, and when she turned seven, her mother gave her a copy of the *Concise Oxford Dictionary* as a birthday gift. The births of her three brothers—Joseph in 1958, Dalma in 1959, and Devon in 1961 (whose death from AIDS in 1996 would provide the focus for *My Brother*)—changed her life, not only because she was no longer an only child but also because she began to realize that her education would never be taken as seriously as her brothers' education would be. While her parents made plans for their sons' university training, she was sent to study with a seamstress twice a week.

When she was seventeen, Elaine left for the United States to become an au pair—although she has stated that she prefers the term "servant"—in Scarsdale, New York. She took classes at Westchester Community College but soon left Scarsdale to take another au pair position looking after the daughters of an Upper East Side, New York, couple (this experience would provide the basic material for *Lucy*). Over the course of the next few years, she would study photography at the New School for Social Research and at Franconia College in New Hampshire before returning to New York to work briefly for the magazine *Art Direction*.

In 1973, she sold her first piece of professional writing to the magazine *Ingenue*; it was an interview with Gloria Steinem that focused on what life was like for the well-known feminist at the age of seventeen. Also in 1973, she changed her name to Jamaica Kincaid, a move probably inspired by her need to create an anonymous, authorial identity; significantly, the pen name marks Kincaid as Caribbean to the American reading audience, something that her birth name does not. Also in 1973, George Trow, a writer for the "Talk of the Town" column in *The New Yorker*, started incorporating quotations from Kincaid in his writing (she was his "sassy black friend"), and her writing career was started.

Kincaid worked as a freelance writer until she became a staff writer for *The New Yorker* in 1976 (a position she held until a 1995 disagreement with then-editor Tina Brown over the direction of the magazine led to her resignation). In 1979, she married Allen Shawn, son of William Shawn, the editor of *The New Yorker* at the time, and the couple moved to North Bennington, Vermont, where Shawn was on the faculty of Bennington College and where Kincaid taught courses in writing. The union produced two children, Annie (born in 1985) and Harold (born in 1989); Kincaid and Shawn divorced after twenty-five years of marriage. In addition to her writing career, Kincaid holds the position of visiting lecturer on African and African American studies and on English and American literature and language at Harvard University.

ANALYSIS

Jamaica Kincaid is known for her impressionistic prose, which is rich with detail presented in a poetic style, her continual treatment of mother-daughter issues, and her relentless pursuit of honesty. More so than many fiction writers, she is an autobiographical writer whose life and art are inextricably woven together. She began her career by mastering the short story, the form from which her longer fiction grew. Most of the pieces that constitute *At the Bottom of the River* and *Annie John* were first published in *The New Yorker*, as were the chapters of *Lucy*. Though the individual pieces in each work have a self-contained unity, *Annie John* and *Lucy* also have a clear continuity from story to story, something less true of the impressionistic writing of *At the Bottom of the River*; thus *At the Bottom of the River* is often considered a collection of short stories, whereas *Annie John* and *Lucy* are clearly novels. *At the Bottom of the River* won for Kincaid the Morton Dauwen Zabel Award for short fiction; the collection includes "Girl," a story written as a stream of instructions from a mother to a daughter, which is probably Kincaid's best-known piece.

Kincaid's native Antigua is central in her writing. This colonial setting strongly relates to her mother-daughter subject matter, because the narrators of her first two novels—Annie and Lucy, respectively—both seem to make connections between their Anglophile mothers and the colonial English, and also because the childhood experiences of both narrators have been shaped by a colonial background that limits their options and makes their relationships with their mothers that much more intense. Kincaid continues this portrayal of Antigua in *Mr. Potter*, a novel that uses her father as its subject. *Mr. Potter* focuses on Roderick Potter and his life as a philandering chauffeur. The narrator of the story, Annie Cynthia Potter, sparked by anger and obligation, examines the life of her detached father by revealing the conditions of his stoic upbringing and links his story with that of the larger community.

Mr. Potter is similar to *Lucy*, in which Kincaid cultivates a detachment with which she explores issues of anger and loss, carefully disallowing any easy resolution. Kincaid seems less interested in solving fictional problems than in exploring contrary states of mind that perceive problems. Admittedly, this style is not to everyone's taste, and even quite a few readers who were seduced by Kincaid's earlier works were less pleased with *Lucy* and *The Autobiography of My Mother*. However, even if her incantatory rhythms and her tight focus on bleak, emotional situations in her post-*Annie John* works are not universally appreciated, few readers deny that Kincaid has an eye for poetic detail and the ability to achieve a shimmering honesty in her prose.

ANNIE JOHN

Kincaid's first novel, *Annie John*, is about a talented young girl in Antigua who, while growing into early womanhood, must separate herself from her mother. Fittingly, the book begins with a story of Annie's recognition of mortality at the age of ten. Fascinated by the knowledge that she or anyone could die at any time, she begins to attend the funerals of people she does not know. At one point, she imagines herself dead and her father, who makes coffins, so overcome with grief that he cannot build one for her, a complex image suggesting her growing separation from her family. When, after attending a funeral for a child she did know, Annie neglects to bring home fish, as her mother demanded, her mother punishes her before giving her a good-night kiss. Though the kiss suggests a continued bond between mother and daughter, the next chapter places it in a different context. The title "The Circling Hand" refers to Annie's mother's hand on her father's back when Annie accidentally spies her parents making love. Almost as if in contradiction to the reassuring maternal kiss of the earlier story, this chapter offers the rising specter of sexuality as a threat that will separate mother and daughter. Annie learns not only that she must stop dressing exactly like her mother but also that she must someday be married and have a house of her own. This is beyond Annie's comprehension.

Though Annie never fully understands this growing distance from her mother, she contributes to it. For instance, when she becomes friends with a girl at school named Gwen, she does not tell her mother. In part, she is transferring her affections to friends as a natural process of growing up, but as the chapters "Gwen" and "The Red Girl" make clear, she is also seeking comfort to ease the pain of her mother's disapproval. Gwen becomes her best friend, and Annie imagines living with her, but Gwen is replaced briefly in Annie's affections by the Red Girl, who is a friend and cohort with whom Annie plays marbles, against the wishes of her mother.

The growing separation from her mother comes to a crisis in the chapter "The Long Rain," when Annie lapses into an extended depression and takes to her bed. When medicine and the cures of a local conjure woman do nothing to help, Annie's grandmother, Ma Chess, also a conjure woman, moves in with her. The weather remains damp the entire time Annie remains bedridden, and she feels herself physically cut off from other people. When she is finally well enough to return to school, she discovers she has grown so much that she needs a new school uniform; symbolically, she has become a new person. Thus it is that the last chapter, "The Long Jetty," begins with Annie thinking, "My name is Annie John," an act of self-naming that is also an act of self-possession. The chapter tells of Annie's last day in Antigua as she prepares to meet the ship that will take her to England, where she plans to study to become a nurse. A sensitive, detailed portrayal of a leave-taking, this chapter serves as a poignant farewell to childhood and to the intimacy with her mother that only a child can know. This last chapter captures perfectly Kincaid's ability to tell a story sensitively without sentimentality.

LUCY

Kincaid's novel *Lucy* is a thematic sequel to *Annie John*. Lucy is seventeen when the novel begins, newly arrived in the United States from Antigua to work as an au pair, watching the four girls of Lewis and Mariah, an upper-middle-class New York couple. Although the novel is set entirely outside Antigua and Lucy's mother never appears in it, Lucy's attempt to separate herself from her mother constitutes the main theme of the novel.

Mariah is presented as a loving but thoroughly ethnocentric white woman. A recurring example of this is her attempt to make Lucy appreciate the Wordsworthian beauty of daffodils, unaware that it is precisely because Lucy had to study Wordsworth's poetry about a flower that does not grow in Antigua that this flower represents the world of the colonizer to her. In fact, Mariah's unselfconscious, patronizing goodwill is exactly what Lucy loves most and yet cannot tolerate about her employer, because it reminds her of her mother.

When Lucy learns that Lewis is having an affair with Mariah's best friend, Dinah, she understands that this idyllic marriage is falling apart. When a letter from home informs her that her father has died, she is unable to explain to Mariah that her anger toward her mother is based on mourning the perfect love she had once felt between them. At the same time, her own sexuality begins to emerge, and she develops interests in young men. Wanting more space, she cuts short her one-year au pair agreement and moves in with her friend Peggy, a young woman who represents a more exciting world to Lucy. The novel ends with Lucy writing her name, Lucy Josephine Potter, in a book and wishing that she could love someone enough to die for that love. This ending clearly signals an act of self-possession (much like the self-naming at the end of *Annie John*), but it also signifies the loneliness of breaking away from others, even to assert oneself. Though *Lucy* is a much angrier novel than *Annie John*, Lucy's anger is best understood in terms of the writer's earlier autobiographical surrogate in *Annie John*; the melancholy that debilitates Annie at the end of her novel is turned into anger by Lucy.

THE AUTOBIOGRAPHY OF MY MOTHER

The Autobiography of My Mother is a tough, bleakly ironic novel, the work of a writer at the full height of her powers. It follows Xuela Claudette Richardson, a Caribbean woman who aborted her only pregnancy. If this fact seems to imply that Kincaid has taken a step away from the style of autobiographical fiction, the self-contradictory title and the main character's last name, Richardson, a name she shares with Jamaica Kincaid, both suggest that this story is not very far removed from the facts of Kincaid's own family.

The novel begins with the narrator proclaiming that her mother died the moment she was born, "and so for my whole life there was nothing standing between myself and eternity." This interesting statement reveals as much about the importance of mothers in Kincaid's writing as about the character Xuela. She lives with her father and a stepmother, who hates her and may have tried to kill her with a poisoned necklace, until she is sent at fifteen to live with a wealthy couple. Ostensibly, she is to be a student, but in fact she is to be the man's mistress.

Though the relationship between the colonizer and the colonized is important in all of Kincaid's writing, *The Autobiography of My Mother* brings it to the foreground in different ways. The first words Xuela learns to read are the words "the British Empire," written across a map. Meanwhile, her stepmother refuses to speak to Xuela in anything other than a patois, or provincial dialect, as if to reduce Xuela to the status of an illegitimate subject of the empire. When Xuela eventually marries (after affairs with many men), it is to a man she identifies as "of the victors"—the British. She takes a cruel satisfaction in refusing to love him, even though, according to her, he lived for the sound of her footsteps. Though it is never a relationship based on love, she lives with him for many years, and he becomes for her "all the children I did not allow to be born." While this is hardly an ideal relationship, it is not a completely empty one.

Toward the end, Xuela declares that her mother's death at the moment of her birth has been the central facet of her life. Her ironic detachment from life seems to have been based on this, as if, devoid of the only buffer between herself and the hardship of life that she can imagine—a mother—she further rejects all other comforts and answers that people wish to propose. If Xuela is the least likable of Kincaid's main characters, her tough-as-nails approach to the world nonetheless makes her among the most compelling.

MR. POTTER

In *Mr. Potter*, Kincaid continues to follow the facts of her own family by introducing readers to a character based on the life of her father, Roderick Nathaniel Potter. The novel traces the subtle happenings of Mr. Potter's life, from his meeting Dr. Weizenger and his wife to his employment with Mr. Shoul. As the story unfolds, the reader learns more about the lives of these characters and their innermost thoughts. Although the characters seem separated and even careless about each other, often looking at each other with disgust, the narrator explores the connections among their lives and explains how history has formed their condition as displaced persons. The story highlights the mundane performance of life and work and the environment that has contributed to the present social state of each of the characters.

The story proceeds through a series of vignettes in which the reader learns about Mr. Potter's love of cars and women and his disdain for his daughters. The narrator's exploration into the lives of Mr. Potter's father and mother suggests an explanation for Mr. Potter's inability to love. Mr. Potter's father, Nathaniel Potter, refused to acknowledge the existence of his son, and his mother, Elfrida Robinson, committed suicide by drowning herself in the ocean. Subsequently, Mr. Potter was sent to live with Mr. and Mistress Shepherd, who treated him with cruelty and indifference. Although Mr. Potter seems unaware of the injustices that have plagued his life and continues to go about life in a rather ordinary manner, he has inherited the inability to love from his surroundings, and so he refuses to acknowledge any of his daughters and fails to sign their birth certificates. Only one child, Louis, the illegitimate child of Mr. Potter's wife, seems to bring out the softer side of Mr. Potter. His affection for this child, a son, suggests that Mr. Potter has a deep emotional problem with women, perhaps sparked by the death of his own mother.

The story is told through the voice of one of Mr. Potter's forsaken daughters, Elaine Cynthia Potter. The prose reflects this character as she tries to understand her father by examining his life through his actions. She notes that all of his daughters inherited his nose but not his name and that his inability to read and write may have prevented him from truly understanding himself. Hence, it has fallen upon her to tell his story. She does not write to defend Mr. Potter or his actions, however; rather, she writes out of a sense of obligation— obligation to herself to reconstruct the life of a man she hardly knew and obligation to him, to give life to a seemingly insignificant man.

This is a richly laced text, with rhythmic patterns enhanced by the repetition of characters, stories, and phrases. Like pieces of a puzzle, each chapter unveils another part of the story that must be connected to the parts that precede it. The story line is circular and often mimics the ebb and flow of the narrator's thoughts and feelings. *Mr. Potter* truly reflects Kincaid's ability to use her poetic style and creativity to paint a portrait of characters and settings that reflect the life and history of Antigua.

Thomas Cassidy
Updated by Renata Harden

OTHER MAJOR WORKS

SHORT FICTION: *At the Bottom of the River*, 1983.

NONFICTION: *A Small Place*, 1988; *My Brother*, 1997; *My Garden (Book)*, 1999; *Talk Stories*, 2001; *Among Flowers: A Walk in the Himalaya*, 2005.

CHILDREN'S LITERATURE: *Annie, Gwen, Lilly, Pam, and Tulip*, 1986 (illustrated by Eric Fischl).

EDITED TEXTS: *The Best American Essays 1995*, 1995; *My Favorite Plant: Writers and Gardeners on the Plants They Love*, 1998; *The Best American Travel Writing 2005*, 2005.

BIBLIOGRAPHY

Bloom, Harold, ed. *Jamaica Kincaid*. Philadelphia: Chelsea House, 1998. Collection of essays provides critical analysis of Kincaid's fiction. Includes bibliographical references and index.

Bouson, J. Brooks. *Jamaica Kincaid: Writing Memory, Writing Back to the Mother*. Albany: State University of New York Press, 2005. Examines Kincaid's life, including her relationship with her mother, the influence of her homeland of Antigua, and her conflicting relations with her father and brother.

Davies, Carole Boyce. *Black Women, Writing, and Identity: Migrations of the Subject*. New York: Routledge, 1994. Focuses on the importance of migration in the construction of identity in black women's fiction in the United States, Africa, and the Caribbean. Presents especially insightful discussion of Kincaid's *Lucy*.

De Abruna, Laura Nielsen. "Jamaica Kincaid's Writing and the Maternal-Colonial Matrix." In *Caribbean Women Writers*, edited by Mary Condé and Thorunn Lonsdale.

New York: St. Martin's Press, 1999. Discusses Kincaid's presentation of women's experience, her use of postmodern narrative strategies, and her focus on the absence of the once-affirming mother or mother country that causes dislocation and alienation.

Forbes, Curdella. "Writing the Autobiography of My Father." Review of *Mr. Potter*, by Jamaica Kincaid. *Small Axe: A Caribbean Journal of Criticism* 7, no. 1 (March, 2003): 172-176. Connects the novel to the events of Kincaid's life and offers analysis of her writing style.

Garis, Leslie. "Through West Indian Eyes." *The New York Times Magazine*, October 7, 1990. Excellent source of information about Kincaid's life contains details about her childhood in Antigua, her relationship with her mother, her early interest in books, her early years in New York, and her marriage to Allen Shawn. Includes illustrations.

Gilmore, Leigh. "There Will Always Be a Mother: Jamaica Kincaid's Serial Autobiography." In *The Limits of Autobiography: Trauma and Testimony.* Ithaca, N.Y.: Cornell University Press, 2001. Discusses Kincaid's work as part of a larger examination of the boundaries of the autobiographical form.

Kincaid). "A Lot of Memory: An Interview with Jamaica Kincaid." Interview by Moira Ferguson. *Kenyon Review* n.s. 16 (Winter, 1994): 163-188. Kincaid discusses the inspiration for her writing and the reasons she wrote her first book in an experimental style, describes the influence of the English tradition on fiction in the Caribbean, and comments on the nature of colonial conquest as a theme she explores through the metaphor of gardening.

Paravisini-Gerbert, Lizabeth. *Jamaica Kincaid: A Critical Companion.* Westport, Conn.: Greenwood Press, 1999. Presents biographical information as well as in-depth analyses of individual novels, including *Annie John*, *Lucy*, and *The Autobiography of My Mother.*

Rhodes-Pitts, Sharifa. "Writing Between the Lines." Review of *Mr. Potter*, by Jamaica Kincaid. *Women's Review of Books* 19 (September, 2002): 11. Focuses on the language used in the novel by the narrator and by Mr. Potter, drawing attention to Mr. Potter's illiteracy and the narrator's verbal prose.

Simmons, Diane. *Jamaica Kincaid.* New York: Twayne, 1994. Provides a clear, lucid critical overview of Kincaid's life and work. A good introduction to her work for nonspecialist readers.

MARGARET LAURENCE

Born: Neepawa, Manitoba, Canada; July 18, 1926
Died: Lakefield, Ontario, Canada; January 5, 1987
Also known as: Jean Margaret Wemyss

Principal long fiction
This Side Jordan, 1960
The Stone Angel, 1964
A Jest of God, 1966
The Fire-Dwellers, 1969
The Diviners, 1974

Other literary forms

Margaret Laurence published two short-story collections, *The Tomorrow-Tamer* (1963) and *A Bird in the House* (1970), and four children's books, *Jason's Quest* (1970), *The Olden Days Coat* (1979), *Six Darn Cows* (1979), and *The Christmas Birthday Story* (1980). She also produced a translation of Somali folktales and poems, *A Tree for Poverty: Somali Poetry and Prose* (1954); a travelogue, *The Prophet's Camel Bell* (1963; also known as *New Wind in a Dry Land*, 1964); and a study of Nigerian novelists and playwrights, *Long Drums and Cannons: Nigerian Dramatists and Novelists, 1952-1966* (1968). A collection of her essays, *Heart of a Stranger*, appeared in 1976. Because of her work on Nigerian fiction and drama, she is well known to students of African literature. Her memoir *Dance on the Earth* appeared posthumously in 1989.

Achievements

From the beginning of her writing career, Laurence received significant popular and critical recognition. *This Side Jordan* won the Beta Sigma Phi Award for best first novel by a Canadian; *The Stone Angel* received both critical and popular acclaim; *A Jest of God* earned Laurence the Governor-General's Literary Award for fiction in 1966 and was adapted for motion pictures as *Rachel, Rachel* (directed by Paul Newman and released in 1968); *The Diviners*, despite less-than-universal critical acclaim, was at the top of the best-seller list for more than sixty consecutive weeks. Along with her popularity, Laurence enjoyed an international reputation as a consistently accomplished fiction writer. Her special contribution to the novel was recognized by Jack McClelland of the Canadian publishing house of McClelland & Stewart when he first read *This Side Jordan*. The stories that were gathered in *The Tomorrow-Tamer* and *A Bird in the House* originally appeared separately in such Canadian, American, and British periodicals as *Prism*, *The Atlantic Monthly*, and *Queen's Quarterly*. Laurence also won respect as a lecturer and critic. United College, University of Winnipeg, made her an Honorary Fellow, the first

woman and the youngest to be so honored. She received honorary degrees from McMaster, Dalhousie, Trent, University of Toronto, and Carleton University and served as writer-in-residence at several Canadian universities. Her works have been translated into French, German, Italian, Spanish, Dutch, Norwegian, Danish, and Swedish.

BIOGRAPHY

Margaret Laurence was born Jean Margaret Wemyss on July 18, 1926, in Neepawa, Manitoba, to Robert Wemyss and the former Verna Jean Simpson. Laurence's mother's family was of Irish descent; her father's, Scottish. Although she was separated from the "old country" on both sides by at least two generations, her early memories, like those of Vanessa MacLeod in the short stories in *A Bird in the House* and of Morag Gunn in *The Diviners*, are of a proud and lively Scottish ancestry.

When Laurence was four, her mother died, and her aunt, Margaret Simpson, left a respected teaching career in Calgary and went home to care for her niece. A year later, she and Robert Wemyss were married. They had one son, Robert, born only two years before his father died of pneumonia. In 1938, Margaret Simpson Wemyss took the two children and moved in with her father, the owner of a furniture store. This domestic situation in slightly altered form provides the setting for the Vanessa MacLeod stories in *A Bird in the House*. Laurence lived in Grandfather Simpson's house until she went to United College, University of Winnipeg, in 1944.

John Simpson was a fierce and autocratic man of eighty-two when his widowed daughter and her two children moved in with him. Laurence resented his authority over her and her stepmother; this relationship fostered Laurence's empathy with women struggling toward freedom. All of her heroines—Hagar Shipley, Rachel Cameron, Vanessa MacLeod, Stacey MacAindra, and Morag Gunn—struggle against oppressive forces, and Laurence's recurring theme of the lack of communication between men and women, as well as between women and women, is rooted in the domestic situation in Grandfather Simpson's house. It appears in her first novel, *This Side Jordan*, as the problem between the colonialists and the Africans, between husbands and wives, and between relatives. At the beginning of her last novel, *The Diviners*, the problem of communication—searching for the right words—is a major frustration that Morag, the protagonist, faces as a writer.

The encouragement and honest criticism given to Laurence by her stepmother were a great help to the girl, who started writing at an early age. At United College, she took honors in English, while her involvement with the "Winnipeg Old Left" during and after her college years reflected her dedication to social reform. Social awareness—the realization that men and women are constrained by social structures and exploit and are exploited by others through these systems—developed from her awareness that the hopes of her parents' generation had been crushed by the Depression and that her own generation's prospects were altered radically by World War II. After she graduated, she worked for one year as a reporter for the *Winnipeg Citizen*. Her experience covering the local labor news consolidated her social and political convictions and advanced theoretical problems to personal ones.

In 1948, Laurence married Jack Laurence, a civil engineer from the University of Manitoba. They left Canada for England in 1949 and went to British Somaliland (part of modern-day Somalia) in 1950, where he was in charge of a dam-building project. In 1952, they moved to the Gold Coast, now Ghana, where they lived until 1957. A daughter, Jocelyn, was born when they were on leave in England in 1952, and a son, David, was born in Ghana in 1955. Out of these African years came several early works, including *The Tomorrow-Tamer, This Side Jordan*, the translations of folktales, and the travel journal *The Prophet's Camel Bell*. Of the last, Laurence said that it was the most difficult work she ever wrote because it was not fiction. The importance of this work lies in its theme— the growth in self-knowledge and humility in an alien environment. During the years in Africa, Laurence read the Pentateuch for the first time, and these books of the Bible became a touchstone for her, especially pertinent to the African works and to a lesser extent to her Manawaka fiction. Here she developed the patience and discipline of a professional writer.

In 1962, Laurence and her children left Jack Laurence in Vancouver and moved to London. They remained in England until 1968, when Laurence returned to Canada to be writer-in-residence at Massey College, University of Toronto. She was affiliated with several other Canadian universities in the years that followed. In 1987, Laurence died in Lakefield, Ontario.

Analysis

The major emphasis of Margaret Laurence's fiction changed considerably between her early and later works. In an article published in *Canadian Literature* in 1969, "Ten Years' Sentences," she notes that after she had grown out of her obsession with the nature of freedom, the theme of the African writings and *The Stone Angel*, her concern "had changed to that of survival, the attempt of the personality to survive with some dignity, toting the load of excess mental baggage that everyone carries." In the same article, she remarks that she became increasingly involved with novels of character, that her viewpoint altered from modified optimism to modified pessimism, and that she had become more concerned with form in writing.

The more profound psychological realism of her later novels developed after a general awareness of the intractable problems of emerging African nations had matured both the Africans and their observers. The characters in the African works were products of a now-dated optimism that forced them into preconceived molds. The later novels reveal modified pessimism, but their vitality comes from Laurence's developing concern with psychological realism, which authenticates the characters and their voices. After *This Side Jordan*, the point of view is consistently in the first person, the protagonist's, and is strictly limited to the protagonist's consciousness. Although Hagar in *The Stone Angel* and Stacey in *The Fire-Dwellers* are stereotypes, a stubborn old lady and a frantic middle-aged housewife, Laurence makes them both compelling protagonists through accurate psychological portrayals.

A theme of major importance that Laurence did not fully develop until *The Diviners* is the nature of language. Rachel's concern with name-calling in *A Jest of God* anticipates the larger exploration in *The Fire-Dwellers*, in which Laurence experiments with a variety of voices, using language in a variety of ways. Exterior voices, many of them bizarre, interrupt and are interrupted by Stacey's inner voices—her monologues, her memories of voices from the past, her challenges, threats, and prayers to God. The exterior voices include radio and television news, snatches of her children's conversations, the characteristic dialects of various socioeconomic groups, the half-truthful promotions of her husband's company, and the meaningfully unfinished conversations between her and her husband. In order to allow language to be discussed explicitly, Laurence makes the protagonist of *The Diviners* a novelist.

In her first three novels Laurence uses biblical allusions to provide a mythic framework for a psychological study of character and situation. All these allusions are from the Old Testament, which made a lasting impression on her when she read it for the first time in Africa. The names she chooses for the characters in the early fiction—Adamo, Jacob, Abraham, Nathaniel, Joshua, Hagar, Ishmael, and Rachel—provide ready-made dilemmas whose traditional solutions appear contrived and psychologically unrealistic. In *This Side Jordan*, Joshua's Ghanian father proclaims that his son will cross the Jordan into the Promised Land, confidently assumed to be both an independent, prosperous Ghana and a Christian heaven. These allusions contribute to the sacramental overtones in the early works, particularly at the end of *The Stone Angel*.

Biblical myth is replaced in *A Bird in the House* and *The Diviners* by the myths of Scottish immigrants and Canadian pioneers and Indians. Vanessa in *A Bird in the House* lives with the sentimentally mythologized memories of her grandparents. The dispossessed Scots and the dispossessed Metis Indians provide a personal mythology for young Morag Gunn in *The Diviners*, which her foster father, Christie Logan, embellishes to give the orphan girl an identity. Christie himself becomes mythologized in the mind of Morag's daughter Pique. The theme of the search for one's true origins plays a prominent part throughout Laurence's fiction, but the issues become increasingly complex. Whereas a clear dichotomy between his Christian and African backgrounds divides Nathaniel Amegbe in *This Side Jordan*, Morag in *The Diviners*, a recognized novelist who was an orphan brought up by a garbage collector, is seriously perplexed by the bases of her identity. Nathaniel hopes for, and apparently receives, both worldly and spiritual rewards in a successful if simplistic reconciliation of his dual heritage. In contrast, Morag painfully learns to reject the heroic Scottish ancestress Christie had invented for her without rejecting him; she realizes that she has invented a hopelessly confused web of self-fabricated personal myth that she has to reconcile with her Canadian roots in her search for self-identity.

Throughout all her works, Laurence explores themes concerning the role of women, the injustices of sex-role stereotyping, and the inequality of opportunity. The changing roles of women in the late twentieth century are a problem for Morag, who is jealous of her daughter's sexual freedom. Although the protagonists of Laurence's later novels are women—women who have not always been treated well by the men in their lives—men are never treated harshly in her work, even though the point of view is limited to the female protagonist's consciousness. Stacey generously concludes that perhaps her uncommunicative husband is tormented by fears and doubts much like her own. Morag never speculates about Jules Tonnerre's motives—a strange lack of curiosity for a novelist. Although Laurence's protagonists are oppressed, they never simply blame the men in their lives or the male-dominated society for their oppression. Men, almost to a man, are given the benefit of the doubt.

THIS SIDE JORDAN

Laurence's first novel, *This Side Jordan*, was begun in Ghana in 1955, finished in Vancouver, and published in 1960. The setting of the novel is Ghana just before independence. The protagonist, Nathaniel Amegbe, had boarded at a Roman Catholic mission school since he was seven and is now caught between two cultures, between loyalty to the fading memory of tribal customs and loyalty to the Christian mission that educated him and gave him the opportunity to better himself, in a European sense, by teaching in the city. His predicament is balanced by that of Johnnie Kestoe, a newly arrived employee of an English-based export-import firm who is trying to forget his slum-Irish background and to rise in the firm despite his antipathy for Africans. Both men have wives expecting their first child. Many of Nathaniel's dilemmas are resolved in the end, even his fears that his father's soul might be assigned to hell. In part, his resolution results from the salvation metaphor of "crossing the Jordan," a feat he hopes his newborn son will accomplish.

Nathaniel's interior monologues reveal the conflicts his dual loyalties have produced. Laurence uses this device more and more in the ensuing novels, and it culminates in *The Diviners* with its complex narrative techniques. Both Johnnie and Nathaniel move through the novel to a greater realization of self by means of humbling experiences, and both achieve worldly success, a naïvely optimistic conclusion made at the expense of psychological realism.

THE STONE ANGEL

The Stone Angel was published in 1964, two years after Laurence and her children moved to London. Laurence, in "A Place to Stand On" from *Heart of a Stranger,* states that the dominant theme of this novel is survival, "not just physical survival, but the preservation of some human dignity and in the end some human warmth and ability to reach out and touch others." The monument Hagar Shipley's father had built for her mother's tomb in the Manawaka cemetery is a stone angel, gouged out by stonemasons who were accustomed to filling the needs of "fledgling pharaohs in an uncouth land." Laurence's horror at the extravagance of the pharaohs' monuments at Luxor, recorded in "Good Morning to the Grandson of Rameses the Second" in *Heart of a Stranger*, is similar to her reaction to the material ambitions of the stern Scotch-Irish prairie pioneers.

The story of Hagar Shipley is told in the first person and covers the three weeks before her death, but in these weeks, long flashbacks depict scenes of Hagar's life in chronological order. Laurence gives sacramental overtones to the events of Hagar's last days: She confesses to a most unlikely priest in a deserted cannery over a jug of wine; in the hospital where she dies, she is able to overcome her pride and to enjoy and empathize with her fellow patients; after she accepts a previously despised minister sent by her son, she has an epiphany—"Pride was my wilderness, and the demon that led me there was fear"; and just before her death, she wrests from her daughter-in-law her last drink. Such sacramental overtones are not unusual in Laurence's works, but in her later works they become more subtle and complex than they are here.

Hagar Shipley is an old woman, an enormously fat, physically feeble old woman, grotesque and distorted in both body and spirit. She is mean spirited as well as mean about her money and her possessions—almost a stereotype, an unlikely heroine, certainly not one who would seem to attract the sympathy of the reader. Hagar does, however, attract the reader; the genuineness of her portrayal makes her believable because of her total honesty, and the reader empathizes with her plight, which she finally recognizes as self-made. The reader feels compassion for her in spite of and because of her pettiness. Her voice, even in her old age, is still strong, willful, and vital, and the development of her self-awareness and self-knowledge is gripping.

The Stone Angel is the first work in which Manawaka, Laurence's fictionalized hometown of Neepawa, Manitoba, serves as the childhood setting of the protagonist. She makes Manawaka a microcosmic world, the childhood home of all her later protagonists, whose memories and friends carry over from one work to another. The mythic heritage of Hagar in *The Stone Angel*—the Scotch-Irish pioneers and Metis Indians in Manitoba—is shared by Vanessa in *A Bird in the House*, Rachel in *A Jest of God*, Stacey in *The Fire-Dwellers*, and Morag in *The Diviners*, although Hagar is old enough to be the grandmother of the other four. Every one of these women leaves Manawaka in a search for identity and spiritual freedom, but none is able to escape her heredity and childhood environment entirely. The effects of environment and heredity were increasingly explored as Laurence became more and more concerned with the nature of identity. The Manawaka setting gave Laurence the opportunity to develop characters whose parents or grandparents engaged in a strenuous battle to open the frontier, founded what they hoped would be dynasties, and lived to see them fall because of the Depression. These stubborn and proud people begot children who had to find their own identities without the visible mansions their parents had built to proclaim theirs. Pride in personal success became in the next generation pride in family and origin, and Hagar's inheritance from her father showed that the strength of the pioneer generation could destroy as well as build. The recognition of the double-edged nature of this strength enables Hagar, a stone angel in her former blindness, to feel at the end some human warmth for those around her.

A JEST OF GOD

A Jest of God was written in Buckinghamshire, England, in 1964 and 1965, and was published the next year. The action takes place during a summer and fall in the 1960's in Manawaka. Laurence creates a woman protagonist learning to break through the entrapments oppressing her.

Only through the first-person point of view could Laurence manage to reenact Rachel Cameron's fearful responses to everything around her and her self-mocking evaluations of her responses; she is afraid even of herself. When she reflects on the way she thinks, on her paranoia and her imagination, she warns herself that through her own distortions of reality she will become strange, weird, an outcast. She continues to tell herself that she must stop thinking that way. Her fear about her own responses to ordinary life keeps her in a state near hysteria. Except for the recognizable quality of her perceptions and the color and richness of her imagination, she could indeed be dismissed as a stereotyped old-maid schoolteacher, the butt of the town's jokes. She lives with her widowed mother, renting the upper story of her dead father's former funeral parlor.

The mythic framework for the psychological study of Rachel is the Old Testament story in which Rachel is "mourning for her children"—in the novel, the children she has never had. When she is confident enough to love Nick Kazlik, whom she needs more as a father for her children than as a lover, he tells her that he is not God; he cannot solve her problems. Neither he nor the possibility of the child he might give her can overcome her sense of isolation, of which the lack of children is only the symbol; her sense of isolation seems to be based on her lack of spiritual fulfillment, isolation from God. God's word is evaded in the church she and her mother attend, and she is totally horrified by fundamentalist irrationality. In the end, Rachel recognizes her own self-pity to be a horrendous sort of pride, and she starts to learn instead to feel compassion for others because they are as isolated as she.

Rachel's situation could set the stage for a tragedy, but Laurence's heroines do not become tragic. They live through their crises, endure, and in enduring gain strength. Rachel gains strength from the loss of Nick, which she never understands, and from the loss of what she hoped and feared would be Nick's baby. After Rachel has decided not to commit suicide when she thinks she is pregnant, she discovers that what she had thought was a baby was a meaningless tumor, not even malignant—a jest of God. Despite, or perhaps because of, this grotesque anticlimax, Rachel is able to make the decision to leave Manawaka; she applies for and earns a teaching position in Vancouver. At the end, she is traveling with her mother, her "elderly child," to a new life in Vancouver.

THE FIRE-DWELLERS

The Fire-Dwellers was written in England between 1966 and 1968; the protagonist of the novel, Stacey MacAindra, is Rachel Cameron's sister. She is an ordinary woman—a middle-class contemporary housewife in Manawaka, anxious over all the possible and impossible perils waiting for her and her family. She overcomes stereotyping through the recognizable, likable, and spontaneous qualities of her narrative voice. Laurence's narrative technique is more complex in *The Fire-Dwellers* than in any of her earlier works. The first-person narration is fragmented by a variety of interruptions—Stacey's inner voices, snatches of Stacey's memories set to the side of the page, italicized dreams and fantasies, incomplete conversations with Mac, her husband, and radio and television news. At times, she is concentrating so completely on her inner voice that she feels a physical jolt when external reality breaks into her inner fantasies.

The title refers, as Stacey's lover Luke implies, to Stacey: She is the ladybird of the nursery rhyme who must fly away home because her house is on fire and her children will burn. Although Sir James George Frazer's *The Golden Bough* (1890) lies unopened beside Stacey's bed at the end of the book, as it did in the beginning, Stacey seems to understand intuitively the explanation of the primitive sexuality of fire. Stacey burns from sexual frustration and fears the burning of an atomic bomb, a threat ever present on the news. Newspaper pictures from Vietnam of a horrified mother trying to remove burning napalm from her baby's face appear again and again in Stacey's mind. Counterpointing the fire metaphor is that of water, here regenerative as well as destructive, which foreshadows its more important position in *The Diviners*.

Unlike the other Manawaka protagonists, Stacey could never be considered grotesque; she views herself as quite ordinary, and, at first glance, most people would agree, despite her apocalyptic fears. The world around her, however, is grotesque. The frightening events in the lives of Stacey's neighbors and friends are counterpointed by the daily news from the Vietnam War. Almost a symbol of Stacey's inability to communicate her fears, her two-year-old, Jen, cannot or will not speak. No wonder Stacey hides her drinks in the Mixmaster. Her interior dialogue convincingly portrays a compassionate woman with a stabilizing sense of humor that makes the limited affirmation of the conclusion believable; Mac and his equally uncommunicative son Duncan are brought together by Duncan's near death, and Jen speaks her first words: "Hi, Mum. Want tea?"

THE DIVINERS

Laurence worked on *The Diviners* from 1969 to 1973, at the old house she bought on the Otonabee River near Peterborough, Ontario. Unlike the earlier Laurence protagonists, apparently ordinary women, almost stereotypes who turn out to be extraordinary in their own ways, Morag Gunn is an extraordinarily gifted writer who has quite ordinary and common concerns. She is also unlike her Manawaka "sisters" in that she is an orphan reared by the town's garbage collector; thus she is an outsider who bears the scorn and taunts of the town's wealthier children, such as Stacey Cameron and Vanessa MacLeod. She shares her humble status with the disreputable half-breed Indians, the Tonnerres, and learns the injustice of the inequality of opportunity at first hand.

The title, *The Diviners*, refers explicitly to gifted individuals, artists such as Morag who contribute to a greater understanding of life, as well as to her friend, Royland, a true water diviner. Indeed, Morag discovers that many of her acquaintances are, in some way, themselves diviners. At the end of the book, when Royland tells Morag he has lost the gift of divining, Morag muses, "At least Royland knew he had been a true diviner. . . . The necessity of doing the thing—that mattered."

The Diviners is the longest and the most tightly structured of Laurence's novels; it has three long parts framed by a prologue and an epilogue. The plot is commonplace; Morag spends a summer worrying about her eighteen-year-old daughter Pique, who has gone west to "find" herself. In this action, Morag is only an observer, as all mothers must be in such situations. Her own story is enclosed within the action in the present, with chronological flashbacks such as those in *The Stone Angel*. The novel is presented in the first person, but with two new techniques: "Snapshots," meditations on the few snapshots Morag has from her youth; and "Memorybank Movies," Morag's memories from her past. The snapshots cover the lives of her parents, before Morag was born through her early childhood and their deaths. Aware that she embroidered stories about the snapshots as a child, Morag looks at a snapshot, remembers her make-believe story, and then muses, "I don't recall when I invented that one." This comment, early in the novel, establishes the mythologizing of one's past as an important motif.

Morag's future as a writer is foreshadowed by her retelling of Christie Logan's tales when just a girl, adapting them to her own needs. In the prologue, Morag the novelist worries about diction, the choice of the proper words: "How could that colour be caught in words? A sort of rosy peach colour, but that sounded corny and was also inaccurate." Morag uses her hometown for setting and characters, just as Laurence herself does; the theme of where one belongs is as important to Morag as a writer as it is to Laurence.

The title of Morag's second novel, *Prospero's Child*, foreshadows the motif of the end frame. Royland loses his gift of witching for water and hopes to pass it on to A-Okay Smith. Morag realizes that she will pass on to Pique her gift, just as Christie Logan's manic prophecies influenced her creativity. Among all Laurence's heroines, Morag Gunn is the closest in experience and interests to Laurence herself. Each successive protagonist, from Hagar and Rachel and Vanessa to Stacy, came closer and closer to Laurence's own identity. She said that she realized how difficult it would be to portray a protagonist so much like herself, but *The Diviners* is a risky novel, an ambitious book that only an established writer could afford to produce.

Because Laurence depicts human problems in terms of sex roles, the gender of the characters in the Manawaka novels is particularly important. The women protagonists of all of these novels clearly demonstrate Laurence's persistent investigation of the role of women in society. The sex lives of Laurence's women are fully integrated parts of their identities without becoming obsessive or neurotic. All of her protagonists enjoy their sexuality but, at the same time, suffer guiltily for it. Laurence did not admit a connection with the women's liberation movement. Morag Gunn, however, a single head of a household with an illegitimate dependent child, could not have been as readily accepted and admired before the feminist movement as she was after.

Similarly, although Laurence employs Christian motifs and themes throughout her fiction, she did not embrace institutional Christianity. Like psychologist Carl Jung, Laurence seems to find God in the human soul, defining religion in terms of a Jungian "numinous experience" that can lead to a psychological change. Salvation is redefined as discovery of self, and grace is given to find a new sense of life direction.

Presenting her characters as beings caught between the determinism of history and their free will, as individuals who are torn between body and spirit, fact and illusion, Laurence portrays life as a series of internal crises. Through the development of her protagonists, Laurence celebrates even the crises as she celebrates her protagonists' progress. The search for self involves both the liberation from and the embracing of the past. Survival with dignity and the ability to love, she remarks in *Heart of a Stranger*, are themes inevitable for a writer of her stern Scotch-Irish background. Since these themes continue to be of immense importance in the modern world, Laurence's works explore problems that have universal appeal, a fact that goes far to explain her tremendous popularity.

Judith Weise

OTHER MAJOR WORKS

SHORT FICTION: *The Tomorrow-Tamer*, 1963; *A Bird in the House*, 1970.

NONFICTION: *The Prophet's Camel Bell*, 1963 (also known as *New Wind in a Dry Land*, 1964); *Long Drums and Cannons: Nigerian Dramatists and Novelists, 1952-1966*, 1968; *Heart of a Stranger*, 1976; *Dance on the Earth*, 1989.

CHILDREN'S LITERATURE: *Jason's Quest*, 1970; *The Olden Days Coat*, 1979; *Six Darn Cows*, 1979; *The Christmas Birthday Story*, 1980.

EDITED TEXT: *A Tree for Poverty: Somali Poetry and Prose*, 1954.

BIBLIOGRAPHY

Coger, Greta M. K., ed. *New Perspectives on Margaret Laurence: Poetic Narrative, Multiculturalism, and Feminism*. Westport, Conn.: Greenwood Press, 1996. Collection of essays examines Laurence's writings. Topics include the female and elderly characters in her works and her use of language, theme, and image. Also presents close readings of *The Stone Angel* and other novels.

Comeau, Paul. *Margaret Laurence's Epic Imagination*. Edmonton: University of Alberta Press, 2005. Focuses on the epic heroism in Laurence's fiction, explaining how she was influenced by the epic elements of the Bible, William Shakespeare, Dante, and

John Milton. Asserts that, for Laurence, "epic heroism" is not a grand saga; rather, it is found more simply in her characters' struggles to survive.

King, James. *The Life of Margaret Laurence.* 1997. Reprint. Toronto, Ont.: Random House Canada, 2002. Biography presents a compassionate account of the events of Laurence's life and discusses how these events and the author's personality influenced her fiction. Includes bibliographical references and index.

Morley, Patricia. *Margaret Laurence.* Boston: Twayne, 1981. Extremely helpful and complete study of Laurence's work argues that Laurence, despite the fact that her work tends to focus on two very disparate places, Africa and Canada, shows consistent development of ideas and themes. Examines the African works, followed by the Manawaka cycle. Includes chronology up to 1980, biographical information, annotated select bibliography, and index.

New, William, ed. *Margaret Laurence: The Writer and Her Critics.* Toronto, Ont.: McGraw-Hill, 1977. Anthology of criticism on Laurence and interviews with her also features an informative introduction by the editor. Includes three central essays by Laurence herself that are invaluable aids to the understanding of her fiction.

Nicholson, Colin, ed. *Critical Approaches to the Fiction of Margaret Laurence.* Vancouver: University of British Columbia Press, 1990. Excellent collection of critical essays on Laurence, most written specifically for this book, covers such topics as Laurence's place in the Canadian tradition in fiction, her work on Africa, and the use of autobiography in her writing. Some essays present close readings of specific works. Includes a helpful preface and an index.

Powers, Lyall. *Alien Heart: The Life and Work of Margaret Laurence.* East Lansing: Michigan State University Press, 2004. Powers, a lifelong friend of Laurence, brings his personal knowledge and extensive research to this study of her life and work. Includes analysis of all her works of fiction, describing how the works expressed her personal conflicts and how her fictional characters affected her life.

Riegel, Christian, ed. *The Writing of Margaret Laurence: Challenging Territory.* Edmonton: University of Alberta Press, 1997. Collection of essays covers areas such as Laurence's African stories, her novels, and her Scots Presbyterian heritage and other early influences on her work. Includes bibliography.

Stovel, Norma. *Rachel's Children: Margaret Laurence's "A Jest of God."* Toronto, Ont.: ECW Press, 1992. Presents analysis of the novel that is both concise and thorough. Includes a brief biography of Laurence and discussions of the novel's critical reception, themes, allusions, imagery, narrative voice, critical reception, and importance.

Verduyn, Christl, ed. *Margaret Laurence: An Appreciation.* Peterborough, Ont.: Broadview Press, 1988. Invaluable collection of essays chronicles the evolution of Laurence's vision in both her fiction and the chief social concerns of her life. Includes an address/essay by Laurence titled "My Final Hour."

Woodcock, George. *Introducing Margaret Laurence's "The Stone Angel": A Reader's*

Guide. Toronto, Ont.: ECW Press, 1989. Presents a close reading of *The Stone Angel*, the first novel of the Manawaka series. Examines plots, characters, themes, and origins and discusses the book's critical reception as well as Laurence's work as a whole. Includes a useful chronology of Laurence's life, a brief biography, and an index.

WENDY LAW-YONE

Born: Mandalay, Burma (now Myanmar); April 1, 1947

PRINCIPAL LONG FICTION
The Coffin Tree, 1983
Irrawaddy Tango, 1993

OTHER LITERARY FORMS

In addition to her novels, Wendy Law-Yone has published short fiction as well as works of memoir, journalism, and technical writing. Like her novels, most of these other pieces are set in or concern her native land, Burma (renamed Myanmar in 1989). For instance, "Drought" (1993) is an erotic short story set on an island *kampung* ("village" in several Southeast Asian languages) about an ostracized Eurasian girl who cares for a European pilot left comatose after a plane crash and who empowers and pleasures herself with his unconscious body. "The Year of the Pigeon" (1994) is a memoir about Law-Yone's wedding in Rangoon, Burma, to Sterling Seagrave on their second date (after two years of intense written correspondence between them) and her attempt to escape Burma's military regime, her imprisonment, and her eventual release into exile.

Several of Law-Yone's most vivid and insightful journalistic pieces spring from visits she has made to her native Burma from exile: For example, "Life in the Hills," which appeared in *The Atlantic Monthly* in December, 1989, details her frustrating visit to a jungle hideout of dissident Burmese students after the brutal suppression of the prodemocracy movement by the military junta in 1988; and "The Outsider," which appeared in the Asia edition of *Time* magazine in August, 2003, tells of her unsentimental journey to the hellscape of her former family home in Rangoon (now known as Yangon) some thirty years after she had fled it. Law-Yone's technical writing has appeared in *Architectural Digest*, and she has also published the business administration text *Company Information: A Model Investigation* (1980).

ACHIEVEMENTS

Wendy Law-Yone's novels have been translated into several European languages, and her works are highly respected, especially by Asian American literary scholars, for their insightful rendering of the problematic issue of immigration in the United States, their sympathetic portrayals of mental illness, their feminist construction of women characters, and their staunch prodemocracy stance on contemporary Burmese politics. Law-Yone has received a number of awards and honors for her writing, including fellowships from the National Endowment for the Arts and the Carnegie Endowment, a Harvard Foundation Award, and a David T. K. Wong Fellowship at the University of East Anglia, England. She was nominated for the Irish Times International Fiction Prize in 1995.

BIOGRAPHY

Wendy Law-Yone was born in 1947 in Mandalay, Burma, and she grew up in Rangoon, the capital city. Her father was Edward Law-Yone, a patriot who played a leading role in Burmese politics; he fought on the side of the Allies during World War II, joining an American OSS (Office of Strategic Services) unit. After the war, he became the editor and publisher of *The Nation*, Burma's leading English-language newspaper during the years before and immediately following Burma's achieving independence from Britain in 1948. When General Ne Win staged a military coup in 1962 and wrested control from the democratically elected U Nu, Law-Yone was imprisoned. He remained in custody for six years before being freed and exiled from Burma; he then attempted to organize armed resistance to the military dictatorship and held the portfolio for foreign affairs in the shadow cabinet of the Burmese government in exile. Edward Law-Yone died in the United States in 1980. These political events, occurring so close to home and family, left a deep, lasting impression on Wendy Law-Yone, and she revisits them frequently in her creative writing.

When growing up, Law-Yone was recognized as being gifted with unusual musical talent, and upon graduation from secondary school (about the time of her father's imprisonment) she was offered scholarships to study music at Leningrad (now St. Petersburg) in the Soviet Union as well as at Mills College in Oakland, California. Her father's arrest and the cancellation of her passport made it impossible for her to accept either offer, however; she was even forced to quit attending the University of Rangoon and could keep herself intellectually occupied only by studying German at a language school.

In 1967 Law-Yone married American journalist Sterling Seagrave; she had met him at a concert in 1965 and then carried on a two-year correspondence with him while he was in the United States. They married in 1967 when the Burmese authorities granted Seagrave a twenty-four-hour visa. After a failed attempt to escape Burma, Law-Yone was incarcerated for several weeks, but eventually she was allowed to leave the country; she then lived temporarily in Bangkok, Singapore, and Kuala Lumpur, Malaysia, where she remained for two years and started drafting the beginnings of *The Coffin Tree*.

In 1973 she emigrated to the United States, where her father had taken up residence in 1971, and she attended Eckerd College in St. Petersburg, Florida. Graduating in 1975, she divorced her husband (she was by then the mother of twins) and went to live in the Washington, D.C., area, where for three decades she freelanced at *The Washington Post* newspaper and worked on her fiction writing. She also married a Washington attorney, Charles A. O'Connor III, and had two children with him. In 2002 she was awarded a fellowship at the University of East Anglia, Norwich, England, and she subsequently took up permanent residence in the United Kingdom while retaining her American citizenship.

ANALYSIS

No fiction writer on the world stage has written as authoritatively and effectively as Wendy Law-Yone about contemporary Burma, that area of political darkness in the heart of a troubled Southeast Asia. Her authority stems from the grit of her experience garnered as she came of age in a family close to the center of political power and ideological foment during a time when the war-torn postcolonial nation of Burma was aborning and then toppling into bloody military dictatorship. The effectiveness of her fiction derives from the myriad facets of a talented imagination: the utterly convincing social and psychological realism of situations and characters, the clever and witty unfolding of plot, the rich and intricate use of archetypal patterns drawn from ancient Asian religion or of iconic prototypes drawn from contemporary American pop culture, the candor with which the problematic of U.S. immigration is explored, the honesty with which the real pain of mental illness is made palpable, the skill with which the malignancies of patriarchy are laid open by an unerring feminist scalpel, and the critical intensity of the light of democratic and humanitarian principles that is shone upon the dark deeds of a military dictatorship.

THE COFFIN TREE

Law-Yone's first novel, *The Coffin Tree*, set partially in Burma and partially in the United States, has received many accolades from reviewers. It has been praised for its supple prose, telling imagery, and compelling presentation of the difficulties that can confront immigrants in the United States as well as for the painfully realistic depiction of the mental illness that afflicts the unnamed Burmese narrator and her elder brother, Shan.

Shan's psychosis is partially attributable to heredity; his mother, a Burmese hill-tribe woman, was mentally ill. Much of the blame for the children's psychosis, however, is justly laid at the door of their father and his treatment (or neglect) of them. He is a legendary freedom fighter and founder of a guerrilla force struggling against Burma's military dictatorship. Of patrician background, he sacrifices his whole life and his family to his unquestionably worthy political cause. Haughty, taciturn, and sudden of action, he is a powerfully distant and largely absent father figure. (Interestingly, the obverse of this portrait of the dynamic and driven Asian male is the relative called Uncle, who only eats, sleeps, and picks at his skin all day.) Their father brings up Shan with a heavy hand—for instance, slapping him to cure him of his stutter. He is perceived as an enigma by his daughter, for he can be deeply affectionate when she falls ill but is profoundly indifferent at other times. The narrator's neurosis is also associated with her feelings of guilt and inferiority toward her mother, who died giving birth to her, and these feelings are exacerbated by her grandmother's calling her "mother-killer" and repeatedly disparaging her plain looks by comparison with her mother's beauty.

For their safety, the narrator and Shan migrate to the United States when their father takes to the jungle to head his guerrilla force. Upon their arrival in New York, however, they find that their father's contacts are unhelpful and uncomprehending, so they must fend for themselves, wandering through Florida, Vermont, and Illinois. Their efforts in the hoped-for promised land are met by failure. Shan is unable to hold a job and sinks into paranoia and cerebral malaria; he finally dies, clutching in pain at his chest, in Chicago.

The narrator is able to hold on to low-level jobs but is so devastated by Shan's death that she attempts suicide herself. She is committed to a mental institution, which is described in vivid detail (one of Law-Yone's brothers worked in a mental institution). She makes a slow and tentative recovery that seems to hold out the possibility of a new life—a process also intimated by the novel's title, which is an allusion to the Tibetan Book of the Dead, which describes the soul's journey toward reincarnation after death.

IRRAWADDY TANGO

In *Irrawaddy Tango*, her second novel, Law-Yone creates a picaresque narrative about female identity formation and empowerment in a context of political repression. Her settings are again Southeast Asia and the United States. This is also a dystopian novel in which much of the action takes place in an imaginary military dictatorship called Daya, which is readily recognized as Burma. Furthermore, Law-Yone seems to be using a witty kind of narrative collage in telling her tale and developing her protagonist.

As the female protagonist-narrator relates her picaresque career, during which her identity as an Asian American woman is formed, the author appears to lead her through several phases of development comprising a collage of iconic female identities drawn from American pop culture. For instance, Tango's career begins chronologically with an "Evita" phase during which she, like the Eva Perón of Andrew Lloyd Webber and Tim Rice's 1970's stage musical, starts out as a winsome and willful village girl who becomes a star tango dance contestant and rises to be the consort of her country's military dictator, Supremo. Then Tango undergoes a "Patty Hearst" phase during which she, now a wealthy socialite, is kidnapped by guerrillas calling themselves the JLA (Jesu Liberation Army) and brainwashed into championing their cause and bedding with their leader; this parallels the 1974 kidnapping of the wealthy California socialite Patty Hearst by the Symbionese Liberation Army, or SLA, which became a huge media event, the subject of several books and films. Tango's kidnappers are eventually destroyed by her husband's forces, who treat her as a traitor and imprison her. From this, Tango is rescued by an American activist named Lawrence (*not* of Arabia) who marries her and brings her to Los Angeles, planning to make a blockbuster film based on her life. Both film project and storybook marriage fall apart, however, and Tango drifts into anomie, alienation, and serial promiscuity as a directionless immigrant in the United States.

In the final empowering phase of her adventures, Tango is invited to return to Daya because Supremo has fallen ill and the Dayan astrologers feel that Tango can help revitalize him. Here Tango morphs into an avatar of the Spider Woman—a reference to Manuel Puig's 1976 novel *El beso de la mujer araña* (*Kiss of the Spider Woman*, 1979) and the 1993 Broadway musical based on the novel. She thus returns to Daya, mates with Supremo after performing a veritable feat of arousal, and then bludgeons the dictator to death, thereby empowering herself and setting her people free.

C. L. Chua

OTHER MAJOR WORKS

SHORT FICTION: "Ankle," 1988 (in *Grand Street*); "Drought," 1993 (in *Slow Hand: Women Writing Erotica*; Michelle Slung, editor).

NONFICTION: *Company Information: A Model Investigation* (1980); "Life in the Hills," 1989 (in *The Atlantic Monthly*); "The Year of the Pigeon," 1994 (in *Without a Guide: Contemporary Women's Travel Adventures*); "The Outsider," 2003 (in *Time,* Asia edition).

BIBLIOGRAPHY

Bow, Leslie. "The Gendered Subject of Human Rights: Domestic Infidelity in *Irrawaddy Tango* and *The Scent of the Gods.*" In *Betrayal and Other Acts of Subversion: Feminism, Sexual Politics, Asian American Women's Literature*. Princeton, N.J.: Princeton University Press, 2001. Employs a postcolonial and feminist perspective to make an illuminating comparison of the treatment of the politics of human rights and domestic infidelity in Law-Yone's *Irrawaddy Tango*, set in Burma, and Fiona Cheong's *The Scent of the Gods* (1991), set in Singapore.

Cowart, David. "Immigration as *Bardo*: Wendy Law-Yone's *The Coffin Tree*." In *Trailing Clouds: Immigrant Fiction in Contemporary America*. Ithaca, N.Y.: Cornell University Press, 2006. Provides a detailed analysis of Law-Yone's first novel, emphasizing the themes of immigrant nostalgia and madness in relationship to the work's allusions to the Tibetan Book of the Dead.

Har, Janie C. "Food, Sexuality, and the Pursuit of a Little Attention." *Hitting Critical Mass* 1, no. 1 (Fall, 1993): 83-92. Presents a close reading of the food imagery in *The Coffin Tree* and argues that the characters compensate for their inability to give love or sex by offering food instead.

Ho, Tamara C. "*The Coffin Tree* by Wendy Law-Yone." In *A Resource Guide to Asian American Literature*, edited by Sau-ling Cynthia Wong and Stephen H. Sumida. New York: Modern Language Association, 2001. Sound and useful guide to the study of *The Coffin Tree*. Includes helpful sections on the historical contexts of the book.

Law-Yone, Wendy. "Beyond Rangoon: An Interview with Wendy Law-Yone." Interview by Leslie Bow. *MELUS* 27, no. 4 (Winter, 2002): 183-200. Wide-ranging interview covers Law-Yone's early life in Burma, the theme of sex and power in her writing (especially in *Irrawaddy Tango*), and her methods of composition. Also discusses her work on a nonfiction book about the history of her family's origins in China.

_____. "Wendy Law-Yone." Interview by Nancy Yoo and Tamara Ho. In *Words Matter: Conversations with Asian American Writers*, edited by King-Kok Cheung. Honolulu: University of Hawaii Press, 2000. Law-Yone discusses her family and her adolescent years in Burma, her feelings about being Asian American, and her treatment of mental illness and immigration as themes in her works.

Lee, Rachel. "The Erasure of Places and the Re-siting of Empire in Wendy Law-Yone's

The Coffin Tree." *Cultural Critique* 35 (Winter, 1996/1997): 149-178. Analyzes the novel's differentiation of space into safe prisons and perilous free spaces, and warns against reading it as universal or transnational, arguing that such readings tend to up-root Asian American works from their Asian roots and dislocate them from their native terrain, which is tantamount to imperialist appropriation.

URSULA K. LE GUIN

Born: Berkeley, California; October 21, 1929
Also known as: Ursula Kroeber

OTHER LITERARY FORMS

In the body of work produced by Ursula K. Le Guin (leh GWIHN) are many books written for children and young adults, among them *A Wizard of Earthsea*, *The Tombs of Atuan*, and *The Farthest Shore* (the first three books of the Earthsea series); *Very Far Away from Anywhere Else*; *Leese Webster*; and *The Beginning Place*. Her other publications include novellas, such as *The Word for World Is Forest* (1972); several volumes of poetry, including *Wild Angels* (1975), *Hard Words, and Other Poems* (1981), *In the Red Zone* (1983), and *Sixty Odd: New Poems* (1999); and a number of volumes of short stories, including *The Wind's Twelve Quarters* (1975), *Orsinian Tales* (1976), *The Compass Rose* (1982), *A Fisherman of the Inland Sea* (1994), *Unlocking the Air, and Other Stories* (1996), and *The Birthday of the World, and Other Stories* (2002).

Many of Le Guin's essays on the nature and meaning of fantasy, her own creative process, science fiction, and gender politics are collected in *From Elfland to Poughkeepsie* (1973), *The Language of the Night: Essays on Fantasy and Science Fiction* (1979; edited by Susan Wood), *Dancing at the Edge of the World: Thoughts on Words, Women, and Places* (1988), and *Napa: The Roots and Springs of the Valley* (1989). Her numerous book reviews have appeared in *The New York Times Book Review*, *The Washington Post Book World*, *The New Republic*, and other respected publications. Her collaboration with the photographer Roger Dorband, *Blue Moon over Thurman Street* (1993), documents in words and pictures the human ecology of the city street on which she lived for more than a quarter of a century.

ACHIEVEMENTS

The high quality of Ursula K. Le Guin's work was apparent from the beginning of her writing career. Brian Attebery, a fellow writer, has stated that even her first published novels are superior to most works of science fiction written at that time. Public recognition of Le Guin's work began with the *Boston Globe* Horn Book Award for *A Wizard of Earthsea* in 1969. Le Guin soon amassed numerous prestigious awards, including the Nebula Award and the Hugo Award for *The Left Hand of Darkness* (1969, 1970); the Newbery Silver Medal Award for *The Tombs of Atuan* (1972); a Hugo Award for *The Word for World Is Forest* (1973); a National Book Award for children's literature for *The Farthest Shore* (1973); a Hugo Award for "The Ones Who Walk Away from Omelas" (1974); a Nebula Award for "The Day Before the Revolution" (1974); Nebula, Jupiter, and Hugo awards for *The Dispossessed* (1974, 1975); a Jupiter Award for "The Diary of the Rose" (1976); and a Gandalf Award for achievement in fantasy (1979). Additional honors include the Kafka Award in 1986; a Hugo Award for "Buffalo Gals, Won't You Come Out Tonight?" (1988); a Pilgrim Award for body of work, awarded by the Science Fiction Research Association (1989); a Pushcart Prize for "Bill Weisler" (1991-1992); a Nebula Award for *Tehanu* (1990); a Nebula Award for "Solitude" (1995); the Tiptree Award for "Mountain Ways" (1996); the Endeavor Award for both *The Telling* (2000) and *Tales from Earthsea* (2001); and the World Fantasy Award for *The Other Wind* (2001).

In 2001, Le Guin was inducted into the Science Fiction Hall of Fame, and in 2003 she was named Grand Master by the Science Fiction and Fantasy Writers of America. In addition to receiving these honors, Le Guin has been a writer-in-residence at the Clarion West workshop at the University of Washington and a teaching participant in a science-fiction workshop at Portland State University. A number of science-fiction conventions, literary conferences, and universities have recognized her literary stature by inviting her to teach and speak.

BIOGRAPHY

Ursula K. Le Guin was born Ursula Kroeber, into a close, intellectual family in Berkeley, California, on October 21, 1929. Her father, Alfred Kroeber, was an anthropologist distinguished for his studies of native California tribes and was curator of the Museum of Anthropology and Ethnology of the University of California. Her mother, Theodora Krackaw Kroeber, was a respected writer with an advanced degree in psychology and a special affinity for Native American subjects and sensibilities. It was Le Guin's father who befriended Ishi, the last survivor of the native Californian Yahi people, and it was her mother who wrote *Ishi in Two Worlds* (1961), an anthropological study of Ishi's life and times, as well as the simpler popular narrative *Ishi, Last of His Tribe* (1964). The interest that Le Guin's fiction shows in communication across great barriers of culture, language, gender, and ideology is a natural offshoot of her parents' lifelong passion for understanding worldviews other than the dominant Euro-American competitive materialism. Her use of songs, stories, folktales, maps, and depictions of material culture to flesh out fictional worlds is also congruent with her parents' professional focus.

The Kroeber family seems to have enjoyed an enviable degree of closeness, reasonable financial security, and an abundance of intellectual stimulation. During the academic year, they lived in a large, airy house in Berkeley. Their summers were spent in their Napa Valley home, Kishamish. To these forty acres flocked writers, scholars, graduate students, relatives, and American Indians.

Living among so many people rich in knowledge and curiosity, and having access to an almost unlimited supply of books, Le Guin began writing and reading quite young. She did not discover science fiction, however, until she was twelve. When she found, while reading Lord Dunsany one day, that people were still creating myths, Le Guin felt liberated, for this discovery validated her own creative efforts.

In 1947, Le Guin entered Radcliffe College in Cambridge, Massachusetts. After she graduated magna cum laude in 1951, she entered Columbia University, where she majored in French and Italian Renaissance literature. After completing her master's degree in 1952, she began work on a doctoral program. En route to France as a Fulbright Fellow, she met Charles Le Guin, a historian from Georgia also on a Fulbright. They were married in Paris on December 22, 1953.

When they returned from France, the Le Guins lived in Georgia. Ursula taught French at Mercer University in Macon, and Charles completed his Ph.D. in French history at Emory University. Afterward, they moved to Idaho, where their first child, Elisabeth, was born in 1957. Caroline, their second daughter, arrived in 1959, the year Charles accepted a position at Portland State University and the family moved to a permanent home in Oregon. A third child, Theodore, would be born in 1964.

Ursula, who had never stopped writing but had yet to find a proper market for her efforts, became reacquainted with science fiction when a friend encouraged her to borrow from his library. Cordwainer Smith's story "Alpha Ralpha Boulevard" (1961) proved to be a catalyst, a type of fiction approaching Le Guin's own attempts. Le Guin began thinking not only about writing but also about publishing her work in something other than obscure magazines.

Since she had begun to write, she had been trying to get her work published, but except for one story, "An die Musick," and a few poems, her work was returned, some of it characterized as "remote." Her breakthrough came when *Fantastic* published "April in Paris" in September, 1962. The following year, *Fantastic* published her first genuine science-fiction story, "The Masters." After that time, Le Guin's literary output steadily increased, and her recognition as one of America's outstanding writers was assured.

Throughout her career, Le Guin has been reserved about the details of her personal life, maintaining that they are expressed best through her fiction. Although she has been involved in political activities, most of Le Guin's efforts are devoted to writing. As her recognition increased, she became a strong advocate for improving the quality of fantasy and science fiction. She seems determined that readers of this genre should not be cheated on their voyages of discovery. She also became a firmer, more definite advocate for feminism as she matured as a writer and as a woman. Early works (such as *The Left Hand of Darkness*) may have grappled delicately with gender issues through "gender-bending" imagination; later works (such as *Tehanu* and *Four Ways to Forgiveness*) have dealt quite explicitly with the impossibility of real love in the absence of equality, the oppression of unshared housework, and the importance of language itself in creating freedom or bondage.

Over the course of her writing career, Le Guin's work has expanded significantly outside the genre of science fiction. From "pro-choice" parables reprinted in *Ms.* magazine to advice to fellow authors (both of which can be found in her book of essays *Dancing at the Edge of the World*), Le Guin has been prolifically diverse in her output.

ANALYSIS

When Ursula K. Le Guin has Genly Ai state in *The Left Hand of Darkness* that "truth is a matter of the imagination," she is indirectly summarizing the essential focus of her fiction: explorations of the ambiguous nature of truth through imaginative means. Few other contemporary authors have described this process with the force and clarity of Le Guin. Her subject is always humankind and, by extension, the human environment, since humanity cannot survive in a vacuum; her technique is descriptive, and her mode is metaphoric. The worlds Le Guin creates are authentic in a profoundly moral sense as her characters come to experience truth in falsehood, return in separation, unity in variety.

Frequently using a journey motif, Le Guin sends her characters in search of shadows, rings, theories, or new worlds—all of which are metaphors for undiscovered elements of the self. Along the way, Le Guin demands that they learn the paradoxes inherent in life, the ambiguous nature of creation, and the interrelatedness of all that seems to be opposed. Once made, these discoveries allow her characters to be integrated into themselves and their worlds. In the end, her characters stand for no one, no concrete meaning; they simply are. Le Guin offers her readers characters who are motivated by intellectual curiosity, humanism, and self-determination, a nonviolent, nonexploitative philosophy capable of encompassing the unknown and complex cultures in relation to one another.

Unity is what Le Guin's characters seek: not a simple sense of belonging but a complex sense of wholeness. Much of her outlook is derived from the Daoist philosopher Laozi (also known as Lao-tzu), who maintained that scientific, ethical, and aesthetic laws, instead of being imposed by any authority, "exist in things and are to be discovered." Le Guin's characters thus must learn to recognize the true natures (or true names) of people or objects—none of which yield easily to the protagonists—before apprehending their essences and roles in the world. Dao is the ultimate unity of the universe, encompassing all and nothing. Built upon paradox, Daoist philosophy proposes that apparently opposing forces actually complete each other. Discovering this in a world enamored of dualist thought, however, requires attaining an attitude of actionless activity, an emptying of the self and at the same time the fullest self-awareness. This compassionate attitude establishes a state of attraction, not compulsion: a state of being, not doing. Indeed, because the cycle of cause and effect is so strong, the Daoist sage never tries to do good at all, for a good action implies an evil action. Discovering the correlation of life/death, good/evil, light/dark, male/female, and self/other requires a relativist judgment. The Native American lore that Le Guin absorbed as a child also contributed to her sense of unity. In her writing, she draws upon her rich knowledge of myths and the work of Carl Jung as well as her own fertile imagination to create intricate metaphors for psychic realities. In her own words, "Outer Space, and the Inner Lands, are still, and will always be, my country."

ROCANNON'S WORLD

Le Guin has described *Rocannon's World*, her first published novel, as "definitely purple," an odd mixture of space age and Bronze Age, the product of an author unsure of her direction and materials. Drawing heavily on Norse mythology, the novel originated from a short story, "Dowry of the Angyar," published in 1964. The story begins when a woman named Semley leaves her husband and child to claim her dowry, a gold and sapphire necklace. During her search, Semley time-travels to another planet, where Rocannon, an ethnologist, struck by Semley's beauty and bearing, gives her the necklace, a museum piece on his planet. Semley returns home, believing that she has been gone only overnight. To her dismay, however, she discovers that she has been gone for sixteen years. Her husband is dead; her daughter, a grown stranger.

The remainder of the novel concerns Rocannon's exploration of Semley's planet, known to him as Formalhaut II, with the aid of Semley's grandson Mogien. After his ship is destroyed by rebels from the planet Farady, Rocannon must warn the League of All Worlds of their rebellion. To do so, he must locate the rebel ship in order to use the rebels' ansible, an instantaneous transmitter, since his has been destroyed.

This episodic tale moves from adventure to adventure, as Rocannon learns that appearance often belies reality, that knowledge is not gained without sacrifice. The price he pays for increased understanding (the gift of mindspeech, through which he can hear the voices of his enemy) is costly: Mogien's life. Through his efforts, however, the planet is saved. Rocannon, a man changed forever by his knowledge, never returns to his own planet, and he dies without knowing that the planet he rescues is given his name.

Often her own best critic, Le Guin has cited this novel to illustrate the flaws of mixing science fiction with fantasy, of ignoring the limitations imposed by plausibility, of excessive caution in creating a new myth, and of reliance on stereotyped characters and situations. While this novel lacks the rich complexity of her later works, it does contain elements that Le Guin developed in subsequent novels. A readily apparent trait is that her focus is not on theoretical or applied science but rather on social science: how different individuals, races, and cultures perpetuate diffusion through lack of communication and how her main character surmounts these genuine yet arbitrary barriers. For example, as an ethnologist, Rocannon is interested in learning about all kinds of human behavior; nevertheless, he assumes superiority over his "primitive" guides. Experience, however, leads him to admire the individual qualities of Mogien, Kyo, and the Fiians. During their journey, his admiration of and loyalty to them increase to such an extent that loyalty becomes a prominent theme, one developed more thoroughly in *The Left Hand of Darkness*, with the relationship of Mogien and Rocannon prefiguring that of Genly Ai and Estraven (as well as other pairs of characters).

The most important goal in the novel, however, is to locate the other, often presented as the enemy, unify it with the self, and thus receive personal gain. The mindspeech Rocannon learns to hear expresses his fear. Though once he listens to the voices of his enemies he will never regain the self-sufficient confidence he had before embarking on his journey, he earns a vital awareness of his human limitations. Rocannon's sense of adventure is tempered by responsibility; his gain requires loss. In the end, Rocannon feels that he is a temporary resident on an alien planet. His sense of displacement denotes his lack of completion as a character. The novel ends without any resolution. In her next two novels, Le Guin shows greater control over her materials: less dependence on others' stories and more considered ideas and direction. Where *Rocannon's World* indicates a major theme of self-exploration, *City of Illusions* develops this theme, bringing it closer to its fullest realization in *The Dispossessed*.

CITY OF ILLUSIONS

City of Illusions begins dramatically in the blank terror of mental darkness experienced by Ramarren and ends in an even larger exterior darkness when Falk-Ramarren, returning to his home planet, departs for his unknown future. In the intervening time, Le Guin presents vivid scenes of an America largely undeveloped and peopled by disparate tribes, all of whom distrust one another and are united only in their universal fear of the Shing, an alien group who maintain division through that terror. Themes of communication, truth, self-discovery, and self-unification are central to this novel.

Using the quest motif, Le Guin has Falk nurtured by the pacific Forest Dwellers, who instill in him their set of values. When he leaves to discover his former identity, Falk confronts differing values, conflicting truths. Along the way, he receives the same warning from those who befriend him: Trust no one; go alone. While he neglects to heed this advice always, these warnings prepare him in part to withstand the considerable powers of the Shing, whose authority depends on self-doubt. Falk is able to recover his past self and retain his present self when he discovers that "there is in the long run no disharmony, only misunderstanding, no chance of mischance but only the ignorant eye." Once he achieves this state of understanding, his two identities merge; he becomes Falk-Ramarren to return to his world with the truth—or rather truths—he apprehends.

Le Guin's Daoist beliefs are given full exposure in this novel, where Falk-Ramarren not only reads Laozi's *Tao Te Ching* (or *Dao De Jing*; third century B.C.E), called the Old Canon, and looks for The Way, but also demonstrates the strength of passivity and enters a state of actionless activity to find himself. Stoic and silent, he prefigures Shevek of *The Dispossessed*. Le Guin's use of setting is also significant as it is employed to reflect psychological states. Her description of the Shing buildings in Es Toch suggests the illusory quality of this alien race and Falk's ambiguous state of mind.

This novel fails, however, to measure up to later works. The Shing, for example, meant to personify evil, are all but unbelievable. Their ambiguity lapses into confusion; their "power" is unsubstantiated. Falk's sudden compassion for them is thus rather surprising. Another mark of this novel's early place in Le Guin's career is her heavy-handedness regarding her source. Not only does she thinly disguise the *Dao De Jing*, but she also employs puns and even paraphrases passages of that work to stress her meaning. In her later novels, she achieves better results through greater restraint and insight.

THE LEFT HAND OF DARKNESS

Le Guin arrived at a denser, more original expression of Daoist thought in *The Left Hand of Darkness*. In this novel, she brings together previously expressed themes in a striking metaphor. Time levels, separate in former books, coexist in this novel, as do polarized political systems, philosophies, and genders. Genly Ai, the man sent to bring the planet of Genthen into the Ekumen (formerly the League of All Worlds), must, like Falk, come to see the relativity of truth. To do so, he must cross barriers of thought, barriers he is at first incapable of recognizing. Even when he does, Ai is reluctant to cross, for he must abandon his masculine-scientific-dualist training to become a relativist. He must believe that "truth is a matter of the imagination."

Ai's difficulty in arriving at this conclusion is complicated by his alien existence on Genthen, where he is not merely an outsider; he is a sexual anomaly, a pervert as far as the natives are concerned. Being a heterosexual male in an androgynous culture adds immeasurably to Ai's sense of distrust, for he cannot bring himself to trust "a man who is a woman, a woman who is a man." The theme of androgyny enriches this novel, not simply because it develops the complex results of an androgynous culture but also because it demonstrates how gender affects—indeed, prejudices—thought and explores the cultural effects of this bias. Initially, Ai can see only one gender, one side at a time. This limited vision leaves him vulnerable to betrayal, both by himself and by others. Through his friendship with Estraven, Ai begins to respect, even require, those qualities he at first denigrates until he and Estraven become one, joined in mindspeech. Ai's varied experiences on Genthen teach him that apparently polarized qualities of light/dark, male/female, rational/irrational, patriot/traitor, life/death are necessary complements. The order of the universe requires both.

The Left Hand of Darkness consolidates Daoist ideas expressed in Le Guin's previous books, places them in a dramatically unique culture, and develops them with a finesse lacking in her earlier novels. Ai discovers what Falk does: a fuller recognition of self through merger with the other. He does so, however, in a much more complete way because Le Guin complicates *The Left Hand of Darkness* with questions of opposing political systems, the nature and consequences of sexism, the issue of personal and political loyalty, and the interrelatedness of different periods of time. While retaining her basic quest structure, Le Guin has Genly Ai construct his "report" by using multiple sources: Estraven's diary, folktales, ancient myths, reports from previous investigatory teams. This adds texture and depth by dramatizing the multiplicity of truth and the unity of time.

In a sense, this mixture of sources, added to the seasonlessness of Genthen, where it is always winter, and the relentless journey over the Gobrin Ice, constructs a center of time for the reader, an objective correlative to Ai's state of mind. Within a circular framework, a sense of wholeness is achieved. Ai will set the keystone in the arch, the image that opens *The Left Hand of Darkness*, by adding Genthen to the Ekumen. Later, he cements his personal bond to Estraven by visiting his home, ostensibly to return Estraven's diary but actually to assuage a sense of betrayal for not having Estraven publicly absolved of his "crime" of supporting the Ekumen instead of his king. At the novel's end, however, when Ai meets in Estraven's son the father's limitless curiosity, Ai's journey begins anew.

Literary critic Robert Scholes has stated that one of the great strengths of *The Left Hand of Darkness* is that it "asks us to broaden our perspectives toward something truly ecumenical, beyond racism and sexism, and even speciesism." Clearly, Le Guin opened up new territory for science-fiction writers to explore.

THE DISPOSSESSED

In *The Dispossessed*, her next novel in what is called her Hainish cycle, Le Guin presses even further, bringing to full realization her heroic figure of the Daoist sage in the protagonist Shevek. Stoic, persistent, curious, and humane, he shares qualities with Falk, Estraven, and Genly Ai. Shevek's character and journey, however, differ from his predecessors' in several important respects. Shevek's sense of alienation is tempered by his mature love for his partner Takver. No matter how alone he is on his journey, Shevek can and does turn to their mutually supportive relationship for solace. Shevek's sense of individual integrity is also more conscious than that of previous characters. Already aware of himself and his value, he is able to expand beyond both. Most important, Shevek has a clearly defined sense of purpose—a need to unbuild walls through communication—and a certainty of return. Early in the novel, Le Guin assures her readers that "he would most likely not have embarked on that years-long enterprise had he not had profound assurance that return was possible . . . that the very nature of the voyage . . . implied return." Buttressed by this conviction, Shevek goes forth, his empty hands signifying his spiritual values, and effects a revolution in both senses of the word: a completed cycle and a dynamic change. When he discovers his theory of temporal simultaneity, Shevek gives it away, for he knows that its value is not in its scarcity but in its general use.

The Dispossessed is not simply a vehicle for Daoist philosophy; it is just as significantly a political novel. Le Guin subtitles the novel *An Ambiguous Utopia*, indicating her focus, and she directs her reader's attention by alternating chapters on Anarres, Shevek's home planet, and Urras, where he resides throughout much of the novel. Scenes from Anarres are recalled through flashback as Shevek, surrounded by an alien political and social system repugnant to much in his nature, reflects upon himself in relation to his culture. Anarres, founded by libertarian followers of Odo, a radical Urrasti thinker, is at once dedicated to individual freedom and to the good of the whole. There is no formal government, only a system of individually initiated syndicates, a Division of Labor to keep track of job needs, and the Production Distribution Committee to oversee production loosely. On Anarres nothing is owned; everything is shared. Since everyone is equal, there is no discrimination, no exploitation, but there are stringent societal responsibilities that all Anarresti share. Because Anarres is virtually a desert, with plant life so scarce that no animals are indigenous, careful conservation, voluntary labor, and a sense of duty to the whole are required of everyone.

By contrast, Urras is wealthy, lush with water, teeming with life. Its capitalistic system, however, encourages exploitation because profit is the motivating force. As a result, Urras has an entrenched class system, with women and workers considered inferior to men and the intellectual and governing classes, and a power structure intent on maintaining control. While much of this authority is exerted by custom, some is imposed by force. Shevek, unaccustomed to any type of exploitation, violence, discrimination, or conspicuous waste, needs to experience fully the benefits and detriments of Urras before he can make necessary connections. Once he recognizes that the seeds of his freedom germinated in the rich soil of Urras, he can declare his brotherhood with the Urrasti and offer them what he can: a way to the only future he knows, that of Anarres. Speaking from deep within himself, Shevek tells Urrasti rebels "You must come to it alone, and naked, as the child comes into his future, without any past, without any property, wholly dependent on other people for his life. . . . You cannot make the Revolution. You can only be the Revolution."

EARTHSEA SERIES

The Earthsea series has been categorized by many as "young adult fiction." Le Guin does write often and well for young audiences, and the fact that the three original books of the series (*A Wizard of Earthsea*, *The Tombs of Atuan*, and *The Farthest Shore*) are quite short, are populated by sorcerers and dragons, and use the vocabulary and syntax of high fantasy has tended to identify them as children's literature, at least on the surface. However, their subtle spiritual, mythic, psychological, and philosophical underpinnings and the elegant simplicity of the writing make the books challenging and satisfying to adult readers as well.

In *A Wizard of Earthsea*, Le Guin introduces Ged, a natural-born wizard whose insensitive family does not realize his innate gift. Ged becomes a sorcerer's apprentice to the mage Ogion but ultimately is forced to leave before completing his studies because he keeps casting spells before learning their complications. His inner conflicts are revealed through his struggle to find and to name what he believes to be a mysterious shadow pursuing him. Le Guin's essay "The Child and the Shadow" (in *The Language of the Night*) discusses her depiction of this archetypal Jungian "dark brother of the conscious mind."

In *The Tombs of Atuan*, Ged meets Tenar (known as Arha), the child priestess of the dark Nameless Ones. Ged has gone to the Labyrinth of the Nameless Ones to recover a Ring that is necessary to the well-being of Earthsea, but he becomes a prisoner in the Labyrinth. Ged and Tenar help each other out of their different sorts of darkness and bondage, return the Ring to its rightful place, and become firm friends. Tenar finds a refuge with Ged's old master, Ogion. Tenar is as powerful as Ged in her own way, yet she too leaves her apprenticeship with Ogion before completing her training, though for a different reason. Ged is forced to leave; Tenar chooses to leave for the fulfillment of married life.

Le Guin's understanding of identity and its relationship to naming is revealed in the theme that runs throughout the Earthsea series: To know the true name of someone is to have power over that person. Hence, characters have "use" names as well as real names. An individual usually tells his or her real name only at the moment of death or to someone who is completely trusted.

TEHANU

In 1990, *Tehanu: The Last Book of Earthsea* was published, formally (or so Le Guin has said) bringing the adventures of Tenar and Ged to an end. *Tehanu* is markedly different from the earlier books in the series, however, in that it is written unequivocally for adults. Perhaps Le Guin wanted to aim it at the audience who had grown up reading her books and was now older and more mature—like Tenar and Ged, no longer rash in their actions and fearless with the immortality of youth.

In *Tehanu*, Tenar has been widowed. She is called to assist in the treatment of a badly burned and sexually abused young girl, whom Tenar adopts and names Therru. A visit to the now-dying mage Ogion elicits the information that there is a powerful and dangerous presence in Therru. The dramatic return of Ged aboard the back of the dragon Kalessin, however, occupies Tenar's mind, as she must nurse him. He has lost the powers of archmagery and is now an ordinary man, vulnerable to violence, grief, depression, aging, and sexual love.

Tehanu is, like much of Le Guin's work, a careful compendium of names, spells, and physical transformations. This novel, however, deals more directly with the dark themes of child molestation and abuse and death than do the earlier volumes in the Earthsea series.

As a venture in world making, *Tehanu* resembles *Always Coming Home*, a work intended primarily for adults. Purporting to write the history of several peoples in the distant future, *Always Coming Home* is accompanied by audio recordings of poems and stories, and the text is supplemented by illustrations and glossaries of terms.

FOUR WAYS TO FORGIVENESS

Just as *Tehanu* deepens Earthsea to include the difficult realities of violence, oppression, sex, and aging, *Four Ways to Forgiveness* deepens Le Guin's exploration of the ways that power creates deep gulfs between the powerful and the powerless. As in *The Dispossessed*, Le Guin again uses the device of two planets, Werel and Yeowe, connected by kinship and history, to illustrate the separate "worlds" created by privilege and exploitation. *Four Ways to Forgiveness* is a novel in the form of four interconnected novellas. Each of the four sections is, in its own way, a love story and could stand alone as a tale of alienation healed. Taken together, the four tales present the larger story of an entire society mending, a new whole being conceived through the union of opposites, and the whole being born through blood and pain.

The first story, "Betrayals," tells of two aging survivors of Yeowe's long, bitter struggle for emancipation. Both have retreated to live in seclusion and "turn to silence, as their religion recommended them to do" in old age. When the man becomes ill, the woman nurses him. When her house burns down, he takes her in. In helping each other, they learn to see each other. Seeing each other, they learn to love each other. Like *Tehanu*, "Betrayals" explores the issues of what loves and graces are left for old age, after the many inevitable losses of life.

The second section, "Forgiveness Day," is the love story of a brash young Ekumenical diplomat on Werel and a stolid, traditional soldier of the ruling class. Their path to partnership gives the author a chance to examine sexism and racism from the point of view of a woman who has been raised in an egalitarian society and from the point of view of a male military defender of the privileged group. To the woman, the rules of behavior that enforce power and powerlessness seem bizarre; to the man, they seem completely natural. Through sharing a difficult ordeal, the two learn to appreciate each other and build a lasting, loving partnership. As they work through the difficulties in their relationship, the author demonstrates for the reader how mental practices of power and privilege make true friendship and love impossible.

The third section, "A Man of the People," follows the career of a Hainish historian as he leaves the comfortable provincial village in which he was born. He studies the history of the diverse cultures of the universe, travels widely, and finally goes to Yeowe as an Ekumenical observer. On Yeowe, he commits himself to the struggle for the long-delayed liberation of women, and in this commitment to a community, he finally experiences the sense of belonging he left behind him when he first left his pueblo. The meditations of the historian on his discipline allow Le Guin to present her ideas on the difference between local cultural knowledge and universal cross-cultural knowledge (both of which she honors), education as revolution, and the interplay between historical observation and activism.

The final piece, "A Woman's Liberation," tells the life story of the Werelian woman who becomes the Hainish historian's wife. This simple first-person telling, reminiscent of the slave narratives collected to support the abolition of slavery in the United States, details the life of an owned woman from childhood in the slave compound to service in the big "House" to the day when she is technically "freed" through the difficulties of staying free and gaining equality. Le Guin uses the final two sections of *Four Ways to Forgiveness* to depict, explicitly and realistically, many of the ugly inhumanities that accompany slavery, such as sexual abuse and other violence. For this author, power and exploitation are not merely theoretical subjects; she seeks to portray the real human suffering that is an essential component of institutionalized privilege.

LAVINIA

In a departure from her earlier novels, Le Guin sets *Lavinia* in Earth's ancient times. Its main character, a young woman named Lavinia, is daughter of King Latinus and Queen Amata of Latium, ancestral Romans of the eighth century B.C.E. She is also a character in Vergil's *Aeneid* (c. 29-19 B.C.E.; English translation, 1553), where she plays a pivotal role. In Vergil's epic, however, she never speaks.

Lavinia gives this character her voice, as narrator. She speaks of her youth and upbringing, her courtship by highborn youths from neighboring cities, the arrival of Aeneas from Troy, and the subsequent battle between the Trojans and the local inhabitants, the latter being led by her rash, spurned suitor, King Turnus.

The novel follows Vergil's narrative, but with distinct departures. Lavinia breaks her narrative with accounts of her brief but happy time immediately after the war, as wife of Aeneas. Also markedly original are her visions at the sacred family shrine, in the forest of Albunea, of the poet Vergil himself. The poet is close to death when he communicates with Lavinia across the gulf of time. Conversing with him over several evenings, Lavinia enlarges the poet's knowledge of her own nature and perspective, which are entirely missing from his poem. Vergil in his turn reveals events in Lavinia's immediate future.

Although Vergil's death ends their communications, Lavinia's story continues. In the last third of the novel she must see her own way through life, without Vergil's prophetic help. It is a time of kingdom building, under Aeneas and his sons, and of the establishment of Rome as a seat of power.

Lavinia's voice provides one of the compelling aspects of the narrative. She is telling her own story not from the viewpoint of maturity or old age but as a spirit in some part of the underworld where people think they are alive, and where they are in communion with others not only of their own time but of others, past and future. Lavinia believes she has been granted this other level of existence because of her having been so slighted by the poet in his work. In this she is different from other characters in the *Aeneid*. Thinking of her husband, Aeneas, she says, "The poet made him live, live greatly, so he must die. I, whom the poet gave so little life to, I can go on." At another time she muses that Vergil "did not sing me enough life to die. He only gave me immortality."

Omens and oracles play an important part in *Lavinia*, as they do in the *Aeneid*. In *Lavinia*, however, the most important oracle is the Latin poet himself. Lavinia recognizes Vergil as not only poet but also "maker." That he is akin to a progenitor is indicated by his spirit's appearing to her in the forest of Abunea, the place where her family's ancestors speak to the family's living members.

Although a departure, *Lavinia* shares with Le Guin's other novels many elements, including the bringing together of different time strands and the struggle of the individual to find meaning within externally imposed order. It presents a powerful portrait of a woman freeing herself of the curse of not being heard, "a curse laid on women more often than on men."

Karen Carmean; Donna Glee Williams
Updated by Mark Rich

OTHER MAJOR WORKS

SHORT FICTION: *The Word for World Is Forest*, 1972; *The Wind's Twelve Quarters*, 1975; *Orsinian Tales*, 1976; *The Water Is Wide*, 1976; *Gwilan's Harp*, 1981; *The Compass Rose*, 1982; *The Visionary: The Life Story of Flicker of the Serpentine, with Wonders Hidden*, 1984; *Buffalo Gals and Other Animal Presences*, 1987; *Fish Soup*, 1992; *A Fisherman of the Inland Sea: Science Fiction Stories*, 1994; *Solitude*, 1994 (novella); *Unlocking the Air, and Other Stories*, 1996; *Tales from Earthsea*, 2001; *The Birthday of the World, and Other Stories*, 2002; *Changing Planes*, 2003.

POETRY: *Wild Angels*, 1975; *Hard Words, and Other Poems*, 1981; *In the Red Zone*, 1983; *Wild Oats and Fireweed: New Poems*, 1988; *Blue Moon over Thurman Street*, 1993; *Going Out with Peacocks, and Other Poems*, 1994; *Sixty Odd: New Poems*, 1999; *Incredible Good Fortune: New Poems*, 2006.

NONFICTION: *From Elfland to Poughkeepsie*, 1973; *The Language of the Night: Essays on Fantasy and Science Fiction*, 1979 (Susan Wood, editor); *Dancing at the Edge of the World: Thoughts on Words, Women, and Places*, 1988; *Napa: The Roots and Springs of the Valley*, 1989; *Steering the Craft: Exercises and Discussions on Story Writing for the*

Lone Navigator or the Mutinous Crew, 1998; *The Wave in the Mind: Talks and Essays on the Writer, the Reader, and the Imagination*, 2004.

TRANSLATIONS: *The Twins, the Dream/Las Gemelas, el sueño*, 1996 (with Diana Bellessi); *Tao Te Ching: A Book About the Way and the Power of the Way*, 1997; *Kalpa Imperial: The Greatest Empire That Never Was*, 2003 (of Angéla Gorodischer's novel); *Selected Poems of Gabriela Mistral*, 2003.

CHILDREN'S LITERATURE: *The Adventure of Cobbler's Rune*, 1982; *The Visionary*, 1984; *Catwings*, 1988; *Solomon Leviathan's 931st Trip Around the World*, 1988; *A Visit from Dr. Katz*, 1988; *Catwings Return*, 1989; *Fire and Stone*, 1989; *A Ride on the Red Mare's Back*, 1992; *Wonderful Alexander and the Catwings*, 1994; *Tales of the Catwings*, 1997; *Tom Mouse*, 1998; *Tom Mouse and Ms. Howe*, 1998; *Jane on Her Own: A Catwings Tale*, 1999; *More Tales of the Catwings*, 2000; *Gifts*, 2004; *Voices*, 2006; *Powers*, 2007.

EDITED TEXTS: *Norton Book of Science Fiction: North American Science Fiction, 1960-1990*, 1993; *Selected Stories of H. G. Wells*, 2005.

BIBLIOGRAPHY

Bernardo, Susan M., and Graham J. Murphy. *Ursula K. Le Guin: A Critical Companion*. Westport, Conn.: Greenwood Press, 2006. Presents critical analysis of many of Le Guin's novels, including *The Lathe of Heaven* and *The Dispossessed*. Includes a brief biography and an essay on Le Guin's place in the "literary genealogy of science fiction."

Cadden, Mike. *Ursula K. Le Guin Beyond Genre: Fiction for Children and Ad2ults*. London: Taylor & Francis, 2004. Explores Le Guin's children's books and fiction for young adults alongside her novels to show shared themes and points of connection. Includes an interview with Le Guin.

Cummins, Elizabeth. *Understanding Ursula K. Le Guin*. Rev. ed. Columbia: University of South Carolina Press, 1993. Analyzes Le Guin's work, with an emphasis on the different worlds she has created and how they provide the structure for all of her fiction.

Freedman, Carl, ed. *Conversations with Ursula K. Le Guin*. Jackson: University Press of Mississippi, 2008. Collection of interviews with Le Guin—conducted by various interviewers over a span of twenty-five years—offers the author's own perspective on her life and her writing.

Le Guin, Ursula K. "I Am a Woman Writer, I Am a Western Writer: An Interview with Ursula Le Guin." Interview by William Walsh. *Kenyon Review* n.s. 17 (Summer/Fall, 1995): 192-205. Le Guin discusses such topics as the genre of science fiction, her readership, the feminist movement, women writers, and the Nobel Prize.

Loy, David R., and Linda Goodhew. "The Dharma of Death and Life: Philip Pullman's *His Dark Materials* and Ursula K. Le Guin's *Earthsea*." In *The Dharma of Dragons and Daemons: Buddhist Themes in Modern Fantasy*. Somerville, Mass.: Wisdom, 2004. Illuminates the themes of Le Guin's Earthsea series and Pullman's trilogy from a Buddhist perspective.

Oziewicz, Marek, *One Earth, One People: The Mythopoeic Fantasy of Ursula K. Le Guin, Lloyd Alexander, Madeleine L'Engle, and Orson Scott Card.* Jefferson, N.C.: McFarland, 2008. Argues that the works of fantasy authors, including Le Guin, have socially transformative power, giving expression to a worldview based on the supernatural or spiritual.

Reid, Suzanne Elizabeth. *Presenting Ursula K. Le Guin.* New York: Twayne, 1997. Critical biography aimed at young adults provides a good introduction to Le Guin's fiction and examines how the events of the author's life have helped to shape her work.

Rochelle, Warren. *Communities of the Heart: The Rhetoric of Myth in the Fiction of Ursula K. Le Guin.* Liverpool, England: University of Liverpool Press, 2001. Analyzes Le Guin's construction of myth and her use of mythological themes in her work.

White, Donna R. *Dancing with Dragons: Ursula K. Le Guin and the Critics.* Columbia, S.C.: Camden House, 1999. Examines Le Guin's works, with a focus on how they have been critically received.

DORIS LESSING

Born: Kermanshah, Persia (now Bakhtaran, Iran); October 22, 1919
Also known as: Doris May Taylor; Jane Somers

PRINCIPAL LONG FICTION

The Grass Is Singing, 1950
Martha Quest, 1952
A Proper Marriage, 1954
Retreat to Innocence, 1956
A Ripple from the Storm, 1958
The Golden Notebook, 1962
Landlocked, 1965, 1991
The Four-Gated City, 1969
Briefing for a Descent into Hell, 1971
The Summer Before the Dark, 1973
The Memoirs of a Survivor, 1974
Shikasta, 1979 (also known as *Re: Colonized Planet 5, Shikasta*)
The Marriages Between Zones Three, Four, and Five, 1980
The Sirian Experiments: The Report by Ambien II, of the Five, 1980
The Making of the Representative for Planet 8, 1982
Documents Relating to the Sentimental Agents in the Volyen Empire, 1983
The Diary of a Good Neighbour, 1983 (as Jane Somers)
If the Old Could . . . , 1984 (as Somers)
The Diaries of Jane Somers, 1984 (includes *The Diary of a Good Neighbour* and *If the Old Could . . .*)
The Good Terrorist, 1985
The Fifth Child, 1988
Canopus in Argos: Archives, 1992 (5-novel cycle includes *Re: Colonized Planet 5, Shikasta, The Marriages Between Zones Three, Four, and Five, The Sirian Experiments, The Making of the Representative for Planet 8*, and *Documents Relating to the Sentimental Agents in the Volyen Empire*)
Playing the Game, 1995
Love, Again, 1996
Mara and Dann, 1999
Ben, in the World, 2000
The Sweetest Dream, 2001
The Story of General Dann and Mara's Daughter, Griot, and the Snow Dog, 2005
The Cleft, 2007
Alfred and Emily, 2008

OTHER LITERARY FORMS

In addition to her works of long fiction, Doris Lessing has published numerous volumes of short stories. She has also published a volume of poetry and has written memoirs, documentaries, essays, reviews, plays, and librettos for operas.

ACHIEVEMENTS

Doris Lessing has been one of the most widely read and influential novelists of the second half of the twentieth century and the early twenty-first. Her works have been translated into many languages and have inspired critical attention around the globe. Generally serious and didactic, Lessing's fiction repeatedly urges the human race to develop a wider consciousness that will allow for greater harmony and less violence. Although known particularly as a master of realism, Lessing is often experimental or deliberately fantastic, as shown in her science-fiction novels. Her interests are wide-ranging, from Marxism and global politics to the mystical teachings of Sufism to the small personal voice of the individual.

In 1999, Lessing was made a Member of the Order of the Companions of Honour (a British honor for those who have done "conspicuous national service"), and in 2001, the Royal Society of Literature named her a Companion of Literature. Among the numerous awards Lessing has received are the Somerset Maugham Award, the German Shakespeare Prize, the Austrian Prize for European Literature, and the French Prix Médicis for Foreigners. In 1995, she won the James Tait Black Memorial Prize and a Los Angeles Times Book Prize for the first volume of her autobiography, *Under My Skin* (1994). In 1999, she received Spain's Premi Internacional Catalunya; in 2001, the David Cohen British Literary Prize as well as Spain's Premio Príncipe de Asturias; and in 2002, the S. T. Dupont Golden PEN Award. In 2007, Lessing was awarded the world's most prestigious honor for literary authors, the Nobel Prize in Literature.

BIOGRAPHY

Doris Lessing was born Doris May Tayler in Kermanshah, Persia (now Bakhtaran, Iran), on October 22, 1919, the first child of Alfred Cook Tayler and Emily Maude McVeagh Tayler, who had emigrated from England to Persia shortly after World War I. A brother, Harry, was born two years later, and in 1925 the family moved to a farm in Southern Rhodesia (now Zimbabwe). Her parents were never financially successful. Her father was a dreamer who became a cynic after he failed at maize farming; her mother was domineering but ineffective. Despite Lessing's love of the African landscape and the isolated veld, she was eager to leave her family behind. She attended a Catholic convent school in Salisbury (now Harare) but left when she was fourteen, saying that she had eye problems, though she continued her voracious reading.

Lessing left home when she was fifteen to become a nursemaid and moved to Salisbury to work in various jobs, mostly clerical, and began writing fiction. She married Frank

Charles Wisdom, a minor civil servant, in 1939, and had a son, John, and a daughter, Jean. Divorced in 1943, she was remarried two years later to a German Jewish refugee, Gottfried Lessing. They had a son, Peter, in 1947. She divorced Gottfried Lessing in 1949 and that same year moved to England, settling in London. In 1950 she published her first novel. She continued to live in London and to make her living as a professional writer, writing reviews, media scripts, and nonfiction in addition to her novels, short stories, drama, and poetry.

Lessing's interest in politics began with a Marxist group in Rhodesia, and in England she was briefly a member of the Communist Party, leaving it officially in 1956. In the late 1950's she participated in mass demonstrations for nuclear disarmament and was a speaker at the first Aldermaston March in 1958. During the early 1960's she worked in the theater, helping to establish Centre 42, a populist art program, and writing her own plays. In the late 1960's Lessing's thinking began to be heavily influenced by the mystical teachings of Indries Shah and Sufism, which emphasizes conscious evolution of the mind in harmony with self and others. Although for many years Lessing resisted the role of public persona, in the mid-1980's she began to make numerous public appearances in many countries.

Lessing received her first major literary award in 1954, and she became increasingly recognized and honored, especially by the 1980's and 1990's. In 1989 she received an honorary doctor of letters degree from Princeton University and in 1995 one from Harvard University, and that year she was also welcomed back into South Africa and Rhodesia, from which she had been banned for four decades because of her political views and her work to end apartheid. She went to visit her daughter and grandchildren and was well received in both countries. Also in 1995, her first volume of autobiography won the prestigious James Tait Black Memorial Prize for best biography as well as the Los Angeles Times Book Prize. The early twenty-first century brought continued awards, and in 2007, two weeks before her eighty-eighth birthday, she received the Nobel Prize in Literature, which included a stipend of approximately one and one-half million dollars. One award she refused, however, was to become a Dame of the British Empire, on the grounds that there is no British Empire.

Lessing has remained one of the most prolific and distinguished writers of the twentieth century and beyond. In the 1990's she made fewer public appearances, devoting herself to more writing. Although she made a fourteen-week tour to promote her autobiography, Lessing has stated that she is more useful to her publisher when she stays at home and writes. When her novel *Love, Again* was published in 1996, she made no public appearances to promote the book.

ANALYSIS

Doris Lessing is a powerful writer committed to the lofty goal of changing human consciousness itself. The narrative voice that weaves throughout her prolific fiction is that of an intense thinker who observes, explores, and describes the contemporary world but whose ultimate sense of human life is that the individual, and indeed the human race, is meant to go beyond mere recognition of perceived reality and to struggle with visions of the possible. Her novels repeatedly suggest that changes in the way humans view themselves, their world, and their relationships with others are imperative if life on this planet is to survive.

Lessing's scope is wide. Her creative imagination is able to provide a close analysis of a character—with all that individual's fears, longings, and contradictions—and to relate that individual not only to his or her circle of acquaintances but to patterns of global economics and politics as well, and then to sweep beyond this planet to the cosmos and a perspective that encompasses the metaphysical questions of existence. Her fictional explorations are multiple, multidimensional, and overlapping, suggesting that no one viewpoint is adequate or complete. This range is also reflected in her varied narrative forms, which include realism, naturalism, science fiction, utopianism and dystopianism, fantasy, fable, transcultural postmodernism, and experimental combinations of these. This heterogeneity of themes, techniques, and perspectives illustrates Lessing's overriding premise that truth and substance cannot easily be compartmentalized or assigned fixed labels: Existence is always process, always in flux.

Lessing's position as an exile is a prominent aspect of her work, both in content and in theme. Born in the Middle East of English parents, she spent her adolescence in Southern Rhodesia, first with her family on an isolated and impoverished farm whose workers were all native black Africans, and then on her own in Salisbury. In the city she became involved with a group interested in international politics whose most specific focus was increased rights for black Rhodesians. Her experiences there in the 1940's, including two marriages and three children, became material for nearly all of her novels for the first twenty years of her writing career.

Lessing has had a wide readership throughout her career. For many years her works have been on best-seller lists, and her novels have been translated into many languages. Her fiction is widely anthologized and has been closely read by many contemporary authors, particularly women writers. The number of critical articles, books, and sections of books about her work is enormous and international in scope, reflecting the wide diversity of Lessing's readers and the serious attention her work continues to command. Lessing's novels, wide-ranging in scope and treatment, resist any easy labels. Her major themes, however, though presented in a variety of ways, have been remarkably consistent. The individual has responsibilities, Lessing always shows, not only to achieve self-knowledge and inner harmony but to contribute to the greater harmony of society as well. Human consciousness must expand and people's attitudes and actions must change if human life is to survive.

THE GRASS IS SINGING

In 1949, Lessing arrived in London with her youngest son and the manuscript of *The Grass Is Singing*. In many ways this first book established a pattern for subsequent novels. Her manuscript was accepted for publication within three days of her submitting it to a publisher. The novel was well received when it appeared and went through seven reprintings within five months. The title comes from part 5 of T. S. Eliot's *The Waste Land* (1922); Lessing's wide reading included the twentieth century writers as well as the great British, French, and Russian novelists of the nineteenth century. She most admired those writers with a sense of moral purpose, a sense of commitment to all humanity. *The Grass Is Singing* clearly shows the horrific effects of apartheid and racial prejudice on both the white colonial rulers and the black people who make up the overwhelming majority of the population of southern Africa.

In a stylistic technique directly opposite to that of a stereotypical detective story, the third-person narrator reveals at the outset of *The Grass Is Singing* that Mary Turner, the wife of a poor farmer, has been killed by a houseboy, Moses, who confessed to the crime. The opening chapter shows the confusion and emotional collapse of Mary's husband, Dick Turner, and the reactions of Charlie Slatter, a neighbor, and Tony Marston, a young recent immigrant from England. The plot then becomes straightforward as it gives the background and chronology of events that led to the murder.

Mary grew up in the city and had established a pleasant though rather meaningless life after the death of her parents. At age thirty she begins to overhear acquaintances' disparaging remarks about the fact that she has never married. Suddenly seeing herself as a failure, she agrees to marry virtually the first man available, an impractical farmer who comes to town for supplies. Dick Turner immediately takes her to his isolated shack, where they are surrounded by black workers; the nearest white neighbor is many miles away. Mary is unprepared for marriage and totally inept at dealing with the series of houseboys Dick brings from the field to do cooking and housework. In exile from her city life, Mary is further hampered by the typical white Southern Rhodesian belief that natives are basically inferior. She cannot handle the day-by-day contact with the native houseboys who seem so alien to her, and with the advent of the arrogant Moses, the many psychological strains lead inexorably to her almost invited death. Mary and all of white culture are guilty, but it is the black Moses who will be hanged. Mary's failures are also a result of her inability to understand herself. She is not a reader. She has dreams and nightmares but makes no exploration of their possible significance. She has never examined social and political realities and has no one with whom to discuss her problems. She is unable to adjust to her current reality and unable to create any alternative reality.

CHILDREN OF VIOLENCE SERIES

Martha Quest, A Proper Marriage, A Ripple from the Storm, Landlocked, and *The Four-Gated City* trace in detail the growth and development of Martha Quest, an autobiographical character who, unlike Mary Turner, is intensely interested in knowing herself and making sense of the world. Together these novels make up Lessing's Children of Violence series. The first four are set in Africa, while *The Four-Gated City*, which nearly equals in length the preceding four, is set in London and traces Martha Quest's life from her arrival there around 1949 to the late 1990's. The novels set in Africa may be categorized as social realism, but *The Four-Gated City* moves beyond that to discuss what are often considered paranormal capacities, and the work concludes after some unspecified disaster has destroyed much of life on earth. Despite forces beyond the control of the individual, Martha Quest and some of the other inhabitants of the postcatastrophic world epitomize the continuing need for individual responsibility and commitment to a more harmonious world.

Martha Quest, as her surname suggests, is a quintessential Lessing heroine, always examining the human condition and searching for a higher consciousness to change herself and her world. The characterization is detailed and frank, including descriptions of Martha's sexual relationships and, in *A Proper Marriage*, a lengthy and explicit description of childbirth. Martha's perceptions and innermost thoughts also provide a historical overview of an entire era and a challenge to the status quo. Central to all of Martha's struggles is her determination to grow and to envision a freer and more responsible world.

THE GOLDEN NOTEBOOK

Lessing interrupted the writing of the Children of Violence series to work on *The Golden Notebook*, published in 1962 and generally acknowledged as her most impressive and influential novel. "The two women were alone in the London flat," begins the long novel, and from this simple statement Lessing creates a fascinating portrait of the modern world. The protagonist is Anna Wulf, a writer who says that she is suffering from writer's block after a successful first novel about racial problems in Africa. Anna's friend Molly is a divorced mother trying to make a life for herself. Through them Lessing perceptively examines the problems of the intelligent and disillusioned modern woman.

Anna tries to create order out of chaos by keeping a diary, which she divides into four notebooks: a black notebook recounting her experiences as a young woman in Africa; a red notebook for her Communist and political activities; a yellow notebook, which includes her fictional attempts to understand herself, including the creation of an autobiographical character named Ella, who is also writing a novel; and a blue notebook to record the factual details of her daily life and her relationships with men. Sections of these notebooks are repeated sequentially four times and are finally superseded by another notebook, the golden one of the novel's title, in which Anna attempts to integrate these compartmentalized and often-conflicting aspects of her life. In the golden notebook section, influenced by the mental breakdown of one of her lovers, Saul Green, Anna goes through layers of madness in herself and questions the idea of reality itself.

The shape of this pivotal metafictional novel is further complicated by sections called

"Free Women," which open and close the book as well as separate the repeated sections of the black, red, yellow, and blue notebooks. The five "Free Women" sections together form a conventional novel about sixty thousand words long. Although it deals with the same characters and events recounted in the various notebook sections, it does so in a reductive and more structured way. It is as though the "Free Women" novel were what Anna is able to produce to end her writer's block, but a novel that shows that fiction is unable to capture the intricacies and complexities of actual existence. Since the sections of this conventional novel frame and appear throughout the larger work, the contrasts and variations with the notebook sections make *The Golden Notebook* as a whole a complex structural and stylistic achievement.

While *The Golden Notebook* elaborates Lessing's attitudes toward racism, sexism, and the interconnections between the personal and the political, it also shows the development of Lessing's thinking to include the benefits of the irrational and the necessity of exploring areas beyond the layers of social pretense and conventionality. These areas are further addressed in *The Four-Gated City* and in three subsequent novels, *Briefing for a Descent into Hell*, *The Summer Before the Dark*, and *The Memoirs of a Survivor*. Each of these novels breaks from traditional versions of realism and insists on a wider definition of the possible.

BRIEFING FOR A DESCENT INTO HELL

Briefing for a Descent into Hell, one of the very few Lessing novels with a male as the central character, presents Charles Watkins, a classics professor at the University of Cambridge, who is found wandering and incoherent in the streets and is hospitalized for treatment of a mental breakdown. While in the hospital, Watkins, who has forgotten even his name, imagines himself taken away in a spaceship, and most of the book relates his various encounters with unfamiliar creatures and situations that seem almost mythological. Many of these experiences are painful or frightening. Often he is alone, yet he feels a sense of urgency and intense anxiety: He must accomplish certain tasks or risk total failure for himself and others. He also has times of exceptional joy, as he sees the beauty of creation and has revelations of a harmony that could prevail if each creature accepted its part in the scheme of things and made its responsible contribution. In the final pages of the book, Watkins is given electroshock treatment and yanked back into his old life, but both he and the reader are left with the sense that, compared to his previous insights, he has been forced back to a shallow and hollow "normalcy."

THE SUMMER BEFORE THE DARK

In *The Summer Before the Dark*, Kate Brown, a woman in her early forties, also goes through a period of "madness" that reveals the extent to which she has previously succumbed to the pressures to become only roles: wife, mother, sex object, efficient organizer, selfless caregiver. During the summer that is the time frame of the novel, Kate's husband and grown children are away from home; at loose ends, Kate accepts a position as translator for an international food organization. She soon finds herself traveling and organizing global conferences. She spends some time in Spain with Jeffrey Merton, a young man whose psychosomatic and psychological illnesses spill over into her own life, and she returns to London to deal with her doubts and confusions.

She stays for a while in a flat with Maureen, a twenty-two-year-old who is establishing her own identity. Through her reactions to Maureen, Kate comes to understand much about herself and her own family, and she finally grasps the relevance of a recurring dream about a seal. The seal dream appears fifteen times in the novel, and the basic image is of Kate struggling to return an abandoned seal to the ocean. When Kate is finally able to finish the dream and return the seal to water, she realizes that what she has been burdened with is her own ego and that she must fight against the power of repressive institutions and roles.

THE MEMOIRS OF A SURVIVOR

Lessing again shows the conjunction between the individual and the larger society, including the importance of responsibility and direction, in *The Memoirs of a Survivor*. In this dystopian rendering of the "near future," the unnamed first-person narrator records her observations of a world in a state of cultural and social decline following an unexplained catastrophe. A stranger consigns into the narrator's care a girl of about twelve, Emily, who has with her Hugo, an ugly cat/dog creature. Much of the novel describes Emily's accelerated development through puberty and her association with Gerald, a young gang leader who, with Emily's help, tries to rebuild some semblance of order or at least some system of survival in a degenerated and nonfunctional society.

From the window of her apartment, the narrator watches groups abandon the city, never to be heard from again, and she witnesses the collapse of civilization, demonstrated particularly in the very young children; for them, not only respect for others but also language itself has broken down, and they attack their victims or one another with barbaric yaps. In the midst of all this collapse, the narrator has become aware of another layer of reality in and through the walls of her apartment. When she enters this space, she is confronted with a variety of scenes from the past, not necessarily her own past, and usually she sees something that she must do. On one journey through the walls she glimpses a figure of a woman, perhaps a goddess or some aspect of herself, who fills her with a sense of hope. Surrounded by despair in the present world, the narrator constructs an alternative visionary world, and at the end of the novel, when even the air is unbreathable, the collapsed world is left behind as the narrator steps through the wall through both a willed and a magical transformation. She takes with her Emily and Gerald and their group of youngsters as well as Hugo, transformed from an ugly beast into something shining with hope and promise.

CANOPUS IN ARGOS SERIES

After a rare gap of five years without a novel, Doris Lessing burst forth with *Shikasta*, which she announced was the first in a series called Canopus in Argos: Archives, and in the next four years she published the other four books in the series. A number of loyal readers were disappointed with what Lessing called her "space fiction," with its undeveloped, stylized characters and strangely unexciting interplanetary rivalries, but the series attracted for Lessing a new audience of science-fiction readers. Taken as a whole, the series continues Lessing's themes: the individual versus the collective, political systems and their interference with racial and sexual equality, the interconnectedness of all life, and the need for a more enlightened consciousness.

Some of the terms that have been used to describe the varied genres in the Canopus in Argos novels—outer-space fiction, science fiction, fantasy, psychomyth, allegory, utopian—indicate the variety within and among these books. They do not even comfortably fit the classification of a series, or *roman-fleuve*, since traditionally a series centers on a single character, as Lessing's Children of Violence centers on Martha Quest. *Shikasta* is filled with reports, journals, and interviews by aliens who discuss the fate of Earth, or Shikasta. *The Marriages Between Zones Three, Four, and Five* does not seem to be set on another planet so much as in the realm of myth and legend as Al·Ith moves between the zones in search of her destiny. *The Sirian Experiments* is told by a woman named Ambien II, who is a leading administrator in the Sirian Colonial Service. She discovers that the rival Canopean Empire is actually in advance of Sirius in every way and more deserving of conducting experiments on Shikasta than is her own empire, though the Sirians certainly do not want to hear this. *The Making of the Representative for Planet 8* is the story of a small planet whose inhabitants live comfortably until the time of The Ice begins, with ice and snow covering most of the globe. The inhabitants are unable to emigrate, but a few of them survive in some nonphysical but essential existence. *Documents Relating to the Sentimental Agents in the Volyen Empire* uses testimonies and histories to show that the Volyen Empire has failed to keep its promises to its inhabitants and to the cosmos. The empire suffers a rhetoric-induced downfall, as its leaders become enamored with the sound of their grand ideas rather than performing the actions that should have accompanied them.

None of the narrators and voices in the Canopus in Argos series is entirely reliable, and many questions are left unanswered. Perhaps this confusion is itself Lessing's goal: to make her readers question and reconsider ideas and actions. As Johor, an emissary to Shikasta, comments on the very first page of the series: "Things change. That is all we may be sure of. . . . This is a catastrophic universe, always; and subject to sudden reversals, upheavals, changes, cataclysms, with joy never anything but the song of substance under pressure forced into new forms and shapes."

THE DIARIES OF JANE SOMERS

The same year the final volume of Canopus in Argos was published, another novel appeared, titled *The Diary of a Good Neighbour*, purportedly by a new British writer, Jane Somers. It was not until the following year, and after the publication of another Jane Somers novel, *If the Old Could...*, that Lessing publicly revealed her authorship with the publication of the two novels together as *The Diaries of Jane Somers*. In her introduction to that book, Lessing discusses some of her reasons for having used a pseudonym. One was to create a new persona as the narrator: How would a real Jane Somers write? Another was to show the difficulties unestablished writers have in getting published, and indeed the first manuscript was rejected by several publishers before it was accepted by Michael Joseph in London, the same firm that had accepted the unknown Doris Lessing's *The Grass Is Singing* nearly four decades earlier. Lessing also says that she wanted the novels to be judged on their own merit, apart from the Lessing canon. When the Jane Somers novels first appeared, they sold in only modest numbers and received favorable but very limited attention from reviewers. Lessing notes that the modern publishing business markets high-volume, high-profile authors rather than new and experimental novelists.

The Diaries of Jane Somers focuses on old age, especially the relationship that develops between the middle-aged Jane Somers, head of a high-fashion magazine, and Maudie Fowler, a poor but proud woman in her nineties. Set in London, the novels, particularly *The Diary of a Good Neighbour*, give an insightful analysis of contemporary health care services and again show the impacts of social attitudes and government policies on the individual. The social realism of the novel, with its discussions of aging and dying, is given contrast by the summaries of novels that Jane writes about Maudie's life. Maudie tells stories of her long, hard life, and Jane transforms them into successful romanticized fictions, which Maudie then enjoys hearing. Jane is repeatedly mistaken for a "Good Neighbour," a social worker, as though there could be no other explanation for her friendship with Maudie.

THE FIFTH CHILD *and* BEN, IN THE WORLD

In her next novel, *The Good Terrorist*, Lessing depicts rather stupid and totally unsympathetic would-be revolutionaries who move from city to city in England planning random bombings. Contrary to the title, no good terrorist appears in the work, and it is just as well that these characters have a tendency to blow up themselves accidentally rather than killing others. A much more interesting novel is *The Fifth Child*, which can be read as an accurate and realistic account of an unfortunate English family, but which other readers have perceived as a science-fiction fantasy, a tale of an alien being born into a human family. The novel hovers on some point that embraces both readings.

The setting of *The Fifth Child* is England in the 1960's. Harriet and David Lovatt want a big family and a settled home life. Everything seems to be working according to their plan until the birth of Ben, their fifth child. Ben has nothing childlike about him. He is gruesome in appearance, insatiably hungry, abnormally strong, demanding, and violent. In no way does he fit into the happy home, but Harriet, steeped in the idea of motherhood, cannot bear to abandon him in some mental institution and insists on keeping him with her. As the years pass, the older children escape, though already harmed by Ben's weirdness and violence, and even David finally recognizes that he cannot continue to live with such a creature. The novel ends in despair, the problems unresolved. Ben is well on his way to becoming a fully grown criminal, a rapist and murderer, with no one able to subdue him. The story of the Lovatts becomes a parable of the modern world, the vision of a simple and happy existence shattered within the family itself and a society unwilling to confront and unable to control its own most brutal aspects.

Twelve years after *The Fifth Child*, Lessing provided a sequel, *Ben, in the World*. Ben does not know how old he is, and when he is told he needs a birth certificate to obtain papers for work or medical care, he tries to find his mother to ask her about this. Harriet Lovatt has moved from place to place to make it impossible for her fifth child to find her. When Ben finally locates her in a park, he cannot ask her, because she is with her favorite son, Paul, the sight of whom always fills Ben with murderous rage. Ben has indeed been in trouble, but for the most part he controls his rages. Lessing in this sequel novel presents Ben as a victim, alienated from society. He is cheated out of wages from one of the few jobs he has ever had and is set up by a con man who uses him as an unwitting drug carrier. Occasionally someone, such as the prostitute Rita, helps him or pities him, but never for long. Ben is so large and physically odd that most people automatically fear and shun him. When Rita first sees him naked, she thinks he is not human: the thick hair over all his body, the hunched shoulders, the long dangling arms, the animal barks and grunts. A mad scientist wants to experiment on Ben, and he cages Ben in a lab where horrific experiments are being conducted on animals. In a sad and unlikely scenario, Ben ends up in the high Andes mountains in South America, where he has been led to believe there are other creatures like himself.

LOVE, AGAIN

Lessing's novel *Love, Again* confronts the uncertainty of love and the decisions made because of love. Sarah, an aging theater manager, writes a play based on the true story of a young, beautiful biracial Frenchwoman named Julie Varion. Julie has many eligible suitors in her life, but none commits himself to her because of family pressures of status and community responsibility. Julie finally becomes engaged to an older gentleman, but she mysteriously dies before the wedding. Writing about this alluring character and her life is emotionally trying for Sarah, who feels that she, unlike Julie, is unable to act on her love interests because of her age. Unable to act on her feelings, Sarah suffers silently through her painful longings for a twenty-eight-year-old actor and a thirty-five-year-old director. Sarah eventually comes to terms with her age through painful moments of realization and acceptance.

MARA AND DANN NOVELS

Mara and Dann is an exciting adventure story set thousands of years in the future. The two main characters, Mara and her brother Dann, were kidnapped from their home with the Mahondi tribe when Mara was seven and Dann was four. In order to stay alive, the two are forced to change their names when they are taken to a village of the Rock People, a tribe considered less advanced than the Mahondi. Mara stays in the village until she becomes a strong young woman who desires to learn as much as possible even as she faces starvation and drought; she is sold into slavery and taken prisoner to be a breeder for other tribes. Dann suffers through abductions and addictions and becomes divided in his desires and duties toward his sister. Through his dreamworld, Dann faces his fears and eventually accepts his past experiences. Although the two are separated many times, they never stop searching for each other even at the risk of slavery and death. The novel suggests the survival of the human mind and spirit even through the most severe times, although issues of racism, greed, and the abuse of power remain.

The Story of General Dann and Mara's Daughter, Griot, and the Snow Dog is a sequel to *Mara and Dann*, and the long title indicates the four main characters. Dann's beloved sister Mara is dead, but her baby, Tamar, has survived, and Dann is finally united with her when she is six years old. When Dann learns Mara is dead, he descends into despair, but through the help of Griot, a soldier who had served under him when Dann was a general, and Ruff, a remarkable white dog that Dann has rescued as a puppy from a frozen lake, Dann survives. He hates the continual, ubiquitous wars, and he turns his interest to trying to learn more about the ancient past, when people had more knowledge available to them and even had things like books and airplanes and big cities. He impresses the need for knowledge on his little niece, Tamar, although the reality of their lives is to be on the move, longing to know more about past cultures and dreaming that somehow future eras can again inhabit a more livable planet, filled with more than ice or deserts, and can create a social order that provides peace for all.

PLAYING THE GAME

Playing the Game is a graphic novel. Its sixty-four pages contain a moralistic fantasy about Spacer Joe Magnifico Simpetco and his hope of love in a soulless, violent urban environment. Accompanying the text are illustrations by Charles Adlard. Lessing was ahead of her time in creating this contribution to what would later become an established genre, again demonstrating her multiple experiments in fiction.

THE SWEETEST DREAM

In *The Sweetest Dream*, Lessing traces the lives of a wide cast of characters for several decades. The novel starts in the 1960's, a decade that brought many changes to the world. Frances Lennox, for lack of money after her husband Johnny has left, lives with her two sons in her former mother-in-law's huge house. Frances serves as a mother figure to an ever-changing group of young people who come to the house for food and shelter, as does Johnny, who sees himself as a charismatic leader who can recruit the motley group to a glorious vision of communism that will save the world, but in reality Johnny will do almost anything to avoid work. Much of the second half of the novel takes place in Africa, where Frances's son Andrew Lennox has become rich working with corrupt African officials, and Sylvia, one of the group, has become a doctor working with extremely poor natives in a scarcely funded bush hospital. The adult lives of Andrew and Sylvia symbolize well the outcome of the youthful "dreams" of the 1960's.

THE CLEFT

In contrast with her futuristic works, in *The Cleft* Lessing depicts a period early in the development of the human race—indeed, a time when there were only females, and female babies. At some point, the women inexplicably found themselves having babies that were different. The story is told by an aging Roman senator, based on some ancient documents that purportedly reveal the past. He deduces that the women first killed the "monsters," but eventually some kindhearted ones left them out on a rock, and big eagles carried them off to a place across the river where the placid women never ventured. Eventually, who knows after how long, the more adventurous group, the "Squirts," as the women called them, met up with the "Clefts," the women, and, as one might say, the rest is history. This speculative fiction allows Lessing to explore the age-old problem of relationships between the sexes, and the use of the Roman narrator reveals the patriarchal views that were common in his time. In fairly obvious allusion to the present, the novel also includes a vast climate change, referred to as "the Noise," which always means hard times for animal species of any sex.

ALFRED AND EMILY

In her 2008 novel *Alfred and Emily*, Lessing combines fiction and memoir. This innovation is reminiscent of *The Golden Notebook*, in which Anna Wulf writes a novel, included in the overall text, based on what happens in the rest of the novel, and of *The Diary of a Good Neighbour*, when Jane Somers fictionalizes the hard life of her aged friend Maudie in a novel that makes Maudie's life romantic and happy. *Alfred and Emily* starts with what is labeled a novella. It presents a fictitious version of what Lessing's parents' lives might have been if World War I had not taken place. The two do meet, but they are only acquaintances. Alfred's leg is not shattered by shrapnel, and the doctor Emily loved did not die when the ship he was on was torpedoed. Alfred farms in his home country, England, and marries a conventional wife, Betsy. Emily abandons her idea of being a singer, becomes a nurse, leaves that career when she marries a wealthy but cold doctor, and, after his death, uses his fortune to help the poor. She is always discontent.

In the second part, Lessing combines biography and autobiography to tell what her parents' life together was really like and how that life affected Lessing as a child. One particular image is of her being roughly bundled by her mother's hard, impatient hands, which Lessing dates to the birth of her younger brother, whom she knows her mother always preferred. It is a nearly primal image, and Lessing describes it in almost the same words she uses in her autobiography, *Under My Skin*. Even earlier, in *The Memoirs of a Survivor*, she wrote a similar scene in which an irritated and impatient mother bundles her little girl into bed and turns quickly to cuddle her baby boy. This coincides with the continuing saga of Lessing's conflicts with her mother, made even more complicated by her pity for her, since she knows her mother is never happy with her husband or her life. Emily's mother had died when Emily was only three, and she was raised by a stepmother who did not love her. Lessing shows that what happens to individuals in childhood shapes their destinies, just as war shapes the destinies of all.

Lois A. Marchino
Updated by Mary A. Blackmon

OTHER MAJOR WORKS

SHORT FICTION: *This Was the Old Chief's Country*, 1951; *Five: Short Novels*, 1953; *No Witchcraft for Sale: Stories and Short Novels*, 1956; *The Habit of Loving*, 1957; *A Man and Two Women*, 1963; *African Stories*, 1964; *The Black Madonna*, 1966; *Winter in July*, 1966; *Nine African Stories*, 1968; *The Temptation of Jack Orkney, and Other Stories*, 1972 (also known as *The Story of a Non-marrying Man, and Other Stories*); *This Was the Old Chief's Country: Volume 1 of Doris Lessing's Collected African Stories*, 1973; *The Sun Between Their Feet: Volume 2 of Doris Lessing's Collected African Stories*, 1973; *Sunrise on the Veld*, 1975; *A Mild Attack of Locusts*, 1977; *Collected Stories*, 1978 (2 volumes; also known as *Stories*); *London Observed: Stories and Sketches*, 1991 (also known as *The Real Thing: Stories and Sketches*, 1992); *Spies I Have Known, and Other Stories*, 1995; *The Old Age of El Magnifico*, 2000; *The Grandmothers*, 2003.

PLAYS: *Each His Own Wilderness*, pr. 1958; *Play with a Tiger*, pr., pb. 1962; *Making of the Representative for Planet 8*, pr. 1988 (libretto); *Play with a Tiger, and Other Plays*, 1996.

POETRY: *Fourteen Poems*, 1959.

NONFICTION: *Going Home*, 1957; *In Pursuit of the English: A Documentary*, 1960; *Particularly Cats*, 1967; *A Small Personal Voice*, 1974; *Prisons We Choose to Live Inside*, 1987; *The Wind Blows Away Our Words*, 1987; *African Laughter: Four Visits to Zimbabwe*, 1992; *Doris Lessing: Conversations*, 1994 (also known as *Putting the Questions Differently: Interviews with Doris Lessing, 1964-1994*, 1996); *Shadows on the Wall of the Cave*, 1994; *A Small Personal Voice: Essays, Reviews, Interviews*, 1994; *Under My Skin*, 1994 (autobiography); *Walking in the Shade*, 1997 (autobiography); *Time Bites: Views and Reviews*, 2005.

MISCELLANEOUS: *The Doris Lessing Reader*, 1988.

BIBLIOGRAPHY

Galen, Müge. *Between East and West: Sufism in the Novels of Doris Lessing*. Albany: State University of New York Press, 1997. Provides an introduction to Sufism and discusses how the ideas of Sufism have influenced Lessing and her novels. Focuses on her space-fiction utopias as an alternative to modern Western lifestyles.

Greene, Gayle. *Doris Lessing: The Poetics of Change*. Ann Arbor: University of Michigan Press, 1997. Examines how Lessing's novels are concerned with change, taking several different critical approaches to the works, including Marxist, feminist, and Jungian approaches.

Klein, Carole. *Doris Lessing: A Biography*. New York: Carroll & Graf, 2000. Unauthorized biography (Lessing specifically refused to cooperate with Klein) nonetheless draws on interviews with Lessing's acquaintances and makes connections between events in Lessing's life and episodes in her novels.

Maslen, Elizabeth. *Political and Social Issues in British Women's Fiction, 1928-1968*. New York: Palgrave Macmillan, 2001. Presents analysis of how British women writers in the mid-twentieth century, including Lessing, chose to represent such issues as war, race, class, and gender.

Perrakis, Phyllis Sternberg, ed. *Spiritual Exploration in the Works of Doris Lessing*. Westport, Conn.: Greenwood Press, 1999. Interesting collection of essays looks at spiritual themes in Lessing's work, touching on both the realistic and the science-fiction novels.

Pickering, Jean. *Understanding Doris Lessing*. Columbia: University of South Carolina Press, 1990. Provides a brief, clear overview of Lessing's work through the late 1980's. Begins with biographical information and an analytical look at Lessing's career, then presents a short but sharp analysis of her fiction through *The Fifth Child*. Includes annotated bibliography and index.

Waterman, David F. *Identity in Doris Lessing's Space Fiction*. Youngstown, N.Y.: Cambria Press, 2000. Discusses the five novels in the Canopus in Argos series and others of Lessing's futuristic works, including *The Memoirs of a Survivor*. Asserts that these novels show the devastating effects of hierarchies in society as individuals and groups violently vie for power instead of striving for cooperation. Includes bibliographical references and index.

Whittaker, Ruth. *Doris Lessing*. New York: St. Martin's Press, 1988. Provides information on Lessing's background and influences as well as a short but excellent overview of Lessing's fiction through *The Good Terrorist*. Includes bibliography and index.

Yelin, Louise. *From the Margins of Empire: Christina Stead, Doris Lessing, Nadine Gordimer*. Ithaca, N.Y.: Cornell University Press, 1998. Discusses how the three authors approach the issue of national identity. Three chapters on Lessing (in a section titled "Doris Lessing: In Pursuit of the English") focus on the process of her "Englishing" after leaving Rhodesia.

BHARATI MUKHERJEE

Born: Calcutta (now Kolkata), West Bengal, India; July 27, 1940

OTHER LITERARY FORMS

Bharati Mukherjee was initially propelled to literary fame with the publication of short stories that provide intense portraits of "immigrant experiences" and cultural collisions through her kaleidoscopic characters; these stories have been published in the collections *Darkness* (1985) and *The Middleman, and Other Stories* (1988). In these brilliant and multifaceted stories, Mukherjee depicts the harsh realities of the "stranger in a strange land" who may find him- or herself confronted with the challenges of understanding new cultures, coping with "otherness," and learning new ways of being. An immigrant herself, Mukherjee delineates in these stories the hardship of and the need for transforming oneself that is inherent in the immigrant experience.

Mukherjee is also recognized for her nonfiction works that deal with the immigrant experience from both political and social perspectives. Her *Days and Nights in Calcutta* (1977), coauthored with her husband, Clark Blaise, demonstrates a bipartite perspective on India: from a returning native (the author) and a foreigner (American-born Blaise). Such a perspective allows for a complex and multilayered look at the complications of being a "citizen" in transition.

Mukherjee has written several studies on political issues and India—studies that demonstrate her continuing interest in placing her fictional concerns within a historical perspective. *The Sorrow and the Terror: The Haunting Legacy of the Air India Tragedy* (1987), coauthored with Blaise, not only examines the personal tragedy of the families involved in the suspected terrorist bombing of an Air India flight in 1985 (to New Delhi from Toronto) but also scrutinizes the role played in the event by the Canadian government's shortsighted immigration policies. Mukherjee also has produced a significant body of work that consists of uncollected essays and articles on women's issues, the intersection of politics and multiculturalism, and the history of India.

ACHIEVEMENTS

In addition to blazing a path for female Indian writers, Bharati Mukherjee has succeeded in initiating a new focus for an entire group of writers: the impact and importance of the immigrant experience. It is an experience that is relevant not only to the immigrant but also to the population of the receiving culture. Mukherjee has been cited as "embracing" American culture and "hopeful" at the regenerative effects of amalgamating her Indian heritage with a constantly metamorphosing American culture.

For both her scholarship and her literary production, Mukherjee has received fellowships, awards, and other recognition, most notably a P.E.O. International Peace Scholarship to the University of Iowa's Writers' Workshop and the National Book Critics Circle Award for fiction (1988) for *The Middleman, and Other Stories*—a work of superbly crafted portraits of a multitude of characters in conflict while acculturating to new homes, families, or cultures. Mukherjee has become known worldwide for her works that somehow define what it means to be an American and, as Radha Chakravarty has noted, what it means to "find a voice to express a complex, cross-cultural sensibility."

BIOGRAPHY

Although born in India to parents of a Bengali Brahman (upper-class) caste, Bharati Mukherjee became a citizen of the world early in life. Born in July, 1940, to a father who was a prosperous pharmaceutical chemist and business owner and to a freethinking mother, both of whom wanted education and freedom of action for their daughters, Mukherjee experienced a rather cosmopolitan education. In 1947, after India won its independence from Great Britain, she was enrolled in boarding schools in England and Switzerland, where she perfected her English. Her native Bengali language and customs were marginalized by her educators, and she returned to Calcutta (now known as Kolkata) somewhat a cultural "outsider" to her native India. There she completed her secondary education at Loreto House, taught by Irish nuns.

Mukherjee continued her education, obtaining a bachelor's degree in English at the University of Calcutta and a master's degree in both English and ancient Indian culture at the University of Baroda (1961). Subsequently, she was part of the Writers' Workshop at the University of Iowa and began her literary and teaching career, the latter of which included positions at Marquette University in Milwaukee, the University of Wisconsin at Madison, McGill University in Montreal, Columbia University in New York, and the University of California at Berkeley.

It was at the University of Iowa that Mukherjee received both an M.F.A. and a Ph.D. In 1963, she married Clark Blaise, with whom she migrated to Toronto. Issues with local racism caused Mukherjee to reevaluate her adopted country and seek residence in the United States. In her essay "An Invisible Woman," published in the Toronto magazine *Saturday Night* in 1981, Mukherjee decried the racism she felt there, presenting a negative picture of Canada's attitude toward its burgeoning immigrant population. As a result, she and her husband sought a more amenable environment for teaching and writing in the United States, which Mukherjee has described as a more fluid environment—one that does not demand passive accommodation but instead allows the immigrant to "help build a culture."

While teaching at McGill, Mukherjee completed her first novel, *The Tiger's Daughter.* It is the story of a conflicted female protagonist who returns to India and is disillusioned by the gap between her memories of her homeland and its reality—a reality even more striking after her sojourn in the West. In the following years, Mukherjee returned repeatedly to India, spending the year 1973 there with her husband on sabbatical. In 1980, the two settled permanently in the United States, and Mukherjee began teaching at a number of institutions while writing. She held the position of writer-in-residence at Emory University in 1984, and her first collection of short fiction, *Darkness*, was published the following year. Many works followed as Mukherjee progressed in her craft and in her vision—the two novels *Wife* and *Jasmine*, short stories, articles, and nonfiction books that entered more directly into political arenas. In 1989, Mukherjee accepted the position of distinguished professor at the University of California at Berkeley, where she has continued to pursue her writing.

ANALYSIS

Bharati Mukherjee has spent many years as a writer and commentator on social issues that involve her native India, immigrants, and the developing "face" of the United States—designating herself first and foremost as an American writer. She has carefully distinguished between herself as an immigrant writer and what is termed an "expatriate writer"; the latter may still be involved in "nostalgia" for a home country instead of redefining him- or herself in an innovative and mutating cultural sense. In fact, some critics have described Mukherjee as both a postcolonialist writer and a feminist writer, but these two "agendas" are not her prime focus, although in redefining their identities in new environments, her protagonists and characters may be shedding "old thought" perceptions of themselves endemic to colonial or gender-oppressive societies. Mukherjee's writing goes beyond these two narrowly defined categories, and her ideas always entail the identity and individuality of transmigrating people and their interactions with old and new worlds.

Furthermore, in her later novels, Mukherjee abandons linear progression and traditional points of view to interweave tales that span centuries, continents, and personal histories. In her long fiction, Mukherjee has progressed from the omnisciently narrated novel (*The Tiger's Daughter*) that, the author has admitted, attempted to imitate British models such as Jane Austen to the intense stream-of-consciousness and first-person personas in *Wife* and *Jasmine*, respectively. This progression of narrative style has been accompanied by greater emphasis on her characters' abilities to negotiate (or attempt to negotiate) the very necessary transformations that form the central focus of her fiction; as she states in her introduction to the short-story collection *Darkness*, "We are a series of fluid identities . . . culture never stops."

Thus, despite violence, racism, and destruction of psychic "selves," the underlying message of Mukherjee's fiction is hope—for a new America, a transformative one, that allows its citizens to create and re-create themselves in myriad ways. Such an attitude characteristically informs her female protagonists, who often take on multiple identities (*Jasmine, The Holder of the World, Desirable Daughters, Leave It to Me*) and liberate themselves metaphorically through separation, expatriation, divorce, and even murder.

Mukherjee's themes, therefore, deal with the forging of identity—both personal and national. For the author, this forging is insistently constant and self-altering, and this state of flux must be accepted, even embraced. This flux and complexity are increasingly mirrored in Mukherjee's long fiction, as the works become progressively more layered and more complex—intermixing time frames and personalities from strikingly different cultures. Mukherjee herself seems to have expanded and extended her narrative goals even further—her two novels *Desirable Daughters* and *The Tree Bride* are in fact a continuing story, the latter a sequel and perhaps the middle of a trilogy that circumscribes an even larger reality, amalgamating history, myth, tradition, and change.

Another aspect explored in Mukherjee's fiction is the nature of female self-identity, which often reflects the larger society in which her heroines are positioned. India, her homeland, has been cited as a constant presence in her work, but it informs her work not merely as a singular cultural stance but also as a particular background of an individual human being. In a 2003 interview, Mukherjee stated that "the writer can only write about the individual self." Mukherjee's themes, however, encompass, paradoxically, both a global and a personal consciousness, and it is this intersection that makes her works so valuable and engrossing. Her style—in both short and long fiction—tends to mix opposites, shuffle ironies, and connect past with present. Mukherjee has been cited as a masterful writer of immigrant literature, but certainly, in the United States, she speaks for all.

WIFE

The narrative of Mukherjee's second novel, *Wife*, focuses on Dimple Dasgupta, who is traditionally united with her husband in an arranged marriage and yet untraditionally transplanted to New York City. Without a support system, Dimple becomes increasingly alienated, an alienation that leaves her as a double outsider—outside her current new culture and outside her old culture. Dimple progressively loses touch with reality until, almost instinctively, she "knows" that to survive she must kill herself (to release herself from the world) or kill her husband (to release herself from incongruent old-world traditions). She chooses the latter, stabbing her husband while he prosaically consumes a bowl of cereal.

The novel is written in the third person, but Mukherjee's focus and tone are deeply personal and totally internal (unlike the more stilted and classic style of *The Tiger's Daughter*), and the only clear, unified perspective received is that of Dimple, who becomes a tragic heroine. Dimple's story depicts one woman's struggle to maintain her sense of self—and her ultimate defeat. Dimple is a victim because she no longer clearly understands her "role" in the world: She has not the strength, stamina, or status of Tara, the heroine of *The Tiger's Daughter.*

Mukherjee emphatically portrays the inner workings of the claustrophobic, paranoid psyche of a culturally deprived young woman who cannot deal with her strange external world. In addition, she does not love her husband, Amit, and subsequently floats between cultures, immersed in a liberating, yet distancing, culture while her partner will not let her partake in it—he denies her freedom to work and, incidentally, to wear slacks. Finally, having nothing with which to fill her "gaps" (except American television), Dimple infuses reality with fantasy and psychically collapses. Deftly, Mukherjee creates a world in which "cultural collisions" have impacts on feminist issues and indicate, in a striking way, the destructiveness of moving from one culture to another—as immigrant, human being, and woman.

JASMINE

Mukherjee's quintessential novel of exploration and self-actualization, *Jasmine* depicts a woman capable of transforming into many selves, assuming a new name that alternately signifies another identity that the heroine is able to assume in her metamorphosis of self. In *Jasmine* Mukherjee departs from linear construction and intermingles time frames and physical space. The protagonist travels from violence in her native village to the United States, where she is raped, where she murders, where she marries, and where she adopts children who, like her, are both global and time travelers.

Jasmine seeks ultimate freedom (a by-product of the American mentality), and in her quest she leaves much behind (her losses) but gains integration of self. Certainly, Jasmine's immigrating self also metaphorically represents the larger self of all humans in their "immigration" through life. Culturally, Jasmine may also adumbrate the Hindu belief in the transmigration of souls. In any case, Jasmine is a survivor and an emblem of the modern immigrant who must "die" in many ways, submit to violence (external racism, emotional loss, or both), and reinvent him- or herself in the "fusion chamber" of a new culture. A masterful, perfect novel, full of lyrical prose, *Jasmine* portrays the odyssey of one woman who is, by extension, all immigrants.

THE HOLDER OF THE WORLD

Mukherjee's supremely complex and intellectual novel *The Holder of the World* takes on the United States and India, juxtaposing them in two narrators: one (of Indian descent) in the form of a researcher or "asset-hunter" who stumbles upon her ancestor in the search for the perfect diamond and the other a Puritan woman (reminiscent of Nathaniel Hawthorne's Hester Prynne—an American woman ahead of her time) who becomes the lover of an Indian raja and transforms herself into "Salem Bibi." This novel displays Mukherjee's powers at an admirable high: Intermixing history and fantasy (verging on Magical

Realism) with dual narrators (Beigh Masters and her ancestor Hannah Easton), the author creates a sense of a journey through time—with two cultures contrapuntally commenting on adaptation and the complexity of self. Mysteries abound and discoveries are made—most important, that across time and geography people are indeed interconnected. Critics have described *The Holder of the World* as a "luminous gem of a novel" that possesses "staggering originality"; it allows readers to glimpse a multifaceted reality of self that has infinite permutations amid a discourse on the magical properties of storytelling (diaries and letters), art (Mughal miniature paintings), and the modern world of computers and virtual reality.

Sherry Morton-Mollo

OTHER MAJOR WORKS

SHORT FICTION: *Darkness*, 1985; *The Middleman, and Other Stories*, 1988.

NONFICTION: *Kautilya's Concept of Diplomacy*, 1976; *Days and Nights in Calcutta*, 1977 (with Clark Blaise); *The Sorrow and the Terror: The Haunting Legacy of the Air India Tragedy*, 1987 (with Blaise); *Political Culture and Leadership in India: A Study of West Bengal*, 1991; *Regionalism in Indian Perspective*, 1992.

BIBLIOGRAPHY

Alam, Fakrul. *Bharati Mukherjee*. New York: Twayne, 1996. Provides a good introduction to the author's life, works, and accomplishments.

Chakravarty, Radha. "Bharati Mukherjee." In *South Asian Writers in English*, edited by Fakrul Alam. Vol. 323 in *Dictionary of Literary Biography*. Detroit, Mich.: Gale Group, 2006. Biographical essay explores Mukherjee's progression thematically and examines her longer works through *Desirable Daughters*.

Chua, C. L. "Passages from India: Migrating to America in the Fiction of V. S. Naipaul and Bharati Mukherjee." In *Reworlding: The Literature of the Indian Diaspora*, edited by Emmanuel S. Nelson. Westport, Conn.: Greenwood Press, 1992. Discussion of Mukherjee's and Naipaul's work is part of a collection of essays that analyze a variety of Indian expatriate writing, scrutinizing the major areas of the diaspora and the "haunting presence" of India in the process of "reworlding."

Dascalu, Cristina Emanuela. *Imaginary Homelands of Writers in Exile: Salman Rushdie, Bharati Mukherjee, and V. S. Naipaul*. Youngstown, N.Y.: Cambria Press, 2007. Places Mukherjee's fiction within the category of the literature of exile, analyzing it along with the works of other postcolonial authors.

Mathur, Suchitra. "Bharati Mukherjee: An Overview." In *Feminist Writers*, edited by Pamela Kester-Shelton. Detroit, Mich.: St. James Press, 1996. Provides an overview of Mukherjee's thematic concerns and examines her position in the canon of American immigrant writers. Briefly discusses her four major novels as well as her short-story collections.

Morton-Mollo, Sherry. "Bharati Mukherjee." In *A Reader's Companion to the Short Story in English*, edited by Erin Fallon et al. Westport, Conn.: Greenwood Press, 2001. Presents biographical information, an overview of Mukherjee's work, and critical analysis of her fiction.

Nelson, Emmanuel S., ed. *Bharati Mukherjee: Critical Perspectives*. New York: Garland, 1993. Collection of essays on Mukherjee's work addresses various topics, including the uses of violence and eroticism in her fiction. Also provides biographical information.

ANAÏS NIN

Born: Paris, France; February 21, 1903
Died: Los Angeles, California; January 14, 1977
Also known as: Angela Anaïs Juana Antolina Rosa Edelmira Nin y Culmell

OTHER LITERARY FORMS

Anaïs Nin (nihn) published numerous volumes of perceptive literary criticism. Her highly acclaimed first book of nonfiction, *D. H. Lawrence: An Unprofessional Study*, appeared in 1932. In 1968, near the end of her career, she wrote *The Novel of the Future*, partly as an attempt to explain the literary philosophy that inspired her innovative fiction. In 1976, she published a collection of her essays, *In Favor of the Sensitive Man, and Other Essays*. During the last decade of her life, Nin was extremely active as a public speaker. *A Woman Speaks: The Lectures, Seminars, and Interviews of Anaïs Nin*, edited by Evelyn J. Hinz, was published in 1975.

Nin's published short stories, like her criticism, span her career. The most distinguished collection is *Under a Glass Bell, and Other Stories* (1944). Her apprentice writing is available in another collection, *Waste of Timelessness, and Other Early Stories* (1977), while two volumes of erotica were published after Nin's death: *Delta of Venus: Erotica* (1977) and *Little Birds: Erotica* (1979).

In addition to her works of fiction and criticism, Nin's extensive diary was published. Edited from a vast manuscript, this autobiographical work appeared in two series. The first series, *The Diary of Anaïs Nin*, comprises seven volumes, with the first volume appearing in 1966. The second series, *The Early Diaries of Anaïs Nin*, contains four volumes and was published between 1978 and 1985.

Anaïs Nin's achievement in literature is of two distinct kinds: artistic and sociological. Strongly influenced by Arthur Rimbaud, Marcel Proust, and D. H. Lawrence, Nin conceived of and developed a uniquely personal approach to style and structure that places her within the modernist tradition as it evolved in the French literature of the early decades of the twentieth century. Nin persisted in articulating, refining, and extending an avowedly "feminine" ideal of the novel; this resulted in lyrical novels in which the imagistic manner of the poet is fused with the psychological penetration of the novelist. In her treatment of character, time, and space, Nin belongs with such writers as Virginia Woolf, Djuna Barnes, and Anna Kavan.

Nin's sociological importance is related to her intention to create a specifically "feminine" novel in which the emphasis is on the evocation of feeling, and to portray as deeply and as honestly as possible an authentically female emotional experience. In this respect, her achievement may be compared with that of Woolf, Dorothy Richardson, Marguerite Duras, and a number of French writers, including Annie LeClerc, Hélène Cixous, Monique Wittig, and Julia Kristeva.

The audience for Nin's novels is smaller than for either her diary or her collections of erotica. As the diary increased Nin's audience, it also brought her fiction to the attention of well-qualified critics and scholars, many of whom have interpreted it in ways that make it more accessible to a general readership accustomed to the conventions of realism. Considering the climate of growing respect for and interest in Nin's novels, it seems that her reputation as a literary artist is now securely established.

Anaïs Nin was born in Paris on February 21, 1903, the oldest child of musicians Joaquin Nin and Rosa Culmell-Nin. Her parents' marriage was turbulent, and in 1913, Joaquin Nin deserted his family at Archachon, France. The following year, Rosa Culmell-Nin transported her daughter and two sons, Thorvald and Joaquin, to the United States. For some years, they lived in New York City and in Queens, actively participating in the lively Cuban community there, many of whose members were musicians. Nin has recorded this period of her life in *Linotte*. What stands out most poignantly is her inconsolable grief at the loss of her father and her intense worship of her mother. At this time, Nin's aspiration to become an artist of one sort or another strongly manifested itself, and her account of her adolescence is a rich study of the formative years of an artist.

In 1918, Nin left school to manage the household for her mother, who worked for Lord and Taylor as a special buyer for the Cuban clientele, and in 1923, Nin married Hugh P. Guiler (known as an engraver and filmmaker under the name of Ian Hugo). As a young married woman, Nin lived in France. Marriage caused her to experience intense conflicts, which she has described and analyzed in her diary. During those years, as in adolescence, Nin continued to write, and in 1932, she published her first book, *D. H. Lawrence*. This work brought about the explosive friendship with June and Henry Miller that she describes in the first published diary. Nin and Miller maintained a relationship until Nin's death.

In Paris during the 1930's, Nin embarked upon a lifelong devotion to psychotherapy. Her therapeutic relationship with the renowned Viennese psychoanalyst Otto Rank is recounted in the first volume of *The Diary of Anaïs Nin*. An independent, original, and forceful thinker whose special area of interest was the artist, Rank was of great assistance to Nin in the fulfillment of her artistic aspirations. His influence on her was so persuasive that for a time she actually considered making a living as a lay psychoanalyst. For a few months in 1934, she lived in New York and assisted Rank with his practice. In 1935, however, she resumed her literary work and returned to France to rejoin her husband, but with the outbreak of World War II, she again returned to the United States. This move in 1939 was to become permanent. It was not easy for Nin to give up her "romantic life" in Paris, as she called it, and her difficulty understanding Americans' disdain for the arts is a recurrent theme of her diary in the 1940's and 1950's.

Throughout her life, Nin maintained many friendships with writers and other artists. Among her friends and acquaintances were Lawrence Durrell, Robert Duncan, James Merrill, and Kenneth Patchen; performers Canada Lee, Josephine Premice, and Louise Rainer; Caresse Crosby, proprietor of the Black Sun Press; composer Edgard Varèse and his wife, translator Louise Varèse; collage artist Janko Varda; and the owner of the influential Gotham Book Mart, Frances Steloff. Even though Nin had widespread contacts among writers and artists in New York City and on the West Coast, she experienced continual frustration in the publishing world. On the whole, editors and critics were either hostile to her work or simply ignored it. The breakthrough of this period was the acceptance by Alan Swallow, founder of the famed Swallow Press, then located in Denver, Colorado, of the five works that constitute *Cities of the Interior: A Continuous Novel*. For many years, Nin was an underground literary figure with a small but enthusiastic following.

In 1966, Nin's status changed suddenly; she had already published all her fiction; the last book, *Collages*, appeared in 1964. When Harcourt Brace and World, with the Swallow Press, brought out the first volume of *The Diary of Anaïs Nin*, Nin quickly became a public figure. Because the content of the work expressed the feelings of many women who were experiencing deep evolutionary changes in their own lives, Nin involuntarily became a spokesperson for the women's movement. She achieved the "dialogue with the world" for which she had longed since childhood.

During the remaining years of Nin's life, individual volumes of her diary continued to appear, and Nin, although viewed as controversial by leaders of the women's movement, received considerable public acclaim. Traveling throughout the United States, she gave hundreds of talks at colleges and universities and undertook trips to various countries, including Sweden and Bali. In 1970, she was awarded the French Prix Sévigné, and in 1974, she was elected to the National Institute of Arts and Letters. Nin's books have been translated into all the major Western languages as well as Serbo-Croatian and Japanese.

ANALYSIS

It was natural that Anaïs Nin should grow up desiring to be an artist. Her father was a friend of Gabriele D'Annunzio. Before Nin's parents separated, their household was filled with the aura of the fin de siècle Symbolist movement. The Symbolists' ideas about art had a decisive and lasting influence on Nin, although she greatly transformed the influences she absorbed in the process of adapting them to the expressive needs of her own temperament.

Like the Symbolists, Nin believed that phenomena possess hidden meanings, significances that escape most people. The artist's task is to penetrate surfaces to reveal the truths they conceal. "The symbol," she wrote, "is an acknowledgement of the emotional and spiritual content of every act and every object around us." Equipped with heightened perception and expressive talent, the artist can interpret the vast confusing world of phenomena, revealing essences in a world of masks and misleading surfaces. Nin described a story as "a quest for meaning."

With the Symbolists, too, and with the later Surrealists, Nin shared a positive attitude toward dream and fantasy. Her books are poetic defenses of her belief in the unconscious as a source of the visions and imaginary experiences that complement verifiable reality, compensating for its limitations and endowing it with the richness of mental play that "reality" is not capable of providing. Nin stressed the positive aspects of fantasy in order to balance what she perceived as American society's mistrust, fear, and even condemnation of any sort of activity that is not directly productive in a materialistic way.

Nin's literary aspiration was formidable; she wanted to express passionately and powerfully that of which others were not aware, or if they were, could not express because they did not possess a creative medium. Throughout her life, Nin was searching for

> another kind of language, the inspirational, which is one that penetrates our unconscious directly and doesn't need to be analyzed or interpreted in a cerebral way. It penetrates us in the way that music does, through the senses.

That is why Nin, like so many other twentieth century writers, borrowed as widely as possible from the nonverbal arts. "My only structure," she wrote,

> is based on three forms of art—painting, dancing, music—because they correspond to the senses I find atrophied in literature today.

Inspired by many artists, including Claude Debussy, Paul Klee, her friend Janko Varda, Richard Lippold, Jean Tinguely, and Edgard Varèse, Nin looked not so much to poets (although Rimbaud influenced her style as well as her ideas) as to those novelists who were masters of a lyrical style: Lawrence, Jean Giraudoux, Pierre Jean Jouve, Barnes, and, above all, Proust. Nin's approach to the novel was that of a poet with a heightened and highly developed sense of language. Oliver Evans, who wrote the first book-length study of her work, called Nin "one of the best imagists writing in this country today." The image was her indispensable medium of expression; free association, which she learned to trust as a patient in psychotherapy, became the process through which she allowed literary structures to emerge. Always, Nin's subject was the self in its evolution, especially the self in relationships with others; her perspective was always psychological (she called psychology her "philosophy" and psychoanalysis her "school"), although her books do not demonstrate any particular school of psychoanalytical thought.

Dispensing with conventional plots and with the framework of linear chronology, Nin portrays her characters in a series of "shots" that derive their power from the carefully selected detail of their imagery. Her language, never purely decorative, is metaphorical in a truly organic sense. It is the language of lyrical poetry; the essence is compressed into a few words or phrases. Nin does not describe; rather, she interprets, and in the act of interpretation, she re-creates her subjects. To know Nin's characters, the reader, too, must interpret their action and their gestures and look beneath the surfaces.

Free association creates its own unique structures. Nin's writing is filled with patterns that are natural and spontaneous, having emerged from the associative flow of images. The form of her books is organic. Repetitions, inversions, and superimpositions are artfully arranged into significant patterns. Increasingly in Nin's later prose, readers will discover improvisatory flights in which images are treated as are themes in jazz. Fluency, fluidity, a sense of motion as well as continuity are what Nin sought in her fiction, an orchestration of a great many elements into a composition that moves through time horizontally and vertically at the same instant, an orchestration that expresses emotion with sensuousness and with emotional power that are impossible, she believed, to achieve in conventional realistic fiction.

HOUSE OF INCEST

House of Incest is not, technically speaking, a novel, but it is pertinent as being the source, as Nin herself said, of all her later fiction. *House of Incest* is the earliest and most extreme example of her "symphonic writing." It also introduces the essential questions of her lifelong exploration of the problem of reconciling human love with the needs of ever-evolving, mobile people, always in the process of transformation, growing through the process of change.

A prose poem, *House of Incest* was envisioned by Nin as a woman's version of Rimbaud's famed confession, *Une Saison en enfer* (1873, *A Season in Hell*, 1932). She wrote the book between 1932 and 1936, when she was intensely involved with psychotherapy, and it is composed entirely of dreams that have been cut, altered, polished, and artfully arranged to express an agonizing journey into the psyche of the nameless first-person narrator. Her suffering is caused by the sundering of feeling from sensuality, of emotion from sexuality, of body from soul. *House of Incest* is filled with images of fragmentation and mutilation.

Like *A Season in Hell*, Nin's prose poem is a confession. The narrator yearns to express her pain and to confess that even when she imagines that she loves another, it is only a projection of herself. In the other, then, she loves only herself. The "house" of the title refers to the self, perhaps specifically to the body; "incest" suggests the sterility of feeling imprisoned inside this self, unable to transcend its boundaries through the supreme act of loving another.

Two types of "incest" are suggested by the book's two personae, both of whom strongly attract the narrator. They are Sabina, lush, sensuous, and irresponsible, freely engaging in sex without emotional commitment; and Jeanne, an aristocrat with a crippled leg, a woman who "strangles" her guitar when she tries to make it produce music. Jeanne is hopelessly in love with her brother. The emotional damage caused by such an inverted fixation is explored in Nin's later works, "The Voice," *Winter of Artifice*, and "Under a Glass Bell" (from the story collection with the same title).

The extreme difficulty of achieving a stable, committed love while continuing to "turn and change" is at the center of all Nin's novels. A positive resolution appears only in the later books *Seduction of the Minotaur* and *Collages*, both of which are lighter in tone than earlier works.

WINTER OF ARTIFICE

Winter of Artifice comprises three "novelettes" (Nin's term): "Stella," *Winter of Artifice*, and "The Voice." Written in 1944, when Nin was planning a series of interconnected novels and struggling with the psychological issues of the woman as artist, "Stella" explores the failure of connection between a woman's personal life and her work; this failure is caused by a neurosis that is unchallenged. As a film star, Stella is much more glamorous, vital, self-assured, and daring than in private life (her "mask" may be said to dominate her "self"). The contrast is so great that when Stella sits in the audience watching one of her own films, she is never recognized. The most important object in her apartment is a "very large, very spacious Movie Star bed of white satin," which she usually occupies alone. The connection that Nin sought between the personal life and the artistic expression of this life does not occur for Stella. Like others, she has been damaged by her childhood, but she has done nothing to repair this damage. Because Stella "did not grow," Nin decided not to include her as one of the major characters in *Cities of the Interior*. Viewed as a psychological portrait of a narcissist, however, "Stella" is an insightful piece of work, and it is brilliantly expressed.

When evaluated exclusively as art, "The Voice" is one of Nin's most original and daring pieces. It is both an extended portrait of a kind and self-neglectful psychotherapist (perhaps suggested by Otto Rank), and an animated essay or exposition of ideas through a seemingly random selection of characters and incidents. "The Voice" is a virtuoso piece that spins off from contrasting motions: soaring, plummeting, floating, sinking, spiraling, rushing, and flowing; it is an excellent example of Nin's deft way of translating characters and incidents into imagery.

The center of this active world is a psychoanalyst's office located in a skyscraper. Tortured New Yorkers, The Voice's patients include Djuna (who becomes one of the principals in *Cities of the Interior*), a young violinist who wishes to be released from her lesbian desires; Mischa, a cellist whose emotions are paralyzed; and Lilith, who suffers from frigidity. The Voice himself falls in love with Lilith, the only one of his patients who can see beyond her own needs to the hungers of the man whose voice is so comforting to the others. As in Nin's later books, Djuna plays the role of comforting confidant to both parties in this impossible dream of love between analyst and patient.

Winter of Artifice is perhaps the most musical of Nin's works; it is also among the most courageous in its subject: an adult daughter's flirtation and near union with the handsome, seductive father who abandoned her when she was a child. The theme is "musique Ancienne," to quote Nin, the Oedipal temptation told from the point of view of the highly intelligent yet vulnerable daughter. *Winter of Artifice* was begun in 1933, when Nin started therapy with Rank, and was completed in 1939, the year of Rank's death.

The novelette is organized in thirteen "movements." A climax of emotional and erotic yearning occurs in the sixth, central movement. From this excruciating height of desire, the work subsides into a slower rhythm and a sadder tone. Eventually, *Winter of Artifice* becomes a solo for the daughter. When she sees her father's "feminine-looking" foot, she imagines that it is really her foot and that he has stolen it. Now she understands that he would like to steal her youth and her capacity for action, her mobility. "Tired of his ballet dancing" (formal, traditional movements), the daughter symbolically reclaims her foot and, with it, her ability to flee from the dangers of the attraction: "*Music runs and I run with it.*"

CITIES OF THE INTERIOR

The five novels found in the final version of *Cities of the Interior*, Nin's "continuous novel," are *Ladders to Fire, Children of the Albatross, The Four-Chambered Heart, A Spy in the House of Love,* and *Seduction of the Minotaur.* They were first published individually during the 1940's and 1950's. Entries in Nin's diary indicate that she began writing *Ladders to Fire* in 1937; she made substantial revisions as late as 1962. *Seduction of the Minotaur,* which was published individually in 1961, was begun in 1938 and expanded in 1958 to include *Solar Barque.* Alan Swallow, a pioneer among small-press publishers, brought out the five novels under their collective title in 1959. When it was first published, *Cities of the Interior* had been growing for twenty years. An extraordinary work, it displays a brilliance of conception, a mastery of image and metaphor, and a refinement of structural technique that make it the equal of many better-known modern masterpieces.

The book's subtitle, *A Continuous Novel*, suggests the timeless scope of this work. The "cities" of the title are both ancient and modern. Nin set out to excavate the buried cities or the psychic worlds of her three main characters: Lillian, Djuna, and Sabina. The idea of "continuity," however, is more complex. It suggests that *Cities of the Interior* is an open work, like certain modern sculptures that extend into and penetrate the space that surrounds them, interacting with their setting.

This multifaceted work is not set apart from life, not carved out of it, not bounded by the conventions of classically written fiction with its concluding "resolution." *Cities of the Interior* remains open to the addition of new parts and to the rearrangement of its five basic novel units. The individual books are entirely self-contained. As Nin uses the word, "continuous" does not mean "to be continued." It does not refer to linear progressive time. There is no fixed starting point and no concluding point. The books have been bound—because books, seemingly, must be bound—in the order in which they were written.

A reader can begin with any one of the five volumes and move to the other four in any order, losing no essential connections. In short, the five novels of *Cities of the Interior* are interchangeable in the total composition, which can be viewed as a type of mobile, an innovation in fiction inspired by the example of modern sculpture. Nin's characters are totally immersed in the flow of internalized psychic time, in the patterns of their own growth. One of the main figures in *Collages* quotes the Qur'an, saying, "Nothing is ever finished."

French philosopher Henri Bergson, whose ideas influenced a number of modern novelists, including Proust, stated the concept of personal evolution succinctly and elegantly: "If matter appeared to us as a perpetual flowering, we should assign no termination to any of our actions." To Nin, life does indeed appear as a "perpetual flowering." In *Cities of the Interior*, she has selected and expressed significant relationships and states of feeling in the ever-changing, continuous process of growth. Life, as distinct from existence, is possible only for those who can accept mutability, knowing that while change promises growth, it also demands inevitable loss.

LADDERS TO FIRE

Lillian's development spans *Cities of the Interior*, opening and closing the work when it is read in conventional sequence. The first part of *Ladders to Fire* describes "This Hunger," Lillian's ravenous need for love. Spontaneous, impetuous, unsure of her physical attractiveness, and compulsively generous, she gives up her career as a pianist so that she can support her lover's ambition to paint, but this sacrifice does not bring her the loyalty and security she desires. Jay repays Lillian's devotion by having affairs with other women.

The most threatening of Lillian's rivals is Sabina. The relationship between these two women is the most compelling in the novel and a superb example of Nin's brilliance at unmasking psychological motivations. When Lillian attempts to stop Sabina's pursuit of Jay by overwhelming the other woman with friendship, she discovers that she, too, is power-fully attracted to Sabina. For different reasons, both women are angry at Jay: Lillian be-cause he has neglected her, Sabina because he would like to conquer her. The two women form an alliance against him. After dancing together in a working-class tavern, they go to Sabina's room to make love, but they discover that it is not sensuality they are seeking in each other so much as an exchange of feminine qualities. They both feel a "mysterious craving . . . to become each other."

During the dazzling party scene with which *Ladders to Fire* closes, Lillian commits "invisible hara-kiri" with an outburst of harmful self-criticism. It is clear to the reader that she has grown, that her anger at herself is partly an expression of this growth, and that she will soon end her unsatisfying relationship with Jay.

CHILDREN OF THE ALBATROSS

A delicate, playful book with an undercurrent of sadness, *Children of the Albatross* traces a theme that is familiar in French literature but something of a novelty in the United States: the initiation of a young man by an older woman. Djuna, in her late twenties, be-comes involved with Paul, who is seventeen years old. The other "children" of the novel's title are their friends, young gay men who meet with Paul and Djuna in her "house of innocence and faith." Here, they dance, paint, and play, celebrating their love of free-dom from responsibility. The young men and Djuna are drawn together by their mutual fear of tyrannical, authoritarian fathers. For Djuna, this figure is represented by the cruel and lecherous watchman who terrified her when she was a child living in an orphanage. The positive creative act of evoking a counterworld to erect against the conventional and materialistic values of the fathers ignites sympathy among the rebellious children.

From the start of *Children of the Albatross*, it is clear that Djuna's affair with Paul will be brief and will provide her with little emotional sustenance. Predictably, Paul's family disapproves of her, not only because she is older but also because she is a dancer. A crucial dream, in which Djuna imagines herself as Ariadne, predicts that after she has guided Paul safely through the passage from adolescence to early adulthood, she will be abandoned. At the novel's end, Paul embarks upon an exciting journey to India, leaving Djuna behind. Feeling empty and dissatisfied, she searches the unexplored "cities" of her self. She be-gins to seek a fuller emotional life with a more mature partner.

THE FOUR-CHAMBERED HEART

In *The Four-Chambered Heart*, Nin explores the psychological complexity of a woman's involvement with a married man. Romantically ensconced in a houseboat on the Seine are Djuna and Rango, a tempestuous vagabond, so she imagines. Their relationship is initially enthralling but ultimately frustrating; both parties are weighed down by responsi-bilities to demanding hypochondriacs: he to his wife, Zora, and Djuna to her father. Heavy rains force the lovers to move their houseboat up and down the river. Like their relationship, the boat does not "go anywhere"; it merely plies its way back and forth over the same area.

Djuna and Rango's passion attains its height in the novel's first thirty pages. After that, there is conflict and threatened violence. Zora makes a bizarre attempt to kill Djuna. Rango comes to the boat very late one night and falls into a heavy depressed sleep. Djuna, desperate to initiate a change of some sort, rips up floorboards in a wild attempt to sink the boat. It is swept down the river; everyone survives, though not in the same form. A fisherman rescues a doll from the water with a joke about its having tried to commit suicide. The doll is a comment on Djuna's passivity with regard to her own life and to the image of conventional femininity that she has been struggling to maintain, at the expense of her "true" self. It is time for her to move beyond the static situation she experiences with Rango, to give up the illusion of her generosity toward Zora, and to recognize and accept the negative qualities she has been "acting out" through Rango. Djuna must grow.

A SPY IN THE HOUSE OF LOVE

In *A Spy in the House of Love*, Sabina is portrayed as a glamorous woman seeking to express herself as "Don Juana." Married to a fatherly, indulgent man, she is free to fulfill her desire for adventure, which she experiences through relationships with men. Each of Sabina's partners embodies an aura, a sense of place, an ambience that lies waiting for her exploration and participation. There is the opera star Philip; he represents "Vienna before the war." There is Mambo, a black musician transplanted to Greenwich Village from a Caribbean island. There is John, a former aviator who has been grounded because of uncontrollable anxiety. Finally, there is Donald, a gay man who returns Sabina's maternal love with an irresistibly flattering letter-portrait of her idealized self. This balances the grossly sexual and cruel portrait given to her by her former lover, Jay, a painter.

A Spy in the House of Love is a musical novel both in style and structure. There is a prelude in which Sabina invites the detection of her "crime" (experiencing sex without feeling) by phoning a "lie detector." There is a coda in which Djuna, Sabina's consoling friend, plays a late Beethoven quartet to soothe and heal the dejected Don Juana. The body of the novel is a series of variations on the central theme: Sabina's attempt to live through her relationships with men who—so she deludes herself into believing—have far more exciting lives than she herself has. Each man is associated with a particular type of music, while Igor Stravinsky's "Firebird" is said to be Sabina's "unerring musical autobiography."

SEDUCTION OF THE MINOTAUR

At once the most mature in theme and the most resplendent in imagery among Nin's novels, *Seduction of the Minotaur* takes up the story of Lillian. She has developed considerably since *Ladders to Fire*. Now a jazz performer instead of an interpreter of the classics, Lillian journeys to Mexico, imagining that she has finally freed herself from everything that imprisoned her in the past.

Traveling alone, Lillian meets a series of men, each of whom becomes a teacher or guide of sorts, revealing something of great significance in her own circuitous passage through the labyrinth of the self. The most engaging of these figures is Dr. Hernandez, a male version of Ariadne. He helps Lillian to see that she is not yet as free as she has imagined, wisely telling her that "we live by a series of repetitions until the experience is solved, understood, liquidated." The monster Lillian confronts is a "masked woman," the part of herself that she has previously been unwilling to recognize.

In Lillian's journey to Mexico and her confrontation with herself, Nin creates a living dream simultaneously in the past, present, and future. The meaning of freedom is not flight, as Sabina imagines, but commitment. If a woman can discover and love the many aspects of one man, she can be fulfilled with a single love. Lillian learns to see her husband, Larry, from whom she has been separated, as a complex, multidimensional person. This discovery brings a new excitement, a forgiveness, the grace of understanding to her feelings about him. Because she untangles the knots in her own past, Lillian rediscovers the love of her husband. Thus, there is reconciliation instead of separation.

COLLAGES

A more ambitious and a deeper book than its easy surface and gentle humor suggest, *Collages* is composed of nineteen short blocks of prose, showing once again Nin's preference for constructed rather than narrated fiction. *Collages* begins and ends with the same passage. Its circular structure encloses twenty-two characters portrayed in a wide variety of quickly sketched settings. The cement that binds these colorful elements into a composition is Renate, an artist who "makes her own patterns." She weaves in and out of the lives of the others, bringing inspiration to not only her paintings but also her friends.

Collage art is shown to work magic transformations. In this book, Nin once again stresses the many ways in which dream and fantasy enrich life. There is an intense relationship, for example, between a young woman and a raven. An elderly man feels closer to seals than to human beings; he finally develops the courage to renounce people in order to live with the animals he loves. A gardener pretends to be a millionaire to fulfill his dream of financing a literary magazine. A woman whose husband has rejected her for a younger woman replaces him with an exotic phantom lover. In *Collages*, imagination is sovereign.

The healing power of genuine relationships is shown as complementary to that of creative fantasy. *Collages* closes with the reluctant emergence of a writer from a bitter, self-imposed isolation. Elderly Judith Sands allows herself to be "courted" by Renate and an Israeli admirer, Dr. Mann. Made more trusting by their friendship, Sands actually shows the visitors one of her manuscripts. Its opening words are the same words with which *Collages* begins. This repetition helps endow *Collages* with its circular form and also underscores Nin's conviction that there is an unbroken connection from one person to another, from one imaginative writer to another, and that life is redeemed through the alchemical transformation of art. *Collages* is an assured and accomplished example of Nin's skill at adapting techniques from the nonverbal arts to literature; it is also the most imaginatively conceived of display of her convictions about the mutually nourishing exchange between art and life.

Sharon Spencer

OTHER MAJOR WORKS

SHORT FICTION: *Under a Glass Bell, and Other Stories*, 1944; *Delta of Venus: Erotica*, 1977; *Waste of Timelessness, and Other Early Stories*, 1977; *Little Birds: Erotica*, 1979.

NONFICTION: *D. H. Lawrence: An Unprofessional Study*, 1932; *Realism and Reality*, 1946; *On Writing*, 1947; *The Diary of Anaïs Nin: 1931-1934*, 1966; *The Diary of Anaïs Nin: 1934-1939*, 1967; *The Novel of the Future*, 1968; *The Diary of Anaïs Nin: 1939-1944*, 1969; *The Diary of Anaïs Nin: 1944-1947*, 1971; *Paris Revisited*, 1972; *The Diary of Anaïs Nin: 1947-1955*, 1974; *A Photographic Supplement to the Diary of Anaïs Nin*, 1974; *A Woman Speaks: The Lectures, Seminars, and Interviews of Anaïs Nin*, 1975 (Evelyn J. Hinz, editor); *In Favor of the Sensitive Man, and Other Essays*, 1976; *The Diary of Anaïs Nin: 1955-1966*, 1976; *Linotte: The Early Diary of Anaïs Nin, 1914-1920*, 1978; *The Diary of Anaïs Nin: 1966-1974*, 1980; *The Early Diary of Anaïs Nin: Volume Two, 1920-1923*, 1982; *The Early Diary of Anaïs Nin: Volume Three, 1923-1927*, 1983; *The Early Diary of Anaïs Nin: Volume Four, 1927-1931*, 1985; *Henry and June: From the Unexpurgated Diary of Anaïs Nin*, 1986; *A Literate Passion: Letters of Anaïs Nin and Henry Miller, 1932-1953*, 1987.

BIBLIOGRAPHY

Bair, Deirdre. *Anaïs Nin: A Biography.* New York: Putnam, 1995. A massive biography by a scholar steeped in the literature of the period and author of biographies of Samuel Beckett and Simone de Beauvoir. Supplements but does not supersede Fitch's shorter but also livelier 1993 biography.

Bloshteyn, Maria R. *The Making of a Counter-Culture Icon: Henry Miller's Dostoevsky.* Toronto, Ont.: University of Toronto Press, 2007. Describes how Fyodor Dostoevski was a model for Nin and her friends, Henry Miller and Lawrence Durrell, who strove to emulate the Russian writer's psychological characterizations and narrative style in their own work.

Fitch, Noel Riley. *Anaïs: The Erotic Life of Anaïs Nin.* Boston: Little, Brown, 1993. As the subtitle suggests, Fitch is concerned with tracing Nin's erotic relationships and close friendships with male and female writers. A biographer of Sylvia Beach and an expert on Paris, Fitch writes with verve and expertise.

Franklin, Benjamin V., and Duane Schneider. *Anaïs Nin: An Introduction.* Athens: Ohio University Press, 1979. A well-balanced study of Nin's work, better than most, which carefully and separately examines her fiction, six volumes of diaries, and her critical and nonfiction work. This study attempts to redress critical neglect of the author and gives her due recognition for her literary achievements.

Jason, Philip K., ed. *The Critical Response to Anaïs Nin*. Westport, Conn.: Greenwood Press, 1996. A selection of essays examining Nin's works. Includes a Freudian interpretation of her novel *Cities of the Interior* and poet William Carlos Williams's analysis of *Winter of Artifice*. Includes bibliographical references and an index.

Knapp, Bettina L. *Anaïs Nin*. New York: Frederick Ungar, 1978. An appreciative examination of Nin's work that explores the psychological depths of her diaries and fiction. Includes a chronology, a bibliography, and an index.

Pierpont, Claudia Roth. *Passionate Minds: Women Rewriting the World*. New York: Alfred A. Knopf, 2000. Evocative interpretive essays on the life paths and works of twelve women, including Nin, connecting the circumstances of their lives with the shapes, styles, subjects, and situations of their art.

Richard-Allerdyce, Diane. *Anaïs Nin and the Remaking of Self: Gender, Modernism, and Narrative Identity*. DeKalb: Northern Illinois University Press, 1998. An examination of the themes of gender and self-creativity in Nin's fiction and diaries, describing how she strove to present a "feminine mode of being" in her work. The first five chapters provide analyses of the majority of Nin's novels.

Scholar, Nancy. *Anaïs Nin*. Boston: Twayne, 1984. A good critical introduction to Nin. The first chapter offers an overview of her life, and succeeding chapters examine the novels, diaries, short stories, and prose pieces. Includes a useful chronology and a select bibliography.

Tookey, Helen. *Anaïs Nin, Fictionality and Femininity: Playing a Thousand Roles*. New York: Oxford University Press, 2003. Examines Nin's work within historical and cultural contexts, focusing on her representations of identity and femininity and her concept of self-creation through various kinds of narratives and performances.

EDNA O'BRIEN

Born: Tuamgraney, county Clare, Ireland; December 15, 1930
Also known as: Josephine Edna O'Brien

PRINCIPAL LONG FICTION

The Country Girls, 1960
The Lonely Girl, 1962 (also known as *Girl with Green Eyes*, 1964)
Girls in Their Married Bliss, 1964
August Is a Wicked Month, 1965
Casualties of Peace, 1966
A Pagan Place, 1970
Zee and Co., 1971
Night, 1972
Johnny I Hardly Knew You, 1977 (also known as *I Hardly Knew You*, 1978)
The Country Girls Trilogy and Epilogue, 1986 (includes *The Country Girls, The Lonely Girl*, and *Girls in Their Married Bliss*)
The High Road, 1988
Time and Tide, 1992
An Edna O'Brien Reader, 1994
House of Splendid Isolation, 1994
Down by the River, 1996
Wild Decembers, 1999
In the Forest, 2002
The Light of Evening, 2006

OTHER LITERARY FORMS

In addition to her novels, Edna O'Brien has published short fiction, plays and screenplays, poetry, children's books, and works of nonfiction. Her short stories have appeared regularly in magazines such as *The New Yorker, The Atlantic Monthly*, and *Cosmopolitan*; collections of her stories include *The Love Object* (1968), *A Scandalous Woman, and Other Stories* (1974), and *Lantern Slides* (1990). Chief among O'Brien's stage plays are *A Cheap Bunch of Nice Flowers* (pr. 1962), *A Pagan Place* (pr. 1972), *Virginia* (pr. 1980), *Triptych* (pr., pb. 2003), and *Iphigenia* (pr., pb. 2003). Her works for film and television include the screenplays *Time Lost and Time Remembered* (1966), *Three into Two Won't Go* (1969), and *X, Y, and Zee* (1971) and the teleplays *The Wedding Dress* (1963), *Mrs. Reinhardt* (1981), and *The Country Girls* (1983). Among her works of nonfiction are the autobiographical *Mother Ireland* (1976); *Arabian Days* (1977), a travel book; *Vanishing Ireland* (1987), a pictorial; and *James Joyce* (1999), a biography.

ACHIEVEMENTS

After moving to London from Dublin, Ireland, in 1959, Edna O'Brien published at a furious pace, mining her early experiences in Ireland and then as a single parent with two sons to rear in England. There was something of a lull in her long fiction, however, from 1977 to 1986. Nearly always from a female narrator's point of view, O'Brien has brilliantly transmuted her personal experiences into art. Her recall and selection of the tiny details that make up the texture of life, particularly in her Irish scenes (*The Country Girls, The Lonely Girl, A Pagan Place*) are most dazzling. Impressive, too, is her evident love and savoring of words—sometimes clearly in a fashion reminiscent of James Joyce—for their own sake, and often in good dialogue. Perhaps because of the speed with which she works, the vivacity and brilliance of her prolific output is frequently marred by awkward grammar, punctuation, and syntax. Apparently, her editors have felt these stylistic lapses are all part of her Irish use of the language and have accordingly let them stand.

O'Brien was a feminist before the term became fashionable, but her works also affirm a wider humanistic sympathy for all people. Early, she took up the topics of women's attitudes toward their bodies, their sexuality, and their roles as mothers and daughters. In Ireland, several of her books have been banned because of their negative commentary on the Roman Catholic Church, more common in her early work, and her frequent use of graphic sexual terms and scenes. Outside Ireland, O'Brien's reputation as a writer of fiction seems assured, although reviewer Marianne Wiggins, writing in *The Nation*, observed that "to the English [she is] a minor self-promoting legend." Despite conflicting critical responses to her work, O'Brien has received numerous awards, including the Kingsley Amis Award in 1962, the Yorkshire Post Award in 1970 for *A Pagan Place*, the Los Angeles Times Book Prize in 1990 for *Lantern Slides* and again in 1992 for *Time and Tide*, the Writers' Guild of Great Britain's Prize for Fiction in 1993, and the European Prize for Literature in 1995; the last of these was presented to O'Brien in tribute to her entire oeuvre.

BIOGRAPHY

Josephine Edna O'Brien was born to Michael and Lena (Cleary) O'Brien in Tuamgraney, county Clare, Ireland, on December 15, 1930. She has one brother and two sisters. Her father was an impractical man who bred horses and squandered his wealth; her mother worked in the United States for eight years, returning to Ireland to marry. O'Brien has characterized her mother as an ambitious, frustrated woman who mistrusted books and was unsympathetic to her daughter's emerging literary interests. (Although O'Brien dedicated her first novel to her mother, she later found her mother's copy with the inscription page torn out and angry comments written throughout.) O'Brien first attended Scarriff National School in 1936, then boarded at the Convent of Mercy, Loughrea, county Galway, in 1941 before going off to the Pharmaceutical College of Ireland in Dublin in 1946, where she worked in a chemist's shop, or drugstore, during the day and attended lectures at night. One of her first purchases in Dublin was a secondhand copy of *Introduc-*

ing James Joyce (1944), edited by T. S. Eliot, which first exposed her to the influence of that Irish literary giant. In 1948, she began to write short pieces for the *Irish Press*.

In 1951, O'Brien married novelist Ernest Gebler and lived for a time in rural county Wicklow (the marriage ended in 1964). Two sons, Carlos and Sasha, were born, in 1952 and 1954. In 1959, the family moved to London, and O'Brien's career as a published writer was quickly launched. In three weeks, far from county Clare, she wrote *The Country Girls*, tracing the development of fourteen-year-old Caithleen Brady. The trilogy begun with that first novel was continued in *The Lonely Girl* and *Girls in Their Married Bliss* (the three novels were published together, appended with *Epilogue*, in 1986). O'Brien composed a second trilogy in the 1990's, made up of *House of Splendid Isolation, Down By the River*, and *Wild Decembers*. In these later works, O'Brien focused on modern Irish life and problems as they affect both men and women. In addition to her prolific career as a writer, O'Brien teaches her craft. She has lectured in numerous countries and has taught creative writing at City College in New York. In 2006, she was appointed adjunct professor of English literature at University College, Dublin, returning home after her self-imposed exile of many years.

ANALYSIS

Edna O'Brien's early years in Ireland profoundly affected her view of the world, and particularly of women's relationships and their place in society. Being Irish, she says in *Mother Ireland*, gives one a unique view of pleasure and punishment, life and death. O'Brien's work is lyrical and lively. Her memory for people and places, for the minutiae of daily living, is prodigious; her zest for language is Joycean. She is frequently on the attack, but at her best, which is often, she transcends her immediate cause to encourage, with a grain of humor, those who still dream of love achieved through kindness and decency—common virtues still no more common than they ever were.

O'Brien's concerns are most readily accessible in her very eccentric travel/autobiography *Mother Ireland*. Her Irishness is something of which O'Brien is proud: "It's a state of mind." She is not, however, blind to Ireland's faults, appreciating that there must be something "secretly catastrophic" about a country that so many people leave. After an iconoclastic opening chapter on Irish history, with its uncanonized patron saint and its paunchy Firbogs, follow six chapters in which are sketched O'Brien's dominant themes: loneliness, the longing for adventure (often sexual), the repressive Irish Roman Catholic Church, family ties (the martyred mother and the rollicking father), and the courageous hopelessness with which life at best must be lived.

It would be a melancholy picture if it were not for O'Brien's saving, ironic sense of humor and the skill with which she roots her observations in the sensual details of the actual world. Her readers share vividly with her a world of wet batteries for radios, ink powder, walls with fragments of bottles embedded in their tops, Fox's (Glacier) Mints, orange-boxes, and lice combed from a child's head onto a newspaper. O'Brien's recurring themes, her experiments with form, and the feeling she succeeds in communicating that this Irish microcosm has its universal significance are all clearly present in *Mother Ireland*.

THE COUNTRY GIRLS

From its detailed, evocative opening page, redolent of genteel poverty, *The Country Girls*, O'Brien's first novel, serves notice of an unusual voice. The shy and sensitive Caithleen tells her first-person story and shares the action with her alter ego, the volatile and malicious Baba. It is a world divided into two warring camps, male and female, where Caithleen's aspirations toward romantic love are doomed to failure. Mr. Gentleman is the first in a long line of rotters (the drunken, brutal father; Eugene Gaillard; Herod; Dr. Flaggler), far outnumbering the few men with decent inclinations (Hickey, Auro); in such a world women stand little chance, single, married in the usual sense, or brides of Christ.

The repressive effects of poverty and a patriarchal society are hardly alleviated by the Church and its proscriptions. Her mother drowned, Caithleen spends her mid-teen years boarding in a strict convent school from which Baba contrives their expulsion for writing a ribald note. In their late teens, joyously, they come up to Dublin, Baba to take a commercial course, Caithleen to work as a grocer's assistant until she can take the civil service examinations. Loneliness, however, follows them: Baba contracts tuberculosis; Caithleen's Mr. Gentleman lets her down. With the resilience of youth, however, her last line in this novel is, "I was almost certain that I wouldn't sleep that night."

THE LONELY GIRL

The Lonely Girl continues the saga two years later, with Baba healthy again. It is, however, largely Caithleen's story; again she is the narrator. The repressive effects of her family, her village community, and her convent education are again in evidence. O'Brien has her heroine involved romantically with Eugene Gaillard, whose face reminds her of a saint and who is about the same height as her father; he is a cultivated snob, and in an often cold fashion he begins the further education of his naïve, prudish "student," both in bed and in the salon. (As Grace Eckley has pointed out, Caithleen's stiff tutor and O'Brien's former husband, Ernest Gebler, share the same initials.) At the novel's conclusion, Caithleen, wild and debased "because of some damned man," is learning, is changing; she is, as she says, finding her feet, "and when I'm able to talk I imagine that I won't be alone." Still seeking their connection, she and Baba sail on the *Hibernia* from Dublin to Liverpool and London.

GIRLS IN THEIR MARRIED BLISS

Girls in Their Married Bliss continues the story of the two in London, where, for the first time, Baba assumes the first-person narration, alternating with an omniscient voice distancing O'Brien and the reader from Caithleen's role—a process O'Brien will carry even further with her protagonist in *A Pagan Place*. The women, now about twenty-five years old, have not left their Irish baggage behind in Dublin; there is a splendid, blustery Celtic quality to the scapegrace Baba's style. Kate (as Caithleen is called), too, has her share of one-liners, word associations, epigrams, and zany metaphors: "Self-interest," she observes on one occasion, "was a common crime"; on another, at a party, she is amused by a girl wearing a strawberry punnet on her head to make herself taller.

In these early novels, O'Brien, like her leading characters, is learning and developing her skills. In *Girls in Their Married Bliss*, the topic is still the female search for love and connection. The novel is a precisely observed account of a marriage failing. People rub exquisitely on one another's nerves in the larger context of women's role in society; in the smaller context of bedroom politics, "Men are pure fools." Marriage, at least on the grounds on which the women enter it here, is evidently no end to the quest. Baba makes a calculated move for comfort; Kate sees that her interest in people is generated solely by her own needs. They have matured to the point where they no longer believe much in romantic plans. Kate's answer to the biological unfairness of God's scheme for women, as Baba sees it, is to have herself sterilized; she will not make the same mistake again: No other child of hers will be abducted by its father; no further child of hers will in its turn become a parent.

In the edition of the complete trilogy that was published in one volume in 1986, O'Brien includes a brief *Epilogue* in the form of a monologue delivered by Baba. Here the ebullient Baba brings the reader up to date: The despairing Kate is dead; she drowned, perhaps deliberately.

AUGUST IS A WICKED MONTH

In O'Brien's next novel, *August Is a Wicked Month*, an omniscient narrator describes the protagonist's abortive attempts at self-liberation, largely through sexual activity. Ellen is something like Kate of the earlier trilogy—a superstitious, convent-bred, twenty-eight-year-old Irish magazine writer, formerly a nurse, living in London when the novel begins. She takes a trip to France when the husband from whom she is separated and their eight-year-old son, Mark, who lives with her, go on a camping holiday together. Her "pathetic struggles towards wickedness" involve rejecting the first sexual invitations she encounters. Eventually, however, when Ellen does become intimately involved with a high-living group, O'Brien subjects her to two catastrophic accidents: She receives a call from her husband, who tells her that her son has been killed by a car in a roadside accident, and she fears, wrongly as it turns out, that she has contracted a venereal disease. The guilt and the judgment are clear; perhaps they are too clear to make this novel an artistic success. Ellen finally finds an uneasy autumnal peace, unlike the women in O'Brien's next novel, who have a genuine joy ripped away from them.

CASUALTIES OF PEACE

In *Casualties of Peace*, Willa McCord, artist in glass, and her earthy domestic, Patsy Wiley, are the protagonists, exemplary victims of male violence. An omniscient narrator views the two unhappy women—Willa having escaped from a nightmarish marriage to the sadistic Herod, Patsy currently suffering her husband Tom's blows. Both have their dreams of happiness outside marriage shattered. There was a chance for peace for them, but accidents prevented them from knowing joy. Patsy blabs to Willa about leaving Tom rather than doing it immediately, as planned, and her lover, Ron, believes she has let him down. Willa, just when a loving connection with Auro seems possible, is murdered by Tom, who mistakes her for Patsy.

Casualties of Peace is second only to *Night*, which it anticipates to some extent, among O'Brien's most Joycean novels. Patsy's love letters to Ron are reminiscent of the earthiest of James Joyce and Nora Barnacle's correspondence; Patsy indeed is a kind of Molly Bloom figure (more clearly developed in *Night*). Willa's letters to Auro, delivered posthumously, share the same stream-of-consciousness qualities: Words pile up into lists; associations trigger other more graphic associations; "memory is the bugger." At times lyrical, at times humorous, O'Brien develops here the Celtic flair with words that is associated with Joyce or Dylan Thomas. Her theme is loneliness and its myriad causes; her characters search to alleviate their pain, to make connections, to overcome their feelings of guilt for being themselves.

A PAGAN PLACE

A Pagan Place is a very odd novel; it is largely a sophisticated rewrite of *The Country Girls*, as O'Brien perhaps would have written that work had she had ten more years of reading, writing, and living behind her at the time. Baba is dropped in favor of one unnamed, preadolescent girl whose sexual arousal when her father beats her accomplishes her move toward adolescence. Getting away from her Irish family and Irish community, with their hereditary guilt, will, it is suggested, take her yet a stage further. At the end of the novel she leaves to the accompaniment of an eerie Hibernian howl.

Throughout the work an omniscient narrator, who sometimes uses dialect forms and sometimes very erudite words, and who is clearly unreliable in matters of fact (putting an English "general" on Nelson's pillar), places the reader at the center of the action by using the second-person narrative. No one but "you," then, is at the center of the action; the narrator and the writer are similarly distanced from the action.

Perhaps in this novel O'Brien exorcised the worst of her Irishness; certainly, very violent feelings surface, all in the consciousness of a young girl. O'Brien, in contrast to her contemporaries among Irish writers of fiction, such as Brian Friel or Benedict Kiely, really seems to dislike her Celtic community. Here is a very bitter indictment of the Church, and perhaps its ultimate rejection in the priest's attempt to seduce "you," masturbating and ejaculating on "you." Here, too, is a savage, repressive, guilt-ridden world of so-called

Christians where unwed mothers receive no _caritas_, and where legally wed mothers and fathers show no love either. It is a world where holy water is sprinkled on thoroughbred foals, where a black dog, chasing a frog that jumps out of the ashes at Della's wake, is seen as one and the same with the devil. All in all, it is, with few exceptions, a nightmarish community, especially for a child. For "you" as a child at the center of this world, deserted even by "your" mother at one period, a thing "you" thought would never happen, the only certainty is that "you" want to escape, whatever the burden of guilt "you" carry.

ZEE AND CO.

The theme of escape is continued in _Zee and Co._, where O'Brien's heroines are back in London, and again a pair. Zee moves increasingly aggressively and ruthlessly to hold her man, Robert, while dominating Stella, her rival. She succeeds in both endeavors. As the war of the sexes heats up, Zee refuses to be a victim; she is no patsy. O'Brien's long preoccupation with the defensive role of women in society appears to be shifting to the offensive in her later works as her heroines themselves become less fragmented. A person needs to be integrated psychically to withstand not only sexual partners and spouses but also all manifestations of phantoms, prejudice, repression, guilt, and loneliness. This new positive attitude is well illustrated in the rambunctious Mary Hooligan, whose nightlong monologue forms O'Brien's next work, _Night_.

NIGHT

In form and style, _Night_ is O'Brien's most Joycean novel. In a harangue from her bed in England, Mary Hooligan—Irish, abused, divorced—delivers herself of an aggressive, courageous, independent, first-person autobiographical statement. Beginning with an Anglo-Saxon monosyllable in the opening paragraph, the nonconciliatory tone of her monologue is established. "I am a woman," Mary affirms, and proceeds to weave, in time and place, the story of her connection with her father and mother, her former husband—"the original Prince of Darkness"—and her son. It is an exuberant linguistic spree: From a "trepidation" of gelatin-like dessert to the welcome "tap o' the mornin'," metaphors and apt words are savored and invented. The pervasive humor is wry; the aggressive tone and confident technique perfectly match the content of a work whose burden is rebellion against loveless unions and ignorance.

Mary Hooligan is another in O'Brien's procession of outsiders, an Irish woman in England, merely house-sitting, so even less important in the community. O'Brien, however, establishes Mary as a force on her own: Mary rejects her friend Madge—Mary needs no Kate figure to complement her being; she is complete on her own. The theme under review remains the eternal search for love in its myriad manifestations; what is new here is the heroine's joyful attack as she continues her pilgrimage to "the higher shores of love." Family, community, and marriage settings are again explored. Many of the details are familiar: the vicious father, the ignoramuses who could not tell cheese from soap, the cold-fish husband. Constant and familiar in O'Brien's work is the warm regard for children, particularly mothers' regard for their sons. This aspect of love leads O'Brien to flirt with incest in her most violent work, *I Hardly Knew You*, in which the narrator has an affair with and then murders her son's friend.

I HARDLY KNEW YOU

Nora, the protagonist of *I Hardly Knew You*, tells her story in yet another night monologue, from her prison cell, as she awaits trial for the murder of Hart, her young lover. Again, O'Brien's narrator is an Irish exile in England, divorced from an overly frugal husband, with a son, and literally in prison, isolated from all society. Loneliness is at the core of her existence, as it is, she remarks, at the core of Celtic songs. Her monologue shuffles time and space more formally than Mary Hooligan's in *Night* and reveals a world of increasing violence. Details and incidents from O'Brien's previous works, as far back even as *The Country Girls*, show up: the drunken father taking the cure, the child-abduction threat, the child scraping the toilet-seat paint, the kicking match engaged in by brutish relatives.

The world has become an increasingly violent place, and the response of O'Brien's narrator matches it. Like Mary's, Nora's personality is integrated, but toward the Kate side. She engages in an explicitly lesbian encounter, but she needs no other woman to complement her. Indeed, she acts increasingly like the worst stereotype of the sadistic male predator, who uses and abuses other people, particularly women and especially wives. This is a chilling picture of a person driven to violence, to kill without regret. Here is a woman who has lost her balance and whose sweeping indictment of men must surely be viewed as just as reprehensible as male chauvinism. "I am proud . . . to have killed one of the breed to whom I owe nothing but cruelty, deceit, and the asp's emission," she avers, ignoring absolutely O'Brien's often-stated support for "human decency" and kindness among people of whatever sex.

THE HIGH ROAD

The graph of O'Brien's fictional split personalities is by no means a straight line. A clearly differentiated pair in the early trilogy, each "Kate" and "Baba" is subsequently given an alternating fictional forum. The *Epilogue* may have seemed to clear the way for Baba and zesty Baba types, but *The High Road*, published two years later, has readers once again seeing a sophisticated society through the moist eyes of a Kate type.

Anna, the narrator of *The High Road*, like many of the women in O'Brien's short stories as well, has come on Easter Sunday to a Mediterranean paradise to get over a London love doomed from its inception. In this exotic setting, she encounters eccentric members of the international set: the superannuated debutante, Portia; the grotesques who make up a German fashion-magazine staff on location; the fading jet-setter, Iris; the itinerant Irish painter, D'Arcy, with the Joycean language flair; and Catalina, the hotel chambermaid, with whom she has an affair. It all ends in murder; D'Arcy, to buy some time, paints

"Lesbos" on a multitude of walls, not merely on Catalina's gable, where the word first appeared, but to no avail. Clutching a scarf full of Catalina's blood-soaked hair, in what in its accumulation of similes seems at times a parody of the gothic romance, Anna sets out, she says, for the last time, for home. Whether she has left behind her the purgatory of motherhood, in its various manifestations, remains to be read.

TIME AND TIDE

O'Brien continues her focus on Irish women's lives and social roles in *Time and Tide*. The title of the work refers to linear progression and cyclical repetition, devices that she incorporates not only thematically (the changeability and sameness of women's lives) but stylistically. The story develops episodically, providing vignettes from the narrator's life. The protagonist, Nell, following a failed marriage to an abusive spouse, has raised two sons independently. Early in the novel it is revealed that her eldest son, Paddy, is enmeshed in drug use. Ironically, it is not an overdose but a boating accident that claims his life. The novel then reverses time to recount earlier family events, contributory tragedies that lead up to and culminate in the loss of Nell's firstborn son.

A powerful image in the novel is that of a barge colliding with a tourist boat on the Thames. That Paddy should be aboard the latter and this random accident claims his life not only reveals the unpredictability of events but also highlights the young man's chosen and quick route through life. Rejecting the misery he associates with his long-suffering mother, he embraces the thrills of drugs and holidays, but his pleasure-seeking life, prematurely ended, only intensifies his family's despair. For O'Brien's characters, there is no respite from the barges of life, from the inevitable hardships that destroy any illusion of happiness.

Despite the desolate events recounted—Nell herself has indulged in narcotics and sexual liaisons, finding solace in neither—the novel ends with a measure of optimism. When her surviving son, Tristan, leaves home to join Paddy's girlfriend (who is pregnant with Paddy's child), Nell is dejected at first by his departure. Eventually, she finds respite in her now quiet home. Having borne the worst, the death of a child, she must accept what is to come, life in all its myriad sorrows and momentary pleasures.

HOUSE OF SPLENDID ISOLATION

O'Brien returns to her native territory with a trilogy of novels set in modern Ireland. The first, *House of Splendid Isolation*, is a stunning book, quite different from her previous work. It reveals a microcosm of divided Ireland, embodied by the patriot-terrorist McGreevy and the widow Josie O'Meara. McGreevy, seeking to free Northern Ireland from British rule, has been sent to the complacent South to murder a prominent English visitor. He plans to hide in Josie's decaying mansion, which he believes is empty. Feared as a coldly efficient terrorist, McGreevy emerges as a surprisingly kind, ordinary man who has been honed to a thin edge by violence.

Josie, ill with pneumonia and high blood pressure, has just been released from a nursing home to her house of isolation. She seems pluckier than most O'Brien heroines, perhaps because she is elderly, although flashbacks illuminate the early life that formed her. The collision of the revolutionary and the antiterrorist, and their gradual sympathy and understanding, defines the conflict of the novel and the hunt that follows. Josie can be seen as the *Shan Van Vocht*, the Poor Old Woman, a historical symbol of Ireland, exemplifying the domestic life of her people. McGreevy represents the bitter fruit of the country's troubled political history. The inevitable conclusion proceeds as well-meaning, patriotic volunteers from both factions struggle with duty, guilt, and grief.

Surprisingly, O'Brien avoids her usual male stereotypes in this novel; she presents imperfect men, both law-abiding and lawless, who are racked by ambivalence. She remains neutral, revealing with rueful detachment the human damage caused by centuries of conflict. *House of Splendid Isolation* offers a portrait of Ireland in all its complexity, with its intense people and its bloody and heartbreaking history.

DOWN BY THE RIVER

The second installment in the trilogy, *Down by the River,* is a less objective book than *House of Splendid Isolation*. The novel was inspired by a controversial incident that took place in Ireland in 1992, when a pregnant fourteen-year-old girl fled to England for an abortion but was brought back and made a ward of the court. O'Brien has changed some details of the case; in her version, Mary MacNamara is impulsively raped by her father as they are picking berries. Mary's dying mother and a female doctor suspect the truth, as do others, but no one acts.

Here again is the world familiar to O'Brien's readers, a world of repression and guilt, in which people do not look directly at each other or say what needs to be said. In a tacit conspiracy of avoidance, everyone knows that Mary is pregnant as a result of the rape, but no one will confront the problem. Worse is the hypocrisy of those quick to judge without mercy. Self-righteous adulterers preen in antiabortion meetings while a shrill speaker waves bloody photographs, even as a retired midwife recalls the dead babies she has found stuffed in drawers and toilets. Other folks are genuinely troubled, torn between religious conviction and pity for the girl. Although a sympathetic neighbor finally agrees to help Mary escape to London to obtain an abortion, the plan is thwarted. People on both sides of the issue exploit Mary for their own purposes, and the novel's ending is tense and melodramatic, though not entirely convincing.

WILD DECEMBERS

Wild Decembers completes the political trilogy begun with *House of Splendid Isolation*. Each of the three novels explores a social issue that has plagued Ireland in its recent history but the origins of which stretch back in time. Whereas the first novel in the series focuses on sectarian violence and the second on abortion rights, the third and final work tills Ireland's very soil. Set in the fictional rural parish of Cloontha, *Wild Decembers* chronicles a series of seemingly petty land disagreements between two farmers: longtime resident Joseph Brennan and his immigrant neighbor, Michael Bugler. Further complications arise from Bugler's growing interest in Brennan's younger sister, Breege, and the unexpected arrival of Bugler's Australian fiancé. By novel's end, one farmer is dead and the other in prison, the land and the women who remain behind abandoned by the men. O'Brien layers the text with numerous references, Irish (the Great Famine), mythological (stories of Greek gods and mortals), and biblical (the struggle between Cain and Abel), thus expanding the significance of this tale of two Irish farmers who feud over territory.

IN THE FOREST

In the Forest explores the childhood trauma and mental frailty that eventually lead a deranged young Irishman to take the lives of three innocent people, including a single mother and her child. As she has in previous novels, notably *House of Splendid Isolation* and *Wild Decembers*, O'Brien incorporates elements of Irish and Greek mythology to imbue her story with universal qualities. Michael O'Kane, whose name (literally "of Cain") carries biblical import, is either a monster or an emotionally disturbed young man. His victims try to relate to him as the latter in a failed attempt to avoid their fates and in an effort to understand the source of his psychosis. As they learn from their captor, O'Kane's childhood was marked by abuse, abandonment, and confinement.

In his youth, Michael O'Kane was identified by his community as an individual capable of great cruelty. His adolescent nickname, *Kinderschreck* (German for "one who scares children"), connotes his designation by society as a monster. Institutionalized and drugged for much of his life, including a final stint in an English facility, Michael is allowed by British authorities to return to Ireland. The multiple murders he commits on his home soil verify that his release was premature and imprudent. In this portrait of a serial killer, O'Brien raises disturbing questions that remain with readers. To what extent does society contribute to the making of its monsters, its sociopaths and violent criminals? Once these dangerous outsiders have been identified, where should society place them? Most pointedly, after such individuals have been labeled *Kinderschrecken*, how should society expect them to behave?

THE LIGHT OF EVENING

In *The Light of Evening*, O'Brien returns to the subject matter of earlier novels: an examination of the troubled and changing lives of Irish women. She also mines biographical material as she depicts the tense relationship between a traditional Irish mother and her less traditional daughter, an emerging writer. Perhaps as a sign of her own maturity as an author and a woman, O'Brien allows the aged Dilly to reminisce about the past from her hospital bed as she awaits the arrival of her adult daughter Eleanora. Recalled in Dilly's mind are events from her life that are similar to episodes in O'Brien's mother's life, including an emigration to America that is followed by a return to Ireland and marriage.

Most revealing of their troubled relationship is Dilly's maternal disappointment when Eleanora marries a foreigner, an act that for a time severs familial and national ties. When Eleanora finally arrives at her bedside, Dilly's anticipated encounter with her daughter proves disappointing; the two women remain estranged. Left behind as counterevidence to Dilly's more positive remembrances is Eleanora's personal journal, which houses a far different and darker perspective on the events of the women's lives.

Archibald E. Irwin; Joanne McCarthy
Updated by Dorothy Dodge Robbins

OTHER MAJOR WORKS

SHORT FICTION: *The Love Object*, 1968; *A Scandalous Woman, and Other Stories*, 1974; *Mrs. Reinhardt*, 1978 (also known as *A Rose in the Heart*, 1979); *Returning*, 1982; *A Fanatic Heart*, 1984; *Lantern Slides*, 1990.

PLAYS: *A Cheap Bunch of Nice Flowers*, pr. 1962; *A Pagan Place*, pr. 1972 (adaptation of her novel); *The Gathering*, pr. 1974; *Virginia*, pr. 1980; *Flesh and Blood*, pr. 1985; *Iphigenia*, pr., pb. 2003 (adaptation of Euripides' play); *Triptych*, pr., pb. 2003.

POETRY: *On the Bone*, 1989.

SCREENPLAYS: *Girl with Green Eyes*, 1964 (adaptation of her novel); *Time Lost and Time Remembered*, 1966 (with Desmond Davis; also known as *I Was Happy Here*); *Three into Two Won't Go*, 1969; *X, Y, and Zee*, 1971 (also known as *Zee and Company*; adaptation of her novel).

TELEPLAYS: *The Wedding Dress*, 1963; *Nothing's Ever Over*, 1968; *Mrs. Reinhardt*, 1981 (adaptation of her short story); *The Country Girls*, 1983 (adaptation of her novel).

NONFICTION: *Mother Ireland*, 1976; *Arabian Days*, 1977; *James and Nora: A Portrait of Joyce's Marriage*, 1981; *Vanishing Ireland*, 1986; *James Joyce*, 1999.

CHILDREN'S LITERATURE: *The Dazzle*, 1981; *A Christmas Treat*, 1982; *The Expedition*, 1982; *The Rescue*, 1983; *Tales for the Telling: Irish Folk and Fairy Stories*, 1986.

EDITED TEXT: *Some Irish Loving*, 1979.

BIBLIOGRAPHY

Byron, Kristine. "'In the Name of the Mother . . . ': The Epilogue of Edna O'Brien's Country Girls Trilogy." *Women's Studies* 31 (July/August, 2002): 447-465. Analyzes the function of O'Brien's epilogue and contrasts it with more traditional literary uses of epilogues in general. Argues that the epilogue does not provide closure to the saga of Kate and Baba, but rather disclosure, allowing for a rereading of the entire trilogy.

Colletta, Lisa, and Maureen O'Connor, eds. *Wild Colonial Girl: Essays on Edna O'Brien*. Madison: University of Wisconsin Press, 2006. Collection of critical essays examines O'Brien's works, assessing the manner in which O'Brien both responds to and undermines traditional Irish literature and figureheads while simultaneously charting a decisively feminist literary course for her native tongue.

Eckley, Grace. *Edna O'Brien*. Lewisburg, Pa.: Bucknell University Press, 1974. Excellent brief study was the first such examination of O'Brien's fiction. Among the themes in O'Brien's extremely personal work discussed are those of love and loss.

Gillespie, Michael Patrick. "(S)he Was Too Scrupulous Always." In *The Comic Tradition in Irish Women Writers*, edited by Theresa O'Connor. Gainesville: University Press of Florida, 1996. Discusses how O'Brien's humor is distinguished from that of Irish male writers; shows the relationship between her humor and that of James Joyce, particularly the relationship between her short stories and those in Joyce's *Dubliners* (1914).

Harris, Michael. "Outside History: Edna O'Brien's *House of Splendid Isolation*." *New Hibernia Review* 10 (March 3, 2006): 111-122. Examines the novel in the context of postmodernism, including the author's use of pastiche, decentering, and fragmentation.

Hooper, Brad. Review of *In the Forest*, by Edna O'Brien. *Booklist*, January 1-15, 2002, 776. Observes that this psychological thriller breaks with previous O'Brien works by exposing a dark side to the human condition that is universal as opposed to uniquely Irish—in this case, the communal fear generated by a killer at large.

Mara, Miriam. "The Geography of Body: Borders in Edna O'Brien's *Down by the River* and Colum McCann's 'Sisters.'" In *The Current Debate About the Irish Literary Canon: Essays Reassessing the Field Day Anthology of Irish Writing*, edited by Helen Thompson. Lewiston: N.Y.: Edwin Mellen Press, 2006. Explores borders as a metaphor for both bodily and national boundaries and notes O'Brien's ability to trespass on and transcend barriers in *Down by the River*.

O'Brien, Edna. "Edna O'Brien." Interview by Caitriona Moloney and Helen Thompson. In *Irish Women Writers Speak Out: Voices from the Field*. Syracuse, N.Y.: Syracuse University Press, 2003. O'Brien discusses her intertwined identities as writer, woman, and postcolonialist.

Quintelli-Neary, Margaret. "Retelling the Sorrows in Edna O'Brien's Country Girls Trilogy." *Nua: Studies in Contemporary Irish Writing* 4, nos. 1/2 (2003): 65-76. Examines O'Brien's treatment of female experiences in relationship to tragedy.

KATE O'BRIEN

Born: Limerick, Ireland; December 3, 1897
Died: Canterbury, England; August 13, 1974

OTHER LITERARY FORMS

Kate O'Brien's first success was a play, *Distinguished Villa*, which had a three-month run in London's West End in 1926. She successfully dramatized her novel *That Lady* for a Broadway production (1949) in which Katherine Cornell played the title role. O'Brien was also the author of two travel books, *Farewell, Spain* (1937) and *My Ireland* (1962). Her *English Diaries and Journals* was published in 1943 and a biography, *Teresa of Avila*, in 1951. Her last major published work was a book of reminiscences, *Presentation Parlour* (1963).

ACHIEVEMENTS

While Kate O'Brien's first novel, *Without My Cloak*, received two of the English literary establishment's most prestigious awards, the Hawthornden Prize and the James Tait Black Memorial Prize, her most notable achievement may best be assessed in the context of contemporary Irish literature. In this context, she remains—together with, though in a much more culturally significant manner than, her perhaps better-known contemporary Elizabeth Bowen—an exemplary representative not only of women's writing but also, through her works and career, of women's potential, broadly considered. Partial recognition of her achievement came in 1947 with her election to the Irish Academy of Letters.

BIOGRAPHY

Kate O'Brien was born in the city of Limerick, Ireland, on December 3, 1897, to a comfortable, middle-class family. Educated at a local convent, she went on to attend University College, Dublin, at a time when Ireland's capital was witnessing the consolidation of the Irish Literary Revival, though the cultural enthusiasm of the time left little or no mark either on O'Brien's student days or on her writing.

The years immediately following graduation seem to have been marked by a degree of

Kate O'Brien
(Library of Congress)

uncertainty. She first worked in England as a journalist for the (then) *Manchester Guardian* and as a teacher. A brief period in Washington, D.C., as a diplomatic aide was followed by a sojourn in Bilbao, Spain, as a governess. Returning to London in 1924, she married Gustav Renier; the marriage was not a success. Spain soon became her second home, though for more than ten years after the completion of her World War II service at the ministry of information in London she was refused admission to Spain, her depiction of King Philip II in *That Lady* having rendered her persona non grata. By this time, O'Brien was no stranger to controversy arising out of her fiction: Her 1941 novel, *The Land of Spices*, was notoriously banned by the Irish censorship board for alleged sexual impropriety. In 1950, she took up residence again in Ireland and lived there until 1961, when she returned to England. She died on August 13, 1974.

Analysis

Kate O'Brien's career emerged and developed during a difficult time for Irish writing; indeed, models of Irish women novelists who might have provided her with beneficial influence and nurturing were virtually nonexistent. Despite these unpromising cultural origins, and despite the obvious struggle O'Brien experienced in order to express herself and command a responsive and sustaining audience, her career can be seen in historical retrospect to be marked with notable integrity, independence of mind and action, and devotion to her art.

In a literary culture where women have not always received sufficient critical attention and have not had their works readily incorporated into the canon of a given generation's achievements, critical responses to O'Brien's life and work have belatedly been seen as manifestations of unwarranted narrowness. The belatedness of this view is perhaps a result of the author's long years of exile, along with the fact that her one major popular success, *That Lady*, published when a fresh audience was ready for her work, is a historical romance rather than another in her sequence of novels about Irish family life. Yet the republication of many of her works during the 1980's not only facilitated a reappraisal of her literary achievements but also had the effect of redrawing the map of Irish literary culture at a crucial period in its development.

The generation of Irish writers to which O'Brien belongs had the unenviable task of following in the pathbreaking footsteps of the principal artists of the Irish Literary Revival—the novelist George Moore, the poet William Butler Yeats, and the playwright John Millington Synge. O'Brien's generation was as different in background and outlook from these three illustrious avatars as it is possible to be. Provincial in upbringing, nationalist in politics, unexperimental in art, and Catholic in cultural formation, this generation had at once a greater intimacy with the actual life of its fellow citizens and a more actively critical perception of the society in whose name it had elected to speak. It also had the not inconsiderable disadvantage of attempting to assert its cultural and artistic validity and viability while the star of the revival had not yet entirely waned, and while Yeats, for example, was willing to co-opt new voices to articulate the agenda of his cultural politics.

The most important writers of this generation—those who went on to establish a somewhat more populist orientation for Irish literature, or at least a more populist role for the Irish writer—have long been considered to be Seán O'Faoláin, Frank O'Connor, and Liam O'Flaherty. The different orientation that they represent may be initially discerned in the fact that they each espoused a form largely neglected by the revival—namely, prose fiction, in particular the short story—and implicitly rejected the formal and ideological explorations of their more modernist forebears. O'Brien is a member of this generation not merely by virtue of her provincial background and conventional education but also because her works reflect this generation's concerns, a reflection that receives added point and importance from the fact of its feminist—or, to be historically accurate, protofeminist—perspectives.

The disillusion and disorientation that emerge as a resonant theme in Irish fiction during the 1930's, the problematized rendering of the independence that the country secured in the late twentieth century in juridical and political terms, and the conflicts between tradition and individuality as the culture seeks not merely aesthetic but moral renewal, far from being neglected by O'Brien, are all the more authentically present in her work through being presented from the standpoint of already marginalized female protagonists. (With the exception of *Pray for the Wanderer*, with its protagonist Matt Costello, all of O'Brien's works feature female protagonists.)

WITHOUT MY CLOAK

O'Brien's first novel, *Without My Cloak*, rehearses a number of the problems that arise from her heritage and anticipates the most important of her fiction's preoccupations. A family saga, it brings to awareness, through the use of an essentially nineteenth century model, the social and psychological forces that gave cultural and moral legitimacy to O'Brien's own class and ideological background. The novel traces the development of the Considine family through three generations from the late eighteenth century, plausibly detailing its establishment in an urban, mercantile setting, for which the author uses her native Limerick.

A major motif in the work is the question of security. The Considine ethos consists of a sublimation of development in consolidation, and the emotional claustrophobia that results from this mode of behavior within the family circle is memorably detailed. The security motif is tensely related to its obverse, a quest for independence; the dynamics of the novel enact the struggle familiar from nineteenth century fiction between individual and society, between the assertion of selfhood and institutional constraints, with the emphasis in this instance falling on the power of institutions.

In particular, the social and moral function of the Catholic Church receives special attention in *Without My Cloak* and retains a particularly important place throughout O'Brien's fiction. Because of its status in her first novel, it is possible to refer to the Considine family as embodying an ethos, since the Church operates as a source of moral and social identity, and alternative sources of such security and self-awareness are nowhere to be found. The power of the Church to authorize selfhood as a tissue of constraints makes of it a second, larger, more absolute family, and the matter of the effect of its power on the individual conscience and consciousness, rather than being resolved in *Without My Cloak*, becomes an increasingly emphatic preoccupation in O'Brien's fiction prior to the publication of *That Lady*. (The fact that O'Brien herself seems to have considered the conflicts of her first novel unresolved may be inferred from their reenactment in condensed and more artistically disciplined form in her next work, *The Anteroom*.)

The role and power of the Church is so central to her work that O'Brien has frequently been thought of as a Catholic, more than as an Irish, novelist. Like most Irish writers, however, she is concerned with the culture of Catholicism; its social, personal, and interpersonal influence; and its significance as a generator of a politics of the spirit rather than as a spiritual convalescent home. Indeed, one of her most fundamental fictional preoccupations is with the difficulty of dealing with impersonal authority, whether conceived as institutional or, as in the portrait of Philip II in *That Lady*, monarchical.

MARY LAVELLE

The fact that O'Brien perceived her preoccupations as continuing difficulty rather than as eventual solution is suggested by the regularity with which her protagonists, for all the author's sympathetic dramatization of their intensity of their struggles, typically fail to attain the independence they desire. An exception to this general outcome is the eponymous heroine of *Mary Lavelle*. This novel, which draws more directly on immediate personal experience than does *Without My Cloak*, tells of a young Irish woman working as a governess for a bourgeois Spanish family. In some sense an account of an innocent abroad—Mary seems to be innocence itself—the novel is also a narrative of conflicting loyalties. The heroine is in many respects an ideal employee, fitting into the Areavaga family with the ease of somebody familiar with a culture in which people know their places. It is Mary's very compliance, however, that is responsible for the novel's central drama.

Mary involuntarily falls for Juanito, the married son of the house, a state of affairs that brings her into conflict not only with the outlook in which she had been rigorously brought up in Ireland but also with its powerfully reinforced presence in Doña Consuelo, the commanding head of the household. The conflict between duty and freedom, between individual desire and ethical obligation, in addition to the novelist's welcome transposition of her concerns to a non-Irish locale and the development of a sexual dimension to Mary's struggle for authentic womanhood, contributes to an impressive sense of the novelist's development. Nevertheless, it is not clear what the overall effect of Mary's experiences has been, whether she accepts or rejects the conflict-laden nature of her experiences. "Anguish and anger for everyone and only one little, fantastic, impossible hope," read the closing lines of *Mary Lavelle*, "was the fruit of her journey to Spain." An unexpected fruit of the publication of *Mary Lavelle*, however, was its banning by Irish censors, an act that may be read now as an unintended tribute to O'Brien's insightful presentation of her heroine's moral authenticity but that, at the time, deepened the alienation from her background that her works articulated with increasing conviction.

THE LAND OF SPICES

This alienation reached its highest level when O'Brien's next novel, *The Land of Spices*, met with a similar fate to that of *Mary Lavelle* at the hands of the censors, as a result of which the novel achieved unjust notoriety—and subsequently, when censorship was relaxed in the early 1970's, a certain amount of popular success. The banning of *The Land of Spices* proved instrumental in calling the censorship board's procedures into question and led indirectly to a revision of its mode of operation. It might be argued that the board's very existence was in itself strongly illustrative of the cultural conflicts and repressions that, from a broader, nonbureaucratic, social perspective, form the core of O'Brien's fictional concerns. The pretext for banning *The Land of Spices* was so slender—consisting of a mere handful of words with potentially homosexual implications—that it came to be seen as a paradigm of the narrow-minded, prurient, and often antifeminist orientation of the official guardians of Irish literary culture.

The Land of Spices can be read as a redeployment and intensification of the mother-and-governess relationship in *Mary Lavelle*, a relationship that is emblematic of relationships conceived throughout O'Brien's work as exercises in power. On this occasion, foreignness of setting and the enclosed nature of the immediate environment are combined to attain a new level of intensity: The action takes place within an Irish convent of a French order of nuns. In addition, this work's animating relationship now has the intimacy of teacher, Mère Marie-Hélène Archer, and pupil, Anna Murphy, with all of its reverberations of nurturing and mastery, the source of which is the overarching presence of Mother Church. The pressures Mary Lavelle felt with regard to her moral development and sense of autonomy are here articulated more dramatically, given how much more difficult it is to escape them, and the sexual component of *Mary Lavelle* is similarly intensified.

The novel, however, has a more meditative than critical tone. Taking its title from the English metaphysical poet George Herbert's "Prayer (1)" ("Church bells beyond the stars heard, the soul's blood,/ The land of spices, something understood"), the emphasis falls on the ritualistic and selfless aspects of the vocational life, on the complexities of agape rather than the challenge of eros, on the willingness to serve rather than the urge to escape, while at the same time remaining crucially sensitive to the urgent presence of humanity and its needs. *The Land of Spices* will seem to many O'Brien's most satisfying production, in which she attains more objective possession of her psychological and spiritual preoccupations without running the risk of compromising them.

THAT LADY

O'Brien's characterization of a woman's fate in the context of power relationships receives its most lavish treatment in her greatest popular success, *That Lady*. As well as being adapted for the stage, *That Lady* was filmed with Olivia de Havilland in the title role in 1955. Set in sixteenth century Spain, the novel tells the story of Ana de Mendoza y de la Cerda, princess of Eboli and duchess of Pastrana; clearly, despite O'Brien's strong Spanish interests, it is an entirely new departure for her as a novelist. Instead of concentrating on the various stages of Ana's life as a woman in an attempt to reconstruct a novel of historical verisimilitude, O'Brien concentrates instead on the years of Ana's unlikely liberation into an experience of womanhood that had hitherto been hidden from her. The reader is explicitly informed in a foreword that this "is not a historical novel"; instead, the imaginative treatment of the material dwells centrally on a dramatization of the psychological and emotional conflicts of the case. Thus, despite a certain amount of costumery, inevitable under the circumstances, *That Lady* achieves an internal consistency with O'Brien's other novels.

That Lady covers the years spent by Ana, now widowed, in state service. To some extent, her work for the Spanish Crown during this brief period recapitulates her early years, when by virtue of her noble birth and excellent marriage she became intimate with affairs of state. Together with the old intimacy, however, there now comes a new, and this development of an additional dimension in Ana's life is at once enhancing and destructive, enriching her personal existence while risking a scandal that would entail the king's serious displeasure. Because of the character of the prevailing power structure, the most significant experience in Ana's personal life—the affair with Don Antonio Pérez—becomes the occasion of her banishment and confinement. The novel's heightened courtly context accentuates rather than dilutes its emphasis on tensions familiar from O'Brien's earlier novels—between passion and form, between desire and responsibility, between a woman's external role and her internal needs. To these tensions and conflicts her work returns again and again, and it is in her identification and negotiation of them that O'Brien's fiction is worthy of the critical attention that, beginning in the late 1980's, it has at length come to receive.

O'Brien's work is noteworthy on two levels. In the first place, it represents significant additions to the history of anglophone women's writing in the period between the two world wars. Her location of her female protagonists in conditions of moral difficulty, emotional complexity, cultural unfamiliarity, and even geographical estrangement provides a comprehensive method of dramatizing women's experience as problematic and unamenable to tidying away by the powers that be. O'Brien's own willingness to live a life as autonomous as that sought by her protagonists testifies to her steadfastness, courage, and integrity. The fact that so much of her writing life was spent in exile is a tribute to both her singularity and her perseverance.

In addition, however, O'Brien's accomplishments become all the more significant when seen in an Irish context. While her novels do not articulate the concerns of her generation as explicitly as the critiques of nationalism and assumption of embattled cultural and ideological positions favored by many of her contemporaries, her work belongs with theirs as part of a concerted effort to render more authentically—that is, with greater respect for individuality and its internal realities—the life of her time. O'Brien's original contributions to this effort make her the first significant female writer of independent Ireland.

George O'Brien

OTHER MAJOR WORKS

PLAYS: *Distinguished Villa*, pr. 1926; *The Bridge*, pr. 1927; *The Schoolroom Window*, pr. 1937; *That Lady*, pr. 1949.

NONFICTION: *Farewell, Spain*, 1937; *English Diaries and Journals*, 1943; *Teresa of Avila*, 1951; *My Ireland*, 1962 (travel); *Presentation Parlour*, 1963 (reminiscence).

BIBLIOGRAPHY

Bloom, Harold, ed. *British Women Fiction Writers, 1900-1960.* 2 vols. Philadelphia: Chelsea House, 1997-1998. Volume 2 includes brief biographies of O'Brien and twelve other authors and critical essays about their work, including analyses of individual books and broader discussions of the authors' place in literary history

Dalsimer, Adele. *Kate O'Brien: A Critical Study.* Dublin: Gill and Macmillan, 1990. The first comprehensive study of O'Brien's entire literary output, with an emphasis on the feminist dimension of her works. Includes a biographical sketch, a bibliography, and an index.

Kiberd, Declan. "Kate O'Brien: *The Ante-Room.*" In *Irish Classics.* Cambridge, Mass.: Harvard University Press, 2001. O'Brien's novel is one of the thirty-five greatest works of Irish literature that Kiberd discusses in her book on the classics of the Irish literary tradition.

Kiely, Benedict. "Love and Pain and Parting: The Novels of Kate O'Brien." In *A Raid into Dark Corners: And Other Essays.* Cork, Ireland: Cork University Press, 1999. Kiely, a popular Irish literary critic and a writer for more than fifty years, includes an analysis of O'Brien's novels in this collection of his essays.

O'Brien, Kate. "The Art of Writing." *University Review* 3 (1965): 6-14. Provides valuable insights into the author's thoughts about the writing process.

Reynolds, Lorna. *Kate O'Brien: A Literary Portrait.* Totowa, N.J.: Barnes & Noble Books, 1987. This study is divided into two parts, the first dealing with the major fiction in chronological order and the second surveying O'Brien's treatment of various major themes. Also contains a valuable treatment of O'Brien's family background.

Walshe, Eibhear. *Kate O'Brien: A Writing Life.* Dublin: Irish Academic Press, 2006. A comprehensive chronicle of O'Brien's life. Walshe maintains that O'Brien was a pioneering writer whose novels depicted independent female protagonists and created a literary identity for the Irish middle class.

_____, ed. *Ordinary People Dancing: Essays on Kate O'Brien.* Cork, Ireland: Cork University Press, 1993. This selection of critical essays examines O'Brien's heritage and feminism, describing how her works challenged the religious and social restrictions of the new Irish republic.

DOROTHY RICHARDSON

Born: Abingdon, Berkshire (now in Oxfordshire), England; May 17, 1873
Died: Beckenham, Kent, England; June 17, 1957
Also known as: Dorothy Odle; Dorothy Miller Richardson

PRINCIPAL LONG FICTION

Pointed Roofs, 1915
Backwater, 1916
Honeycomb, 1917
Interim, 1919
The Tunnel, 1919
Deadlock, 1921
Revolving Lights, 1923
The Trap, 1925
Oberland, 1927
Dawn's Left Hand, 1931
Clear Horizon, 1935
Dimple Hill, 1938
March Moonlight, 1967
Pilgrimage, 1938, 1967 (includes all previous titles)

OTHER LITERARY FORMS

Dorothy Richardson's literary reputation rests on the single long novel *Pilgrimage*. She referred to the parts published under separate titles as "chapters," and they were the primary focus of her energy throughout her creative life. The first appeared in 1915; the last—unfinished and unrevised—was printed ten years after her death. Before 1915, she wrote some essays and reviews for obscure periodicals edited by friends and also two books growing out of her interest in the Quakers. She contributed descriptive sketches on Sussex life to the *Saturday Review* between 1908 and 1914. During the years writing *Pilgrimage*, Richardson did an enormous amount of miscellaneous writing to earn money—columns and essays in the *Dental Record* (1912-1922), film criticism and translations as well as articles on various subjects for periodicals including *Vanity Fair*, *Adelphi*, *Little Review*, and *Fortnightly Review*. She also wrote a few short stories, chiefly during the 1940's. None of this material has been collected. A detailed bibliography is included in *Dorothy Richardson: A Biography* by Gloria G. Fromm (1977).

ACHIEVEMENTS

The term "stream of consciousness," adapted from psychology, was first applied to literature in a 1918 review of Dorothy Richardson's *Pointed Roofs*, *Backwater*, and *Honey-*

comb. In the twentieth century, novels moved from outward experience to inner reality. The experiments that marked the change were made almost simultaneously by three writers unaware of one another's work: The first volume of Marcel Proust's *À la recherche du temps perdu* (1913-1927; *Remembrance of Things Past*, 1922-1931) appeared in 1913, James Joyce's *Portrait of the Artist as a Young Man* began serial publication in 1914, and Richardson's manuscript of *Pointed Roofs* was finished in 1913.

Richardson was the first novelist in England to restrict the point of view entirely to the protagonist's consciousness, to take for content the experience of life at the moment of perception, and to record the development of a single character's mind and emotions without imposing any plot or structural pattern. Her place in literature (as opposed to literary history) has been less certain; some critics feel that her work is interesting only because it dates the emergence of a new technique. The absence of story and explanation make heavy demands on the reader. Since the protagonist's own limited understanding controls every word of the narrative, readers must also do the work of evaluating the experience in order to create meaning.

Richardson wrote what Virginia Woolf called "the psychological sentence of the feminine gender"; a sentence that expanded its limits and tampered with punctuation to convey the multiple nuances of a single moment. She deliberately rejected the description of events, which she thought was typical of male literature, in order to convey the subjective understanding that she believed was the reality of experience. The autobiographical basis of *Pilgrimage* was not known until 1963. Richardson, like her protagonist and like other women of her period, broke with the conventions of the past, sought to create her own being through self-awareness, and struggled to invent a form that would communicate a woman's expanding conscious life.

BIOGRAPHY

Dorothy Richardson, born on May 17, 1873, was the third of four daughters. Her father, Charles Richardson, worked in the prosperous grocery business that his father had established, but he wanted to be a gentleman. He abandoned Nonconformity for the Church of England and, in 1874, sold the family business to live on investments. During Dorothy's childhood, periods of upper-middle-class luxury (a large house, servants, gardens, membership in a tennis club) alternated with moves arising from temporarily reduced circumstances.

Charles had hoped for a son, and he took Dorothy with him to lectures in Oxford and meetings of scientific associations. She was sent at age eleven to a private day school for the daughters of gentlemen. It was late enough in the century for the curriculum to emphasize academic subjects; her studies included logic and psychology. In 1890, realizing that her family's financial condition had become seriously straitened, Dorothy looked to the example of Charlotte Brontë and *Villette* (1853) and applied for a post as pupil-teacher in a German school. Six months in Hanover were followed by two years teaching in a North

London private school and a brief spell as governess for a wealthy suburban family.

By the end of 1893, Richardson's father was declared bankrupt; in 1895, two of her sisters married. Her mother, Mary Richardson, was troubled by an unusually severe bout of the depression that had gripped her for several years. Richardson took her mother to stay in lodgings near the sea and found that she required almost constant companionship and supervision. On November 30, 1895, while her daughter was out for a short walk in the fresh air, Mary committed suicide.

At the age of twenty-two, responsible for her own support and severely shaken by the past two years' events, Richardson moved to an attic room in a London lodging house and took a job as secretary and assistant to three Harley Street dentists. For young women at that time, such a step was unusual; by taking it Richardson evaded the restraint, protection, and religious supervision that made teaching an acceptable profession for young women of good family. The nineteenth century was drawing to a close and London was alive with new ideas. Richardson explored the city, made friends with women who worked in business offices, and lived on eggs and toast so that she could afford concert tickets.

Soon after moving to London, she was invited for a Saturday in the country by an old school friend, Amy Catherine Robbins, who had married her science instructor at London University: That instructor's name was H. G. Wells. He had just published *The Time Machine* (1895). Richardson was fascinated by Wells and by the people and ideas she encountered at his house but angered by his way of telling her what to do. She was aware that she stood outside the class system and between the Victorian and modern worlds. She was drawn both to picnics with cousins at Cambridge and to anarchist and Fabian meetings. She sampled various churches (including Unitarian and Quaker) but refrained from committing herself to any group or cause.

In 1902, Richardson began contributing occasional articles and reviews to *Crank* and other magazines edited by a vegetarian friend. She refused a proposal from a respectable physician and broke her engagement to a Russian Jew, Benjamin Grad. Her friendship with Wells passed at some point into physical intimacy, but she continued to struggle against being overwhelmed by his ideas and personality. In 1906, finding herself pregnant, she brought the affair to an end; she looked forward to raising the child on her own and was distressed when she suffered a miscarriage.

Exhausted physically and mentally, Richardson left her dental job and went to Sussex to recover and think. In 1908, she began writing sketches for the *Saturday Review*. Then, as her fortieth year approached, she began deliberately searching for the form that would allow her to create what she called "a feminine equivalent of the current masculine realism."

Pointed Roofs was at first rejected by publishers. When it was published in 1915 it puzzled readers, distressed some reviewers, and failed to make money. Richardson persisted, however, on the course she had set, even while living an unsettled life in YWCA hostels and borrowed rooms and earning a minimal income by proofreading and by writing a monthly column for the *Dental Record*. In 1917, she married artist Alan Odle, who was fifteen years younger than she and had been rejected for military service by a doctor who told him he had six months to live.

Richardson's books attracted some critical recognition in the years after World War I, but they never earned money; she was usually in debt to her publishers. She supported herself and Odle (who lived until 1948) and also coped with all the practical details of their life—housekeeping, paying taxes, writing checks, doing his business with publishers and exhibitors. The couple moved frequently, spending the off-season (when lodgings were less expensive) in Cornwall and going to rooms in London for the summer. During the early 1930's, Richardson took on the burden of five full-length translations from French and German. Returning to *Pilgrimage* and the state of mind in which it was begun became increasingly difficult for Richardson; the later volumes were weakened by extraliterary distractions and also by the psychological difficulty for the author in concluding the work that was based on her own life. The final segment, *March Moonlight*, was found unfinished among her papers after she died on June 17, 1957, at the age of eighty-four.

ANALYSIS

Pilgrimage is a quest. The novel's protagonist, Miriam Henderson, seeks her self and, rejecting the old guideposts, makes her own path through life. The book remains a problem for many readers, although since 1915 most of Dorothy Richardson's technical devices have become familiar: unannounced transitions from third-person narration to the first person for interior monologue, shifts between present and past as experience evokes memory, and disconnected phrases and images and fragmentary impressions representing the continuous nonverbal operations of the mind.

Looking back on the period when she was trying to find a way to embody Miriam Henderson's experience, Richardson described her breakthrough as the realization that no one was "*there* to *describe* her." Impressed by Henry James's control of viewpoint, she went one step further. The narrator and the protagonist merge; the narrator knows, perceives, and expresses only what comes to Miriam's consciousness. Furthermore, the narrator does not speak to any imagined reader and therefore does not provide helpful explanations. The scenes and people are presented as they impinge on Miriam's awareness—thus the most familiar circumstances are likely to be undescribed and the most important people identified only by name, without the phrases that would place them or reveal their relationship to Miriam.

Many readers are discouraged by the attempt to follow the book and make meaning of it; some are tempted to use Richardson's biography to find out what "really" happened and others prefer to read isolated sections without regard to sequence, responding to the feeling and imagery as if it were poetry. Because there is no narrative guidance, meaning is continually modified by the reader's own consciousness and by the extent of identification.

MIRIAM HENDERSON NOVELS

The first three titles show Miriam Henderson in the last stages of her girlhood and form the prelude to her London life. *Pointed Roofs* covers her experience in Hanover; in *Backwater*, she is resident teacher in a North London school and still drawn to the possibility of romance with a young man from her suburban circle; in *Honeycomb*, she briefly holds a post as governess before her sisters' weddings and her mother's death complete the disintegration of her girlhood family.

The Tunnel begins Miriam's years in London and introduces situations and characters that reappear in the next several volumes: the dental job; the room at Mrs. Bailey's lodging house; the new women, Mag and Jan; and the dependent woman, Eleanor Dear; and a visit to her school friend, Alma, who has married the writer Hypo Wilson. In *Interim*, Miriam perceives the difficulty of communicating her current thoughts and experiences to her sister and other old friends. *Deadlock* treats her acquaintance—growing into an engagement—with Michael Shatov. In *Revolving Lights*, she has decided not to marry Shatov and becomes increasingly involved with Wilson.

The Trap shows her sharing a cramped flat with a spinster social worker and growing despondent about the isolation that, she realizes, she imposes on herself to avoid emotional entanglements. *Oberland* is a lyrical interlude about a holiday in Switzerland. In *Dawn's Left Hand*, Miriam has an affair with Wilson and an intense friendship with a young woman (Amabel) who becomes a radical suffragist. *Clear Horizon* concludes much of the practical and emotional business that has occupied Miriam for several years; she disentangles herself from Wilson, Shatov, and Amabel and prepares to leave London. In *Dimple Hill*, she lives on a farm owned by a Quaker family, absorbs their calm, and works at writing. *March Moonlight* rather hastily takes Miriam up to the point of meeting the artist who would become her husband and to the beginning of her work on a novel.

This summary of events is the barest framework. Life, for Miriam Henderson, exists not in events but in the responses that create her sense of awareness. The books are made up of relatively independent sections, each treating a single segment of experience or reflection. Because of the depth with which single moments are recorded, the overall narrative line is fragmentary. Despite *Pilgrimage*'s length, it embodies isolated spots of time. Frequently, neither narration nor the memories evoked by subsequent experience indicate what events may have taken place in the gaps between. Furthermore, the book concentrates on those moments important to Miriam's interior experience, and it leaves out the times when she acts without self-awareness—which may include significant actions that take place when Miriam is so engrossed by events that she does not engage in thought or reflection.

Richardson disliked the phrase "stream of consciousness" because it implies constant movement and change. She preferred the image of a pool—new impressions are added, and sometimes create ripples that spread over the previously accumulated consciousness. Thus, Miriam's interior monologue becomes steadily more complex as she grows older.

Her consciousness widens and deepens; fragmentary phrases show her making connections with her earlier experiences and perceptions; her understanding of past events alters with later awareness. The earlier volumes have more sensory impression and direct emotion; later, as Miriam grows more self-aware, she has greater verbal skill and is more likely to analyze her responses. Because of her more sophisticated self-awareness, however, she also grows adept, in the later volumes, at suppressing impressions or fragments of self-knowledge that she does not want to admit to consciousness.

In many ways, Miriam is not likable—readers are sometimes put off by the need to share her mind for two thousand pages. In the early books, she is a self-preoccupied, narrow-minded adolescent, oppressively conscious of people's appearance and social class, annoyingly absorbed in wondering what they think about her, defensively judgmental. The wild swings in mood and the ebb and flow of her energies during the day appear to have little cause and to be unworthy of the attention she gives them. Most people, however, would appear unpleasantly selfish if their minds were open for inspection. Miriam creates her self by deliberate consciousness. The danger is that she tends to withdraw from experience in order to contemplate feeling.

PILGRIMAGE

The events of *Pilgrimage* span the decades at the turn of the century but, because of the interior focus, there is relatively little physical detail or explicit social history to create an objective picture of the era. Women's developing self-awareness, however, must be seen as one of the period's significant events. Miriam reflects the mental life of her times in her range of responses to religion, the books she reads, and the people, ideas, and movements she encounters.

A good deal of life's texture and even its choices take place at levels that are not verbalized. Richardson's first publisher described her work as "female imagism." Miriam responds particularly and constantly to the quality of light. Readers are also aware of her reaction to places, objects, and physical surroundings; ultimately, it is through mastering the emotional content of this response that she is able to discover what she needs to have in her life.

Another continuing thread is created by Miriam's thoughts about men, about men and women together, and about the roles of women in society. Her basic animosity toward men gives shape to a series of statements on their personal, emotional, social, and intellectual peculiarities that falls just short of a formal feminist analysis. Each possible romance, each rejected or forestalled proposal amounts to a choice of a way of life. The matter is, however, complicated by Miriam's sexual reticence. Even though she can talk about free love, she is not conscious—or perhaps will not permit herself to become conscious—of overt sexual urges or of physical attraction to men or to women. She struggles not to let her feeling for certain women lead her to be absorbed by their lives or roles. In *Backwater,* Miss Perne's religion is dangerously comfortable; Eleanor Dear's passive feminine helplessness forces Miriam to become her protector; Amabel's possessiveness is as stifling as Hypo Wilson's. At the end—in *March Moonlight*—there is a hint of emotional involvement with the unidentified Jane. Struggling to know herself, Miriam is constantly faced with the problem of knowing other women.

POINTED ROOFS

Pointed Roofs comes close to being a structural whole—it begins with Miriam Henderson's journey to Hanover and ends with her return home six months later. She is on her first trip away from home, looking at new scenes, anxious about her ability to do her job and earn her wages, having her first taste of independence. Since Miriam is seventeen years old—and, as a Victorian daughter, a relatively innocent and sheltered seventeen—the reader often understands more than Miriam does and can interpret the incidents that develop her sense of who she is and where she fits in the world. Some of Miriam's reactions are cast in the form of mental letters home or imaginary conversations with her sisters, which provide a structured way to verbalize mental processes. Miriam pays attention to the sights and sounds and smells of Hanover because they are new, giving readers a sense of the physical setting absent in many of the later books.

Miriam's moods are typically adolescent. An incident or object can set off a homesick reverie or a bout of self-recrimination; the sound of music or the sight of rain on paving stones can create an inexpressible transport of joy. She is alternately rebellious and anxious for approval; she is glad to learn that her French roommate is Protestant (because she could not bear living with a Catholic), proud of the skill in logic that allows her to criticize the premises of a sermon, moved by the sound of hymns in German. She worries about her plainness, her intellectual deficiencies, her inability to get close to people. Observing class and cultural differences lets her begin to understand that she has unthinkingly absorbed many of her tastes and ideas; she starts to grow more deliberate. This portrait of Miriam at the age of seventeen—which forms the essential background for the rest of *Pilgrimage*—is also interesting for its own sake.

Because the narrative is limited to Miriam's consciousness, the reader is able to supply interpretation. In one key scene, the middle-aged Pastor Lahmann, chaplain to the school, quotes a verse describing his ambition for "A little land, well-tilled,/ A little wife, well-willed" and then asks Miriam to take off her glasses so that he can see how nearsighted her eyes really are. Miriam, who is both furious at being "regarded as one of a world of little tame things to be summoned by little man to be well-willed wives" and warmed by the personal attention that makes her forget, for a moment, that she is a governess, is oblivious to the sexual implications of Pastor Lahmann's behavior, and she cannot understand why the headmistress is angry when she walks in upon the scene. Although Miriam's consciousness will develop in subsequent volumes, her combination of receptivity to male attention, anger at male assumptions, and blindness to sexual nuance will remain.

DEADLOCK

Deadlock contains a greater proportion of direct internal monologue than the earlier books. Miriam has grown more articulate; she interprets her emotional states and examines the premises underlying her conflicts. During her first years in London, she had cherished the city for the independence it gave her. By such acts as smoking, eating alone in restaurants, and dressing without regard to fashion, she deliberately rejected Victorian womanhood. In *Honeycomb*, she refused a marriage that would have satisfied her craving for luxuries because she could not accept a subordinate role. In *Deadlock*, Miriam is faced by the loneliness that seems inextricably linked to independence. Her work has become drudgery because she no longer has the sense of a social relationship with her employer. A Christmas visit to her married sister reveals the distance that has grown between them; Miriam had not even realized that Harriet's marriage was unhappy.

Deadlock is shaped by the course of Miriam's relationship with Michael Shatov. The romance forces her conflicts to the surface. Shatov is a young Jew recently arrived from Russia; a lodger at Mrs. Bailey's arranges for Miriam to tutor him in English. As she shows Shatov London, tired scenes recapture their original freshness. Miriam is excited by her ability to formulate ideas when she argues about philosophy or works on a translation. Yet, although Miriam is buoyed by the joy of sharing her thoughts with another person, Shatov's continual presence comes between her and the life that was her own. Her love has a maternal quality: Though Shatov is only three years younger than Miriam, he is a foreigner and also, Miriam finds, rather impractical; she feels protective. She is also sexually reticent: Because she has despised traditional femininity, she does not know how to behave as the object of a courtship. The romance ends when Miriam deliberately engages Shatov in an argument that reveals his views of woman's limited nature. (The final scene restates the problem more concretely when Miriam visits an Englishwoman married to a Jewish man.)

Beneath these specific difficulties lies the friction between Miriam's individualism and Shatov's tendency to see problems in the abstract—she talks about herself, he dwells on the future of the race. For Richardson, the conflict reflects the irreconcilable difference between masculine objectivity (or materialism) and feminine subjectivity. The images of darkness accumulate as Miriam realizes the extent of her deadlock; unable to be a woman in the sense that men see women, she seems to have no path out of loneliness and alienation.

DAWN'S LEFT HAND

Dawn's Left Hand is a prelude to the deliberate detachment and observation that would turn Miriam into a writer. *Oberland* (the preceding book) vibrates with the sensory detail of a two-week holiday in Switzerland that makes London complications seem far away; returning, Miriam sees people objectively even when she is with them. The transitions between third-person narrative and internal monologue are less noticeable; Miriam and the narrator have virtually merged. The visual content of scenes reveals their meaning. Miriam looks at pictorial relationships and examines gesture and tone for the nonverbal communications that, to women, are often more meaningful than words. (During the years that she worked on *Dawn's Left Hand*, Richardson wrote regularly about films—which were still silent—for the magazine *Close Up*.)

Images of light carry emotional and symbolic content throughout *Pilgrimage*. When Miriam visits Densley's medical office early in *Dawn's Left Hand*, the drawn shades are keeping out the light; she refuses his proposal—one last offer of conventional marriage—with a momentary wistfulness that is immediately replaced by a great sense of relief. She is increasingly aware of herself as an actor in the scenes of her life. Self-observation allows physical compositions to reveal power relationships: When Wilson comes into Miriam's room, she notices that he stands over her like a doctor, and when he embarks on a program of seduction to the music of Richard Wagner, she disputes his control by rearranging the chairs. On another occasion, in a hotel room, Miriam looks in the mirror to observe herself and Wilson. Her own position blocks the light and thus the scene is chilled even before she begins to see him as a pathetic naked male.

During the final stages of the Wilson affair, Miriam is increasingly preoccupied by a beautiful young woman—soon to be a radical suffragist—who pursues her ardently and pays homage to her as a woman in ways that bring home to Miriam the impossibility of real communion with men. Yet the deep commitment demanded by Amabel is frightening; her intense adoration forces Miriam into a role that threatens her independence more crucially than Wilson's overt attempts at domination. The advantage of being with people who interact only on superficial levels, Miriam realizes, is that she can retain her freedom.

MARCH MOONLIGHT

Although Richardson struggled to bring the events in *March Moonlight* up to 1912, the year that she began writing *Pilgrimage*, her form and subject virtually required the book to remain without conclusion. The narrative techniques of *March Moonlight* grow more deliberate; when Miriam begins to write, she thinks and sees differently and is aware of selecting and arranging details. Thus, the book's ending is only a middle: Miriam's sense of self would inevitably change as she reexamined and re-created her experiences in order to write novels. Once traditional formulas are rejected and *being* itself becomes the subject, there can be no ending; there is no epiphany, no coming-of-age, no final truth but rather a continuous process of self-making through self-awareness.

Sally Mitchell

OTHER MAJOR WORKS

NONFICTION: *Gleanings from the Works of George Fox*, 1914; *The Quakers Past and Present*, 1914; *John Austen and the Inseparables*, 1930.

BIBLIOGRAPHY

Bloom, Harold, ed. *British Women Fiction Writers, 1900-1960.* 2 vols. Philadelphia: Chelsea House, 1997. A brief biography and critical essays about Richardson's work and place in literary history is included in volume 2 of this survey of British women writers.

Bluemel, Kristin. *Experimenting on the Borders of Modernism: Dorothy Richardson's "Pilgrimage."* Athens: University of Georgia Press, 1997. The first chapter assesses Richardson and previous studies of her. Subsequent chapters explore Richardson's handling of gender, the problems of the body, science in *Pilgrimage*, and the author's quest for an ending to this long work. Includes notes and a bibliography.

Fromm, Gloria G. *Dorothy Richardson: A Biography.* Champaign: University of Illinois Press, 1977. An objective biography, which carefully draws distinctions between the events of Richardson's life and those of her fictional characters, but also identifies clear correlations between the two. Extensively researched and well written and supplemented by illustrations, chapter endnotes, a comprehensive bibliography, and an index.

Garrity, Jane. "'Neither English nor Civilized': Dorothy Richardson's Spectatrix and the Feminine Crusade for Global Intervention." In *Step-Daughters of England: British Women Modernists and the National Imaginary.* New York: St. Martin's Press, 2003. Garrity examines works by Richardson and three other modernist women writers to demonstrate how these works express the writers' ambivalent and complex feelings about English national culture.

Gevirtz, Susan. *Narrative's Journey: The Fiction and Film Writing of Dorothy Richardson.* New York: Peter Lang, 1996. A probing discussion of Richardson's aesthetic. This is a challenging study for advanced students. *Pilgrimage* receives detailed discussion throughout the book. Includes an extensive bibliography not only on Richardson but also on feminist theory, literary and cultural theory, poetics and phenomenology, theology and spirituality, travel and travel theories, and narrative.

McCracken, Scott. "Editorial." *Pilgrimages: The Journal of Dorothy Richardson Studies* 1, no. 1 (2008). Richardson scholar Scott McCracken introduces the first issue of a new academic journal focusing on Richardson's life and works.

Parsons, Deborah L. *Theorists of the Modernist Novel: James Joyce, Dorothy Richardson, Virginia Woolf.* New York: Routledge, 2007. A study of the aesthetic theories of Richardson and two other modernist writers. Parsons examines realism, characterization, gender representation, and other elements of Richardson's work.

Radford, Jean. *Dorothy Richardson.* Bloomington: Indiana University Press, 1991. An excellent introductory study, with chapters on reading in *Pilgrimage*, the author's quest for form, London as a space for women, and Richardson as a feminist writer. Includes notes and a bibliography.

Randall, Bryony. "Dailiness in Dorothy Richardson's *Pilgrimage.*" In *Modernism, Daily*

Time, and Everyday Life. New York: Cambridge University Press, 2007. Argues that the temporal notion of "the day" partly structures Richardson's fiction. Also examines Richardson's attempts at rendering time without beginnings and endings.

Rosenberg, John. *Dorothy Richardson, the Genius They Forgot: A Critical Biography.* New York: Alfred A. Knopf, 1973. The strength of Rosenberg's biography lies in his scholarly credibility, as he aptly parallels events in *Pilgrimage* to Richardson's life. His concluding analysis of Richardson's pioneering impact upon the development of the novel, however, lacks the impact of his earlier writing but is still perceptive. Includes an index and a bibliography.

Winning, Joanne. *The Pilgrimage of Dorothy Richardson*. Madison: University of Wisconsin Press, 2000. Winning argues that Richardson's thirteen-volume novel contains a subtext of lesbian desire and sexuality, and she compares this novel to works by other lesbian modernist writers.

CAROL SHIELDS

Born: Oak Park, Illinois; June 2, 1935
Died: Victoria, British Columbia, Canada; July 16, 2003
Also known as: Carol Ann Warner

PRINCIPAL LONG FICTION
Small Ceremonies, 1976
The Box Garden, 1977
Happenstance, 1980
A Fairly Conventional Woman, 1982
Swann: A Mystery, 1987
A Celibate Season, 1991 (with Blanche Howard)
The Republic of Love, 1992
Happenstance, 1993 (contains *Happenstance* and *A Fairly Conventional Woman*)
The Stone Diaries, 1993
Larry's Party, 1997
Unless, 2002

OTHER LITERARY FORMS

Carol Shields began her writing career as a poet with the publication of *Others* in 1972 and *Intersect* in 1974; she would return to her poetic roots with 1992's *Coming to Canada*. Shields wrote in various genres; in addition to composing novels and poetry, she was a short-story writer, an essayist, a playwright, a literary critic, and a biographer. Shields collaborated on a number of projects across genres with other writers. She coauthored the novel *A Celibate Season* with Blanche Howard, cowrote the drama *Anniversary* (pr., pb. 1998) with Dave Williamson, and edited two essay anthologies with Marjorie Anderson, *Dropped Threads: What We Aren't Told* (2001) and its sequel, *Dropped Threads 2: More of What We Aren't Told* (2003). Long an admirer of the British novelist Jane Austen, Shields researched and wrote a literary biography of the author that was published in 2001 to great acclaim.

ACHIEVEMENTS

The success that Carol Shields experienced as a novelist is remarkable given that she did not publish her first novel until she was forty, although her talent as a writer was apparent much earlier. In 1965 she received recognition from the Canadian Broadcasting Corporation (CBC) for a poem she entered in a contest; by the mid-1970's, she had published two volumes of poetry. It was her first novel, *Small Ceremonies*, however, that captured the attention of critics and the reading public. In the three decades of her career as a novelist, her works met with both popular and critical approval. *Small Ceremonies* won the Canadian Authors' Association Award for the Best Novel of 1976. Shields's popular *The Stone Diaries* was short-listed for the Booker Prize, won the National Book Critics Circle Award in 1994, and received the Pulitzer Prize in 1995. Her other award-winning novels include *Larry's Party*, recipient of the Orange Prize for women's fiction, and *Swann: A Mystery*, recipient of the Arthur Ellis Award for Best Canadian Mystery. Her final novel, *Unless*, was nominated for the Booker Prize and the Orange Prize and won the Ethel Wilson Fiction Prize. In other genres, Shields received the CBC Prize for Drama in 1983, and her biography *Jane Austen* was awarded the Charles Taylor Prize for Literary Non-Fiction in 2002. In recognition of her talents as an author, Shields was named a fellow of both the Guggenheim Foundation and the Royal Society of Canada. In 2003 she received an honorary doctorate from the University of Manitoba.

BIOGRAPHY

Carol Shields was born Carol Ann Warner in Oak Park, Illinois, on June 2, 1935, the third and youngest child of Robert Warner and Inez Warner (née Selgren). Her father supervised a candy company, and her mother taught grade school. Carol grew up in a household in which books were treasured by her parents and her older twin siblings; she taught herself to read before she began formal schooling. After completing her studies at Oak Park High School in 1953, she left Illinois to attend Hanover College in Indiana. She spent her junior year abroad, studying in England at the University of Exeter, where she met and fell in love with Donald Shields. Following her graduation from Hanover, they married and returned to England so that Donald, a civil engineer, could enter a doctoral program at the University of Manchester. Their union produced four children, a son and three daughters.

In 1963, Shields and her family settled in Toronto, Canada, where in 1971 the transplanted American became a Canadian citizen. In the midst of raising a family and running a household, Shields carved out time for her writing. In 1964 she submitted a poem to the Young Writers Competition, sponsored by the Canadian Broadcasting Corporation, and won. Encouraged by her success, Shields continued to write and to submit her work for publication. Her poems appeared in print in various Canadian journals, and several were broadcast on CBC programs. Her output as a poet resulted in the publication of two collections of poetry: *Others* in 1972 and *Intersect* in 1974. In 1973, Shields began graduate studies at the University of Manitoba and found part-time employment as an editorial assistant at the journal *Canadian Slavic Papers*. She completed her master of arts degree in 1975; her master's thesis was a study of female sexuality and social roles in works by nineteenth century Canadian author Susanna Moodie.

Following her graduation, Shields obtained teaching positions at a number of universities, including the University of Ottawa, the University of British Columbia in Vancouver, and the University of Manitoba in Winnipeg. She continued to write poetry but found greater success as a writer of novels. Beginning with her 1976 debut novel, *Small Ceremonies*, and ending with the publication of *Unless* in 2002, Shields would experience twenty-five years of increasing acclaim as a novelist. In her final years, aware that she had terminal cancer, Shields wrote at a prodigious rate, completing several works, including *Unless* and her Austen biography. She died of cancer on July 16, 2003.

ANALYSIS

Critics generally divide Carol Shields's novels into two groups: those novels written prior to her Pulitzer Prize-winning *The Stone Diaries* and those following. Shields's first four novels, *Small Ceremonies*, *The Box Garden*, *Happenstance*, and *A Fairly Conventional Woman*, are domestic in focus and realistic in style. Set in her adopted Canada, they trace the lives of ordinary women in commonplace circumstances who are striving to discover who they are through relationships with other people in their lives. The search for identity is a common theme in these works. The titles of the works suggest the insularity of the women's lives through words like "small," "box," and "conventional." What marks Shields's early work is the contrast between the quiet personalities and lives of her protagonists and the strong impression they make on readers, who see versions of their own lives, those of ordinary women, represented on the pages.

Shields's later novels bear trademarks of postmodernism, a literary style characterized by fragmentation and multiple narrative voices. Whereas modern novelists quest after meaning in their works, postmodern writers question the very possibility of creating meaning through words. Shields's use of multigeneric forms and multiple, competing narrators places her within this movement. Even prior to *The Stone Diaries*, her 1987 novel *Swann* exhibited traits of postmodernism. In *Swann*, the questionable circumstances surrounding the title character's death are relayed by four separate narrators, and the final chapter is written as a script. Using this unconventional format, Shields unravels the mystery genre even as she reconstructs the murder of Swann, a once obscure Canadian poet made famous in death. *Swann* is a precursor to *The Stone Diaries*, a novel that, in its unconventional approach to chronicling the life of Daisy Goodwill, deconstructs the genre of fictional autobiography. Increasingly, in her later works, including *Larry's Party* and *Unless*, Shields became more emboldened in the use of structures and styles associated with postmodernism.

SMALL CEREMONIES

While at the University of Manitoba, Shields was encouraged by her professors to try her hand at fiction in addition to literary criticism. Her first novel, *Small Ceremonies*, published in 1976, manages to blend both elements. Inspired by Shields's scholarly thesis, the novel features a narrator who, mirroring her creator, conducts research on Canadian author Susanna Moodie in order to write a literary biography of Moodie's life. Although classified as realistic fiction, the novel nevertheless hints at the more postmodern forms that emerge in Shields's later works. Present already is the metatextual element: Shields writes about a writer who writes about a writer.

Clearly this novel draws on autobiographical elements. Similar to Shields at the time, the novel's protagonist, Judith Gill, is a literary scholar who is married with children. Reminiscent of Shields's relocation to England during her husband's graduate studies, Gill's husband's sabbatical takes his family to Birmingham and to the residence of a family that has traveled to Greece. These parallel circumstances offer a family living abroad in the home of a family living abroad. The novel begins with the Gill family recently returned to Canada and traces events across three seasons, autumn through spring. A central theme in the novel is identity, both personal and national. In the process of researching the life of Susanna Moodie, Gill examines her own. Both inquiries lead to reflections on what it means to be a writer, mother, wife, Canadian, and traveler abroad. Gill contemplates the effects of life abroad on her family's return to Canadian life and on her writing. In another connection between author and character, Shields has Gill step aside from her scholarly book on Moodie to attempt to write a novel.

THE STONE DIARIES

In *The Stone Diaries*, Shields's multilayered narration reinvents the fictional biography. The story of Daisy Goodwill is told at intervals in the first and the third person. Wherever Daisy leaves off telling her version of events, or is unable to speak for herself, a second narrator steps in and continues her story. In this manner, Shields blends together biography and autobiography in a fictional setting to create a hybrid genre. Witnessing is a major motif in the novel, beginning with the neighbors who view Daisy's birth and her mother's resultant death. Shields suggests that a person's life is too complex for a single voice to be sufficient—to acknowledge a life, there must be outside observers. The third-person narrator, in addition to recounting scenes from Daisy's life, offers commentary on that life and on the nature of autobiography. The metatextual elements that emerge—an autobiography that explores the nature of autobiography—are a continuation of techniques that Shields began employing in *Small Ceremonies*.

Divided into ten chapters, *The Stone Diaries* records life stages. Chapter titles such as "Birth," "Childhood," "Marriage," "Love," and "Illness and Decline" progress until "Death" is reached. The novel ends with the nondescript eulogy delivered at Daisy's funeral, one that appears to negate her existence. This last testimonial to Daisy's life offers little that is memorable. We learn from the minister that she was a wife, a mother, and a citizen, but who Daisy was when she was not filling these roles is omitted. From her own account, what gave her the greatest satisfaction in life was not marriage or children but writing a gardening column, a job taken from her and given to a man. In the final verdict of her life, Daisy becomes simultaneously an everywoman and a no woman. The novel is unsettling as it leaves readers with little comprehension of the value of Daisy's life. There remains a sense that it was worth more than what was recorded. The character's own dissatisfaction with the remembrances accorded her is clear in her dying thought, "I am not at peace." In her chronicle of Daisy, Shields manages to create a fictional biography about the invisibility of most women's lives.

UNLESS

In her final novel, one written with knowledge of her own impending death, Shields returns to the life of a woman writer, the subject of her first novel. In *Unless*, Shields expands the scope and intensifies the depth of her inquiry. The lead character, Reta Winters, despite her facility with words, which has allowed her to pen a successful first novel and begin a second, finds herself unable to communicate with friends and, more painfully, with her reclusive college-age daughter. Complicating matters is an envious editor who insists she rewrite her female heroine into the background of her second novel in order to elevate the status of a minor male character. *Unless* explores the role of women in modern society and culture, and the pain that often accompanies women's efforts to achieve visibility and voice. Critics consider *Unless* to be Shields's most postmodern and most feminist work.

Dorothy Dodge Robbins

OTHER MAJOR WORKS

SHORT FICTION: *Various Miracles*, 1985; *The Orange Fish*, 1989; *Dressing Up for the Carnival*, 2000; *Collected Stories*, 2004.

PLAYS: *Departures and Arrivals*, pr., pb. 1990; *Thirteen Hands*, pr., pb. 1993; *Fashion, Power, Guilt, and the Charity of Families*, pr., pb. 1995 (with Catherine Shields); *Anniversary: A Comedy*, pr., pb. 1998 (with Dave Williamson); *Thirteen Hands, and Other Plays*, 2002.

POETRY: *Others*, 1972; *Intersect*, 1974; *Coming to Canada*, 1992.

NONFICTION: *Susanna Moodie: Voice and Vision*, 1976; *Jane Austen*, 2001.

EDITED TEXTS: *Dropped Threads: What We Aren't Told*, 2001 (with Marjorie Anderson); *Dropped Threads 2: More of What We Aren't Told*, 2003 (with Anderson and Catherine Shields).

BIBLIOGRAPHY

Atwood, Margaret. "A Soap Bubble Floating over the Void." *Virginia Quarterly Review* 81, no. 1 (Winter, 2005): 139-142. Tribute to Shields characterizes her as intelligent, witty, and observant, a writer equally capable of creating images of intense joy and images of despair.

Besner, Neil K., ed. *Carol Shields: The Arts of a Writing Life*. Winnipeg, Man.: Prairie Fire Press, 2003. Collection of essays takes an anecdotal, rather than critical, approach to Shields's life as a writer, connecting her fiction to events in her own life. Focuses primarily on Shields's poetry and novels.

Ciabattari, Jane. "The Goodbye Girl." Review of *Unless*, by Carol Shields. *Los Angeles*

Times, May 12, 2002. Assesses the novel in terms of its postmodern conceits. Includes discussion of its metatextual format (a novel about a woman writing a novel about a woman writing a novel) and its juxtaposition of fact and fiction.

Eden, Edward, and Dee Goertz, eds. *Carol Shields, Narrative Hunger, and the Possibilities of Fiction.* Toronto, Ont.: University of Toronto Press, 2003. Collection of essays addresses Shields as a complex and significant author. Presents critical examination of Shields's oeuvre in relation to realist and postmodern narratives. Includes extensive annotated bibliography.

Schwartz, Lynn Sharon. "The Allures of Form." Review of *Dressing Up for the Carnival*, by Carol Shields. *New Leader* 83, no. 2 (May/June, 2000): 35-37. Compares the stories in the collection *Dressing Up for the Carnival* to Shields's novels *The Stone Diaries* and *Larry's Party* and asserts that the stories are rich in ideas but insufficient in character development, a trademark of the novels.

Stovel, Nora Foster. "'Because She's a Woman': Myth and Metafiction in Carol Shields's *Unless.*" *English Studies in Canada* 32, no. 4 (December, 2006): 51-73. Examines the blend of feminism and modernism in *Unless*, a novel about a woman on the margins of society. Categorizes the novel as Shields's most experimental in form and most daring in content.

Weese, Katherine. "The 'Invisible Woman': Narrative Strategies in *The Stone Diaries.*" *Journal of Narrative Theory* 36, no. 1 (Winter, 2006): 90-120. Applies feminist theories to the complex narrative techniques used in *The Stone Diaries* to reveal a main character who is simultaneously central to and distant from her own story.

GERTRUDE STEIN

Born: Allegheny (now in Pittsburgh), Pennsylvania; February 3, 1874
Died: Neuilly-sur-Seine, France; July 27, 1946

PRINCIPAL LONG FICTION
Three Lives, 1909
The Making of Americans: Being a History of a Family's Progress, 1925
   (abridged 1934)
Lucy Church Amiably, 1930
A Long Gay Book, 1932
The World Is Round, 1939
Ida, a Novel, 1941
Brewsie and Willie, 1946
Blood on the Dining-Room Floor, 1948
Things as They Are, 1950 (originally known as *Q.E.D.*)
Mrs. Reynolds, and Five Earlier Novelettes, 1931-1942, 1952
A Novel of Thank You, 1958

OTHER LITERARY FORMS

Any attempt to separate Gertrude Stein's novels from her other kinds of writing must be highly arbitrary. Stein thought the novel to be a failed literary form in the twentieth century, claiming that no real novels had been written after Marcel Proust, even including her own novelistic efforts in this assessment. For this and other reasons, it might be claimed that few, if any, of Stein's works are novels in any traditional sense. In fact, very few of Stein's more than six hundred titles in more than forty books can be adequately classified into any traditional literary forms. Her philosophy of composition was so idiosyncratic, her prose style so seemingly nonrational, that her writing bears little resemblance to whatever genre it purports to represent.

Depending on one's definition of the novel, Stein wrote anywhere between six and twelve novels, ranging in length from less than one hundred to 925 pages. The problem is that none of Stein's novels has a plot in any conventional sense, that few have conventionally developed and sustained characters, and that several seem almost exclusively autobiographical, more diaries and daybooks than anything else.

It is not any easier to categorize Stein's other pieces of writing, most of which are radically sui generis. If references to literary forms are made very loosely, Stein's work can be divided into novels, autobiographies, portraits, poems, lectures, operas, plays, and explanations. Other than her novels, her best-known works are *The Autobiography of Alice B. Toklas* (1933); *Tender Buttons* (1914); *Four Saints in Three Acts* (pr., pb. 1934); *Lectures in America* (1935); *Everybody's Autobiography* (1937); and *Portraits and Prayers*, 1934.

Gertrude Stein
(Library of Congress)

ACHIEVEMENTS

Whether towering or crouching, Gertrude Stein is ubiquitous in contemporary litera-ture. A child of the nineteenth century who staunchly adhered to many of its values half-way through the twentieth, she nevertheless dedicated her creative life to the destruction of nineteenth century concepts of artistic order and purpose. In her own words, she set out to do nothing less than to kill a century, to lay the old ways of literary convention to rest. She later boasted that "the most serious thinking about the nature of literature in the twen-tieth century has been done by a woman," and her claim has great merit.

During the course of her career, Stein finally managed to convince almost everyone that there was indeed some point, if not profundity, in her aggressively enigmatic style. The ridicule and parody that frustrated so much of her early work had turned to grudging tolerance or outright lionizing by 1934, when Stein made her triumphant American lecture tour; for the last fifteen or so years of her life, she was published even if her editor had not the vaguest idea of what she was doing (as Bennett Cerf later admitted he had not). On the most concrete level, Stein's distinctive prose style is remarkably significant even when its philosophical dimensions are ignored. William H. Gass has observed, Stein "did more with sentences, and understood them better, than any writer ever has."

More important was Stein's influence on other leaders in the development of modernism. As a student of William James and as a friend of Alfred Alfred North Whitehead and Pablo Picasso, Stein lived at the center of the philosophical and artistic revolutions of the twentieth century. She was the natural emblem for modernism, and in her person, career, and legend, many of its salient issues converged.

In the light of more recent developments in the novel and in literary theory, it has also been argued that Stein was the first postmodernist, the first writer to claim openly that the instance of language is itself as important as the reality to which it refers. Among major writers, Ernest Hemingway was most obviously influenced by his association with her, but her genius was freely acknowledged by F. Scott Fitzgerald, Sherwood Anderson, and Thornton Wilder. William Saroyan explained her influence most directly when he asserted that no American writer could keep from coming under it, a sentiment reluctantly echoed by Edmund Wilson in *Axel's Castle* (1931), even before Stein's great popular success in the mid-1930's.

BIOGRAPHY

Gertrude Stein was born on February 3, 1874, in Allegheny, Pennsylvania, but she was seven years old before her family settled into permanent residence in Oakland, California, the city she was later to describe as having "no there there." Her birth itself was contingent on the deaths of two of her five brothers and sisters: Her parents had decided to have only five children, and only after two children had died in infancy were Gertrude and her older brother, Leo, conceived. Identity was to become one of the central preoccupations of her writing career, and the tenuous nature of her own birth greatly influenced that concern.

Stein's early years were comfortably bourgeois and uneventful. Her father, a vice president of the Union Street Municipal Railway System in San Francisco, was authoritarian, moody, and aggressive, but vacillating, and he may have helped foster her sense of independence, but he undoubtedly left her annoyed by him in particular and by fatherhood in general. Her mother barely figured in her life at all: A pale, withdrawn, ineffectual woman, she left most of the rearing of her children to governesses. By the time Stein was age seventeen, both parents had died and she had grown even closer to her immediate older brother, Leo. In 1893, she entered Harvard Annex (renamed Radcliffe College the following year), thus rejoining Leo, who was a student at Harvard. There, Stein studied with William James and Hugo Munsterberg and became involved in research in psychology. Together with the great influence exerted on her thinking by James, this early work in psychology was to provide her with both a subject and a style that would continue in many forms throughout her career. She was awarded her bachelor of arts degree by Harvard in 1898, almost a year after she had entered medical school at Johns Hopkins University. Her interest in medicine rapidly waned, and she left Johns Hopkins in 1901, failing four courses in her final semester.

After leaving medical school, Stein spent two years moving back and forth between Europe and the United States. During that time, she was involved in an agonizing love affair with another young woman student at Johns Hopkins, May Bookstaver. The affair was painfully complicated, first by Stein's naïveté then by the presence of a more sophisticated rival for May's love, Mabel Haynes. The resulting lover's triangle led Stein, in an effort to understand May, to begin formulating the theories of personality that dominated her early writing. The frustration and eventual despair of this lesbian relationship profoundly influenced Stein's view of the psychology of personality and of love. Most directly, Stein's troubled affair with May provided her with many, if not most, of the concerns of three of her books, *Q.E.D.*, *The Making of Americans*, and *Three Lives*, the first two of which she began while living in New York in the winter of 1903.

After a brief stay in New York, she lived with Leo, first in Bloomsbury in London and then, beginning in 1903, in Paris at 27 rue de Fleurus, the address she was to make so well known to the world. In Paris, Gertrude and Leo became more and more interested in painting, buying works by new artists such as Henri Matisse and Picasso. Leo's preference was for works by Matisse, while Gertrude favored the more experimental works of Picasso, marking the beginning of a distancing process that would lead to Leo's complete separation from his sister in 1913. Leo was bright and opinionated, and fancied himself by far the greater creative talent of the two, but his brilliance and energy never produced any creative or significant critical work, and he grew to resent both his sister's independent thinking and her emerging ability to write. Later in his life, he would dismiss Gertrude as "dumb" and her writing as "nonsense."

In 1907, Stein met another young American woman in Paris, Alice Toklas, and Alice began to displace Leo as the most important personal influence in Gertrude's life. Alice learned to type so she could transcribe Stein's handwritten manuscripts, beginning with portions of *The Making of Americans* in 1908. In 1909, Alice moved in with Gertrude and Leo at 27 rue de Fleurus, and by 1913, Alice had replaced Leo as Gertrude's companion and as the manager of her household. Stein later referred to her relationship with Alice as a "marriage," and few, if any, personal relationships have ever influenced a literary career so profoundly. Apart from providing Stein with the persona for her best-known work, *The Autobiography of Alice B. Toklas*, Alice typed, criticized, and valiantly worked to publish all of Stein's work for the rest of her career and for the twenty years that Alice lived after Stein's death. While it is doubtful that Alice was directly responsible for any of Stein's writing, her influence on its composition and on Stein's life was tremendous.

Gertrude and Alice spent the first months of World War I in England as houseguests of Alfred North Whitehead, returning to Paris briefly in 1914, then spending more than a year in Spain. They joined the war effort in 1917 when Stein ordered a Ford motor van from America for use as a supply truck for the American Fund for French Wounded, an acquisition that began Stein's lifelong fascination with automobiles, particularly with Fords. She and Alice drove this van, named Auntie, until the war ended, work for which she was later awarded the Medaille de la Reconnaissance Française.

Modernism had burst on the American consciousness when the Armory Show opened in New York in 1913, and this show, which had confronted Americans with the first cubist paintings, also led to the association in the public mind of Stein's writing with this shockingly new art, particularly since Stein's first periodical publications had been "Matisse" and "Picasso" in *Camera Work* the year before. Stein's mammoth, 925-page novel, *The Making of Americans*, was published in 1925, and in 1926, she lectured at Oxford and Cambridge, attempting to explain her idiosyncratic writing style. Her "landscape" novel, *Lucy Church Amiably*, appeared in 1930, but it was in 1933, with the publication of the best-selling *The Autobiography of Alice B. Toklas*, that Stein first captured the public's interest. She became front-page news the following year when her opera *Four Saints in Three Acts* was first performed and when she embarked on a nationwide lecture tour, later described in *Everybody's Autobiography* and *Lectures in America*.

Stein and Toklas spent World War II in Bilignin and then in Culoz, France. Although Stein and Toklas were both Jewish, they were never persecuted by occupying forces, owing in part to the influence of Bernard Fay, an early admirer of Stein's work who directed the Bibliothèque Nationale for the Vichy regime. When, after the war, Fay was sentenced to life imprisonment for his Vichy activities, Stein was one of his few defenders. That her art collection survived Nazi occupation virtually intact can only have been through Fay's intercession. During the war, Stein finished another novel, *Mrs. Reynolds*, and *Wars I Have Seen* (1945), an autobiographical work. Her novel *Brewsie and Willie*, a series of conversations among American soldiers, was published in 1946.

Stein died following an operation for cancer in the American Hospital in Neuilly-sur-Seine, France, on July 27, 1946. While Toklas's account of Stein's last words may be apocryphal, it certainly is in keeping with the spirit of her life. As Toklas later reconstructed their last conversation, Stein had asked her "What is the answer?" Then, when Toklas remained silent, Stein added, "In that case, what is the question?"

ANALYSIS

While Gertrude Stein's persistence finally earned her access to readers, it could never guarantee her readers who would or could take her strange writing seriously. As a result, more confusing and contradictory information surrounds her career than that of any other twentieth century writer of comparable reputation. Usually responding in any of four basic ways, readers and critics alike seemed to view her as one, a literary charlatan of the P. T. Barnum ilk, interested in publicity or money rather than in art; two, something of a naïve child-woman incapable of comprehending the world around her; three, a fiery-eyed literary revolutionary, den mother of the avant-garde; or four, an ageless repository of wisdom and genius. Ultimately, the reader's acceptance or rejection of these various categories will greatly determine his or her response to Stein's writing, which forces the reader to make as many cognitive choices as does that of any major writer.

Stein's many explanations of her writing further complicate its interpretation: Even her "explanations" frustrate as much as they reveal, explicitly setting her up in cognitive competition with her reader, a competition suggested by her favorite cryptogram, which works out to read "I understand you undertake to overthrow my undertaking." Stein proposes a rhetoric not of misunderstanding, but of anti-understanding; that is, her explanations usually argue precisely against the desirability of explaining.

As Stein bluntly put the matter, "understanding is a very dull occupation." "Understanding" has a special denotation for Stein, sometimes meaning as little as "paying attention to" or "reading." "To understand a thing means to be in contact with that thing," she proclaimed. Central to her mistrust of explanations and interpretations was her often anguished belief that her thoughts could never really be matched to anyone else's. She was deeply troubled by this doubt as she wrote *The Making of Americans*, referring in that work to "the complete realization that no one can believe as you do about anything" as "complete disillusionment in living." Starting from this assumption that no one can ever really understand what someone else says or writes because of the inherent ambiguity of language, Stein not only decided to force her readers to confront that ambiguity but also claimed it as a primary virtue of her writing. She announced triumphantly that

> if you have vitality enough of knowing enough of what you mean, somebody and sometimes a great many will have to realize that you know what you mean and so they will agree that you mean what you know, which is as near as anybody can come to understanding any one.

Stein's focus here is on relationships or process rather than on product—on the act of trying to become one with, rather than focusing on the ultimate result of that act.

Stein's thinking about understanding manifests itself in a number of distinctive ways in her writing, as do her theories of perception and of human psychology. Moreover, during the nearly fifty years of her writing career, her style developed in many related but perceptibly different stages, such as her "cubist" or her "cinema" phases. As a result, no single analysis can do more than describe the primary concerns and features of one of her stylistic periods. There are, however, three central concerns that underlie and partially account for all the stages in the development of her style. These concerns are with the value of individual words, with repetition as the basic rhythm of existence, and with the related concept of "movement" in writing. Her articulations of these central concerns all run counter to her reader's expectations about the purpose and function of language and of literature. Her writing surprised her readers in much the same way that her penchant for playing only the black keys on a piano surprised and frustrated all but the most patient of her listeners.

One of Stein's goals was to return full meaning, value, and particularity to the words she used. "I took individual words and thought about them until I got their weight and volume complete and put them next to another word," she explained of seemingly nonsense phrases such as "toasted Susie is my ice cream," or "mouse and mountain and a quiver, a quaint statue and pain in an exterior and silence more silence louder shows salmon a mischief intender." This sort of paratactic juxtaposition of seemingly unrelated words rarely occurs in Stein's novels but represents a problem for her reader in many other ways in her writing. She frequently chose to stress or focus on a part or aspect of the object of her description that the reader normally does not consider. The "things" Stein saw and wrote of were not the "things" with which readers are familiar: Where another observer might see a coin balanced on its edge, Stein might choose either of the descriptive extremes of seeing it literally as a thin rectangle, or figuratively as the essence of money. Characteristically, her most opaque parataxis refers to essences or processes rather than to objects or static concepts.

A related quirk in Stein's style results from her intellectual or emotional attachment to particular words and phrases at certain stages of her career. As she admitted in *The Making of Americans,*

> To be using a new word in my writing is to me a very difficult thing. . . . Using a word I have not yet been using in my writing is to me a very difficult and a peculiar feeling. Sometimes I am using a new one, sometimes I feel a new meaning in an old one, sometimes I like one I am very fond of that one that has many meanings many ways of being used to make different meanings to everyone.

Stein said she had learned from Paul Cézanne that everything in a painting was related to everything else and that each part of the painting was of equal importance—a blade of grass as important to the composition of the painting as a tree. She attempted to apply these two principles to the composition of her sentences, taking special delight in using normally "overlooked" words, arguing that articles, prepositions, and conjunctions—the transitive elements in grammar—are just as important and more interesting than substantives such as nouns and verbs. Her reassessment both of the value of words and of the conventions of description resulted in what Michael J. Hoffman, in *The Development of Abstractionism in the Writings of Gertrude Stein* (1965), has described as Stein's "abstractionism." It also resulted in her including in her writing totally unexpected information in perplexing paratactic word strings.

A second constant in Stein's style is the pronounced repetition of words, phrases, and sentences, with no changes or with only incremental progressions of sounds or associations. Works such as *The Making of Americans* and *Three Lives* contain long passages in which each sentence is a light variation on some core phrase, with great repetition of words even within a single sentence. Stein termed this phenomenon "insistence" rather than repetition, citing her former teacher, James, as her philosophical authority. James's argument in his *The Principles of Psychology* (1890) that one must think of the identical recurrence of a fact in a fresh manner remarkably resembles Stein's contention that

> in expressing anything there can be no repetition because the essence of that expression is insistence, and if you insist you must each time use emphasis and if you use emphasis it is not possible while anybody is alive that they should use exactly the same emphasis.

Repetition or insistence is perhaps the central aspect of what has been called Stein's "cinema style," based on her claim that in writing *The Making of Americans* she was "doing what the cinema was doing." She added that her writing in that book was "like a cinema picture made up of succession and each moment having its own emphasis that is its own difference and so there was the moving and the existence of each moment as it was in me."

Stein's discussion of "what the cinema was doing" appears in her *Lectures in America* and also suggests the third basic concern of her writing: movement. By "movement," she referred not to the movement of a message to its conclusion or the movement of a plot or narrative, but to "the essence of its going" of her prose, a timeless continuous present in the never-ending motion of consciousness. Stein also credits Cézanne with discovering this concern, "a feeling of movement inside the painting not a painting of a thing moving but the thing painted having inside it the existence of moving." She seemed to understand Cézanne's achievement in terms of James's model of consciousness as an ever-flowing stream of thought.

Accordingly, Stein used her writing not to record a scene or object or idea (products of thought), but to try to capture the sense of the process of perceiving such things. Her subject is almost always really two things at once: whatever attracted her attention—caught her eye, entered her ear, or crossed her mind—and the mobile nature of reality, particularly as it is perceived by human consciousness. In fact, Stein was usually more concerned with the nature of her own perception and with that of her reader than she was with its objects. She wanted to escape the conventions of linguistic representation, arbitrary arrangements similar to the "rules" for perspective in painting, and to present "something moving as moving is not as moving should be." As confusing as her resulting efforts sometimes are, her concern with motion makes sense as an attempt to mimic or evoke the nature of consciousness as she understood it.

From James at Harvard and possibly from Henri Bergson in Paris, Stein had learned that the best model for human consciousness was one that stressed the processual, ever-flowing nature of experience. She added to this belief her assumption that the essence of any subject could only be perceived and should only be represented through its motion, echoing Bergson's claim that "reality is mobility." Unfortunately, this belief led her writing into one of its many paradoxes: She could only attempt to represent the continuous stream of experience through the segmented, inherently sequential nature of language. Streams flow; words do not. Instead, they proceed one by one, like the cars pulled by a train engine. While James would certainly have objected to Stein's sequential cinema

model as an approximation of the stream of consciousness, her motion-obsessed writing probably suggests the flow of consciousness as well as does any literary style.

THINGS AS THEY ARE

Written in 1903 as *Q.E.D.*, but set aside until 1932 and not published until 1950, *Things as They Are* is Stein's most conventional novel. Its sentences employ no unexpected syntax or diction, its central concerns are clear, its time scheme is linear, and its characters are conventionally drawn. If anything, Stein's style in this first novel is markedly old-fashioned, including highly formal sentences that frequently sport balanced serial constructions. She writes, for example, "Adele vehemently and with much picturesque vividness explained her views and theories of manners, people and things, in all of which she was steadily opposed by Helen who differed fundamentally in all her convictions, aspirations and illusions." While its conventional style (crudely reminiscent of that of Henry James) is completely unlike that of any other Stein novel, *Things as They Are* is a very significant work for the consideration of Stein's career. Apart from convincingly refuting the suspicion of some of her detractors that Stein was incapable of rational writing, this book establishes her preoccupation with psychological typecasting and vaguely hints at the importance of repetition in her thinking and writing.

Things as They Are charts the growth, turbulence, and eventual dissolution of the relationships among three young women: Adele, the book's central consciousness, an obviously autobiographical figure; Helen Thomas, the object of Adele's love; and Mabel Neathe, Adele's calculating rival for Helen's affection. These three characters closely parallel Stein, May Bookstaver, and Mabel Haynes, and the story of their relationship is the story of Stein's first, agonizing love affair. While the novel follows these three young women for three years, not much happens. Most of the book relates conversations and correspondence between Adele and Helen, showing Adele's torment first from her not yet understood desire for Helen, then from her growing realization that she is losing Helen to Mabel. Of principal interest to the reader is Stein's self-characterization in her portrayal of Adele.

THREE LIVES

Three Lives is easily Stein's best-known and most respected piece of fiction. Technically three novellas, this work is unified by its three subjects, by its central concern with the nature of consciousness, and by its attempt to blend colloquial idioms with Stein's emerging style, here based largely on her understanding of Cézanne's principles of composition, particularly that "one thing was as important as another thing."

"The Good Anna," "Melanctha," and "The Gentle Lena" are the three sections of this work. Anna and Lena are poor German immigrants who patiently work as servants in Bridgepoint, Baltimore; Melanctha is a young black woman who discovers sexuality and love, then turns from a frustrating relationship with a sincere young black doctor to a

dissipative affair with a gambler. Because all three women are essentially victimized by their surroundings and die at the end of their stories, this work is deterministic in the naturalist tradition, but *Three Lives* marks the transition from naturalism to modernism as Stein departs from nineteenth century literary conventions. She abandons conventional syntax to try to follow the movement of a consciousness rather than of events, and she develops a new narrative style only partially tied to linear chronology. The result is an interior narrative of consciousness in which Stein's prose style serves as the primary carrier of knowledge. Through the rhythms of her characters' speech and the rhythms of her narration, Stein gives her reader a sense of the basic rhythms of consciousness for these three women—what Stein would elsewhere refer to as their "bottom natures."

Possibly Stein's most widely celebrated piece of writing, "Melanctha" recasts the anguishing love triangle of *Q.E.D.* into the conflict between Melanctha and Jeff Campbell, whose inherently conflicting "bottom natures" or personality types parallel the conflict between Helen and Adele in the earlier work. "Melanctha" has been praised by Richard Wright, among others, as one of the first realistic and sympathetic renderings of black life by a white American author, but Melanctha's race is actually incidental to Stein's central concerns with finding a style to express the rhythms of personality and the frustrating cycles of love.

THE MAKING OF AMERICANS

Although it was not published until 1925, Stein's *The Making of Americans* occupied her as early as 1903 and was in fact begun before *Q.E.D.* and *Three Lives*. This mammoth novel began as a description of the creation of Americans from a representative immigrant family: "The old people in a new world, the new people made out of the old, that is the story that I mean to tell, for that is what really is and what I really know." Stein's projected family chronicle soon lost its original focus, becoming first a history of everyone, then a study of character types rather than of characters. Leon Katz, who has worked with this book more than has anyone else, calls it "a massive description of the psychological landscape of human being in its totality."

Although the book ostensibly continues to follow events in the lives of two central families, the Herslands and the Dehnings, its real concern is almost always both larger and smaller, ranging from Stein's questions about her own life and identity to questions about the various personality types of all of humanity. As Richard Bridgman suggests, this is "an improvised work of no identifiable genre in which the creator learned by doing," one "full of momentary wonders and botched long-range schemes, lyrical outbursts and anguished confessions." Accordingly, Bridgman concludes that *The Making of Americans* is best thought of "not as a fictional narrative nor a philosophic tract, but as a drama of self-education." In a way, the book chronicles the "making" of Stein, presenting a phenomenology of her mind as it works its way through personal problems toward the distinctive "cinema style."

Underlying a great part of the writing in this book is Stein's belief that human personality consists of variations on a few basic "bottom natures" or kinds of identity that can be perceived through a character's repeated actions:

> There are then many things every one has in them that come out of them in the repeating everything living have always in them, repeating with a little changing just enough to make of each one an individual being, to make of each repeating an individual thing that gives to such a one a feeling of themselves inside them.

There are two basic personality types: "dependent independent" and "independent dependent." These are polarities identified in part by the way the person fights: the first kind by resisting, the second by attacking.

Concerns with character-typing dominate the book's first two sections, "The Dehnings and the Herslands" and "Martha Hersland" (the character most closely modeled on Stein's own life), while the third section, "Alfred and Julia Hersland," contains mostly digressions about contemporary matters in Stein's life. The fourth section, "David Hersland," becomes a meditation on the nature of aging and death ("He was dead when he was at the beginning of being in middle living."), and the final section, "History of a Family's Progress," is—even for Stein—an incredibly abstract and repetitive series of reflections on the concerns that had given rise to the novel. This final section contains no names, referring only to "some," "any," "every," or "very many."

Stein later described her efforts in this book as an attempt "to do what the cinema was doing"; that is, to give a sense of motion and life through a series of highly repetitive statements, each statement only an incremental change from the preceding one, like frames in a strip of film. One of the main effects of this technique is to freeze all action into a "continuous present." Not only do Stein's sentences exist in overlapping clusters, depending more for their meaning on their relationships to one another than on individual semantic content, but also her verbs in *The Making of Americans* are almost exclusively present participles, suspending all action in the present progressive tense. "The business of Art," Stein later explained, "is to live in the actual present, that is the complete actual present." As a result, while *The Making of Americans* does ostensibly present a history of four generations of the Hersland family, there exists in it little or no sense of the passage of time. Instead, the book presents a sense of "existence suspended in time," a self-contained world existing quite independent of the "real world," a basic modernist goal that has also become one of the hallmarks of postmodernism.

A 416-page version, abridged by Stein, was published in 1934 but has not been accepted by Stein scholars as adequately representative of the longer work. For all its difficulty, *The Making of Americans* is one of modernism's seminal works and an invaluable key to Stein's literary career.

LUCY CHURCH AMIABLY

Described by its author as "a novel of Romantic beauty and nature and which Looks Like an Engraving," *Lucy Church Amiably* shares many characteristics with Stein's best-known play *Four Saints in Three Acts* and with the several works she called "geographies." The book was Stein's response to the area around Belley, France, where she and Alice spent many summers. Stein's title plays on the existence of the church in a nearby village, Lucey. As Richard Bridgman has observed, Lucy Church refers throughout the book to both that church and to a woman who resembles a relaxed Stein. As Bridgman also notes, "the book is essentially a long, lyric diary," with Stein including in it information about the geography, residents, and flora of the surrounding area. This information appears, however, in Stein's distinctive paratactic style:

> In this story there is to be not only white black tea colour and vestiges of their bankruptcy but also well wishing and outlined and melodious and with a will and much of it to be sure with their only arrangement certainly for this for the time of which when by the way what is the difference between fixed.

This novel can perhaps best be thought of as a pastoral and elegiac meditation on the nature of place.

THE WORLD IS ROUND *and* IDA, A NOVEL

In 1939, Stein's novel for children, *The World Is Round*, was published, with illustrations by Clement Hurd. The book focuses on a series of events in the lives of a nine-year-old girl, Rose, and her cousin, Willie. These events are more enigmatic than dramatic but seem to move both children through several kinds of initiations. Identity worries both Rose and Willie ("Would she have been Rose if her name had not been Rose and would she have been Rose if she had been a twin"), as does the contrast between the uncertainties of their lives and the advertised verities of existence, emblemized by the "roundness" of the world. Comprising both the children's meditations and their songs, the book is, for Stein, relatively conventional. Although its sentences are highly repetitive and rhythmic, they present a compelling view of a child's consciousness, and Stein scholars agree on the importance and success of this little-known work.

Originally intended as "a novel about publicity," *Ida, a Novel* expands many of the concerns of *The World Is Round*, extending them from Ida's birth well into her adult life. As is true of all of Stein's novels, there is not anything resembling a plot, and many of the things that happen in Ida's life are surrealistically dreamlike. "Funny things" keep happening to the young Ida, and while the nature of these things is never explained, most of them seem to involve men. Frequently, these men have nothing at all to do with her, or they only glance at her, but Ida sees them as vaguely threatening, and insofar as her novel can be said to have a central concern, it is with certain problems of sexuality. Although Stein later described Ida as having been based on the duchess of Windsor, this connection is only superficial, and Ida is better seen as another in the long line of Stein's autobiographical characters.

BREWSIE AND WILLIE

Stein's novel *Brewsie and Willie* redirected her revolutionary spirit from literary to social and economic problems. In this series of conversations among American soldiers and nurses awaiting redeployment from France to the United States after World War II, Stein pessimistically considered the future of her native land. Stein had long held that the United States was "the oldest country in the world" because it had been the first to enter the twentieth century. By 1945, she felt that America had grown "old like a man of fifty," and that its tired, middle-aged economic system had become stale and repressive.

In *Brewsie and Willie*, she describes that economic system as "industrialism," portraying a stultifying cycle of depleting raw materials for overproduction and installment buying. This cycle also locked the worker into "job thinking," making of him a kind of automaton, tied to his job, locked into debt, and, worst of all, robbed of freedom of thought. Through conversations involving Brewsie (Stein's spokesperson), Willie, and several other soldiers and nurses, Stein portrays an apprehensive generation of young Americans who see the potential dangers of postwar America but who fear they do not "have the guts to make a noise" about them. These conversations cover a wide range of subjects, from a comparison of French and American baby carriages to the tentative suggestion that the American system must be torn down before "pioneering" will again be possible.

Stein makes little or no effort in this book to differentiate the voices of her speakers, but she does rather amazingly blend her own voice with those of the soldiers. The result is a style that is characteristically Stein's but that also has the rhythm and the randomness of overheard conversation. Often overlooked, *Brewsie and Willie* is one of the most remarkable documents in Stein's writing career.

However idiosyncratic Stein's writing may seem, it must be remembered that a very strong case can be made for its substantial philosophical underpinnings. To her way of thinking, language could refuse few things to Stein, and the limitations of language were exactly what she refused to accept. She bent the language to the very uses that process philosophers such as James and Bergson and Whitehead feared it could not be put. Her stubborn emphasis on the individual word—particularly on transitive elements—her insistent use of repetition, and her ever-present preoccupation with the essential motion of words were all part of Stein's monumental struggle with a language she felt was not accurately used to reflect the way people perceive reality or the motion of reality itself. In a narrow but profound sense, she is the most serious realist in literary history. Stein was not a philosopher—her magpie eclecticism, associational flights, and thundering *ex cathedra* pronouncements ill suited her for systematic explanation—but in her writing a wealth of philosophy appears.

Brooks Landon

OTHER MAJOR WORKS

SHORT FICTION: *As Fine as Melanctha*, 1954; *Painted Lace, and Other Pieces, 1914-1937*, 1955; *Alphabets and Birthdays*, 1957.

PLAYS: *Geography and Plays*, 1922; *Operas and Plays*, 1932; *Four Saints in Three Acts*, pr., pb. 1934; *In Savoy: Or, Yes Is for a Very Young Man (A Play of the Resistance in France)*, pr., pb. 1946; *The Mother of Us All*, pr. 1947; *Last Operas and Plays*, 1949; *In a Garden: An Opera in One Act*, pb. 1951; *Lucretia Borgia*, pb. 1968; *Selected Operas and Plays*, 1970.

POETRY: *Tender Buttons: Objects, Food, Rooms*, 1914; *Before the Flowers of Friendship Faded Friendship Faded*, 1931; *Two (Hitherto Unpublished) Poems*, 1948; *Bee Time Vine, and Other Pieces, 1913-1927*, 1953; *Stanzas in Meditation, and Other Poems, 1929-1933*, 1956.

NONFICTION: *Composition as Explanation*, 1926; *How to Write*, 1931; *The Autobiography of Alice B. Toklas*, 1933; *Matisse, Picasso, and Gertrude Stein, with Two Shorter Stories*, 1933; *Portraits and Prayers*, 1934; *Lectures in America*, 1935; *Narration: Four Lectures*, 1935; *The Geographical History of America*, 1936; *Everybody's Autobiography*, 1937; *Picasso*, 1938; *Paris, France*, 1940; *What Are Masterpieces?*, 1940; *Wars I Have Seen*, 1945; *Four in America*, 1947; *Reflections on the Atomic Bomb*, 1973; *How Writing Is Written*, 1974; *The Letters of Gertrude Stein and Thornton Wilder*, 1996 (Edward Burns and Ulla E. Dydo, editors); *Baby Precious Always Shines: Selected Love Notes Between Gertrude Stein and Alice B. Toklas*, 1999 (Kay Turner, editor).

MISCELLANEOUS: *The Gertrude Stein First Reader and Three Plays*, 1946; *The Yale Edition of the Unpublished Writings of Gertrude Stein*, 1951-1958 (8 volumes; Carl Van Vechten, editor); *Selected Writings of Gertrude Stein*, 1962; *The Yale Gertrude Stein*, 1980.

BIBLIOGRAPHY

Bowers, Jane Palatini. *Gertrude Stein*. New York: St. Martin's Press, 1993. A succinct, feminist-oriented introduction to Stein, with separate chapters on the novels, short fiction, and plays. Includes notes and a bibliography.

Brinnin, John Malcom. *The Third Rose: Gertrude Stein and Her World*. Boston: Little, Brown, 1959. Aside from its significant biographical value, this study contains provocative comments on Stein's writing, twentieth century painting, and modern intellectual and artistic movements. Includes a useful bibliography.

Curnutt, Kirk, ed. *The Critical Response to Gertrude Stein*. Westport, Conn.: Greenwood Press, 2000. While including quintessential pieces on Stein by Carl Van Vechten, William Carlos Williams, and Katherine Anne Porter, this guide to her critical reception also includes previously obscure estimations from contemporaries such as H. L. Mencken, Mina Loy, and Conrad Aiken.

DeKoven, Marianne. *A Different Language: Gertrude Stein's Experimental Writing.*

Madison: University of Wisconsin Press, 1983. DeKoven's feminist study focuses on Stein's experimental work published after *Three Lives* and before *The Autobiography of Alice B. Toklas.* She argues that this period of Stein's writing is important not so much because of its influence on other writers but because of its attempt to redefine patriarchal language and provide alternatives to conventional modes of signification.

Dydo, Ulla E., with William Rice. *Gertrude Stein: The Language that Rises, 1923-1934.* Evanston, Ill.: Northwestern University Press, 2003. Dydo, a renowned Stein scholar, provides a comprehensive analysis of the letters, manuscripts, and notebooks Stein generated over a twenty-year period. Includes a bibliography and an index.

Hoffman, Michael J. *Critical Essays on Gertrude Stein.* Boston: G. K. Hall, 1986. A collection of reviews and essays, most of which appeared during and immediately after Stein's long career in letters. Diverse literary criticisms, such as new criticism, structuralism, feminism, and deconstruction are represented. Among the contributors are Sherwood Anderson, Marianne Moore, William Carlos Williams, B. F. Skinner, Katherine Anne Porter, Edmund Wilson, and W. H. Auden.

Kellner, Bruce, ed. *A Gertrude Stein Companion: Content With the Example.* New York: Greenwood Press, 1988. Kellner supplies a helpful introduction on how to read Stein. The volume includes a study of Stein and literary tradition, her manuscripts, and her various styles, and included biographical sketches of her friends and critics. Provides an annotated bibliography of criticism.

Knapp, Bettina. *Gertrude Stein.* New York: Continuum, 1990. A general introduction to Stein's life and art. Discusses her stylistic breakthrough in the stories in *Three Lives,* focusing on repetition and the use of the continuous present. Devotes a long chapter to *Tender Buttons* as one of Stein's most innovative and esoteric works.

Malcolm, Janet. *Two Lives: Gertrude and Alice.* New Haven, Conn.: Yale University Press, 2007. An account of Stein's relationship with Alice B. Toklas, in which Malcolm provides new information about the couple's lives during the German occupation of France. She explains how Stein and Toklas were allowed to survive because of their friendship with Bernard Fay, a wealthy, anti-Semitic Frenchman.

Souhami, Diana. *Gertrude and Alice.* London: Pandora, 1991. The most frank account of Stein's lesbian relationship with Toklas, this book shows Toklas's strength and how she dominated many aspects of her forty-year marriage to Stein.

Sutherland, Donald. *Gertrude Stein: A Biography of Her Work.* Westport, Conn.: Greenwood Press, 1951. The first substantial critical book on Stein's writing, this work treats Stein's radical writings as an illustration of her own modernist philosophy and aesthetics. The book also justifies the modern movement in writing and painting. Includes a useful appendix, which catalogs Stein's writing according to stylistic periods.

FAY WELDON

Born: Alvechurch, Worcestershire, England; September 22, 1931
Also known as: Franklin Birkinshaw

PRINCIPAL LONG FICTION

The Fat Woman's Joke, 1967 (also known as *. . . And the Wife Ran Away*, 1968)
Down Among the Women, 1971
Female Friends, 1974
Remember Me, 1976
Words of Advice, 1977 (also known as *Little Sisters*, 1978)
Praxis, 1978
Puffball, 1980
The President's Child, 1982
The Life and Loves of a She-Devil, 1983
The Shrapnel Academy, 1986
The Heart of the Country, 1987
The Hearts and Lives of Men, 1987
The Rules of Life, 1987
Leader of the Band, 1988
The Cloning of Joanna May, 1989
Darcy's Utopia, 1990
Growing Rich, 1992
Life Force, 1992
Affliction, 1993 (also known as *Trouble*)
Splitting, 1995
Worst Fears, 1996
Big Women, 1997 (also known as *Big Girls Don't Cry*)
Rhode Island Blues, 2000
The Bulgari Connection, 2001
Mantrapped, 2004
She May Not Leave, 2005
The Spa Decameron, 2007 (also known as *The Spa*)

OTHER LITERARY FORMS

Fay Weldon began her writing career with plays for radio, television, and theater, but she soon transferred her efforts to novels, and it is her novels for which she has become best known. She has also published short stories and a good deal of nonfiction. The latter includes a biography of Rebecca West; an introduction to the work of Jane Austen in fictional form, *Letters to Alice on First Reading Jane Austen* (1984); an "advice book" for modern women, *What Makes Women Happy* (2006); an autobiography, *Auto da Fay* (2002); and a collection of her journalism, *Godless in Eden* (1999). Her collections of short fiction include *Moon over Minneapolis: Or, Why She Couldn't Stay* (1991) and *Wicked Women* (1995). She has also put her comic gifts to work in three books for children, *Wolf the Mechanical Dog* (1988), *Party Puddle* (1989), and *Nobody Likes Me* (1997).

Achievements

In addition to a successful career as an advertising copywriter, Fay Weldon has enjoyed a long career as a television scriptwriter, a playwright (for television, radio, and theater), and a novelist. Her radio play *Spider* (1972) won the Writers' Guild Award for Best Radio Play in 1973, and *Polaris* (1978) won the Giles Cooper Award for Best Radio Play in 1978. Weldon has earned growing acclaim for her humorous fictional explorations of women's lives and her biting satires that expose social injustice, and her novel *Praxis* was nominated for the prestigious Booker Prize. In 1983, Weldon became the first woman chair of judges for the Booker Prize. She was recognized for her many achievements in 1997, when she received the Women in Publishing Pandora Award. In 2000, she was made a Commander of the Order of the British Empire.

Biography

Fay Weldon was born Franklin Birkinshaw in the village of Alvechurch, England, in 1931. Her mother, who wrote under the name Pearl Bellairs, her maternal grandfather, Edwin Jepson, and one of her uncles were all novelists. While still a child, Weldon emigrated with her family to New Zealand, where her father worked as a doctor. When she was six years old, her parents divorced, and Weldon eventually returned to England with her mother and sister to live with her grandmother. This experience of being reared by a single mother in an era that did not easily accommodate single-parent families gave Weldon early insight into the lot of women living beyond the pale of the nuclear family; she was able to observe, at first hand, both the trials women faced and the importance of family and of humor in overcoming these difficulties.

In 1949, Weldon earned a scholarship to St. Andrews University in Scotland, and in 1952 she graduated with an M.A. in economics and psychology. Her first marriage, to Ronald Bateman, a man twenty years her senior, lasted less than two years, leaving her to support her son, Nicholas, as a single mother. She drifted through a series of jobs involving writing of various sorts: writing propaganda for the Foreign Office, answering problem letters for a newspaper, and, finally, composing advertising copy. In this last career she was quite successful, producing many jingles and slogans—a few of which stuck in the memory beyond their use in specific campaigns—and honing her talent for concision, wit, and catchy, memorable phrasing.

In 1960, she married Ronald Weldon, a London antiques dealer; they settled in a North

London suburb, where they had three children: Daniel (born 1963), Thomas (born 1970), and Samuel (born 1977). Beginning in the mid-1960's, Weldon combined professional and family responsibilities with a burgeoning career as a writer. Her first efforts were directed toward writing plays. Her one-act play *Permanence* was produced in London in 1969 and was followed by many successes. For British television, Weldon wrote more than fifty screenplays, including an award-winning episode of the series *Upstairs, Downstairs*. Writing for television led to fiction: Weldon's first novel, *The Fat Woman's Joke*, in 1967, began life as a television play. Her third novel, *Female Friends*, solidified her reputation, and Weldon quit her job in advertising. She earned further acclaim for *Praxis* and *The President's Child*, but *The Life and Loves of a She-Devil* proved a breakthrough work, introducing her work to a mass audience when it was made into a motion picture, *She-Devil* (1989), starring Meryl Streep and Roseanne Barr.

Her eventual divorce from Ronald Weldon in 1994 caused a certain amount of bitterness, which she expressed in some of her subsequent fiction. She later married poet Nicholas Fox; they lived briefly in Hampstead before moving to Shaftesbury in Dorset. Weldon seemed to mellow after her marriage to Fox, and she experienced something of an existential break when she had a vision of "the gates of paradise" (or possibly Hell) during a near-death experience suffered in 2005 when an allergic reaction caused her heart to stop. Even though the gates in question seemed hideously tacky and vulgar, she subsequently had herself baptized after being a committed atheist for most of her life. She had already begun to suggest in both her fiction and her nonfiction that she had recanted some of her earlier views, although she sacrificed none of her acerbic sarcasm in making the point. Her widely quoted opinion that men had gotten a rough deal as a result of the advancement of feminism seemed to some of her former admirers a particularly painful item of moral treason. Her combative "advice book," *What Makes Women Happy*—a title that suggests, perhaps presumptuously, that she now knows the answer—argues that the apparent reply is sex, chocolate, and shopping but that slightly deeper analysis would suggest a more refined alliterative triad of family, friends, and food.

ANALYSIS

Fay Weldon's fiction explores women's lives with wit and humor in the cause of a determined opposition to the clichés of romantic fiction. Weldon is caustic in her implicit condemnation of injustice but avoids preaching by satirizing both sides of every issue and by revealing the gulf between what characters say and what they do. Despite their realistic settings, her novels blend fable, myth, and the fantastic with satire, farce, and outlandish coincidence; the combination produces highly distinctive tragicomedies of manners.

Weldon's admiration for writers such as Jane Austen (whose work she has adapted for television) is expressed openly in *Letters to Alice on First Reading Jane Austen*, but it is also evident from the parallels in Weldon's own work. In a typical early Weldon novel, a limited cast of characters interacts in a defined setting. A series of misunderstandings or trivial coincidences initiates the action, which then takes on a momentum of its own, carrying all along with it until an equally trivial series of explanations or coincidences brings closure and a resolution that restores all to their proper place. The theme is often a minor domestic drama, such as a marital crisis, rather than an epic upheaval, but such personal interactions are seen to represent in microcosm society as a whole and therefore have a universal appeal.

Over time, her novels have become more wide-ranging in their settings, narrative devices, and claims, sometimes recruiting fantastic devices in order to attempt deeper analyses of the issues at stake, but generally her works still convey the impression that Weldon is not much given to elaborate planning, preferring to allow her characters and story lines to develop their own momentum. This has sometimes taken her into unexpected narrative terrain, but she always retains a keen intelligence and a trenchant wit. Although her works focus primarily on the lives of women, Weldon comments on a wide-ranging number of issues with relevance to all. Her work reveals a deep yet unsentimental compassion for all human beings, an understanding of their weaknesses and foibles, and a celebration of their continued survival and ability to love one another in the face of adversity.

... AND THE WIFE RAN AWAY

This structure is present even in Weldon's early work, no doubt because it is a formula that works well for television. In her first novel, originally titled *The Fat Woman's Joke* but renamed *... And the Wife Ran Away* for its American publication in 1968, Weldon takes as her subject the crisis in the marriage of a middle-aged, middle-class couple, Esther and Alan Wells, when Alan decides to have an affair with his young and attractive secretary, Susan. The beginning of Alan's affair coincides with Esther and Alan's joint decision to go on a diet, a symbolic attempt, Weldon suggests, to recapture not only their lost youthful figures but also their youthful love, ambition, and optimism. Infidelity, the novel therefore subtly suggests, is related to aging and to a more deep-seated identity crisis. Weldon frequently uses hunger or the satisfaction of food as a metaphor for other, more metaphysical and intangible, needs, and this theme recurs in a number of her works (for example, in the short story "Polaris," 1985).

The influence of Weldon's background as a scriptwriter (and the novel's origin as a play) is also evident in this book's form. Esther, who has left her husband at the opening of the novel, recounts her version of events to her friend Phyllis as she gorges herself on food to compensate for the self-denial she has suffered during the diet. Esther's narrative is intercut with scenes of Susan telling her version of events to her friend Brenda. The novel is thus almost entirely conveyed through dialogue describing flashbacks seen from the perspectives of the female characters. This technique is evident elsewhere in Weldon's early work—for example, in *Female Friends*, where parts of the novel are presented in the form of a script.

THE LIFE AND LOVES OF A SHE-DEVIL

The Life and Loves of a She-Devil stands as one of Weldon's most accomplished works. It represents the themes that are the hallmark of Weldon's fiction (a concern with women's lives and the significance of human relationships such as marriage) while encompassing her use of fantasy in one of her most carefully constructed and formally satisfying novels. The plot tells the story of a middle-class, suburban housewife, Ruth, whose accountant husband leaves her for a rich and attractive writer of romance novels. Unlike the typical wife, however, Ruth does not simply bow to the inevitable. When her husband calls her a "she-devil" in a moment of anger, this becomes her new identity, and she musters a formidable array of resources to live up to it. Through a series of picaresque adventures, she makes the life of her husband, Bobbo, and his new love, Mary Fisher, impossible. She has Bobbo framed and then imprisoned for embezzlement, destroys Mary's ability and will to write, and finally undergoes massive plastic surgery so that she looks just like her now-dead rival and can assume her place in Bobbo's broken life. The configuration at the end of the novel thus mirrors the beginning, but with the variation that the power dynamics of the relationship have been inverted: Ruth is now in command, while Bobbo has been humiliated and accepts his fate like a downtrodden wife.

The tale not only presents a certain kind of symmetry reminiscent of fairy stories but also evokes a poetic magic in the telling of it. Many of the chapters begin with a variation on the opening line of the novel: "Mary Fisher lives in a High Tower, on the edge of the sea." These incantations, repeated with variations, have the hypnotic quality of a witch's spell, reinforcing both Ruth's supernatural power and her obsession with Mary Fisher (whose residence in a tower evokes a fairy-tale princess). This poetic refrain also unifies the narrative and gives a cyclical structure to the plot.

THE SHRAPNEL ACADEMY

On the surface, *The Shrapnel Academy* is a variation on the stale British motif of the "country house weekend." A group of characters, most of them unknown to one another, are seen arriving at the Shrapnel Academy, a military institute, for a weekend. Bad weather will ensure that they remain confined to the academy, cut off from the outside world and forced to confront one another and the problems that arise.

While many novelists fail to acknowledge the presence of the host of servants who make such country weekends possible, Weldon's novel takes the reader below stairs and into the lives of the hundreds of illegal immigrant servants and their extended families and camp followers—as in *Upstairs, Downstairs*, the early 1970's television series about an upper-class Edwardian family and its servants to which Weldon contributed an award-winning episode. *The Shrapnel Academy* ventures beyond realist conventions by presenting a clash between shortsighted, class-based militarism and the struggle for survival and dignity in the microcosm of the academy, eventually extending into quasi-apocalyptic allegory.

As in most of Weldon's novels, no single villain is responsible for the misfortunes that befall the characters in *The Shrapnel Academy*; all the characters bear some degree of responsibility for the accumulation of trivial choices and decisions that combine to make up the climactic "frightful tidal wave of destiny." Many continual thematic elements of Weldon's work recur in *The Shrapnel Academy,* including revenge fantasy, food symbolism, and transfigurations of myth and fable. Formally, too, the novel displays typical characteristics of Weldon's work (short narrative passages with aphoristic asides, the use of dialogue) as well as innovative and experimental qualities. The author interrupts the narrative at frequent intervals, sometimes to offer satirical summaries of military history, highlighting advances in warfare or giving accounts of famous battles. Weldon brings out the absurdity of celebrating such "progress" and uses her fine wit to draw the reader's attention to the Orwellian doublespeak and underlying assumptions of military thinking. At other times, Weldon interpellates the reader directly, apologizing for the delay in getting on with the story or inviting the reader to put him- or herself in the place of one of the characters—invitations that pointedly drive home the lesson that the reader is no better than the characters he or she is inclined to judge.

LIFE FORCE

Weldon also breaks strategically with her readers' expectations in *Life Force,* which, instead of being an indictment of male callousness and infidelity, is a lusty tribute to male sexuality. The central figure in the book is Leslie Beck, a man with no virtues except his power to please women through the skillful use of his huge genitalia and his equally outsized imagination. Structurally, *Life Force* follows the pattern established in Weldon's earlier novels: It begins with a seemingly unimportant incident that stimulates the narrator to relive and reassess complex relationships; that incident eventually becomes a crucial element in a dramatic resolution, in which a woman avenges herself upon a man who has wronged her.

When Leslie Beck turns up at the Marion Loos Gallery, carrying a large painting by his late wife Anita, it does not seem possible that this unappealing, sixty-year-old man could for so long have been the Lothario of upper-middle-class London. However, the owner of the gallery, who at this point is the first-person narrator, explains to the reader why she is so shocked when she sees the unimpressive painting that her former lover expects her to sell on his behalf. Its subject is the bedroom and the bed in which Leslie once gave Marion so much pleasure. Naturally, the painting prompts Marion to recall her involvement with Leslie and to wonder how much Anita knew about the affair.

Nothing in this novel is as straightforward as it seems, however. In the second chapter, Weldon not only changes narrators—now telling the story through the eyes of Nora, another of Beck's former lovers—but also has Nora admit that it was she, not Marion, who actually wrote the first chapter, simply imagining herself as Marion. Although the two narrators continue to alternate as the book progresses, from time to time the author reminds us that Marion's narrative is Nora's fiction, based as much on gossip and guesses as on fact. Weldon thus suggests that since the only approach to truth is through what human beings see and say, what we call reality will always include as much fiction as fact.

GROWING RICH

Growing Rich describes the harassment of three adolescent girls by a Mephistophelian figure who has promised one of them as a prize to the wealthy businessman with whom he has made a Faustian pact. Cast in the same mock-folkloristic mode as *The Life and Loves of a She-Devil*, this novel seems to be casting around for a different moral but cannot in the end discover one. The demon is incarnate as the businessman's chauffeur and is thus referred to as "the Driver," which implies that the novel's presiding proverb is "Needs must when the devil drives"—and, indeed, even the novel's primary heroine, Carmen, cannot in the end avoid his driving. Carmen withstands his subtler temptations easily enough, although her friends Annie and Laura are not nearly so fortunate, but she cannot ultimately prevail against his nastier threats. In the end, the fact that she is not required to yield everything demanded by his blackmail cannot conceal the fact that she does yield.

The Driver is an intriguing literary creation: an apt devil for the modern age, whose acid observations reveal as strong a kinship with Alain-René Lesage's Asmodeus as with Christopher Marlowe's Mephistopheles. *Growing Rich*, like most of Weldon's works, is so exuberantly good-humored that even its blackest comedy is little more than black-edged, and the same is true of the marginal gothic elements of many of its predecessors and successors among her long fiction, including the mock-Dickensian melodrama *The Hearts and Lives of Men*, the mock-science-fictional *The Cloning of Joanna May*, and the similarly fantasized *Splitting* and *Mantrapped*. Like many modern authors, Weldon simply cannot take the fantastic seriously enough to make the most of its inherent narrative energy, but the frothy frivolity with which she invests it carries its own rewards.

TROUBLE

In *Trouble*, Weldon again turns her attention to a society that permits men to victimize women. The protagonist of this novel, which was first published in England under the title *Affliction*, is Annette Horrocks, a woman who, after ten years of trying, has finally become pregnant, only to find that her once-devoted husband, Spicer, has become monstrous. Not only does he now seem to loathe Annette, but also none of his tastes, opinions, and prejudices are what they were just a few months before.

Eventually, Annette discovers the source of the problem: Spicer has been seduced by a pair of unscrupulous, sadistic New Age psychiatrists. Before she is finally cured of what she comes to recognize as her addiction to Spicer, Annette loses her home, her baby, and very nearly her mind. If in *Life Force* Weldon shows the battle of the sexes as essentially comic, in *Trouble* she tells a story with tragic overtones. Again she points out how vulnerable women are in a society that believes men have a monopoly on the truth, but in this case she shows what can happen when the male version of reality is reinforced by the self-seeking therapy industry, the primary target of satire in this novel.

WORST FEARS

Worst Fears is one of Weldon's novels most clearly marked by the scars of her 1994 divorce. Its protagonist, Alexandra, an actor, is suddenly precipitated into crisis by the unexpected death of her husband, Ned, and is required, as conventional parlance has it, to "put his affairs in order." This involves her in a disquieting sequence of discoveries about the "true identity" Ned had succeeded in hiding from her for many years, which eventually extend to nightmarish extremes. Members of all of the professions that Weldon learned to hate in the course of her own divorce—especially therapists and lawyers—become targets for her bile here, although the burden of the role of primary traitor within the plot falls on a child-care provider: a dangerous cuckoo in the domestic nest.

RHODE ISLAND BLUES

In *Rhode Island Blues*, Weldon presents an elaborate examination of female family ties, dominated by the character of eighty-five-year-old Felicity, whose granddaughter Sophie, a film editor—the novel's primary protagonist—undertakes a quixotic quest to find the old woman's "lost" granddaughter. In the process, Sophie uncovers a great deal of family history extended over the generations and begins to reassess her relationship with her own mother. The novel's transatlantic movements, occasioned by the fact that Felicity was a war bride, add an extra dimension of cultural comparison, while a fantastic edge is added by Felicity's consolatory delusions.

THE BULGARI CONNECTION

The Bulgari Connection is an interesting experiment in novelistic product placement, as the writing of the work was financed by the Italian jewelry company. This connection is, however, incidental to the network of the plot, which develops a version of the eternal triangle. Businessman Barney Salt deserts his wife, Grace, for television personality Doris Dubois, thus inviting a she-devil-like revenge. The revenge in question is duly visited after Grace takes up with artist Walter Wells and receives a new lease on life that is quite literal—an aspect of the plot explicitly modeled on Oscar Wilde's *The Picture of Dorian Gray* (1890).

As on several previous occasions, Weldon picked up themes from this novel for further extrapolation in her next work, the identity-exchange comedy *Mantrapped*, whose heroine awakes one morning to find herself in a man's body. There, as in *The Bulgari Connection*, elements of Weldon's own autobiography are clearly recycled, but the fantastic embellishments in both books serve as useful distancing devices for putting "reality" into a broader and more comfortable perspective.

SHE MAY NOT LEAVE

She May Not Leave is an elaborate expansion of the child-care-worker subplot from *Worst Fears*, complicated by intergenerational issues echoing those in *Rhode Island Blues*, both elements being carefully ameliorated by a conscientious attempt to strike an evenhanded balance. The protagonist, Hattie, is busily employed in a literary agency and has trouble juggling her relationships with her partner, Martin, a political journalist; her grandmother, Frances, who is busy tracing the family history; and her daughter, Kitty. Polish au pair Agnieszka is an extremely dubious godsend, but she might well be indispensable no matter how problematic she eventually proves to be. As in many Weldon novels, the eventual "resolution" of *She May Not Leave* is unashamedly artificial and rather tokenistic, but the breezy tone illustrates the author's recovered sense of well-being and the essential irrepressibility of her character.

THE SPA DECAMERON

In a plot that echoes *The Shrapnel Academy* but lacks that novel's male/militaristic component, *The Spa Decameron* features wealthy female guests who are snowed in for ten days at a Cumbrian health spa over the Christmas/New Year holidays. As the facilities gradually begin to fail and the staff who maintain the guests' comforts and privileges begin to desert or rebel, the women pass the time by telling one another their instructive life stories, somewhat after the fashion of the plague-beleaguered characters in Giovanni Boccaccio's classic *Decameron: O, Prencipe Galeotto* (1349-1351; *The Decameron*, 1620). *The Spa Decameron* is, however, much more tightly organized around a thematic core than is its model; it really is a novel in spite of its discursive structure.

The characters' experiences gradually add up to a grotesque survey of the possibilities open to modern women and the threats facing them, including adultery, gender reassignment surgery, incest, abortion, husband murder, lesbian sexuality, and child abuse—to name but a few. The principal viewpoint character, Phoebe, is able to supplement the tales she hears further by virtue of her (possibly imaginary) ability to hear other people's thoughts; she does not tell her own story, partly—the reader suspects—because it cannot withstand melodramatic comparison with the stories the other characters tell, but also, and more appropriately, because it still remains to be equipped with a satisfactory sense of closure.

Melanie Hawthorne;
Rosemary M. Canfield Reisman
Updated by Brian Stableford

OTHER MAJOR WORKS

SHORT FICTION: *Watching Me, Watching You*, 1981; *Polaris, and Other Stories*, 1985; *Moon over Minneapolis: Or, Why She Couldn't Stay*, 1991; *Angel, All Innocence, and Other Stories*, 1995; *Wicked Women: A Collection of Short Stories*, 1995; *A Hard Time to Be a Father*, 1998.

PLAYS: *Permanence*, pr. 1969; *Time Hurries On*, pb. 1972; *Words of Advice*, pr., pb. 1974; *Friends*, pr. 1975; *Moving House*, pr. 1976; *Mr. Director*, pr. 1978; *Action Replay*, pr. 1979 (also known as *Love Among the Women*); *After the Prize*, pr. 1981 (also known as *Woodworm*); *I Love My Love*, pr. 1981; *Tess of the D'Urbervilles*, pr. 1992 (adaptation of Thomas Hardy's novel); *The Four Alice Bakers*, pr. 1999; *The Reading Group*, pb. 1999.

TELEPLAYS: *The Fat Woman's Tale*, 1966; *Wife in a Blonde Wig*, 1966; *Dr. De Waldon's Therapy*, 1967; *Fall of the Goat*, 1967; *The Forty-fifth Unmarried Mother*, 1967; *Goodnight Mrs. Dill*, 1967; *What About Me*, 1967; *Hippy Hippy Who Cares*, 1968; *Ruined Houses*, 1968; *£13083*, 1968; *The Three Wives of Felix Hull*, 1968; *Venus Rising*, 1968; *Smokescreen*, 1969; *The Loophole*, 1969; *Office Party*, 1970; *Poor Mother*, 1970; "On Trial," 1971 (episode of television series *Upstairs, Downstairs*); *Hands*, 1972; *The Lament of an Unmarried Father*, 1972; *A Nice Rest*, 1972; *Old Man's Hat*, 1972; *A Splinter of Ice*, 1972; *Comfortable Words*, 1973; *Desirous of Change*, 1973; *In Memoriam*, 1974; *Aunt Tatty*, 1975 (adaptation of Elizabeth Bowen's story); *Poor Baby*, 1975; *The Terrible Tale of Timothy Bagshott*, 1975; *Act of Rape*, 1977; "Married Love," 1977 (episode of television series *Six Women*); *Honey Ann*, 1980; *Life for Christine*, 1980; *Pride and Prejudice*, 1980 (adaptation of Jane Austen's novel); "Watching Me, Watching You," 1980 (episode of television series *Leap in the Dark*); *Little Miss Perkins*, 1982; *Loving Women*, 1983; *Redundant! Or, The Wife's Revenge*, 1983.

RADIO PLAYS: *Spider*, 1972; *Housebreaker*, 1973; *Mr. Fox and Mr. First*, 1974; *The Doctor's Wife*, 1975; *Polaris*, 1978; *All the Bells of Paradise*, 1979; "Weekend," 1979 (episode in radio series *Just Before Midnight*); *I Love My Love*, 1981.

NONFICTION: *Letters to Alice on First Reading Jane Austen*, 1984; *Rebecca West*, 1985; *Sacred Cows: A Portrait of Britain, Post-Rushdie, Pre-Utopia*, 1989; *Godless in Eden: A Book of Essays*, 1999; *Auto da Fay*, 2002; *What Makes Women Happy*, 2006.

CHILDREN'S LITERATURE: *Wolf the Mechanical Dog*, 1988; *Party Puddle*, 1989; *Nobody Likes Me*, 1997.

EDITED TEXT: *New Stories Four: An Arts Council Anthology*, 1979 (with Elaine Feinstein).

BIBLIOGRAPHY

Barreca, Regina, ed. *Fay Weldon's Wicked Fictions*. Hanover, N.H.: University Press of New England, 1994. Collection of eighteen essays, five by Weldon herself, deals with leading themes and techniques in Weldon's fiction and various issues raised by her work, such as her relation to feminism and her politics and moral stance.

Cane, Aleta F. "Demythifying Motherhood in Three Novels by Fay Weldon." In *Family Matters in the British and American Novel*, edited by Andrea O'Reilly Herrera, Elizabeth Mahn Nollen, and Sheila Reitzel Foor. Bowling Green, Ohio: Bowling Green State University Popular Press, 1997. Points out that in *Puffball*, *The Life and Loves of a She-Devil*, and *Life Force*, dysfunctional mothers produce daughters who are also dysfunctional mothers. Argues that Weldon agrees with the feminist position that mothering cannot be improved until women cease to be marginalized.

Dowling, Finuala. *Fay Weldon's Fiction*. Rutherford, N.J.: Fairleigh Dickinson University Press, 1998. Examines the themes and techniques in Weldon's fiction, with the principal emphasis on the novels.

Faulks, Lana. *Fay Weldon*. New York: Twayne, 1998. Provides a good introduction to Weldon's life and work, with a focus on the novels. Describes Weldon's fiction as "feminist comedy," contrasting with feminist writing that depicts women as oppressed. Also examines Weldon's experiments with narrative techniques.

Ferreira, Maria Aline Salgueiro Seabra. "Cloning and Biopower: Joanna Russ and Fay Weldon." In *I Am the Other: Literary Negotiations of Human Cloning*. Westport: Conn.: Greenwood Press, 2005. Presents a critical discussion of the role of cloning in Weldon's novel *The Cloning of Joanna May*.

Mitchell, Margaret E. "Fay Weldon." In *British Writers*, Supplement 4 in *Contemporary British Writers*, edited by George Stade and Carol Howard. New York: Charles Scribner's Sons, 1997. Presents detailed information on Weldon's life and work, divided into sections titled "Weldon's Feminism," "The Personal as Political," "Nature, Fate, and Magic," "Self and Solidarity," and "Fictions."

Paloge, Helen. *The Silent Echo: The Middle-Aged Female Body in Contemporary Women's Fiction*. Lanham, Md.: Lexington Books, 2007. Discusses the depiction of middle-aged women in the novels of Weldon, Margaret Atwood, Joan Barfoot, Joyce Carol Oates, and others.

Weldon, Fay. "Nature, Science, and Witchcraft: An Interview with Fay Weldon." Interview by Joanna Zylinska. *Critical Survey* 12, no. 3 (2000): 108-122. Weldon discusses her writing, particularly her novels and their inspirations.

Wilde, Alan. "'Bold, But Not Too Bold': Fay Weldon and the Limits of Poststructuralist Criticism." *Contemporary Literature* 29, no. 3 (1988): 403-419. Focuses primarily on literary theory, using *The Life and Loves of a She-Devil* as an arena to pit poststructuralism against New Criticism, offering some useful comments regarding moderation versus extremism in this novel.

REBECCA WEST
Cicily Isabel Fairfield

Born: London, England; December 21, 1892
Died: London, England; March 15, 1983
Also known as: Cicily Isabel Fairfield

PRINCIPAL LONG FICTION
The Return of the Soldier, 1918
The Judge, 1922
Harriet Hume: A London Fantasy, 1929
War Nurse: The True Story of a Woman Who Lived, Loved, and Suffered on the Western Front, 1930
The Harsh Voice, 1935
The Thinking Reed, 1936
The Fountain Overflows, 1956
The Birds Fall Down, 1966
This Real Night, 1984
Cousin Rosamund, 1985
Sunflower, 1986
The Sentinel: An Incomplete Early Novel, 2002 (Kathryn Laing, editor)

OTHER LITERARY FORMS

Although Rebecca West excelled in a variety of literary genres, she first came to prominence as a book reviewer, a role that she continued throughout her life. From her first critique, which appeared in *The Freewoman* in 1911, to her last, which appeared in the *London Sunday Telegraph* on October 10, 1982, West wrote almost one thousand reviews. Several of these appear in the collection *The Young Rebecca* (1982). Her first book, *Henry James* (1916), which is an evaluation of Henry James's contributions to literature, was considered an audacious project for a young woman. This fearless honesty and willingness to write bluntly about sacrosanct persons and ideas marked West's entire career. After that bold debut, West published several other notable works of literary criticism. *The Strange Necessity: Essays and Reviews* (1928), a collection of essays from the *New York Herald Tribune* and the *New Statesman*, introduced one of West's recurring themes: the necessity of art in human life. *The Court and the Castle* (1957), based on lectures she delivered at Yale University, describes the role of the arts in government and society from the time of William Shakespeare to Franz Kafka.

West was also a prominent journalist and social commentator. Her coverage of the Nuremberg Trials (the trials of Nazi war criminals following World War II) appeared in *A Train of Powder* (1955). One of her most famous books, *Black Lamb and Grey Falcon: A*

Journey Through Yugoslavia (1941), a combination travelogue, history, and sociopolitical commentary on the Balkans, is still considered essential reading for those who wish to understand the complexities of that area.

ACHIEVEMENTS

Rebecca West was a writer of great perception, encyclopedic knowledge, extensive interests, and great curiosity. It is hard to categorize her work because of its variety and complexity. As a result, West's individual works, both fiction and nonfiction, have not received the critical analysis and acclaim that they deserve. She often received recognition for the body of her work, however. Certain universal themes permeate her writing: the nature of art, the frauds and weaknesses of the social system, the causes and results of treason and betrayal. West received numerous honors because of her ability to portray accurately the social milieu of the twentieth century. In 1937, West was made a member of the Order of St. Sava by Yugoslavia. The French government named her a Chevalier of the Legion of Honor in 1959. She became Dame Commander, Order of the British Empire, in 1959 and was made a Companion of Literature for the Royal Society of Literature in 1968. The American Academy of Arts and Letters inducted West as an honorary member in 1972. She also received the Women's National Press Club Award for journalism.

BIOGRAPHY

Rebecca West was born Cicily "Cissie" Isabel Fairfield, the youngest of three daughters of Charles Fairfield and Isabella Mackenzie. Charles Fairfield pursued several careers, including journalism, yet failed to succeed at any of them. In 1901, he abandoned his family in order to pursue yet another dream in Sierra Leone. Although he returned to England after a few months, he never again lived with his family. Still, West admired her father's Anglo-Irish gentility and charm, finding him a strong and romantic figure. Throughout her life she wrote fondly of him and frequently justified his poor treatment of his family.

After her father's departure, the family was forced to move to Isabella Mackenzie's family home in Edinburgh. West described this as a period of deprivation. Although the family had enough income to survive, they were caught between social classes, not fitting into any established social level. All three of the Fairfield daughters embraced feminism. West's first job, in 1911, was writing for *The Freewoman*, a weekly publication focusing on women's issues. In the spring of 1912, she adopted a pseudonym, Rebecca West, the name of a character she had once played in Henrik Ibsen's play *Rosmersholm* (pb. 1886; English translation, 1889). The character, a strong woman, mistress of a married man, convinces her lover to join her in suicide. Later, West said that this had been a hasty decision and that she liked neither the play nor the character. However, the name took hold, and to all but her family, Cissie had become Rebecca West.

West's reviews gained for her the attention of the London literary establishment. After

Rebecca West
(Library of Congress)

reading her review of his novel *Marriage* (1912), H. G. Wells wished to meet its author. Although he was married, the two embarked on an intense ten-year affair. On August 4, 1914, West gave birth to a son, Anthony Panther West. Both West and Wells kept his true parentage from their son for many years, primarily since Wells did not wish to make the affair public. West even acquired adoption papers for Anthony in order to formalize her status as his parent. Anthony West was particularly bitter about his mother's role in his life, often criticizing her in the press. The relationship between West and Wells was a tempestuous one. They frequently disagreed on social, political, and literary issues, as well as the details of their relationship and on child rearing. In addition, West often felt trapped by motherhood and was resentful of the freedom Wells had. Her literary career, however, met with growing success in both England and the United States. Her first novels received favorable comment. By 1923, her affair with Wells was ending, and she began a brief, unsuccessful liaison with newspaper magnate Max Beaverbrook.

In 1930, West married Henry Andrews, a banker she had met the previous year. Andrews worked for Schroder, a German banking firm. Both he and West became increasingly disturbed by the growing Nazi influence. Andrews, sympathetic to the plight of the

Jews, helped many escape from Germany, a role that eventually caused the bank to fire him. During the 1930's, West became fascinated with the politics, history, and social mores of Yugoslavia. This increased her determination to encourage Britain to adopt an active role in combating the Nazi threat. In 1941, *Black Lamb and Grey Falcon*, West's monumental portrait of Yugoslavia, appeared and garnered popular acclaim.

After World War II, West published several works examining treason and justice. Her stance during the late 1940's and 1950's isolated her from many of her literary acquaintances because she felt Communism was a greater threat than Senator Joseph McCarthy and the actions of the U.S. House Committee on Un-American Activities. On November 3, 1968, Henry Andrews died. In spite of illnesses that crippled her during the 1970's, West continued working until her death in 1983.

ANALYSIS

Rebecca West never received the same acclaim for her novels as she did for her critical and journalistic work. While her novels were praised for their complexity, West was often criticized for overintellectualizing her stories. Critics have frequently asserted that her novels lack action. In fact, all her novels are characterized by extended internal monologues. In addition, West uses long, complex sentences; she has frequently been compared to Henry James in both subject matter and style. A West novel demands the reader's close attention. Most of her novels take place during the Edwardian era or explore the values and social behaviors of that period. Within this background, her fiction examines the relationships between men and women, most of which seem doomed to failure. Her stories are presented through a feminine perspective; West's usual narrator is a young woman who is intelligent, sensitive, and clever.

THE RETURN OF THE SOLDIER

The title character of her first short novel, *The Return of the Soldier*, is Chris Baldry, a shell-shocked soldier who is suffering from amnesia. This is a story about love rather than war, however. The novel opens as Chris's wife, Kitty, and his cousin Jenny, the narrator, wait to receive a letter from the war front. Instead they are visited by Margaret Grey, a shabbily dressed woman, who tells them that she has received a message from Chris. As a result of his injuries, Chris has forgotten the last fifteen years of his life, including his marriage, the death of his child, and his comfortable life in Baldry Hall. He remembers only Margaret, whom he had loved passionately fifteen years earlier, despite the difference in their social classes.

When Chris returns, he fails to recognize his wife, and he is desperately unhappy; the present has become a prison, keeping him from the person he loves—Margaret. Eventually he arranges to see her, finding that in spite of the ravages that years of poverty have caused, he is truly at ease only with her. Margaret, however, recognizes that because of their obvious class differences the two of them cannot hope for a life together, and she helps him regain his memory. Ironically, this allows him to resume his former life, and he realizes that he was never content. In addition, since he is now cured, he can return to his life as a soldier. The recovery of memory proves to be more tragic than its loss. *The Return of the Soldier* has the strengths common to West's novels: insight into the nature of romantic relationships, vivid descriptions of the influence of social background, and insightful examination of human nature.

THE JUDGE

West's second novel, *The Judge*, a longer, more complex work than *The Return of the Soldier*, is divided into two sections: The first explores a young woman's coming-of-age, and the second centers on the tortured relationships in her fiancé's family. Several critics have complained that these sections differ so much in style and content that they do not form a satisfactory whole. The first part of the novel, set in Edinburgh, contains many autobiographical elements. The main character, Ellen Melville, a secretary for a law firm, is clever, independent, and involved in the woman suffrage movement. She emerges from youth into womanhood, dealing with problem employers and becoming involved with Richard Yaverland, whom she sees as a romantic hero. Ellen is both charming and intriguing as she learns somewhat bitter lessons about a woman's role in society. The engagement between Ellen and Richard leads to the second section of the novel, where the subject and mood shift dramatically.

The focus moves from Ellen to Richard's mother, Marion, as West concentrates on Richard's illegitimate birth and its consequences. During her pregnancy, Marion is attacked by a group of villagers. In desperation, she allows herself to be married to Peacey, the butler of the man she loves. He eventually rapes her, and she bears a second child, Roger, a pale and pathetic figure beside his more vigorous brother. Marion, whose relationship with Richard contains strong sexual overtones, commits suicide in order to allow Richard and Ellen to be free of his ties to her and to his past. Roger blames his brother for the death. The two fight, and Richard kills his brother. In spite of this novel's dramatic content, it has been criticized for its lack of action as well as for its length.

HARRIET HUME

West's previous novels utilized the Freudian psychological realism of many twentieth century novels. In her third novel, *Harriet Hume*, she changed her style, creating a fantasy. The two main characters, Harriet, a pianist, and Arnold Condorex, a politician, both have weaknesses that jeopardize their careers: Harriet's hands are too small to span the keys of the piano as she would like; Arnold was not born to a family with power and social class. Both succeed in spite of their difficulties, however. Their relationship is complicated by Arnold's need to be involved with a woman who will aid his political career and by the fact that Harriet possesses psychic powers, which enable her to read the mind of her lover. The novel traces their meetings throughout the years, describing both the fascination they have for each other and the differences in the values that they have embraced. The novel is a fable illustrating some of the main themes of West's work: the necessity of art in love and life as well as the complex reasons men give to justify betrayal.

THE THINKING REED

The Thinking Reed focuses on the lives of the wealthy, in particular, a young widow and the men she pursues and who pursue her. Critics have noted that West deviates from other writers of her time in her depiction of this moneyed social class. *The Thinking Reed* has often been compared with *The Portrait of a Lady* (1881), Henry James's novel that associates wealth with personal liberty, and *The Great Gatsby* (1925), F. Scott Fitzgerald's morality tale that links wealth with decadence. West, in contrast to her American predecessors, compares persons of wealth to wild animals, attributing to them an instinctive desire for power and a dangerous disregard for the well-being of others.

The title of this novel is drawn from Blaise Pascal's seventeenth century defense of Christianity, *Pensées* (1670; *Monsieur Pascal's Thoughts, Meditations, and Prayers*, 1688), and West begins with an epigram selected from this work. The passage likens man to a vulnerable "thinking reed," noble in pursuing life with passion despite knowledge of certain death. West's heroine is Isabella Terry, a young American who distracts herself from the recent loss of her husband by pursuing a series of men in France, her ancestral country. Isabella is, in succession, the mistress of a French noble, whom she rejects for being controlling; the love interest of a Virginian abroad, who rejects her for her own unseemly behavior; and finally the wife of a French industrialist, whom she marries to spite the rejecting American. Her marriage is unhappy and, following a miscarriage, she considers obtaining a divorce. Her meditations on her situation, however, cause her to reconsider. Eventually, Isabella places the needs of another, her husband, ahead of her own, and she finds in this abnegation of self a measure of happiness.

THE FOUNTAIN OVERFLOWS

The Fountain Overflows is the first of a four-novel series West planned to write centering on the Aubrey family, patterned on her own family. Only the first of these works appeared before her death; two more, *This Real Night* and *Cousin Rosamund*, were published posthumously. She never completed the fourth novel. *The Fountain Overflows* is a childhood memory. It describes the Aubrey children's survival after their father deserts them: Cordelia, the eldest; the twins Mary and Rose; and Richard Quin, the youngest member of the family. Filled with vivid detail, this novel contains not only a rich portrait of family life but also a murder and several supernatural occurrences, all presented from a child's perspective. West's subject matter and style in this novel have been compared to the richly textured writings of Charles Dickens and Arnold Bennett.

THE BIRDS FALL DOWN

The Birds Fall Down, one of the most popular of West's novels, marks another departure in subject matter. The story, set in 1905, is narrated by Laura Rowen, an eighteen-year-old whose grandfather, a Russian grand duke, has been unfairly exiled by the czar. The main plot deals with treachery and betrayal, set against the backdrop of the political turmoil in Russia during this period. Clearly, however, West is developing themes she explores in her history book *The Meaning of Treason* (1947). As Laura journeys through France with her grandfather, he learns that his trusted aide is a double agent responsible for his disgrace. Her grandfather has a stroke and dies, and Laura has to struggle to escape from the traitor. The secondary plot line describes her father's affair, a betrayal of his wife and family that runs a parallel course to the treachery on the international level.

THIS REAL NIGHT

Published after West's death, *This Real Night* is the second installment in the chronicles of the Aubrey family. The children featured in *The Fountain Overflows* are now young adults beset by problems associated with the modern age. Conflicts in the novel range from the local to the global, from family disputes to world war, with the former acting as a microcosm of the latter. Richard Quin, the only son in the family, remains the favorite sibling of his older sisters. Central to the novel's exploration of modern life is the crisis of World War I. Richard Quin is no warrior, but following his enlistment, he goes to war. His interest in sports—the fencing, boxing, tennis, and cricket of his youth—fails to arm him effectively for battle. After Richard Quin dies at the front, his sisters confront the effects of his permanent absence. For them there is no glory, only loss.

This Real Night continues the psychological exploration of sibling relations begun in *The Fountain Overflows*. West describes Richard Quin in both feminine and masculine terms. Raised in a matriarchy comprising sisters and a mother, Richard Quin develops a feminine sensitivity while embracing the socially prescribed role of man of the house. At home, he is the de facto protector of his sisters. Unfortunately, when Richard Quin is out in the war-torn world, his older sisters can offer no protection to their brother in return. Their isolation as women on the home front, far from the scene of their brother's death, intensifies their grief.

SUNFLOWER

Sunflower, a fictional account of the author's affair with H. G. Wells, was begun in 1925 and later discarded. It is likely that West never intended for the manuscript to be published, but three years after her death it appeared in print, an incomplete sketch. The writing is unique for its dreamlike qualities, and the story shifts between descriptions of events and the character's interpretations of those events relayed through interior monologues. When West began the novel, she was undergoing psychotherapy to reduce her post-Wells trauma. Notes that she composed for those sessions may have made their way into the book in a curious convergence of fiction and life writing. The title character, Sybil Fassendyll, nicknamed Sunflower, is patterned after West. Sunflower is a young actor engaged in an affair with an older, married intellectual, Lord Essington, a depiction of Wells. While the novel chronicles certain events in the author's life, critics have noted that West was far superior to her fictional alter ego. Sunflower appears a bit dimwitted in certain passages, a trait never associated with the intellectual West.

Mary E. Mahony
Updated by Dorothy Dodge Robbins

OTHER MAJOR WORKS

NONFICTION: *Henry James*, 1916; *The Strange Necessity: Essays and Reviews*, 1928; *Ending in Earnest: A Literary Log*, 1931; *St. Augustine*, 1933 (biography); *Black Lamb and Grey Falcon: A Journey Through Yugoslavia*, 1941; *The Meaning of Treason*, 1947 (revised as *The New Meaning of Treason*, 1964); *A Train of Powder*, 1955; *The Court and the Castle*, 1957; *The Young Rebecca: Writings of Rebecca West*, 1982; *Family Memories*, 1987; *Selected Letters of Rebecca West*, 2000; *Survivors in Mexico*, 2003; *Woman as Artist and Thinker*, 2005.

MISCELLANEOUS: *Rebecca West: A Celebration*, 1977.

BIBLIOGRAPHY

Glendinning, Victoria. *Rebecca West: A Life*. New York: Alfred A. Knopf, 1986. Presents a detailed account of West's life, focusing particularly on the early years. Provides insight into West's development as a writer.

Lesinska, Zofia. *Perspectives of Four Women Writers on the Second World War: Gertrude Stein, Janet Flanner, Kay Boyle, and Rebecca West*. New York: Peter Lang, 2002. Relies on textual evidence drawn from West's novels, essays, political writings, and correspondence to reveal how her written responses to warfare are distinct from those of her contemporaries.

Norton, Ann V. *Paradoxical Feminism: The Novels of Rebecca West*. Lanham, Md.: International Scholars, 1999. Offers comprehensive analysis of West's novels in terms of their feminist themes, plots, and characters. Includes discussion of the author as a problematic feminist.

Rollyson, Carl E. *Rebecca West: A Life*. New York: Charles Scribner's Sons, 1996. Detailed biography discusses West's importance to twentieth century literature, tracing the development of her long career and illustrating the connections between her fiction and nonfiction.

Schweizer, Bernard. *Rebecca West: Heroism, Rebellion, and the Female Epic*. Westport, Conn.: Greenwood Press, 2002. Argues that West, in her novels and her travel writing, reinvents the epic tradition to serve the cause of feminism. Presents West as a philosopher whose ideas are more spiritual than political in origin.

_____, ed. *Rebecca West Today: Contemporary Critical Approaches*. Newark: University of Delaware Press, 2006. Nearly all of West's works are discussed in this volume, the first published collection of essays devoted to her writing. Included are in-depth analyses of ten novels, two short stories, one essay, and two of her journalistic writings. The chapter that West omitted from her novel *The Real Night* is also discussed at length.

Scott, Bonnie Kime. *Refiguring Modernism*. 2 vols. Bloomington: Indiana University Press, 1995. First volume of this set discusses women of 1928; second volume offers postmodern feminist readings of the works of Virginia Woolf, Djuna Barnes, and West.

Varney, Susan. "Oedipus and the Modern Aesthetic: Reconceiving the Social in Rebecca West's *The Return of the Soldier*." In *Naming the Father: Legacies, Genealogies, and Explorations of Fatherhood in Modern and Contemporary Fiction*, edited by Eva Paulino Bueno, Terry Caesar, and William Hummel. Lanham, Md.: Rowman & Littlefield, 2000. Examines events and characters in West's *Return of the Soldier* in relation to the story of Oedipus. Contends that West updated the tragic Greek character to serve a new age and a new art.

VIRGINIA WOOLF

Born: London, England; January 25, 1882
Died: The River Ouse, near Rodmell, Sussex, England; March 28, 1941
Also known as: Adeline Virginia Stephen

PRINCIPAL LONG FICTION

The Voyage Out, 1915
Night and Day, 1919
Jacob's Room, 1922
Mrs. Dalloway, 1925
To the Lighthouse, 1927
Orlando: A Biography, 1928
The Waves, 1931
Flush: A Biography, 1933
The Years, 1937
Between the Acts, 1941
Melymbrosia, 1982 (wr. 1912;
  revised 2002)

OTHER LITERARY FORMS

To say that Virginia Woolf lived to write is no exaggeration. Her output was both prodigious and varied; counting her posthumously published works, it fills more than forty volumes. Beyond her novels, her fiction encompasses several short-story collections. As a writer of nonfiction, Woolf was similarly prolific, her book-length works including *Roger Fry: A Biography* (1940) and two influential feminist statements, *A Room of One's Own* (1929) and *Three Guineas* (1938). Throughout her life, Woolf also produced criticism and reviews; the best-known collections are *The Common Reader: First Series* (1925) and *The Common Reader: Second Series* (1932). In 1966 and 1967, the four volumes of *Collected Essays* were published. Additional books of essays, reviews, and sketches continue to appear, most notably the illuminating selection of autobiographical materials, *Moments of Being* (1976). Her letters—3,800 of them survive—are available in six volumes; when publication was completed, her diaries stood at five. Another collection, of Woolf's essays, also proved a massive, multivolume undertaking.

ACHIEVEMENTS

From the appearance of her first novel in 1915, Virginia Woolf's work was received with respect—an important point, since she was extremely sensitive to criticism. Descendant of a distinguished literary family, member of the avant-garde Bloomsbury Group, herself an experienced critic and reviewer, she was taken seriously as an artist. Nevertheless, her early works were not financially successful; she was forty before she earned a living from her writing. From the start, the rather narrow territory of her novels precluded broad popularity, peopled as they were with sophisticated, sexually reserved, upper-middle-class characters, finely attuned to their sensibilities and relatively insulated from the demands of mundane existence. When in *Jacob's Room* she first abandoned the conventional novel to experiment with the interior monologues and lyrical poetic devices that characterize her mature method, she also began to develop a reputation as a "difficult" or "highbrow" writer, though undeniably an important one. Not until the brilliant fantasy *Orlando* was published did she enjoy a definite commercial success. Thereafter, she received both critical and popular acclaim; *The Years* was even a bona fide best seller.

During the 1930's, Woolf became the subject of critical essays and two book-length studies; some of her works were translated into French. At the same time, however, her novels began to be judged as irrelevant to a world beset by growing economic and political chaos. At her death in 1941, she was widely regarded as a pioneer of modernism but also reviewed by many as the effete, melancholic "invalid priestess of Bloomsbury," a stereotype her friend and fellow novelist E. M. Forster dismissed at the time as wholly inaccurate; she was, he insisted, "tough, sensitive but tough."

Over the next twenty-five years, respectful attention to Woolf's work continued, but in the late 1960's, critical interest accelerated dramatically and has remained strong. Two reasons for this renewed notice seem particularly apparent. First, Woolf's feminist essays *A Room of One's Own* and *Three Guineas* became rallying documents in the growing women's movement; readers who might not otherwise have discovered her novels were drawn to them via her nonfiction and tended to read them primarily as validations of her feminist thinking. Second, with the appearance of her husband Leonard Woolf's five-volume autobiography from 1965-1969, her nephew Quentin Bell's definitive two-volume biography of her in 1972, and the full-scale editions of her own diaries and letters commencing in the mid-1970's, Woolf's life has become one of the most thoroughly documented of any modern author. Marked by intellectual and sexual unconventionality, madness, and suicide, it is for today's readers also one of the most fascinating; the steady demand for memoirs, reminiscences, and photograph collections relating to her has generated what is sometimes disparagingly labeled "the Virginia Woolf industry." At its worst, such insatiable curiosity is morbidly voyeuristic, distracting from and trivializing Woolf's achievement; on a more responsible level, it has led to serious, provocative reevaluations of the political and especially the feminist elements in her work, as well as to redefinitions of her role as an artist.

BIOGRAPHY

Daughter of the eminent editor and critic Sir Leslie Stephen and Julia Jackson Duckworth, both of whom had been previously widowed, Virginia Woolf was born Adeline Virginia Stephen in 1882 into a solidly late Victorian intellectual and social milieu. Her father's first wife had been William Makepeace Thackeray's daughter, James Russell Lowell was her godfather, and visitors to the Stephens' London household included Henry James, George Meredith, and Thomas Hardy. From childhood on, she had access to her father's superb library, and she benefited from her father's guidance and commentary on her rigorous, precocious reading. Nevertheless, unlike her brothers, she did not receive a formal university education, a lack she always regretted and that partly explains the anger in *Three Guineas*, in which she proposes a "university of outsiders." (Throughout her life she declined all academic honors.)

In 1895, when Woolf was thirteen, her mother, just past fifty, suddenly died. Altruistic, self-sacrificing, totally devoted to her demanding husband and large family, the beautiful Julia Stephen fulfilled the Victorian ideal of womanhood and exhausted herself doing so; her daughter would movingly eulogize her as Mrs. Ramsay in *To the Lighthouse*. The loss devastated Woolf, who experienced at that time the first of four major mental breakdowns in her life, the last of which would end in death.

Leslie Stephen, twenty years his wife's senior and thus sanguinely expecting her to pilot him comfortably through old age, was devastated in another way. Retreating histrionically into self-pitying but deeply felt grief, like that of his fictional counterpart, Mr. Ramsay, he transferred his intense demands for sympathetic attention to a succession of what could only seem to him achingly inadequate substitutes for his dead wife: first, his stepdaughter Stella Duckworth, who herself died suddenly in 1897, then, Virginia's older sister Vanessa. The traditional feminine role would eventually have befallen Virginia had Leslie Stephen not died in 1904. Writing in her 1928 diary on what would have been her father's ninety-sixth birthday, Woolf reflects that, had he lived, "his life would have entirely ended mine. . . . No writing, no books;—inconceivable."

On her father's death, Woolf sustained her second incapacitating breakdown, but she also gained, as her diary suggests, something crucial: freedom. That freedom took an immediate and, to her parents' staid friends and relatives, shocking form. Virginia, Vanessa, and their brothers Thoby and Adrian abandoned the Stephen house in respectable Kensington to set up a home in the seedy bohemian district of London known as Bloomsbury. There, on Thursday evenings, a coterie of Thoby Stephen's Cambridge University friends regularly gathered to talk in an atmosphere of free thought, avant-garde art, and sexual tolerance, forming the nucleus of what came to be called the Bloomsbury Group. At various stages in its evolution over the next decade, the group included such luminaries as biographer Lytton Strachey, novelist E. M. Forster, art critic Roger Fry, and economist John Maynard Keynes. In 1911, they were joined by another of Thoby's Cambridge friends, a colonial official just returned from seven years in Ceylon, Leonard Woolf; Virginia Stephen married him the following year. Scarcely twelve months after the wedding, Virginia Woolf's third severe breakdown began, marked by a suicide attempt; her recovery took almost two years.

The causes of Woolf's madness have been much debated and the treatment she was prescribed—bed rest, milk, withdrawal of intellectual stimulation—much disputed, especially since Woolf apparently never received psychoanalytic help, even though the Hogarth Press, founded by the Woolfs in 1917, was one of Sigmund Freud's earliest English publishers. A history of insanity ran in the Stephen family; if Virginia was afflicted with a hereditary nervous condition, it was thought, then, that must be accepted as unalterable. On the other hand, the timing of these three breakdowns prompts speculation about more subtle causes. About her parents' deaths she evidently felt strong guilt; of *To the Lighthouse*, the fictionalized account of her parents' relationship, she would later say, "I was obsessed by them both, unhealthily; and writing of them was a necessary act." Marriage was for her a deliberately sought yet disturbing commitment, representing a potential loss of autonomy and a retreat into what her would-be novelist Terence Hewet envisions in *The Voyage Out* as a walled-up, firelit room. She found her own marriage sexually disappointing, perhaps in part because she had been molested both as a child and as a young woman by her two Duckworth stepbrothers.

In the late twentieth century, feminist scholars especially argued as a cause of Woolf's madness the burden of being a greatly talented woman in a world hostile to feminine achievement, a situation Woolf strikingly depicts in *A Room of One's Own* as the plight of William Shakespeare's hypothetical sister. Indeed, the young Virginia Stephen might plunder her father's library all day, but by teatime she was expected to don the role of deferential Victorian female in a rigidly patriarchal household. Once she settled in Bloomsbury, however, she enjoyed unconventional independence and received much sympathetic encouragement of her gifts, most of all from her husband.

Leonard Woolf, himself a professional writer and literary editor, connected his wife's madness directly with her genius, saying that she concentrated more intensely on her work than any writer he had ever known. Her books passed through long, difficult gestations; her sanity was always most vulnerable immediately after a novel was finished. Expanding on his belief that the imagination in his wife's books and the delusions of her breakdowns "all came from the same place in her mind," some critics have gone so far as to claim her madness as the very source of her art, permitting her to make mystical descents into inner space from which she returned with sharpened perception.

It is significant, certainly, that although Woolf's first publication, an unsigned article for the newspaper *The Guardian*, appeared just two months after her 1904 move to Bloomsbury, her first novel, over which she labored for seven years, was only completed shortly after her marriage; her breakdown occurred three months after its acceptance for publication. Very early, therefore, Leonard Woolf learned to keep a daily record of his wife's health; throughout their life together, he would be alert for those signs of fatigue or erratic behavior that signaled approaching danger and the need for her customary rest cure. Rational, efficient, uncomplaining, Leonard Woolf has been condemned by some disaffected scholars as a pseudosaintly nurse who benignly badgered his patient into crippling dependence. The compelling argument against this extreme interpretation is Virginia Woolf's astonishing productivity after she recovered from her third illness. Although there were certainly periods of instability and near disaster, the following twenty-five years were immensely fruitful as she discarded traditional fiction to move toward realizing her unique vision, all the while functioning actively and diversely as a fine critic, too.

After Woolf's ninth novel, *The Years*, was finished in 1936, however, she came closer to mental collapse than she had been at any time since 1913. Meanwhile, a larger pattern of breakdown was developing in the world around her as World War II became inevitable. Working at her Sussex home on her last book, *Between the Acts*, she could hear the Battle of Britain being fought over her head; her London house was severely damaged in the Blitz. Strangely, however, that novel was her easiest to write; Leonard Woolf, ever watchful, was struck by her tranquillity during this period. The gradual symptoms of warning were absent this time; when her depression began, he would recall, it struck her "like a sudden blow." She began to hear voices and knew what was coming. On February 26, 1941, she finished *Between the Acts*. Four weeks later, she went out for one of her usual walks across the Sussex downs, placed a heavy stone in her pocket, and stepped into the River Ouse. Within minutes Leonard Woolf arrived at its banks to find her walking stick and hat lying there. Her body was recovered three weeks later.

ANALYSIS

In one of her most famous pronouncements on the nature of fiction—as a practicing critic, she had much to say on the subject—Virginia Woolf insists that "life is not a series of gig lamps symmetrically arranged; but a luminous halo, a semi-transparent envelope surrounding us from the beginning of consciousness to the end." In an ordinary day, she argues, "thousands of ideas" course through the human brain; "thousands of emotions" meet, collide, and disappear "in astonishing disorder." Amid this hectic interior flux, the trivial and the vital, the past and the present, are constantly interacting; there is endless tension between the multitude of ideas and emotions rushing through one's consciousness and the numerous impressions scoring on it from the external world. Thus, even personal identity becomes evanescent, continually reordering itself as "the atoms of experience . . . fall upon the mind." It follows, then, that human beings must have great difficulty communicating with one another, for of this welter of perceptions that define individual personality, only a tiny fraction can ever be externalized in word or gesture. Yet, despite—in fact, because of—their frightening isolation as unknowable entities, people yearn to unite both with one another and with some larger pattern of order hidden behind the flux, to experience time standing still momentarily, to see matches struck that briefly illuminate the darkness.

Given the complex phenomenon of human subjectivity, Woolf asks, "Is it not the task of the novelist to convey this varying, this unknown and uncircumscribed spirit . . . with as little mixture of the alien and external as possible?" The conventional novel form is plainly inadequate for such a purpose, she maintains. Dealing sequentially with a logical set of completed past actions that occur in a coherent, densely detailed physical and social environment, presided over by an omniscient narrator interpreting the significance of it all, the traditional novel trims and shapes experience into a rational but falsified pattern. "Is life like this?" Woolf demands rhetorically. "Must novels be like this?"

In Woolf's first two books, nevertheless, she attempted to work within conventional modes, discovering empirically that they could not convey her vision. Although in recent years some critics have defended *The Voyage Out* and *Night and Day* as artistically satisfying in their own right, both novels have generally been considered interesting mainly for what they foreshadow of Woolf's later preoccupations and techniques.

THE VOYAGE OUT

The Voyage Out is the story of Rachel Vinrace, a naïve and talented twenty-four-year-old amateur pianist who sails from England to a small resort on the South American coast, where she vacations with relatives. There, she meets a fledgling novelist, Terence Hewet; on a pleasure expedition up a jungle river, they declare their love. Shortly thereafter, Rachel falls ill with a fever and dies. The novel's exotic locale, large cast of minor characters, elaborate scenes of social comedy, and excessive length are all atypical of Woolf's mature work. Already, however, many of her later concerns are largely emerging. The resonance of the title itself anticipates Woolf's poetic symbolism; the "voyage out" can be the literal trip across the Atlantic or up the South American river, but it also suggests the progression from innocence to experience, from life to death, which she later depicts using similar water imagery. Her concern with premature death and how survivors come to terms with it prefigures *Jacob's Room*, *Mrs. Dalloway*, *To the Lighthouse*, and *The Waves*. Most significant is her portrayal of a world in which characters are forever striving to overcome their isolation from one another. The ship on which Rachel "voyages out" is labeled by Woolf an "emblem of the loneliness of human life." Terence, Rachel's lover, might be describing his creator's own frustration when he says he is trying "to write a novel about Silence, the things people don't say. But the difficulty is immense."

Moments of unity amid seemingly unconquerable disorder do occur, however. On a communal level, one such transformation happens at a ball being held to celebrate the engagement of two English guests at the resort's small hotel. When the musicians go home, Rachel appropriates the piano and plays Mozart, hunting songs, and hymn tunes as the guests gradually resume dancing, each in a newly expressive, uninhibited way, eventually to join hands in a gigantic round dance. When the circle breaks and each member spins away to become individual once more, Rachel modulates to Bach; her weary yet exhilarated listeners sit quietly and allow themselves to be soothed by the serene complexity of the music. As dawn breaks outside and Rachel plays on, they envision "themselves and their lives, and the whole of human life advancing nobly under the direction of the music." They have transcended their single identities temporarily to gain a privileged glimpse of some larger pattern beyond themselves.

If Rachel through her art briefly transforms the lives of a small community, she herself privately discerns fleeting stability through her growing love for Terence. Even love is insufficient, however; although in the couple's newfound sense of union "divisions disappeared," Terence feels that Rachel seems able "to pass away to unknown places where she had no need of him." In the elegiac closing scenes of illness (which Woolf reworked many times and which are the most original as well as moving part of the novel), Rachel "descends into another world"; she is "curled up at the bottom of the sea." Terence, sitting by her bedside, senses that "they seemed to be thinking together; he seemed to be Rachel as well as himself." When she ceases breathing, he experiences "an immense feeling of peace," a "complete union" with her that shatters when he notices an ordinary table covered with crockery and realizes in horror that in this world he will never see Rachel again. For her, stability has been achieved; for him, the isolating flux has resumed.

NIGHT AND DAY

Looking back on *The Voyage Out*, Woolf could see, she said, why readers found it "a more gallant and inspiring spectacle" than her next and least known book *Night and Day*. This second novel is usually regarded as her most traditional in form and subject—in its social satire, her obeisance to Jane Austen. Its dancelike plot, however, in which mismatched young couples eventually find their true loves, suggests the magical atmosphere of William Shakespeare's romantic comedies as well. References to Shakespeare abound in the book; for example, the delightfully eccentric Mrs. Hilbery characterizes herself as one of his wise fools, and when at the end she presides over the repatterning of the couples in London, she has just arrived from a pilgrimage to Stratford-upon-Avon. Coincidentally, *Night and Day* is the most conventionally dramatic of Woolf's novels, full of dialogue, exits and entrances; characters are constantly taking omnibuses and taxis across London from one contrived scene to the next.

Like *The Voyage Out*, *Night and Day* does point to Woolf's enduring preoccupations. It is, too, a novel depicting movement from innocence to maturity and escape from the conventional world through the liberating influence of love. Ralph Denham, a London solicitor from a large, vulgar, middle-class family living in suburban Highgate, would prefer to move to a Norfolk cottage and write. Katharine Hilbery measures out her days serving tea in her wealthy family's beautiful Chelsea home and helping her disorganized mother produce a biography of their forebear, a great nineteenth century poet. Her secret passions, however, are mathematics and astronomy. These seeming opposites, Ralph and Katharine, are alike in that both retreat at night to their rooms to pursue their private visions. The entire novel is concerned with such dualities—public selves and private selves, activity and contemplation, fact and imagination; but Woolf also depicts the unity that Ralph and Katharine can achieve, notwithstanding the social and intellectual barriers separating them. At the end, as the couple leaves Katharine's elegant but constraining home to walk in the open night air, "they lapsed gently into silence, travelling the dark paths side by side towards something discerned in the distance which gradually possessed them both."

The sustained passages of subtle interior analysis by which Woolf charts the couple's growing realization of their need for each other define her real area of fictional interest, but they are hemmed in by a tediously constrictive traditional structure. Except for her late novel, *The Years*, also comparatively orthodox in form, her first two books took the longest to finish and underwent the most extensive revisions, undoubtedly because she was writing against her grain. Nevertheless, they represented a necessary apprenticeship; as she would later remark of *Night and Day*, "You must put it all in before you can leave out."

JACOB'S ROOM

Woolf dared to leave out a great deal in the short experimental novel she wrote next. Described in conventional terms, *Jacob's Room* is a bildungsroman, or "novel of formation," tracing its hero's development from childhood to maturity: Jacob Flanders is first portrayed as a small boy studying a tide pool on a Cornish beach; at twenty-six, he dies fighting in World War I. In structure, style, and tone, however, *Jacob's Room* defies such labeling. It does not move in steady chronological fashion but in irregular leaps. Of the fourteen chapters, two cover Jacob's childhood, two, his college years at Cambridge, the remainder, his life as a young adult working in London and traveling abroad. In length, and hence in the complexity with which various periods of Jacob's existence are treated, the chapters range from one to twenty-eight pages. They vary, that is, as the process of growth itself does.

Individual chapters are likewise discontinuous in structure, broken into irregular segments that convey multiple, often simultaneous perspectives. The ten-page chapter 8, for example, opens with Jacob's slamming the door of his London room as he starts for work in the morning; he is then glimpsed at his office desk. Meanwhile, on a table back in his room lies his mother's unopened letter to him, placed there the previous night by his lover, Florinda; its contents and Mrs. Flanders herself are evoked. The narrator then discourses on the significance of letter writing. Jacob is next seen leaving work for the day; in Greek Street, he spies Florinda on another man's arm. At eight o'clock, Rose Shaw, a guest at a party Jacob attended several nights earlier, walks through Holburn, meditating bitterly on the ironies of love and death. The narrator sketches London by lamplight. Then, Jacob is back in his room reading by the fire a newspaper account of the Prime Minister's speech on Home Rule; the night is very cold. The narrator abruptly shifts perspective from congested London to the open countryside, describing the snow that has been accumulating since midafternoon; an old shepherd crossing a field hears a distant clock strike. Back in London, Jacob also hears the hour chiming, rakes out his fire, and goes to bed. There is no story here in any conventional sense, no action being furthered; in the entire ten pages, only one sentence is direct dialogue. What Woolf delineates is the *texture* of an ordinary day in the life of Jacob and the world in which he exists. Clock time moves the chapter forward, while spatially the chapter radiates outward from the small area Jacob occupies. Simultaneously, in the brief reference to the Prime Minister, Woolf suggests the larger procession of modern history that will inexorably sweep Jacob to premature death.

Such indirection and understatement characterize the whole novel: "It is no use trying to sum people up," the narrator laments. "One must follow hints." Thus, Jacob is described mainly from the outside, defined through the impressions he makes on others, from a hotel chambermaid to a Cambridge don, and by his surroundings and possessions. Even his death is conveyed obliquely: Mrs. Flanders, half asleep in her Yorkshire house, hears "dull sounds"; it cannot be guns, she thinks, it must be the sea. On the next page, she stands in her dead son's London room, holding a pair of Jacob's old shoes and asking his friend pathetically, "What am I to do with these, Mr. Bonamy?" The novel ends.

To construct Jacob's ultimately unknowable biography out of such fragments, Woolf evolves not only a new structure but a new style. Long, fluid sentences contain precise physical details juxtaposed with metaphysical speculations on the evanescence of life and the impossibility of understanding another person. Lyrical descriptions of nature—waves, moths, falling snow, birds rising and settling—are interspersed to suggest life's beauty and fragility. Images and phrases recur as unifying motifs: Jacob is repeatedly associated with Greek literature and myth and spends his last fulfilling days visiting the Parthenon. Most important, Woolf begins to move freely in and out of her characters' minds to capture the flow of sense impressions mingling with memory, emotion, and random association, experimenting with that narrative method conveniently if imprecisely labeled "stream of consciousness."

Jacob's Room is not a mature work, especially with its intrusive narrator, who can be excessively chatty, archly pedantic, and sententious. Woolf protests the difficulties of her task ("In short, the observer is choked with observations") and cannot quite follow the logic of her new method; after an essaylike passage on the necessity of illusion, for example, she awkwardly concludes, "Jacob, no doubt, thought something in this fashion." Even the lovely passages of poetic description at times seem self-indulgent. The book definitely shows its seams. Woolf's rejection of traditional novel structure, however, and her efforts to eliminate "the alien and the external" make *Jacob's Room* a dazzling advance in her ability to embody her philosophical vision: "Life is but a procession of shadows, and God knows why it is that we embrace them so eagerly, and see them depart with such anguish, being shadows."

MRS. DALLOWAY

Within three years, Woolf had resolved her technical problems superbly in *Mrs. Dalloway*. The intruding narrator vanishes; though the freedom with which point of view shifts among characters and settings clearly posits an omniscient intelligence, the narrator's observations are now subtly integrated with the thoughts of her characters, and the transitions between scenes flow organically. Woolf's subject is also better suited to her method: Whereas *Jacob's Room* is a story of youthful potential tragically cut off, *Mrs.*

Dalloway is a novel of middle age, about what people have become as the result of choices made, opportunities seized or refused. Jacob Flanders had but a brief past; the characters in *Mrs. Dalloway* must come to terms with theirs, sifting and valuing the memories that course through their minds.

The book covers one June day in the life of Clarissa Dalloway, fifty-two years old, an accomplished London political hostess and wife of a Member of Parliament. A recent serious illness from which she is still recovering has made her freshly appreciate the wonder of life as she prepares for the party she will give that evening. Peter Walsh, once desperately in love with her, arrives from India, where he has had an undistinguished career; he calls on her and is invited to the party, at which another friend from the past, Sally Seton, formerly a romantic and now the conventional wife of a Manchester industrialist, will also unexpectedly appear. Running parallel with Clarissa's day is that of the mad Septimus Warren Smith, a surviving Jacob Flanders, shell-shocked in the war; his suicide in the late afternoon delays the arrival of another of Clarissa's guests, the eminent nerve specialist Sir William Bradshaw. Learning of this stranger's death, Clarissa must confront the inevitability of her own.

Mrs. Dalloway is also, then, a novel about time itself (its working title at one point was *The Hours*). Instead of using chapters or other formal sectioning, Woolf structures the book by counterpointing clock time, signaled by the obtrusive hourly tolling of Big Ben, against the subjective flow of time in her characters' minds as they recover the past and envision the future. Not only does she move backward and forward in time, however; she also creates an effect of simultaneity that is especially crucial in linking Septimus's story with Clarissa's. Thus, when Clarissa Dalloway, buying flowers that morning in a Bond Street shop, hears "a pistol shot" outside and emerges to see a large, official automobile that has backfired, Septimus is standing in the crowd blocked by the car and likewise reacting to this "violent explosion" ("The world has raised its whip; where will it descend?"). Later, when Septimus's frightened young Italian wife Rezia guides him to Regents Park to calm him before their appointment with Bradshaw, he has a terrifying hallucination of his dead friend Evans, killed just before the Armistice; Peter Walsh, passing their bench, wonders, "What awful fix had they got themselves in to look so desperate as that on a fine summer morning?" This atmosphere of intensely populated time and space, of many anonymous lives intersecting briefly, of the world resonating with unwritten novels, comic and tragic, accounts in part for the richly poignant texture of nearly all Woolf's mature work.

In her early thinking about *Mrs. Dalloway*, Virginia Woolf wanted to show a "world seen by the sane and the insane, side by side." Although the novel definitely focuses on Clarissa, Septimus functions as a kind of double, representing her own responses to life carried to an untenable extreme. Both find great terror in life and also great joy; both want to withdraw from life into blissful isolation, yet both want to reach out to merge with others. Clarissa's friends, and indeed she herself, sense a "coldness" about her, "an impenetrability"; both Peter and Sally believe she chose safety rather than adventure by marrying the unimaginative, responsible Richard Dalloway. The quiet attic room where she now convalesces is described as a tower into which she retreats nunlike to a virginal narrow bed. Yet Clarissa also loves "life; London; this moment of June"—and her parties. Though some critics condemn her party giving as shallow, trivial, even corrupt (Peter Walsh could make her wince as a girl by predicting that she would become "the perfect hostess"), Clarissa considers her parties a form of creativity, "an offering," "her gift" of bringing people together. For Septimus, the war has destroyed his capacity to feel; in his aloneness and withdrawal, he finds "an isolation full of sublimity; a freedom which the attached can never know"—he can elude "human nature," "the repulsive brute, with the blood-red nostrils." Yet just watching leaves quivering is for him "an exquisite joy"; he feels them "connected by millions of fibres with his own body" and wants to reveal this unity to the world because "communication is health; communication is happiness."

Desperate because of his suicide threats, Septimus's wife takes him to see Sir William Bradshaw. At the center of the novel, in one of the most bitter scenes in all of Woolf's writing (certainly one with strong autobiographical overtones), is Septimus's confrontation with this "priest of science," this man of "lightning skill" and "almost infallible accuracy" who "never spoke of 'madness'; he called it not having a sense of proportion." Within three minutes, he has discreetly recorded his diagnosis on a pink card ("a case of complete breakdown . . . with every symptom in an advanced stage"); Septimus will be sent to a beautiful house in the country where he will be taught to rest, to regain proportion. Rezia, agonized, understands that she has been failed by this obtuse, complacently cruel man whom Woolf symbolically connects with a larger system that prospers on intolerance and sends its best young men to fight futile wars. Septimus's suicide at this point becomes inevitable.

The two stories fuse when Bradshaw appears at the party. Learning of the reason for his lateness, Clarissa, deeply shaken, withdraws to a small side room, not unlike her attic tower, where she accurately imagines Septimus's suicide: "He had thrown himself from a window. Up had flashed the ground; through him, blundering, bruising, went the rusty spikes. . . . So she saw it." She also intuits the immediate cause: Bradshaw is "capable of some indescribable outrage—forcing your soul, that was it"; seeing him, this young man must have said to himself, "they make life intolerable, men like that." Thus, she sees, "death was defiance," a means to preserve one's center from being violated, but "death was an attempt to communicate," and in death, Septimus's message that all life is connected is heard by one unlikely person, Clarissa Dalloway. Reviewing her own past as she has reconstructed it this day, and forced anew to acknowledge her own mortality, she realizes that "he had made her feel the beauty." Spiritually regenerated, she returns to her party "to kindle and illuminate" life.

TO THE LIGHTHOUSE

In her most moving, complexly affirmative novel, *To the Lighthouse*, Woolf portrays another woman whose creativity lies in uniting people, Mrs. Ramsay. For this luminous evocation of her own parents' marriage, Woolf drew on memories of her girlhood summers at St. Ives, Cornwall (here transposed to an island in the Hebrides), to focus on her perennial themes, the difficulties and joys of human communication, especially as frustrated by time and death.

The plot is absurdly simple: An expedition to a lighthouse is postponed, then completed a decade later. Woolf's mastery, however, of the interior monologue in this novel makes such a fragile plot line quite sufficient; the real "story" of *To the Lighthouse* is the reader's gradually increasing intimacy with its characters' richly depicted inner lives; the reader's understanding expands in concert with the characters' own growing insights.

Woolf again devises an experimental structure for her work, this time of three unequal parts. Approximately the first half of the novel, titled "The Window," occurs during a single day at the seaside home occupied by an eminent philosopher, Mr. Ramsay, his wife, and a melange of children, guests, and servants, including Lily Briscoe, an amateur painter in her thirties, unmarried. Mrs. Ramsay's is the dominant consciousness in this section. A short, exquisitely beautiful center section, "Time Passes," pictures the house succumbing to time during the family's ten-year absence and then being rescued from decay by two old women for the Ramsays' repossession. Periodically interrupting this natural flow of time are terse, bracketed, clock-time announcements like news bulletins, telling of the deaths of Mrs. Ramsay, the eldest son Andrew (in World War I), and the eldest daughter Prue (of childbirth complications). The final third, "The Lighthouse," also covers one day; the diminished family and several former guests having returned, the lighthouse expedition can now be completed. This section is centered almost entirely in Lily Briscoe's consciousness.

Because Mr. and Mrs. Ramsay are both strong personalities, they are sometimes interpreted too simply. Particularly in some readings by feminist critics, Mr. Ramsay is seen as an insufferable patriarch, arrogantly rational in his work but almost infantile emotionally, while Mrs. Ramsay is a Victorian earth mother, not only submitting unquestioningly to her husband's and children's excessive demands but actively trying to impose on all the other female characters her unliberated way of life. Such readings are sound to some extent, but they undervalue the vivid way that Woolf captures in the couple's monologues the conflicting mixture of motives and needs that characterize human beings of either sex. For example, Mrs. Ramsay is infuriated that her husband blights their youngest son James's anticipation of the lighthouse visit by announcing that it will storm tomorrow, yet his unflinching pursuit of truth is also something she most admires in him. Mr. Ramsay finds his wife's irrational habit of exaggeration maddening, but as she sits alone in a reverie, he respects her integrity and will not interrupt, "though it hurt him that she should look so distant, and he could not reach her, he could do nothing to help her." Lily, a shrewd observer who simultaneously adores and resists Mrs. Ramsay, perceives that "it would be a mistake . . . to simplify their relationship."

Amid these typical contradictions and mundane demands, however, "little daily miracles" may be achieved. One of Woolf's finest scenes, Mrs. Ramsay's dinner, provides a paradigm (though a summary can scarcely convey the richness of these forty pages). As she mechanically seats her guests at the huge table, Mrs. Ramsay glimpses her husband at the other end, "all in a heap, frowning": "She could not understand how she had ever felt any emotion of affection for him." Gloomily, she perceives that not just the two of them but everyone is separate and out of sorts. For example, Charles Tansley, Mr. Ramsay's disciple, who feels the whole family despises him, fidgets angrily; Lily, annoyed that Tansley is always telling her "women can't paint," purposely tries to irritate him; William Bankes would rather be home dining alone and fears that Mrs. Ramsay will read his mind. They all sense that "something [is] lacking"—they are divided from one another, sunk in their "treacherous" thoughts. Mrs. Ramsay wearily recognizes that "the whole of the effort of merging and flowing and creating rested on her."

She instructs two of her children to light the candles and set them around a beautiful fruit centerpiece that her daughter Rose has arranged for the table. This is Mrs. Ramsay's first stroke of artistry; the candles and fruit compose the table and the faces around it into an island, a sheltering haven: "Here, inside the room, seemed to be order and dry land; there, outside, a reflection in which things wavered and vanished, waterily." All the guests feel this change and have a sudden sense of making "common cause against that fluidity out there." Then the maid brings in a great steaming dish of *boeuf en daube* that even the finicky widower Bankes considers "a triumph." As the guests relish the succulent food and their camaraderie grows, Mrs. Ramsay, serving the last helpings from the depths of the pot, experiences a moment of perfect insight: "There it was, all around them. It partook . . . of eternity." She affirms to herself that "there is a coherence in things, a stability; something, she meant, that is immune from change, and shines out . . . in the face of the flowing, the fleeting." As is true of so much of Woolf's sparse dialogue, the ordinary words Mrs. Ramsay then speaks aloud can be read both literally and symbolically: "Yes, there is plenty for everybody." As the dinner ends and she passes out of the room triumphantly— the inscrutable poet Augustus Carmichael, who usually resists her magic, actually bows in homage—she looks back on the scene and sees that "it had become, she knew . . . already the past."

The burden of the past and the coming to terms with it are the focus of part 3. Just as "a sort of disintegration" sets in as soon as Mrs. Ramsay sweeps out of the dining room, so her death has left a larger kind of wreckage. Without her unifying artistry, all is disorder, as it was at the beginning of the dinner. In a gesture of belated atonement for quarreling with his wife over the original lighthouse trip, the melodramatically despairing Mr. Ramsay insists on making the expedition now with his children James and Cam, although both hate his tyranny and neither wants to go. As they set out, Lily remains behind to paint. Surely mirroring the creative anxiety of Woolf herself, she feels "a painful but exciting ecstasy" before her blank canvas, knowing how ideas that seem simple become "in practice immediately complex." As she starts making rhythmic strokes across the canvas, she loses "consciousness of outer things" and begins to meditate on the past, from which she gradually retrieves a vision of Mrs. Ramsay that will permit her to reconstruct and complete the painting she left unfinished a decade ago, one in which Mrs. Ramsay would have been, and will become again, a triangular shadow on a step (symbolically echoing the invisible "wedge-shaped core of darkness" to which Mrs. Ramsay feels herself shrinking during her moments of reverie). Through the unexpectedly intense pain of recalling her, Lily also comprehends Mrs. Ramsay's significance, her ability "to make the moment something permanent," as art does, to strike "this eternal passing and flowing . . . into stability." Mrs. Ramsay is able to make "life stand still here."

Meanwhile, Mr. Ramsay and his children are also voyaging into the past; Cam, dreamily drifting her hand in the water, begins, as her mother did, to see her father as bravely pursuing truth like a tragic hero. James bitterly relives the childhood scene when his father thoughtlessly dashed his hopes for the lighthouse visit, but as they near the lighthouse in the present and Mr. Ramsay offers his son rare praise, James too is reconciled. When they land, Mr. Ramsay himself, standing in the bow "very straight and tall," springs "lightly like a young man . . . on to the rock," renewed. Simultaneously, though the boat has long since disappeared from her sight and even the lighthouse itself seems blurred, Lily intuits that they have reached their goal and she completes her painting. All of them have reclaimed Mrs. Ramsay from death, and she has unified them; memory can defeat time. "Yes," Lily thinks, "I have had my vision." Clearly, Woolf had achieved hers too and transmuted the materials of a painful past into this radiant novel.

Although Woolf denied intending any specific symbolism for the lighthouse, it resonates with almost infinite possibilities, both within the book and in a larger way as an emblem of her work. Like the candles at the dinner party, it can be a symbol of safety and stability amid darkness and watery flux, its beams those rhythmically occurring moments of illumination that sustain Mrs. Ramsay and by extension everyone. Perhaps, however, it can also serve as a metaphor for human beings themselves as Woolf portrays them. The lighthouse signifies what can be objectively perceived of an individual—in Mrs. Ramsay's words, "our apparitions, the things you know us by"; but it also signals invisible, possibly tragic depths, for, as Mrs. Ramsay knew, "beneath it is all dark, it is all spreading, it is unfathomably deep."

THE WAVES

In *The Waves*, widely considered her masterpiece, Woolf most resolutely overcomes the limits of the traditional novel. Entirely unique in form, *The Waves* cannot perhaps be called a novel at all; Woolf herself first projected a work of "prose yet poetry; a novel and a play." The book is a series of grouped soliloquies in varying combinations spoken by six friends, three men and three women, at successive stages in their lives from childhood to late middle age. Each grouping is preceded by a brief, lyrical "interlude" (Woolf's own term), set off in italic type, that describes an empty house by the sea as the sun moves across the sky in a single day.

The texture of these soliloquies is extremely difficult to convey; the term "soliloquy," in fact, is merely a critical convenience. Although each is introduced in the same straightforward way ("Neville said," "Jinny said"), they obviously are unspoken, representing each character's private vision. Their style is also unvarying—solemn, formal, almost stilted, like that of choral figures. The author has deliberately translated into a rigorously neutral, dignified idiom the conscious and subconscious reality her characters perceive but cannot articulate on their own. This method represents Woolf's most ambitious attempt to capture the unfathomable depths of separate human personalities, which defy communication in ordinary life—and in ordinary novels. The abstraction of the device, however, especially in combination with the flow of cosmic time in the interludes, shows that she is also concerned with depicting a universal pattern that transcends mere individuals. Thus, once more Woolf treats her theme of human beings' attempts to overcome their isolation and to become part of a larger stabilizing pattern; this time, however, the theme is embodied in the very form of her work.

It would be inaccurate, however, to say that the characters exist only as symbols. Each has definable qualities and unique imagery; Susan, as an example, farm-bred and almost belligerently maternal, speaks in elemental images of wood smoke, grassy paths, flowers thick with pollen. Further, the characters often evoke one another's imagery; the other figures, for example, even in maturity picture the fearful, solitary Rhoda as a child rocking white petals in a brown basin of water. They are linked by intricately woven threads of common experience, above all by their shared admiration for a shadowy seventh character, Percival. Their gathering with him at a farewell dinner before he embarks on a career in India is one of the few actual events recorded in the soliloquies and also becomes one of those miraculous moments of unity comparable to that achieved by Mrs. Ramsay for her dinner guests; as they rise to leave the restaurant, all the characters are thinking as Louis does: "We pray, holding in our hands this common feeling, 'Do not move, do not let the swing-door cut to pieces this thing that we have made, that globes itself here.'" Such union, however, is cruelly impermanent; two pages later, a telegram announces Percival's death in a riding accident. Bernard, trying to make sense of this absurdity, echoes the imagery of encircling unity that characterized their thoughts at the dinner: "Ideas break a thousand times for once that they globe themselves entire."

It is Bernard—identified, significantly, throughout the book as a storyteller—who is given the long final section of *The Waves* in which "to sum up," becoming perhaps a surrogate for the author herself. (As a young man at school, worrying out "my novel," he discovers how "stories that follow people into their private rooms are difficult.") It is he who recognizes that "I am not one person; I am many people," part of his friends as they are part of him, all of them incomplete in themselves; he is "a man without a self." Yet it is also he who on the novel's final page, using the wave imagery of the universalizing interludes, passionately asserts his individuality: "Against you I will fling myself, unvanquished and unyielding, O Death!" Life, however obdurate and fragmented, must be affirmed.

The Waves is without doubt Woolf's most demanding and original novel, her most daring experiment in eliminating the alien and the external. When she vowed to cast out "all waste, deadness, and superfluity," however, she also ascetically renounced some of her greatest strengths as a novelist: her wit and humor, her delight in the daily beauty, variety, and muddle of material existence. This "abstract mystical eyeless book," as she at one point envisioned it, is a work to admire greatly, but not to love.

The six years following The Waves were a difficult period for Woolf both personally and artistically. Deeply depressed by the deaths of Lytton Strachey and Roger Fry, two of her oldest, most respected friends, she was at work on an "essay-novel," as she first conceived of it, which despite her initial enthusiasm became her most painfully frustrating effort—even though it proved, ironically, to be her greatest commercial success.

THE YEARS

In *The Years*, Woolf returned to the conventional novel that she had rejected after *Night and Day*; she planned "to take in everything" and found herself "infinitely delighting in facts for a change." Whereas *The Waves* had represented the extreme of leaving out, *The Years* suggests the opposite one of almost indiscriminate putting in. Its very subject, a history of the Pargiter clan spanning fifty years and three generations, links it with the diffuse family sagas of John Galsworthy and Arnold Bennett, whose books Woolf was expressly deriding when she demanded, "Must novels be like this?"

Nevertheless, *The Years* is more original than it may appear; Woolf made fresh use of her experimental methods in her effort to reanimate traditional form. The novel contains eleven unequal segments, each standing for a year; the longest ones, the opening "1880" section and the closing "Present Day" (the 1930's), anchor the book; the nine intermediate sections cover the years between 1891 and 1918. Echoing *The Waves*, Woolf begins each chapter with a short panoramic passage describing both London and the countryside. Within the chapters, instead of continuous narrative, there are collections of vignettes, somewhat reminiscent of *Jacob's Room*, depicting various Pargiters going about their daily lives. Running parallel with the family's history are larger historical events, including Edward VII's death, the suffrage movement, the Irish troubles, and especially World War I. These events are usually treated indirectly, however; for example, the "1917" section takes place mainly in a cellar to which the characters have retreated, dinner plates in hand, during an air raid. It is here that Eleanor Pargiter asks, setting a theme that suffuses the rest of the novel, "When shall we live adventurously, wholly, not like cripples in a cave?"

The most pervasive effect of the war is felt in the lengthy "Present Day" segment, which culminates in a family reunion, where the youngest generation of Pargiters, Peggy and North, are lonely, cynical, and misanthropic, and their faltering elders are compromised either by complacency or failed hopes. Symbolically, Delia Pargiter gives the party in a rented office, not a home, underscoring the uprooting caused by the war. Yet the balancing "1880" section is almost equally dreary: The Pargiters' solid Victorian house shelters a chronically ailing mother whose children wish she would die, a father whose vulgar mistress greets him in hair curlers and frets over her dog's eczema, and a young daughter traumatized by an exhibitionist in the street outside. One oppressive way of life seems only to have been superseded by another, albeit a more universally menacing one.

The overall imagery of the novel is likewise unlovely: Children recall being scrubbed with slimy washcloths; a revolting dinner of underdone mutton served by Sara Pargiter includes a bowl of rotting, flyblown fruit, grotesquely parodying Mrs. Ramsay's *boeuf en daube* and Rose's centerpiece; London is populated with deformed violet-sellers and old men eating cold sausages on buses. Communication in such a world is even more difficult than in Woolf's earlier books; the dialogue throughout is full of incomplete sentences, and a central vignette in the "Present Day" section turns on one guest's abortive efforts to deliver a speech toasting the human race.

Despite these circumstances, the characters still grope toward some kind of transforming unity; Eleanor, the eldest surviving Pargiter and the most sympathetic character in the novel, comes closest to achieving such vision on the scale that Lily Briscoe and Clarissa Dalloway do. At the reunion, looking back over her life, she wonders if there is "a pattern; a theme recurring like music . . . momentarily perceptible?" Casting about her, trying to connect with her relatives and friends but dozing in the process, she suddenly wakes, proclaiming that "it's been a perpetual discovery, my life. A miracle." Answering by implication her question posed fifteen years earlier during the air raid, she perceives that "we're only just beginning . . . to understand, here and there." That prospect is enough, however; she wants "to enclose the present moment . . . to fill it fuller and fuller, with the past, the present and the future, until it shone, whole, bright, deep with understanding."

Even this glowing dream of eventual unity is muted, however, when one recalls how Eleanor's embittered niece Peggy half pities, half admires her as a person who "still believed with passion . . . in the things man had destroyed," and how her nephew North, a captain in the trenches of World War I, thinks, "We cannot help each other, we are all deformed." It is difficult not to read the final lines of this profoundly somber novel ironically: "The sun had risen, and the sky above the houses wore an air of extraordinary beauty, simplicity and peace."

BETWEEN THE ACTS

Woolf's final work, *Between the Acts*, also deals with individual lives unfolding against the screen of history, but her vision and the methods by which she conveys it are more inventive, complex, and successful than in *The Years*. Covering the space of a single day in June, 1939, as world war threatens on the Continent, *Between the Acts* depicts the events surrounding a village pageant about the history of England, performed on the grounds of Pointz Hall, a country house occupied by the unhappily married Giles and Isa Oliver. The Olivers' story frames the presentation of the pageant, scenes of which are directly reproduced in the novel and alternate with glimpses of the audience's lives during the intervals between the acts. The novel's title is hence richly metaphorical: The acts of the drama itself are bracketed by the scenes of real life, which in turn can be viewed as brief episodes in the long pageant of human history. Equally ambiguous, then, is the meaning of "parts," connoting clearly defined roles within a drama but also the fragmentation and incompleteness of the individuals who play them, that pervasive theme in Woolf's work.

In *The Years*, Woolf had focused on the personal histories of her characters; history in the larger sense made itself felt as it impinged on private lives. This emphasis is reversed in *Between the Acts*. Though the novel has interesting characters, Woolf does not provide much information about their backgrounds, nor does she plumb individual memory in her usual manner. Instead, the characters possess a national, cultural, communal past—finally that of the whole human race from the Stone Age to the present. That Woolf intends her characters to be seen as part of this universal progression is clear from myriad references in the early pages to historical time. For example, from the air, the "scars" made by the Britons and the Romans can be seen around the village as can the Elizabethan manor house; graves in the churchyard attest that Mrs. Haines's family has lived in the area "for many centuries," whereas the Oliver family has inhabited Pointz Hall for "only something over a hundred and twenty years"; Lucy Swithin, Giles's endearing aunt, enjoys reading about history and imagining Piccadilly when it was a rhododendron forest populated by mastodons, "from whom, presumably, she thought . . . we descend."

The pageant itself, therefore, functions in the novel as more than simply a church fundraising ritual, the product of well-meaning but hapless amateurs (though it exists amusingly on that level too). It is a heroic attempt by its author-director, the formidable Miss La Trobe, to make people see themselves playing parts in the continuum of British history. Thus, the audience has an integral role that blurs the lines "between the acts"; "Our part," says Giles's father, Bartholomew, "is to be the audience. And a very important part too." Their increasing interest in the pageant as they return from the successive intermissions signals their growing sense of a shared past and hence of an identity that both binds and transcends them as individuals.

The scenes of the pageant proceed from bathos to unnerving profundity. The first player, a small girl in pink, announces, "England am I," then promptly forgets her lines, while the wind blows away half the words of the singers behind her. Queen Elizabeth, splendidly decorated with six-penny brooches and a cape made of silvery scouring pads, turns out to be Mrs. Clark, the village tobacconist; the combined applause and laughter of delighted recognition muffle her opening speech. As the pageant progresses from a wicked though overlong parody of Restoration comedy to a satiric scene at a Victorian picnic, however, the audience becomes more reflective; the past is now close enough to be familiar, triggering their own memories and priming them for the last scene, Miss La Trobe's inspired experiment in expressionism, "The Present Time. Ourselves." The uncomprehending audience fidgets as the stage remains empty, refusing to understand that they are supposed to contemplate their own significance. "Reality too strong," Miss La Trobe mutters angrily from behind the bushes, "Curse 'em!" Then, "sudden and universal," a summer shower fortuitously begins. "Down it rained like all the people in the world weeping." Nature has provided the bridge of meaning Miss La Trobe required. As the rain ends, all the players from all the periods reappear, still in costume and declaiming fragments of their parts while flashing mirrors in the faces of the discomfited audience. An offstage voice asks how civilization is "to be built by orts, scraps and fragments like ourselves," then dies away.

The Reverend Streatfield, disconcerted like the rest of the audience, is assigned the embarrassing role of summing up the play's meaning. Tentatively, self-consciously, he ventures, "To me at least it was indicated that we are members of one another. . . . We act different parts; but are the same. . . . Surely, we should unite?" Then he abruptly shifts into a fund-raising appeal that is drowned out by a formation of war planes passing overhead. As the audience departs, a gramophone plays a valedictory: "Dispersed are we; we who have come together. But let us retain whatever made that harmony." The audience responds, thinking "There is joy, sweet joy, in company."

The qualified optimism of the pageant's close, however, is darkened by the bleak, perhaps apocalyptic postscript of the framing story. After the group disperses, the characters resume their usual roles. Lucy Swithin, identified earlier as a "unifier," experiences a typically Woolfian epiphany as she gazes on a fishpond, glimpsing the silver of the great carp below the surface and "seeing in that vision beauty, power and glory in ourselves." Her staunchly rational brother Bartholomew, a "separatist," goes into the house. Miss La Trobe, convinced that she has failed again, heads for the local pub to drink alone and plan her next play; it will be set at midnight with two figures half hidden by a rock as the curtain rises. "What would the first words be?"

It is the disaffected Giles and Isa, loving and hating each other, who begin the new play. In a remarkable ending, Woolf portrays the couple sitting silently in the dark before going to bed: "Before they slept, they must fight; after they had fought they would embrace." From that embrace, they may create another life, but "first they must fight, as the dog fox fights the vixen, in the heart of darkness, in the fields of night." The "great hooded chairs" in which they sit grow enormous, like Miss La Trobe's rock. The house fades, no longer sheltering them; they are like "dwellers in caves," watching "from some high place." The last lines of the novel are, "Then the curtain rose. They spoke."

This indeterminate conclusion implies that love and hate are elemental and reciprocal, and that such oppositions on a personal level are also the polarities that drive human history. Does Woolf read, then, in the gathering European storm, a cataclysm that will bring the pageant of history full circle, back to the primitive stage of prehistory? Or, like W. B. Yeats in "The Second Coming," does she envision a new cycle even more terrifying than the old? Or, as the faithful Lucy Swithin does, perhaps she hopes that "*all* is harmony could we hear it. And we shall."

Eight years earlier, Virginia Woolf wrote in her diary, "I think the effort to live in two spheres: the novel; and life; is a strain." Miss La Trobe, a crude alter ego for the author, is obsessed by failure but always driven to create anew because "a vision imparted was relief from agony . . . for one moment." In her brilliant experimental attempts to impart her own view of fragmented human beings achieving momentary harmony, discovering unity and stability behind the flux of daily life, Woolf repeatedly endured such anguish, but after *Between the Acts* was done, the strain of beginning again was too great. Perhaps the questions Virginia Woolf posed in this final haunting novel, published posthumously and unrevised, were answered for her in death.

Kristine Ottesen Garrigan

OTHER MAJOR WORKS

SHORT FICTION: *Two Stories*, 1917 (one by Leonard Woolf); *Kew Gardens*, 1919; *The Mark on the Wall*, 1919; *Monday or Tuesday*, 1921; *A Haunted House, and Other Short Stories*, 1943; *Mrs. Dalloway's Party*, 1973 (Stella McNichol, editor); *The Complete Shorter Fiction of Virginia Woolf*, 1985.

NONFICTION: *The Common Reader: First Series*, 1925; *A Room of One's Own*, 1929; *The Common Reader: Second Series*, 1932; *Three Guineas*, 1938; *Roger Fry: A Biography*, 1940; *The Death of the Moth, and Other Essays*, 1942; *The Moment, and Other Essays*, 1947; *The Captain's Death Bed, and Other Essays*, 1950; *A Writer's Diary*, 1953; *Letters: Virginia Woolf and Lytton Strachey*, 1956; *Granite and Rainbow*, 1958; *Contemporary Writers*, 1965; *Collected Essays, Volumes 1-2*, 1966; *Collected Essays, Volumes 3-4*, 1967; *The Flight of the Mind: The Letters of Virginia Woolf, Vol. I, 1888-1912*, 1975 (Nigel Nicolson, editor; also known as *The Letters of Virginia Woolf, Vol. I: 1888-1912*); *The London Scene: Five Essays*, 1975; *Moments of Being*, 1976 (Jeanne Schulkind, editor); *The Question of Things Happening: The Letters of Virginia Woolf, Vol. II, 1912-1922*, 1976 (Nicolson, editor; also known as *The Letters of Virginia Woolf, Vol. II: 1912-1922*); *A Change of Perspective: The Letters of Virginia Woolf, Vol. III, 1923-1928*, 1977 (Nicolson, editor; also known as *The Letters of Virginia Woolf, Vol. III: 1923-1928*, 1978); *Books and Portraits*, 1977; *The Diary of Virginia Woolf*, 1977-1984 (5 volumes; Anne Olivier Bell, editor); *A Reflection of the Other Person: The Letters of Virginia Woolf, Vol. IV, 1929-1931*, 1978 (Nicolson, editor; also known as *The Letters of Virginia Woolf, Vol. IV: 1929-1931*, 1979); *The Sickle Side of the Moon: The Letters of Virginia Woolf, Vol. V, 1932-1935*, 1979 (Nicolson, editor; also known as *The Letters of Virginia Woolf, Vol. V: 1932-1935*); *Leave the Letters Til We're Dead: The Letters of Virginia Woolf, Vol. VI,*

1936-1941, 1980 (Nicolson, editor); *The Essays of Virginia Woolf*, 1987-1994 (4 volumes); *Carlyle's House, and Other Sketches*, 2003 (David Bradshaw, editor).

BIBLIOGRAPHY

Barrett, Eileen, and Patricia Cramer, eds. *Virginia Woolf: Lesbian Readings*. New York: New York University Press, 1997. Part 2 of this collection of conference papers focuses on Woolf's novels, with lesbian interpretations of *The Voyage Out*, *Mrs. Dalloway*, *To the Lighthouse*, *Orlando*, *The Waves*, *The Years*, and *Between the Acts*.

Beja, Morris, ed. *Critical Essays on Virginia Woolf*. Boston: G. K. Hall, 1985. Collection is divided into two sections: reviews of Woolf's major works and essays on Woolf's art and artistic vision. The various interpretations reflect the editor's premise that Woolf, although claimed by several ages and schools of criticism, was unique and thus cannot be pigeonholed in any specific way.

Blair, Emily. *Virginia Woolf and the Nineteenth-Century Domestic Novel*. Albany: State University of New York Press, 2007. Describes the influence of nineteenth and early twentieth century literature, particularly its descriptions of femininity, on Woolf's work and compares her novels to those of Elizabeth Gaskell and Margaret Oliphant, two popular Victorian novelists.

Briggs, Julia. *Virginia Woolf: An Inner Life*. Orlando, Fla: Harcourt, 2005. Biography focuses on Woolf's work in relation to her fascination with the workings of the mind. Traces the creation of each of Woolf's books, from *The Voyage Out* through *Between the Acts*, combining literary analysis with details of Woolf's life.

Goldman, Jane. *The Cambridge Introduction to Virginia Woolf*. New York: Cambridge University Press, 2006. Provides a wealth of information designed to help students and other readers better understand Woolf's writings. One section places Woolf's life and work within historical, political, and cultural context, including information about the Bloomsbury Group; another section focuses on critical reception of the works from the 1940's through the 1990's and includes contemporary reviews.

_____. *The Feminist Aesthetics of Virginia Woolf: Modernism, Post-impressionism, and the Politics of the Visual*. New York: Cambridge University Press, 2001. Feminist reading of Woolf's works focuses on the influence of literary and artistic modernism and places the works within their historical and cultural context.

Gordon, Lyndall. *Virginia Woolf: A Writer's Life*. New York: W. W. Norton, 1985. Biography looks not only at Woolf's life in Bloomsbury but also at her works, including her unfinished memoirs, the drafts of novels, and some lesser-known and unpublished pieces. Divides Woolf's life into three phases: her childhood, her time of literary apprenticeship and recurring illness, and her mature period of artistic achievement.

King, James. *Virginia Woolf*. New York: W. W. Norton, 1995. Literary biography relates Woolf's life to her works, showing how the chief sources of material for her writing were her life, her family, and her friends.

Lee, Hermione. *Virginia Woolf.* New York: Alfred A. Knopf, 1997. Detailed biography describes Woolf's complex family relationships, her lifelong battle with mental illness, and her relationship to the Bloomsbury Group.

Marder, Herbert. *The Measure of Life: Virginia Woolf's Last Years.* Ithaca, N.Y.: Cornell University Press, 2000. Biography focuses on the events of the final decade of Woolf's life and analyzes the changes in her writings during this period.

Reid, Panthea. *Art and Affection: A Life of Virginia Woolf.* New York: Oxford University Press, 1996. Biography draws on the vast amount of material available about Woolf and her circle to examine Woolf's desires to write and to be loved. Especially strong in providing a psychological explanation for Woolf's artistic choices, such as her decision to abandon conventional representation in her fiction.

Roe, Sue, and Susan Sellers, eds. *The Cambridge Companion to Virginia Woolf.* New York: Cambridge University Press, 2000. Collection of essays by leading scholars addresses Woolf's life and work from a wide range of intellectual perspectives. Includes analyses of her novels and discussions of Woolf in relation to modernism, feminism, and psychoanalysis.

BIBLIOGRAPHY

Every effort has been made to include studies published in 2000 and later. Most items in this bibliography contain a listing of secondary sources, making it easier to identify other critical commentary on novelists, movements, and themes.

THEORETICAL, THEMATIC, AND HISTORICAL STUDIES

Altman, Janet Gurkin. *Epistolarity: Approaches to a Form.* Columbus: Ohio State University Press, 1982. Examines the epistolary novel, explaining how novelists use the letter form to develop characterization, further their plots, and develop meaning.

Beaumont, Matthew, ed. *Adventures in Realism.* Malden, Mass.: Blackwell, 2007. Fifteen essays explore facets of realism, which was critical to the development of the novel. Provides a theoretical framework for understanding how novelists attempt to represent the real and the common in fiction.

Brink, André. *The Novel: Language and Narrative from Cervantes to Calvino.* New York: New York University Press, 1998. Uses contemporary theories of semiotics and narratology to establish a continuum between early novelists and those of the postmodern era in their conscious use of language to achieve certain effects. Ranges across national boundaries to illustrate the theory of the development of the novel since the seventeenth century.

Bruzelius, Margaret. *Romancing the Novel: Adventure from Scott to Sebald.* Lewisburg, Pa.: Bucknell University Press, 2007. Examines the development of the adventure novel, linking it with the medieval romance tradition and exploring readers' continuing fascination with the genre.

Cavallaro, Dani. *The Gothic Vision: Three Centuries of Horror, Terror, and Fear.* New York: Continuum, 2005. Study of the gothic novel from its earliest manifestations in the eighteenth century to the early twenty-first century. Through the lenses of contemporary cultural theories, examines readers' fascination with novels that invoke horror, terror, and fright.

Doody, Margaret Anne. *The True Story of the Novel.* New Brunswick, N.J.: Rutgers University Press, 1996. Traces the roots of the novel, traditionally thought to have been developed in the seventeenth century, to classical Greek and Latin texts that exhibit characteristics of modern fiction.

Hale, Dorothy J., ed. *Social Formalism: The Novel in Theory from Henry James to the Present.* Stanford, Calif.: Stanford University Press, 1998. Emphasizes the novel's special ability to define a social world for readers. Relies heavily on the works of contemporary literary and cultural theorists. Provides a summary of twentieth century efforts to identify a theory of fiction that encompasses novels of many kinds.

Hart, Stephen M., and Wen-chin Ouyang, eds. *A Companion to Magical Realism.* London: Tamesis, 2005. Essays outlining the development of Magical Realism, tracing its roots from Europe through Latin America to other regions of the world. Explores the political dimensions of the genre.

Hoffman, Michael J., and Patrick D. Murphy, eds. *Essentials of the Theory of Fiction.* 2d ed. Durham, N.C.: Duke University Press, 1996. Collection of essays by influential critics from the late nineteenth century through the twentieth century. Focuses on the essential elements of fiction and the novel's relationship to the world it depicts.

Lodge, David. *The Art of Fiction: Illustrated from Classic and Modern Texts.* New York: Viking Press, 1993. Short commentaries on the technical aspects of fiction. Examples from important and minor novelists illustrate literary principles and techniques such as point of view, suspense, character introduction, irony, motivation, and ending.

Lynch, Deirdre, and William B. Walker, eds. *Cultural Institutions of the Novel.* Durham, N.C.: Duke University Press, 1996. Fifteen essays examine aspects of long fiction produced around the world. Encourages a redefinition of the genre and argues for inclusion of texts not historically considered novels.

Moretti, Franco, ed. *The Novel.* 2 vols. Princeton, N.J.: Princeton University Press, 2006. Compendium exploring the novel from multiple perspectives, including as an anthropological, historical, and sociological document; a function of the national tradition from which it emerges; and a work of art subject to examination using various critical approaches.

Priestman, Martin, ed. *The Cambridge Companion to Crime Fiction.* New York: Cambridge University Press, 2003. Essays examine the nature and development of the genre, explore works by writers (including women and ethnic minorities) from several countries, and establish links between crime fiction and other literary genres. Includes a chronology.

Scaggs, John. *Crime Fiction.* New York: Routledge, 2005. Provides a history of crime fiction, explores key subgenres, and identifies recurring themes that suggest the wider social and historical context in which these works are written. Suggests critical approaches that open crime fiction to serious study.

Shiach, Morag, ed. *The Cambridge Companion to the Modernist Novel.* New York: Cambridge University Press, 2007. Essays explaining the concept of modernism and its influence on the novel. Detailed examination of works by writers from various countries, all influenced by the modernist movement. Includes a detailed chronology.

Vice, Sue. *Holocaust Fiction.* New York: Routledge, 2000. Examines controversies generated by novels about the Holocaust. Focuses on eight important works, but also offers observations on the polemics surrounding publication of books on this topic.

Zunshine, Lisa. *Why We Read Fiction: Theory of Mind and the Novel.* Columbus: Ohio State University Press, 2006. Applies theories of cognitive psychology to novel reading, explaining how experience and human nature lead readers to constrain their interpretations of a given text. Provides numerous examples from well-known novels to illustrate how and why readers find pleasure in fiction.

FEMINIST FICTION

Brownstein, Rachel. *Becoming a Heroine: Reading About Women in Novels*. New York: Viking Press, 1982. Feminist survey of novels from the eighteenth century through the latter half of the twentieth century. Examines how "becoming a heroine" defines for women a sense of value in their lives. Considers novels by both men and women, and discusses the importance of the traditional marriage plot.

Hale, Dorothy J., ed. *The Novel: An Anthology of Criticism and Theory, 1900-2000*. Malden, Mass.: Blackwell, 2006. Collection of essays by theorists and novelists. Includes commentary on the novel form from the perspective of formalism, structuralism, poststructuralism, Marxism, and reader response theory. Essays also address the novel through the lenses of sociology, gender studies, and feminist theory.

Kenyon, Olga. *Women Novelists Today: A Survey of English Writing in the Seventies and Eighties*. New York: St. Martin's Press, 1988. Extensive critical commentary on six important English women novelists. Introductory chapter examines the effect of the feminist movement on women novelists and reviews the importance of techniques such as realism in English fiction.

O'Gorman, Francis, ed. *The Victorian Novel*. Malden, Mass.: Blackwell, 2002. Excerpts from dozens of influential twentieth century studies of Victorian fiction. Organized thematically; includes materials on formalist approaches, feminist readings, issues involving realism, historical approaches to fiction, postcolonial readings, discussions focusing on language and form, the impact of science on the novel, and the importance of publication practices.

Peters, Joan Douglas. *Feminist Metafiction and the Evolution of the British Novel*. Gainesville: University Press of Florida, 2002. Uses feminist theory to reexamine the development of English fiction, demonstrating the key role women writers played in shaping the genre. Also discusses novels written by men that feature female protagonists.

Whelehan, Imelda. *The Feminist Bestseller: From "Sex and the Single Girl" to "Sex and the City."* New York: Palgrave Macmillan, 2005. Analyzes popular women's literature of the second half of the twentieth century. Explains how these works are in dialogue with contemporary feminist ideas.

Laurence W. Mazzeno

GLOSSARY OF LITERARY TERMS

absurdism: A philosophical attitude, pervading much of modern drama and fiction, that underlines the isolation and alienation that humans experience, having been thrown into what absurdists see as a godless universe devoid of religious, spiritual, or metaphysical meaning. Conspicuous in its lack of logic, consistency, coherence, intelligibility, and realism, the literature of the absurd depicts the anguish, forlornness, and despair inherent in the human condition. Counter to the rationalist assumptions of traditional humanism, absurdism denies the existence of universal truth or value.

allegory: A literary mode in which a second level of meaning, wherein characters, events, and settings represent abstractions, is encoded within the surface narrative. The allegorical mode may dominate an entire work, in which case the encoded message is the work's primary reason for being, or it may be an element in a work otherwise interesting and meaningful for its surface story alone. Elements of allegory may be found in Jonathan Swift's *Gulliver's Travels* (1726) and Thomas Mann's *Der Zauberberg* (1924; *The Magic Mountain*, 1927).

anatomy: Literally the term means the "cutting up" or "dissection" of a subject into its constituent parts for closer examination. Northrop Frye, in his *Anatomy of Criticism* (1957), uses the term to refer to a narrative that deals with mental attitudes rather than people. As opposed to the novel, the anatomy features stylized figures who are mouthpieces for the ideas they represent.

antagonist: The character in fiction who stands as a rival or opponent to the *protagonist.*

antihero: Defined by Seán O'Faoláin as a fictional figure who, deprived of social sanctions and definitions, is always trying to define himself and to establish his own codes. Ahab may be seen as the antihero of Herman Melville's *Moby Dick* (1851).

archetype: The term "archetype" entered literary criticism from the psychology of Carl Jung, who defined archetypes as "primordial images" from the "collective unconscious" of humankind. Jung believed that works of art derive much of their power from the unconscious appeal of these images to ancestral memories. In his extremely influential *Anatomy of Criticism* (1957), Northrop Frye gave another sense of the term wide currency, defining the archetype as "a symbol, usually an image, which recurs often enough in literature to be recognizable as an element of one's literary experience as a whole."

atmosphere: The general mood or tone of a work; atmosphere is often associated with setting but can also be established by action or dialogue. A classic example of atmosphere is the primitive, fatalistic tone created in the opening description of Egdon Heath in Thomas Hardy's *The Return of the Native* (1878).

bildungsroman: Sometimes called the "novel of education," the bildungsroman focuses on the growth of a young *protagonist* who is learning about the world and finding his or her place in life; typical examples are James Joyce's *A Portrait of the Artist as a*

Young Man (1914-1915, serial; 1916, book) and Thomas Wolfe's *Look Homeward, Angel* (1929).

biographical criticism: Criticism that attempts to determine how the events and experiences of an author's life influence his or her work.

bourgeois novel: A novel in which the values, preoccupations, and accoutrements of middle-class or bourgeois life are given particular prominence. The heyday of the bourgeois novel was the nineteenth century, when novelists as varied as Jane Austen, Honoré de Balzac, and Anthony Trollope both criticized and unreflectingly transmitted the assumptions of the rising middle class.

canon: An authorized or accepted list of books. In modern parlance, the literary canon comprehends the privileged texts, classics, or great books that are thought to belong permanently on university reading lists. Recent theory—especially feminist, Marxist, and poststructuralist—critically examines the process of canon formation and questions the hegemony of white male writers. Such theory sees canon formation as the ideological act of a dominant institution and seeks to undermine the notion of canonicity itself, thereby preventing the exclusion of works by women, minorities, and oppressed peoples.

character: Characters in fiction can be presented as if they were real people or as stylized functions of the plot. Usually characters are a combination of both factors.

classicism: A literary stance or value system consciously based on the example of classical Greek and Roman literature. While the term is applied to an enormous diversity of artists in many different periods and in many different national literatures, "classicism" generally denotes a cluster of values including formal discipline, restrained expression, reverence for tradition, and an objective rather than a subjective orientation. As a literary tendency, classicism is often opposed to *Romanticism*, although many writers combine classical and romantic elements.

climax/crisis: The term "climax" refers to the moment of the reader's highest emotional response, whereas "crisis" refers to a structural element of plot, a turning point at which a resolution must take place.

complication: The point in a novel when the *conflict* is developed or when the already existing conflict is further intensified.

conflict: The struggle that develops as a result of the opposition between the *protagonist* and another person, the natural world, society, or some force within the self.

contextualist criticism: A further extension of *formalist criticism*, which assumes that the language of art is constitutive. Rather than referring to preexistent values, the artwork creates values only inchoately realized before. The most important advocates of this position are Eliseo Vivas (*The Artistic Transaction*, 1963) and Murray Krieger (*The Play and Place of Criticism*, 1967).

conventions: All those devices of stylization, compression, and selection that constitute the necessary differences between art and life. According to the Russian Formalists, these conventions constitute the "literariness" of literature and are the only proper concern of the literary critic.

deconstruction: An extremely influential contemporary school of criticism based on the works of the French philosopher Jacques Derrida. Deconstruction treats literary works as unconscious reflections of the reigning myths of Western culture. The primary myth is that there is a meaningful world that language signifies or represents. The deconstructionist critic is most often concerned with showing how a literary text tacitly subverts the very assumptions or myths on which it ostensibly rests.

defamiliarization: Coined by Viktor Shklovsky in 1917, this term denotes a basic principle of Russian Formalism. Poetic language (by which the Formalists meant artful language, in prose as well as in poetry) defamiliarizes or "makes strange" familiar experiences. The technique of art, says Shklovsky, is to "make objects unfamiliar, to make forms difficult, to increase the difficulty and length of perception. . . . Art is a way of experiencing the artfulness of an object; the object is not important."

detective story: The so-called classic detective story (or mystery) is a highly formalized and logically structured mode of fiction in which the focus is on a crime solved by a detective through interpretation of evidence and ratiocination; the most famous detective in this mode is Arthur Conan Doyle's Sherlock Holmes. Many modern practitioners of the genre, however, such as Dashiell Hammett, Raymond Chandler, and Ross Macdonald, have de-emphasized the puzzlelike qualities of the detective story, stressing instead characterization, theme, and other elements of mainstream fiction.

determinism: The belief that an individual's actions are essentially determined by biological and environmental factors, with free will playing a negligible role. (See *naturalism.*)

dialogue: The similitude of conversation in fiction, dialogue serves to characterize, to further the *plot*, to establish *conflict*, and to express thematic ideas.

displacement: Popularized in criticism by Northrop Frye, this term refers to the author's attempt to make his or her story psychologically motivated and realistic, even as the latent structure of the mythical motivation moves relentlessly forward.

dominant: A term coined by Roman Jakobson to refer to that which "rules, determines, and transforms the remaining components in the work of a single artist, in a poetic canon, or in the work of an epoch." The shifting of the dominant in a *genre* accounts for the creation of new generic forms and new poetic epochs. For example, the rise of *realism* in the mid-nineteenth century indicates realistic conventions becoming dominant and *romance* or fantasy conventions becoming secondary.

doppelgänger: A double or counterpart of a person, sometimes endowed with ghostly qualities. A fictional character's doppelgänger often reflects a suppressed side of his or her personality. One of the classic examples of the doppelgänger motif is found in

Fyodor Dostoevski's novella *Dvoynik* (1846; *The Double*, 1917); Isaac Bashevis Singer and Jorge Luis Borges, among others, offer striking modern treatments of the doppelgänger.

epic: Although this term usually refers to a long narrative poem that presents the exploits of a central figure of high position, the term is also used to designate a long novel that has the style or structure usually associated with an epic. In this sense, for example, Herman Melville's *Moby Dick* (1851) and James Joyce's *Ulysses* (1922) may be called epics.

episodic narrative: A work that is held together primarily by a loose connection of self-sufficient episodes. *Picaresque novels* often have episodic structure.

epistolary novel: A novel made up of letters by one or more fictional characters. Samuel Richardson's *Pamela: Or, Virtue Rewarded* (1740-1741) is a well-known eighteenth century example. In the nineteenth century, Bram Stoker's *Dracula* (1897) is largely epistolary. The technique allows for several different points of view to be presented.

euphuism: A style of writing characterized by ornate language that is highly contrived, alliterative, and repetitious. Euphuism was developed by John Lyly in his *Euphues, the Anatomy of Wit* (1578) and was emulated frequently by writers of the Elizabethan Age.

existentialism: A philosophical, religious, and literary term, emerging from World War II, for a group of attitudes surrounding the pivotal notion that existence precedes essence. According to Jean-Paul Sartre, "Man is nothing else but what he makes himself." Forlornness arises from the death of God and the concomitant death of universal values, of any source of ultimate or a priori standards. Despair arises from the fact that an individual can reckon only with what depends on his or her will, and the sphere of that will is severely limited; the number of things on which he or she can have an impact is pathetically small. Existentialist literature is antideterministic in the extreme and rejects the idea that heredity and environment shape and determine human motivation and behavior.

exposition: The part or parts of a fiction that provide necessary background information. Exposition not only provides the time and place of the action but also introduces readers to the fictive world of the story, acquainting them with the ground rules of the work.

fantastic: In his study *The Fantastic* (1970), Tzvetan Todorov defines the fantastic as a *genre* that lies between the "uncanny" and the "marvelous." All three genres embody the familiar world but present an event that cannot be explained by the laws of the familiar world. Todorov says that the fantastic occupies a twilight zone between the uncanny (when the reader knows that the peculiar event is merely the result of an illusion) and the marvelous (when the reader understands that the event is supposed to take place in a realm controlled by laws unknown to humankind). The fantastic is thus essentially unsettling, provocative, even subversive.

feminist criticism: A criticism advocating equal rights for women in political, economic, social, psychological, personal, and aesthetic senses. On the thematic level, the feminist reader should identify with female characters and their concerns. The object is to provide a critique of phallocentric assumptions and an analysis of patriarchal ideologies inscribed in a literature that is male-centered and male-dominated. On the ideological level, feminist critics see gender, as well as the stereotypes that go along with it, as a cultural construct. They strive to define a particularly feminine content and to extend the *canon* so that it might include works by lesbians, feminists, and women writers in general.

flashback: A scene in a fiction that depicts an earlier event; it may be presented as a reminiscence by a character in the story or may simply be inserted into the narrative.

foreshadowing: A device to create suspense or dramatic irony in fiction by indicating through suggestion what will take place in the future.

formalist criticism: Two particularly influential formalist schools of criticism arose in the twentieth century: the Russian Formalists and the American New Critics. The Russian Formalists were concerned with the conventional devices used in literature to defamiliarize that which habit has made familiar. The New Critics believed that literary criticism is a description and evaluation of its object and that the primary concern of the critic is with the work's unity. Both schools of criticism, at their most extreme, treated literary works as artifacts or constructs divorced from their biographical and social contexts.

genre: In its most general sense, this term refers to a group of literary works defined by a common form, style, or purpose. In practice, the term is used in a wide variety of overlapping and, to a degree, contradictory senses. Tragedy and comedy are thus described as distinct genres; the novel (a form that includes both tragic and comic works) is a genre; and various subspecies of the novel, such as the *gothic* and the *picaresque,* are themselves frequently treated as distinct genres. Finally, the term "genre fiction" refers to forms of popular fiction in which the writer is bound by more or less rigid conventions. Indeed, all these diverse usages have in common an emphasis on the manner in which individual literary works are shaped by particular expectations and conventions; this is the subject of genre criticism.

genre fiction: Categories of popular fiction in which the writers are bound by more or less rigid conventions, such as in the *detective story,* the *romance,* and the *Western.* Although the term can be used in a neutral sense, it is often used dismissively.

gothic novel: A form of fiction developed in the eighteenth century that focuses on horror and the supernatural. In his preface to *The Castle of Otranto* (1765), the first gothic novel in English, Horace Walpole claimed that he was trying to combine two kinds of fiction, with events and story typical of the medieval romance and character delineation typical of the realistic novel. Other examples of the form are Matthew Gregory

Lewis's *The Monk: A Romance* (1796; also known as *Ambrosio: Or, The Monk*) and Mary Wollstonecraft Shelley's *Frankenstein: Or, The Modern Prometheus* (1818).

grotesque: According to Wolfgang Kayser (*The Grotesque in Art and Literature*, 1963), the grotesque is an embodiment in literature of the estranged world. Characterized by a breakup of the everyday world by mysterious forces, the form differs from fantasy in that the reader is not sure whether to react with humor or with horror and in that the exaggeration manifested exists in the familiar world rather than in a purely imaginative world.

Hebraic/Homeric styles: Terms coined by Erich Auerbach in *Mimesis: The Representation of Reality in Western Literature* (1953) to designate two basic fictional styles. The Hebraic style focuses only on the decisive points of narrative and leaves all else obscure, mysterious, and "fraught with background"; the Homeric style places the narrative in a definite time and place and externalizes everything in a perpetual foreground.

historical criticism: In contrast to *formalist criticism*, which treats literary works to a great extent as self-contained artifacts, historical criticism emphasizes the historical context of literature; the two approaches, however, need not be mutually exclusive. Ernst Robert Curtius's *European Literature and the Latin Middle Ages* (1940) is a prominent example of historical criticism.

historical novel: A novel that depicts past historical events, usually public in nature, and features real as well as fictional people. Sir Walter Scott's *Waverley* novels established the basic type, but the relationship between fiction and history in the form varies greatly depending on the practitioner.

implied author: According to Wayne Booth (*The Rhetoric of Fiction*, 1961), the novel often creates a kind of second self who tells the story—a self who is wiser, more sensitive, and more perceptive than any real person could be.

interior monologue: Defined by Édouard Dujardin as the speech of a character designed to introduce the reader directly to the character's internal life, the form differs from other kinds of monologue in that it attempts to reproduce thought before any logical organization is imposed on it. See, for example, Molly Bloom's long interior monologue at the conclusion of James Joyce's *Ulysses* (1922).

irrealism: A term often used to refer to modern or postmodern fiction that is presented self-consciously as a fiction or a fabulation rather than a mimesis of external reality. The best-known practitioners of irrealism are John Barth, Robert Coover, and Donald Barthelme.

local colorists: A loose movement of late nineteenth century American writers whose fiction emphasizes the distinctive folkways, landscapes, and dialects of various regions. Important local colorists include Bret Harte, Mark Twain, George Washington Cable, Kate Chopin, and Sarah Orne Jewett. (See *regional novel*.)

Marxist criticism: Based on the nineteenth century writings of Karl Marx and Friedrich Engels, Marxist criticism views literature as a product of ideological forces determined by the dominant class. However, many Marxists believe that literature operates according to its own autonomous standards of production and reception: It is both a product of ideology and able to determine ideology. As such, literature may overcome the dominant paradigms of its age and play a revolutionary role in society.

metafiction: This term refers to fiction that manifests a reflexive tendency, such as Vladimir Nabokov's *Pale Fire* (1962) and John Fowles's *The French Lieutenant's Woman* (1969). The emphasis is on the loosening of the work's illusion of reality to expose the reality of its illusion. Other terms used to refer to this type of fiction include "irrealism," "postmodernist fiction," "antifiction," and "surfiction."

modernism: An international movement in the arts that began in the early years of the twentieth century. Although the term is used to describe artists of widely varying persuasions, modernism in general was characterized by its international idiom, by its interest in cultures distant in space or time, by its emphasis on formal experimentation, and by its sense of dislocation and radical change.

motif: A conventional incident or situation in a fiction that may serve as the basis for the structure of the narrative itself. The Russian Formalist critic Boris Tomashevsky uses the term to refer to the smallest particle of thematic material in a work.

motivation: Although this term is usually used in reference to the convention of justifying the action of a character from his or her psychological makeup, the Russian Formalists use the term to refer to the network of devices that justify the introduction of individual *motifs* or groups of motifs in a work. For example, "compositional motivation" refers to the principle that every single property in a work contributes to its overall effect; "realistic motivation" refers to the realistic devices used to make a work plausible and lifelike.

multiculturalism: The tendency to recognize the perspectives of those traditionally excluded from the canon of Western art and literature. In order to promote multiculturalism, publishers and educators have revised textbooks and school curricula to incorporate material by and about women, members of minority groups, persons from non-Western cultures, and homosexuals.

myth: Anonymous traditional stories dealing with basic human concepts and antinomies. According to Claude Lévi-Strauss, myth is that part of language where the "formula *tradutore, traditore* reaches its lowest truth value. . . . Its substance does not lie in its style, its original music, or its syntax, but in the story which it tells."

myth criticism: Northrop Frye says that in myth "we see the structural principles of literature isolated." Myth criticism is concerned with these basic principles of literature; it is not to be confused with mythological criticism, which is primarily concerned with finding mythological parallels in the surface action of the *narrative.*

narrative: Robert Scholes and Robert Kellogg, in *The Nature of Narrative* (1966), say that by "narrative" they mean literary works that include both a story and a storyteller. The term "narrative" usually implies a contrast to "enacted" fiction such as drama.

narratology: The study of the form and functioning of *narratives*; it attempts to examine what all narratives have in common and what makes individual narratives different from one another.

narrator: The *character* who recounts the *narrative*, or story. Wayne Booth describes various dramatized narrators in *The Rhetoric of Fiction* (1961): unacknowledged centers of consciousness, observers, narrator-agents, and self-conscious narrators. Booth suggests that the important elements to consider in narration are the relationships among the narrator, the author, the characters, and the reader.

naturalism: As developed by Émile Zola in the late nineteenth century, naturalism is the application of the principles of scientific *determinism* to fiction. Although it usually refers more to the choice of subject matter than to technical conventions, those conventions associated with the movement center on the author's attempt to be precise and scientifically objective in description and detail, regardless of whether the events described are sordid or shocking.

New Criticism: See *formalist criticism.*

novel: Perhaps the most difficult of all fictional forms to define because of its multiplicity of modes. Edouard, in André Gide's *Les Faux-monnayeurs* (1925; *The Counterfeiters*, 1927), says the novel is the freest and most lawless of all *genres*; he wonders if fear of that liberty is the reason the novel has so timidly clung to reality. Most critics seem to agree that the novel's primary area of concern is the social world. Ian Watt (*The Rise of the Novel*, 2001) says that the novel can be distinguished from other fictional forms by the attention it pays to individual characterization and detailed presentation of the environment. Moreover, says Watt, the novel, more than any other fictional form, is interested in the "development of its characters in the course of time."

novel of manners: The classic examples of this form might be the novels of Jane Austen, wherein the customs and conventions of a social group of a particular time and place are realistically, and often satirically, portrayed.

novella, novelle, nouvelle, novelette, novela: Although these terms often refer to the short European tale, especially the Renaissance form employed by Giovanni Boccaccio, the terms often refer to that form of fiction that is said to be longer than a short story and shorter than a novel. "Novelette" is the term usually preferred by the British, whereas "novella" is the term usually used to refer to American works in this *genre*. Henry James claimed that the main merit of the form is the "effort to do the complicated thing with a strong brevity and lucidity."

phenomenological criticism: Although best known as a European school of criticism practiced by Georges Poulet and others, this so-called criticism of consciousness is also propounded in the United States by such critics as J. Hillis Miller. The focus is less on individual works and *genres* than it is on literature as an act; the work is not seen as an object but rather as part of a strand of latent impulses in the work of a single author or an epoch.

picaresque novel: A form of fiction that centers on a central rogue figure, or picaro, who usually tells his or her own story. The plot structure is normally *episodic*, and the episodes usually focus on how the picaro lives by his or her wits. Classic examples of the mode are Henry Fielding's *The History of Tom Jones, a Foundling* (1749; commonly known as *Tom Jones*) and Mark Twain's *Adventures of Huckleberry Finn* (1884).

plot/story: "Story" refers to the full *narrative* of *character* and action, whereas "plot" generally refers to action with little reference to character. A more precise and helpful distinction is made by the Russian Formalists, who suggest that "plot" refers to the events of a narrative as they have been artfully arranged in the literary work, subject to chronological displacement, ellipses, and other devices, while "story" refers to the sum of the same events arranged in simple, causal-chronological order. Thus story is the raw material for plot. By comparing the two in a given work, the reader is encouraged to see the narrative as an artifact.

point of view: The means by which the story is presented to the reader, or, as Percy Lubbock says in *The Craft of Fiction* (1921), "the relation in which the narrator stands to the story"—a relation that Lubbock claims governs the craft of fiction. Some of the questions the critical reader should ask concerning point of view are the following: Who talks to the reader? From what position does the narrator tell the story? At what distance does he or she place the reader from the story? What kind of person is he or she? How fully is he or she characterized? How reliable is he or she? For further discussion, see Wayne Booth, *The Rhetoric of Fiction* (1961).

postcolonialism: Postcolonial literature emerged in the mid-twentieth century when colonies in Asia, Africa, and the Caribbean began gaining their independence from the European nations that had long controlled them. Postcolonial authors, such as Salman Rushdie and V. S. Naipaul, tend to focus on both the freedom and the conflict inherent in living in a postcolonial state.

postmodernism: A ubiquitous but elusive term in contemporary criticism, "postmodernism" is loosely applied to the various artistic movements that followed the era of so-called high modernism, represented by such giants as James Joyce and Pablo Picasso. In critical discussions of contemporary fiction, the term "postmodernism" is frequently applied to the works of writers such as Thomas Pynchon, John Barth, and Donald Barthelme, who exhibit a self-conscious awareness of their modernist predecessors as well as a reflexive treatment of fictional form.

protagonist: The central *character* in a fiction, the character whose fortunes most concern the reader.

psychological criticism: While much modern literary criticism reflects to some degree the impacts of Sigmund Freud, Carl Jung, Jacques Lacan, and other psychological theorists, the term "psychological criticism" suggests a strong emphasis on a causal relation between the writer's psychological state, variously interpreted, and his or her works. A notable example of psychological criticism is Norman Fruman's *Coleridge, the Damaged Archangel* (1971).

psychological novel: A form of fiction in which *character,* especially the inner lives of characters, is the primary focus. This form, which has been of primary importance at least since Henry James, characterizes much of the work of James Joyce, Virginia Woolf, and William Faulkner. For a detailed discussion, see *The Modern Psychological Novel* (1955) by Leon Edel.

realism: A literary technique in which the primary convention is to render an illusion of fidelity to external reality. Realism is often identified as the primary method of the novel form: It focuses on surface details, maintains a fidelity to the everyday experiences of middle-class society, and strives for a one-to-one relationship between the fiction and the action imitated. The realist movement in the late nineteenth century coincides with the full development of the novel form.

reception aesthetics: The best-known American practitioner of reception aesthetics is Stanley Fish. For the reception critic, meaning is an event or process; rather than being embedded in the work, it is created through particular acts of reading. The best-known European practitioner of this criticism, Wolfgang Iser, argues that indeterminacy is the basic characteristic of literary texts; the reader must "normalize" the text either by projecting his or her standards into it or by revising his or her standards to "fit" the text.

regional novel: Any novel in which the character of a given geographical region plays a decisive role. Although regional differences persist across the United States, a considerable leveling in speech and customs has taken place, so that the sharp regional distinctions evident in nineteenth century American fiction have all but disappeared. Only in the South has a strong regional tradition persisted to the present. (See *local colorists.*)

rhetorical criticism: The rhetorical critic is concerned with the literary work as a means of communicating ideas and the means by which the work affects or controls the reader. Such criticism seems best suited to didactic works such as satire.

roman à clef: A fiction wherein actual people, often celebrities of some sort, are thinly disguised.

romance: The romance usually differs from the novel form in that the focus is on symbolic events and representational characters rather than on "as-if-real" characters and events. Richard Chase says that in the romance, character is depicted as highly stylized, a function of the plot rather than as someone complexly related to society. The romancer is more likely to be concerned with dreamworlds than with the familiar world, believing that reality cannot be grasped by the traditional novel.

Romanticism: A widespread cultural movement in the late eighteenth and early nineteenth centuries, the influence of which is still felt. As a general literary tendency, Romanticism is frequently contrasted with *classicism*. Although many varieties of Romanticism are indigenous to various national literatures, the term generally suggests an assertion of the preeminence of the imagination. Other values associated with various schools of Romanticism include primitivism, an interest in folklore, a reverence for nature, and a fascination with the demoniac and the macabre.

scene: The central element of *narration*; specific actions are narrated or depicted that make the reader feel he or she is participating directly in the action.

science fiction: Fiction in which certain givens (physical laws, psychological principles, social conditions—any one or all of these) form the basis of an imaginative projection into the future or, less commonly, an extrapolation in the present or even into the past.

semiotics: The science of signs and sign systems in communication. According to Roman Jakobson, semiotics deals with the principles that underlie the structure of signs, their use in language of all kinds, and the specific nature of various sign systems.

sentimental novel: A form of fiction popular in the eighteenth century in which emotionalism and optimism are the primary characteristics. The best-known examples are Samuel Richardson's *Pamela: Or, Virtue Rewarded* (1740-1741) and Oliver Goldsmith's *The Vicar of Wakefield* (1766).

setting: The circumstances and environment, both temporal and spatial, of a *narrative*.

spatial form: An author's attempt to make the reader apprehend a work spatially in a moment of time rather than sequentially. To achieve this effect, the author breaks up the *narrative* into interspersed fragments. Beginning with James Joyce, Marcel Proust, and Djuna Barnes, the movement toward spatial form is concomitant with the *modernist* effort to supplant historical time in fiction with mythic time. For the seminal discussion of this technique, see Joseph Frank, *The Widening Gyre* (1963).

stream of consciousness: The depiction of the thought processes of a *character*, insofar as this is possible, without any mediating structures. The metaphor of consciousness as a "stream" suggests a rush of thoughts and images governed by free association rather than by strictly rational development. The term "stream of consciousness" is often used loosely as a synonym for *interior monologue*. The most celebrated example of stream of consciousness in fiction is the monologue of Molly Bloom in James Joyce's *Ulysses* (1922); other notable practitioners of the stream-of-consciousness technique include Dorothy Richardson, Virginia Woolf, and William Faulkner.

structuralism: As a movement of thought, structuralism is based on the idea of intrinsic, self-sufficient structures that do not require reference to external elements. A structure is a system of transformations that involves the interplay of laws inherent in the system itself. The study of language is the primary model for contemporary structuralism. The structuralist literary critic attempts to define structural principles that operate intertextually throughout the whole of literature as well as principles that operate in *genres* and in individual works. One of the most accessible surveys of structuralism and literature available is Jonathan Culler's *Structuralist Poetics* (1975).

summary: Those parts of a fiction that do not need to be detailed. In *Tom Jones* (1749), Henry Fielding says, "If whole years should pass without producing anything worthy of . . . notice . . . we shall hasten on to matters of consequence."

thematics: According to Northrop Frye, when a work of fiction is written or interpreted thematically, it becomes an illustrative fable. Murray Krieger defines thematics as "the study of the experiential tensions which, dramatically entangled in the literary work, become an existential reflection of that work's aesthetic complexity."

tone: The dominant mood of a work of fiction. (See *atmosphere*.)

unreliable narrator: A narrator whose account of the events of the story cannot be trusted, obliging readers to reconstruct—if possible—the true state of affairs themselves. Once an innovative technique, the use of the unreliable narrator has become commonplace among contemporary writers who wish to suggest the impossibility of a truly "reliable" account of any event. Notable examples of the unreliable narrator can be found in Ford Madox Ford's *The Good Soldier* (1915) and Vladimir Nabokov's *Lolita* (1955).

Victorian novel: Although the Victorian period extended from 1837 to 1901, the term "Victorian novel" does not include the later decades of Queen Victoria's reign. The term loosely refers to the sprawling works of novelists such as Charles Dickens and William Makepeace Thackeray—works that frequently appeared first in serial form and are characterized by a broad social canvas.

vraisemblance/verisimilitude: Tzvetan Todorov defines vraisemblance as "the mask which conceals the text's own laws, but which we are supposed to take for a relation to reality." Verisimilitude refers to a work's attempts to make the reader believe that it conforms to reality rather than to its own laws.

Western novel: Like all varieties of *genre fiction*, the Western novel—generally known simply as the Western—is defined by a relatively predictable combination of *conventions*, *motifs*, and recurring themes. These predictable elements, familiar from many Western films and television series, differentiate the Western from *historical novels* and idiosyncratic works such as Thomas Berger's *Little Big Man* (1964) that are also set in the Old West. Conversely, some novels set in the contemporary West are regarded as Westerns because they deal with modern cowboys and with the land itself in the manner characteristic of the *genre*.

Charles E. May

GUIDE TO ONLINE RESOURCES

WEB SITES

The following sites were visited by the editors of Salem Press in 2009. Because URLs frequently change, the accuracy of these addresses cannot be guaranteed; however, long-standing sites, such as those of colleges and universities, national organizations, and government agencies, generally maintain links when sites are moved or updated.

American Literature on the Web

http://www.nagasaki-gaigo.ac.jp/ishikawa/amlit

Among this site's features are several pages providing links to Web sites about specific genres and literary movements, southern and southwestern American literature, minority literature, literary theory, and women writers, as well as an extensive index of links to electronic text collections and archives. Users also can access information for five specific time periods: 1620-1820, 1820-1865, 1865-1914, 1914-1945, and since 1945. A range of information is available for each period, including alphabetical lists of authors that link to more specific information about each writer, time lines of historical and literary events, and links to related additional Web sites.

Books and Writers

http://www.kirjasto.sci.fi/indeksi.htm

This broad, comprehensive, and easy-to-use resource provides access to information about hundreds of authors throughout the world, extending from 70 B.C.E to the twenty-first century. Links take users from an alphabetical list of authors to pages featuring biographical material, lists of works, and recommendations for further reading about individual authors; each writer's page also includes links to related pages on the site. Although brief, the biographical essays provide solid overviews of the authors' careers, their contributions to literature, and their literary influences.

The Canadian Literature Archive

http://www.umanitoba.ca/canlit

Created and maintained by the English Department at the University of Manitoba, this site is a comprehensive collection of materials for and about Canadian writers. It includes an alphabetical listing of authors with links to additional Web-based information. Users also can retrieve electronic texts, announcements of literary events, and videocasts of author interviews and readings.

A Celebration of Women Writers

http://digital.library.upenn.edu/women

This site presents an extensive compendium of information about the contributions of women writers throughout history. The "Local Editions by Authors" and "Local Editions by Category" pages include access to electronic texts of the works of numerous writers, including Louisa May Alcott, Djuna Barnes, Grazia Deledda, Edith Wharton, and Virginia Woolf. Users can also access biographical and bibliographical information by browsing lists arranged by writers' names, countries of origin, ethnicities, and the centuries in which they lived.

Contemporary Writers

http://www.contemporarywriters.com/authors

Created by the British Council, this site offers "up-to-date profiles of some of the U.K. and Commonwealth's most important living writers (plus writers from the Republic of Ireland that we've worked with)." The available information includes biographies, bibliographies, critical reviews, news about literary prizes, and photographs. Users can search the site by author, genre, nationality, gender, publisher, book title, date of publication, and prize name and date.

Internet Public Library: Native American Authors

http://www.ipl.org/div/natam

Internet Public Library, a Web-based collection of materials, includes this index to resources about writers of Native American heritage. An alphabetical list of authors enables users to link to biographies, lists of works, electronic texts, tribal Web sites, and other online resources. The majority of the writers covered are contemporary Indian authors, but some historical authors also are featured. Users also can retrieve information by browsing lists of titles and tribes. In addition, the site contains a bibliography of print and online materials about Native American literature.

LiteraryHistory.com

http://www.literaryhistory.com

This site is an excellent source of academic, scholarly, and critical literature about eighteenth, nineteenth, and twentieth century American and English writers. It provides numerous pages about specific eras and genres, including individual pages for eighteenth, nineteenth, and twentieth century literature and for African American and postcolonial literature. These pages contain alphabetical lists of authors that link to articles, reviews, overviews, excerpts of works, teaching guides, podcast interviews, and other materials. The eighteenth century literature page also provides access to information about the eighteenth century novel.

Literary Resources on the Net

http://andromeda.rutgers.edu/~jlynch/Lit

 Jack Lynch of Rutgers University maintains this extensive collection of links to Internet sites that are useful to academics, including numerous Web sites about American and English literature. This collection is a good place to begin online research about the novel, as it links to hundreds of other sites with broad ranges of literary topics. The site is organized chronically, with separate pages for information about the Middle Ages, the Renaissance, the eighteenth century, the Romantic and Victorian eras, and twentieth century British and Irish literature. It also has separate pages providing links to Web sites about American literature and to women's literature and feminism.

LitWeb

http://litweb.net

 LitWeb provides biographies of more than five hundred world authors throughout history that can be accessed through an alphabetical listing. The pages about each writer contain a list of his or her works, suggestions for further reading, and illustrations. The site also offers information about past and present winners of major literary prizes.

The Modern Word: Authors of the Libyrinth

http://www.themodernword.com/authors.html

 The Modern Word site, although somewhat haphazard in its organization, provides a great deal of critical information about writers. The "Authors of the Libyrinth" page is very useful, linking author names to essays about them and other resources. The section of the page headed "The Scriptorium" presents "an index of pages featuring writers who have pushed the edges of their medium, combining literary talent with a sense of experimentation to produce some remarkable works of modern literature." The site also includes sections devoted to Samuel Beckett, Umberto Eco, Gabriel García Márquez, James Joyce, Franz Kafka, and Thomas Pynchon.

Novels

http://www.nvcc.edu/home/ataormina/novels/default.htm

 This overview of American and English novels was prepared by Agatha Taormina, a professor at Northern Virginia Community College. It contains three sections: "History" provides a definition of the novel genre, a discussion of its origins in eighteenth century England, and separate pages with information about genres and authors of nineteenth century, twentieth century, and postmodern novels. "Approaches" suggests how to read a novel critically for greater appreciation, and "Resources" provides a list of books about the novel.

Outline of American Literature

http://www.america.gov/publications/books/outline-of-american-literature.html

This page of the America.gov site provides access to an electronic version of the ten-chapter volume *Outline of American Literature*, a historical overview of prose and poetry from colonial times to the present published by the U.S. Department of State. The work's author is Kathryn VanSpanckeren, professor of English at the University of Tampa. The site offers links to abbreviated versions of each chapter as well as access to the entire publication in PDF format.

Voice of the Shuttle

http://vos.ucsb.edu

One of the most complete and authoritative places for online information about literature, Voice of the Shuttle is maintained by professors and students in the English Department at the University of California, Santa Barbara. The site provides thousands of links to electronic books, academic journals, association Web sites, sites created by university professors, and many, many other resources about the humanities. Its "Literature in English" page provides links to separate pages about the literature of the Anglo-Saxon era, the Middle Ages, the Renaissance and seventeenth century, the Restoration and eighteenth century, the Romantic age, the Victorian age, and modern and contemporary periods in Britain and the United States, as well as a page focused on minority literature. Another page on the site, "Literatures Other than English," offers a gateway to information about the literature of numerous countries and world regions.

ELECTRONIC DATABASES

Electronic databases usually do not have their own URLs. Instead, public, college, and university libraries subscribe to these databases, provide links to them on their Web sites, and make them available to library card holders or other specified patrons. Readers can visit library Web sites or ask reference librarians to check on availability.

Canadian Literary Centre

Produced by EBSCO, the Canadian Literary Centre database contains full-text content from ECW Press, a Toronto-based publisher, including the titles in the publisher's Canadian fiction studies, Canadian biography, and Canadian writers and their works series, *ECW's Biographical Guide to Canadian Novelists*, and *George Woodcock's Introduction to Canadian Fiction*. Author biographies, essays and literary criticism, and book reviews are among the database's offerings.

Literary Reference Center

EBSCO's Literary Reference Center (LRC) is a comprehensive full-text database designed primarily to help high school and undergraduate students in English and the humanities with homework and research assignments about literature. The database contains massive amounts of information from reference works, books, literary journals, and other materials, including more than 31,000 plot summaries, synopses, and overviews of literary works; almost 100,000 essays and articles of literary criticism; about 140,000 author biographies; more than 605,000 book reviews; and more than 5,200 author interviews. It also contains the entire contents of Salem Press's MagillOnLiterature Plus. Users can retrieve information by browsing a list of authors' names or titles of literary works; they can also use an advanced search engine to access information by numerous categories, including author name, gender, cultural identity, national identity, and the years in which he or she lived, or by literary title, character, locale, genre, and publication date. The Literary Reference Center also features a literary-historical time line, an encyclopedia of literature, and a glossary of literary terms.

MagillOnLiterature Plus

MagillOnLiterature Plus is a comprehensive, integrated literature database produced by Salem Press and available on the EBSCO*host* platform. The database contains the full text of essays in Salem's many literature-related reference works, including *Masterplots*, *Cyclopedia of World Authors*, *Cyclopedia of Literary Characters*, *Cyclopedia of Literary Places*, *Critical Survey of Long Fiction*, *Critical Survey of Short Fiction*, *World Philosophers and Their Works*, *Magill's Literary Annual*, and *Magill's Book Reviews*. Among its contents are articles on more than 35,000 literary works and more than 8,500 writers, poets, dramatists, essays, and philosophers, more than 1,000 images, and a glossary of more than 1,300 literary terms. The biographical essays include lists of authors' works and secondary bibliographies, and almost four hundred overview essays offer information about literary genres, time periods, and national literatures.

NoveList

NoveList is a readers' advisory service produced by EBSCO. The database provides access to 155,000 titles of both adult and juvenile fiction as well information about literary awards, book discussion guides, feature articles about a range of literary genres, and "recommended reads." Users can search by author name, book title, or series title or can describe the plot to retrieve the name of a book, information about the author, and book reviews; another search engine enables users to find titles similar to books they have enjoyed reading.

Rebecca Kuzins

GEOGRAPHICAL INDEX

SUBJECT INDEX